A Bibliography on

Historical Organization Practices

Research

Edited by

Frederick L. Rath, Jr.,
and
Merrilyn Rogers O'Connell

American Association for State and Local History
Nashville, Tennessee

We are grateful for the generous support of the American Conservation Association, Inc., and the Surdna Foundation for their assistance in the preparation of this volume.
Publication of this book was made possible in part by funds from the sale of the Bicentennial State Histories, which were supported by the National Endowment for the Humanities..

Library of Congress Cataloguing-in-Publication Data
Rath, Frederick L
  A bibliography on historical organization practices.

  Vols. 2–   compiled by R. S. Reese.
  Includes indexes.
  CONTENTS: v.1. Historic preservation—v. 2. Care and conservation of collections.—[etc.]—v. 6. Research.
    1. Historic buildings—United States—Conservation and restoration—Bibliography. 2. Architecture—United States—Conservation and restoration—Bibliography. 3. Historic buildings—Conservation and restoration—Bibliography. 4. United States—History, Local—Bibliography. 5. Historical museums—United States—Bibliography. 6. Museum techniques—Bibliography.
  I. O'Connell, Merrilyn Rogers, joint author.   II. Title.
  Z1251.A2R35   [E159]   016.973   75–26770
  ISBN 0–910050–17–1 (v. 1)
  ISBN 0–910050–48–1 (v. 6)

Printed in the United States of America

Contents

Preface

In 1972, when the decision was made to undertake the third edition of this bibliography, the editors had to make some important decisions. One led to an expansion of concept from a narrow view of subjects covered in earlier editions to a broad view of the subjects central to all the interests of historical organizations. This led to a decision to publish, *seriatim*, six volumes embracing the major categories, disciplines, and subjects within the purview of historical organization activity. The result was volumes on Historic Preservation (1975), Conservation of Collections (1977), Interpretation (1978), Documentation of Collections (1979), Administration (1980), all published by the American Association for State and Local History. This volume on Research concludes the edition and ends the series.

When work on the third edition started, it was realized that the technology of data-collection and data-retrieval was changing. The possibility of computerization was investigated and had to be rejected at the time simply because the technology had not progressed quite far enough then to conquer the problems of distance. The data could be stored, but only at a crippling distance from those who were collecting and analyzing; the terminals so readily available today were not financially feasible within the framework of a limited budget. As a result, as stated in the first volume of this series, a punch card retrieval system was adopted for immediate flexibility and future conversion to computerization.

Happily, the fundamental principles of bibliographical compilation have remained the same. Nonetheless, it is necessary to note several things. Once again we must comment on the astonishing proliferation of references, including a growing number of guides to sources and monographs on specialized subjects in the disciplines covered in this volume. Some volumes in this edition, therefore, have taken longer to compile and publication was delayed. Massive funding to speed the pace of production simply was not available. It is unfortunately true that a bibliographical project, while always deemed worthy and necessary, is not a popular item for funding. And that makes us even more grateful to those organizations that aided so significantly in recent years to keep the project alive, the American Conservation Association, Inc., and Surdna Foundation. Without their help this six-volume series would never have been completed.

The sad fact is that all of the volumes in this bibliography, even this, the latest, are out-of-date. The cut-off date for compilation of this volume, for example, was December 1981, although a few important, readily verified 1982 references have been included. Thus, we feel that the next step is the establishment of an historical organization bibliographical center, based on new data-collection and data-retrieval methodology and designed to be in continuous operation. Only in this way will historical organizations be able to keep pace with the evident changes and growth of their profession. Given the possibility that the six main subject divisions established for this series were retained, it might then be possible to have a finding tool that renewed itself every third year, with two revised volumes or supplements being released each year. We can only hope that the challenge can be met, for if it is not and if the printing and publication of significant materials continues at the same rate, those who have established a career in the field and those who plan to be students in the field will be hampered in their efforts. A profession simply cannot survive without a key to its literature—a bibliography.

The heart of the matter is an understanding of the research method, the best way to unravel the snarled and often elusive threads of the past in order to illuminate the present and to offer hope for the future. It is not easy, as Jacques Barzun and Henry Graff again and again point out in their admirable book *The Modern Researcher*, for "the art of exploiting the full resources of present-day libraries has become more demanding as the adjuncts to books on shelves—data banks, joint repositories, micro-collections, and the like—have grown in number and variety." But it is not impossible if one knows where to look, how to look, how to verify, and how to report, whether in spoken words or written report.

In this volume we have attempted to lay out paths to comprehensive research into four main branches of historical organization practice: history, archeology, architecture, and technology and crafts. This accentuates the fact that the volume is interdisciplinary and underscores the need for interrelating the data. In passing we would note that in Volume 4 of this series, Documentation of Collections, there can be found extensive reference to research in artifacts, decorative arts, fine arts, and folk arts. Together the two volumes should set a solid base under the vital research program of every historical organization, local, state, regional, or national.

Like its predecessors, this volume on research aids seeks to offer the better reference, whether that is a handbook, a monograph, a guide to sources, or an address. It is selective rather than definitive. The compilers, aided by expert advisers, have concentrated on citing the most significant, currently available references, although some early definitive references and standard sources have been included. Articles in periodicals, except for special issues on a topic, and monographs in unattainable editions have not been included. No attempt has been made to repeat innumerable citations already available in published subject bibliographies, again with the exception of those selected references considered as classics in their field. For many subject areas, there are a growing number of annual bibliographic compilations to assist researchers in keeping up-to-date. Other sources for keeping abreast of the growing number of revised editions, reprints of important works and current periodicals include *Books In Print: An Author-Title-Series Index to the Publishers' Trade List Annual . . .* (annual), *Ulrich's International Periodicals Directory* (biennial and quarterly supplements), and book reviews in scholarly journals and book review digests.

All published references follow the Library of Congress card catalog information for main entry. Thus, all include number of pages or number of volumes; illustrations, with notations of any drawings, diagrams, maps, plans, or other graphic materials; bibliography or bibliographical references; appendices; index.

The primary purpose of the bibliography is to be a working tool, providing the first steps on research trails. To this end, there is a detailed table of contents; cross-reference notes to other chapters and sections within the volume and, for supplemental information, to related chapters in other volumes in the bibliography series; and, a deliberately comprehensive author/editor-title-subject index. In a sense, the researcher can start at the front or the back of the volume. At the end of many sections there are descriptive notes and periodical citations to provide more information sources and services that cannot be cited as standard bibliographic references. Listed in the appendix are all the periodicals cited throughout the volume, with addresses and subscription information and notations where necessary if a journal has ceased, been superseded or renamed.

A single Basic Reference Shelf, followed by a descriptive section on national and international historical organizations, became an important feature in previous volumes. For practicality and usefulness in this volume, each chapter starts with a Basic Reference Shelf for that discipline, followed by a section on related organizations and periodicals. The periodicals are repeated in the cumulative appendix. Refer to previous volumes for full descriptions of major national and international organizations; brief, updated material is included in the history chapter.

The format for the rest of each chapter includes: methodology; reference books and guides to sources; surveys and general works; topical studies; and, regional studies (except in Technology and Crafts). Again, the index incorporates the vital and necessary cross-referencing.

To produce a bibliography series of this kind, the support and assistance of many organizations and individuals was necessary. The expanded project would not have been possible without the initial funding of the Smithsonian Institution as administrator of National Museum Act funds. We are indeed grateful to the Advisory Council and Paul N. Perrot. Research libraries throughout the country have played an important role in the compilation and verification of materials. In particular, we are indebted to the New York State Historical Association, the Fine Arts Library of Cornell University, the library of the National Trust for Historic Preservation, and the Gannett Library of Utica College of Syracuse University, for all their fine services and staff assistance.

One of the pleasures of compiling a bibliography is the opportunity to work with so many colleagues who willingly reviewed references, tracked down details, sorted out superseded and outdated works, so that the final compilation would bring the researcher closer to the most useful sources. For their time, sharing of expertise, and encouragement, we are deeply grateful to Langdon G. Wright, Cooperstown Graduate Programs; Willa Baum, The Bancroft Library, University of California at Berkeley; Wiley Williams, George Peabody College for Teachers, Nashville; Virginia Lyle, librarian and genealogist, Commerce Union Bank, Nashville; Ron Greenberg, National Register Programs, National Park Service; Stuart W. Stein, Department of City and Regional Planning, Cornell University; Anatole Senkevitch, Jr., Department of Architecture, Cornell University; Leonard Mirin, Department of Landscape Architecture, Cornell University; Michael and Mary Tomlan, and Julee Marie Johnson, Graduate Program in Historic Preservation, Cornell University; Dell Upton, architectural historian, Cleveland Heights, Ohio; James Ramsey, Fine Arts Department, Vanderbilt University; John L. Cotter, bibliographer/associate curator emeritus, American Historical Archeology, The University Museum, University of Pennsylvania; Paul R. Huey, senior scientist/archeology, Bureau of Historic Sites, New York State Office of Parks, Recreation and Historic Preservation; Minor Wine Thomas, former director, New York State Historical Association; John S. Watson, Geoffrey N. Stein, Robert E. Mulligan, Peter D. Shaver, curatorial staff, Division of Historical and Anthropological Services, New York State Education Department; David Gould, Division of Museum Services, New York State Museum. Since the references for the four disciplines have been drawn from many related sources and organizations, we extend our thanks to all individuals who responded promptly to our inquiries about publications, programs, and services.

The technical compilation of such a complex volume has also been the effort of many able assistants. Throughout the duration of this project, our associate editor, Rosemary S. Reese, has provided efficient, scholarly assistance, and a special understanding of the scope and purpose of the bibliography series. On this volume, we have been assisted by Marjorie Searl and Maria Quinlan Leiby, summer research project students when they attended the Cooperstown Graduate Programs, and Deborah Cooney and Katherine H. Davis, who worked on the association's staff in Nashville. A special thank you goes to Betty Eastman, New Hartford village librarian and friend, for that extra effort with the verification process in order to meet the deadline.

As we noted in the earlier volumes, the American Association for State and Local History undertook the support of the bibliographic project in recognition that this growing field needed a reference guide to the literature that is defining and refining the field. The project has been ably guided by association director Gerald W. George and former director William T. Alderson, and production of the finished volumes has been thoughtfully and meticulously directed by publications director Betty Doak Elder, editor Martha I. Strayhorn, and designer and former publications director Gary G. Gore.

Frederick L. Rath, Jr.
Executive Secretary
Eastern National Park &
Monument Association

Merrilyn R. O'Connell
Director, Bibliographic Project

A Special Note from Merrilyn Rogers O'Connell

As project director, one cannot overlook the importance of perspective in the overall field of historical organization practices. For this reason, I have valued my association with several state and local organizations—New York State Historical Association, former Office of State History (Albany), Regional Conference of Historical Agencies (Manlius), Oneida Historical Society (Utica), Herkimer County Historical Society (Herkimer), and the Town of Middlefield Historical Association (Otsego County)—in order to maintain my awareness of the needs of staff, volunteers, and community. And the many individuals with whom I worked have provided special resources, such as ideas and practical application, that put life and direction in a bibliography that could easily become mired in esoteric minutiae. If they and their counterparts across the country find some measure of assistance from the sources and references provided in these volumes, it will indeed be a great satisfaction to the editors that those jobs were made a bit easier. In addition to my experience with historical and library resources, I have gained a new appreciation for the art of producing the printed word through my work with the craftsmen at Utica Typesetting Company. I especially thank Gene Canfield for his understanding of the need to complete the final volume and for his patience in awaiting my return.

Compiling and editing a work of this magnitude for over a decade deserves a dedication—to a wonderfully patient and supportive husband. The disruptions of family life, the travels, the deadlines were always met with understanding, words of encouragement, and sharing in the excitement of receiving each published volume.

A Special Note from Frederick L. Rath, Jr.

The trail that leads to this, the sixth volume in the third edition of the *Bibliography*, began after World War II when I acquired a small box to hold the precious few 3" x 5" cards that constituted the bibliography for the relatively new field of historic preservation. Over the years it grew until, in the mid-1960's, Louis C. Jones, director of the New York State Historical Association, and I were discussing the setting up of the Cooperstown Graduate Programs; it was then that we realized that graduate students would need a locating tool, a bibliography. He (and the association) then made it possible for me to work with Merrilyn Rogers O'Connell on the paperback volume that we called the *NYSHA Selective Reference Guide to Historic Preservation*. Published by NYSHA in 1966, it was called a pilot project and we promised to follow through.

We did and in 1970 NYSHA published the *Guide to Historic Preservation, Historical Agencies, and Museum Practices: A Selective Bibliography*. Like its predecessor, it was well received. Encouraged, we planned a third edition, which, as you have been told, the AASLH adopted and to which the Smithsonian Institution gave initial support. Now some 12 years later we near the end of the trail.

It has been a long, arduous, and sometimes discouraging trail for my colleague and co-editor, Merrilyn Rogers O'Connell, who had of necessity become the project director because I was actively and fully employed in other projects. It was her lot to struggle with the problems of compilation, analysis, and presentation; it was my lot to share the planning, to revive her spirits upon occasion, and finally to find the money that would enable her to continue. That is why I'm so grateful to George Lamb, Paul Brenner, and Lindsley Homrighausen, all of whom were willing to listen to someone who believed the project was important.

Now it's done. Reviewers have found remarkably few omissions and imperfections, but we know they exist. And that is why we express the hope again that a way will be found to build on this base in the future through an historical organization bibliographical center.

As we have said so many times in the past, to our friends and our colleagues, to our students, and to our successors, happy hunting! May these volumes make your work easier and may you have the same satisfaction and pleasure in your work that we have had in these, the earlier years.

1

History

Completely understanding the past may be impossible; but studying the past in order to arrive at some reasonable truths is not. At least, it is not for those who take seriously the historical method, the way in which evidence is unearthed, balanced, verified, and exposed for the benefit of others. Cumbersome though the procedure may seem to be at times to the layman, it is the only way we have to expose our yesterdays so that we will not be caught forever in the act of repeating our mistakes. This, at least, is a move toward understanding. And understanding may yield enough wisdom to assure a tomorrow.

The professional historian is trained in the handling of evidence; he/she will use that capability to the best of his or her ability. Those who have not had a rigorous or extensive training must learn the method from available sources and then indulge in self-training exercises that not only satisfy self but also meet the test of the marketplace. They will be helped most if they take seriously the wise words of Jacques Barzun and Henry Graff, who for several decades now have guided the untutored along straight and comprehensible paths toward clear and reasonable expositions of historical themes.

Here, in this chapter, will be found citations to basic handbooks, many serving as introductions to the new disciplines and "ologies," which spring from the art and science of history. But the focus, as always, is on the how-to of local history and on community studies, for we value and bespeak the importance of the microcosmic as the best way to understand the cosmic. Accordingly, we proceed in what we conceive to be logical order to the bibliographic aids and reference works and guides to sources dealing with all (or almost all) aspects of American history, including folklife, which today is a portmanteau word embracing every aspect of our culture.

In effect, the thrust of the chapter is to start research trails by including something about just about everything, from agriculture to women's rights. How it is used will test the mettle and the patience, as well as the intelligence, of the researcher-reporter. How it is used will also serve to assess the standing of the parent historical organizations, for they surely will be "rated on the thoroughness of the scholarship behind them as well as the care with which they have carried out their findings," as the *Harvard Guide to American History* points out. History is an unfolding story, made from complex and intertwined materials laboriously gathered and artfully woven to produce a comprehensible whole. It is the warp and the woof of all that is presented today to the hosts of the curious who flock to history museums, battlefields, and historic places. Without a knowledge of the research process there is no chance that a search for historical truth can succeed, and without historical truth there is nothing.

Basic Reference Shelf

Barzun, Jacques, and Henry F. Graff. *The Modern Researcher.* 3rd ed. New York: Harcourt, Brace Jovanovich, c1977. 378 pp., illus., diagrams, bibliog., index. ◆ Manual of research methods, essay on evaluation and interpretation of facts, text on writing of acceptable expository English.

Baum, Willa K. *Oral History for the Local Historical Society.* 2nd ed., rev. Nashville, Tenn.: American Association for State and Local History, 1971, 1977. 62 pp., illus., bibliog. ◆ How to start a program, interviewing, ethics, transcribing and preservation of tapes, use of oral history materials, and updated recommendations regarding equipment.

Brunvand, Jan H. *Folklore: A Study and Research Guide.* M. Thomas Inge, general editor. New York: St. Martin's Press, 1976. 144 pp., bibliog., index.

Degler, Carl N. *At Odds: Women and Family in America from the Revolution to the Present.* New York: Oxford University Press, 1980. 527 pp., bibliog. references. ◆ Surveys two centuries of history of women and history of family; includes children, families of Afro-Americans and immigrants, women's sexuality in 19th century America, suffrage, women at work.

Dinnerstein, Leonard; Roger L. Nichols; and David M. Reimers. *Natives and Strangers: Ethnic Groups and the Building of America.* New York: Oxford University Press, 1979. 333 pp., illus., bibliog., index. ◆ Surveys chronologically the role of ethnic minorities; concentrates on blacks, Indians and immigrants.

Doane, Gilbert H., and James B. Bell. *Searching for Your Ancestors: The How and Why of Genealogy.* 5th ed. Minneapolis: University of Minnesota Press, 1980. 208 pp., bibliog., appendices, index. ◆ Manual and guide to genealogical searching; includes finding and use of family papers, town records,

cemeteries, church records; information on over 35 ethnic groups; bibliographies of most-used materials and guides to sources.

Dorson, Richard M., ed. *Folklore and Folklife, An Introduction.* Chicago: University of Chicago Press, 1972. 561 pp., illus., bibliog. ◆ In two parts: The Fields of Folklife Studies; The Methods of Folklife Study.

Driver, Harold E. *The Indians of North America.* 2nd rev. ed. Chicago: University of Chicago Press, 1969. 632 pp., illus., bibliog. ◆ An anthropological textbook, organized by subject. Offers comprehensive comparative description and interpretation of native American cultures from the Arctic to Panama.

The Encyclopedia of Southern History. Edited by David C. Roller and Robert W. Twyman; Avery O. Craven, Dewey W. Grantham, Jr., general consultants. Baton Rouge: Louisiana State University Press, c1979. 1421 pp., illus., bibliog. references, index. ◆ Compendium of articles; lengthy treatment of each of the region's 16 states; biographical articles, entries for towns and cities, state and regional associations devoted to the study of the South, brief bibliographies with many entries.

Everton, George B., ed. *The Handy Book for Genealogists.* 7th ed., rev. and enl. Logan, Utah: Deseret Book Co., 1981. 392 pp., bibliog., index. ◆ Contains state and county histories, maps, a list of libraries, where to write for records, etc.; kept up-to-date by revisions.

Felt, Thomas E. *Researching, Writing, and Publishing Local History.* 2nd ed. Nashville, Tenn.: American Association for State and Local History, 1981. 165 pp., bibliog., index. ◆ In three parts: researching, including note taking and organization, use of libraries, oral history, other research sources; writing, including the writing process, footnotes and quotes, editing; publishing, including design and type styles, production processes, revisions to copyright information, promotion and marketing.

Franklin, John Hope. *From Slavery to Freedom: A History of Negro Americans.* 5th ed. New York: Knopf, 1980. 554 pp., illus., bibliog., index. ◆ Survey of the history of the American Negro from African background to the present.

Goldstein, Kenneth S. *A Guide for Field Workers in Folklore.* 1964. Reprint. Detroit: Gale Research Co., 1974. 199 pp., bibliog. ◆ Practical advice about how to start and to conduct fieldwork in folklore; discusses observation vs. interview methods in collecting.

Harvard Guide to American History. Rev. ed. Edited by Frank Freidel. Cambridge, Mass.: Belknap Press of Harvard University Press, c1974, 1975. 2 vols., index of names. ◆ Volume 1 is topical; volume 2 is chronological; sections on methods and materials; cut-off date 1970.

Hechinger, Fred M., and Grace Hechinger. *Growing Up in America.* New York: McGraw-Hill, 1975. 451 pp., bibliog., index. ◆ Survey of American education, and critical role of public education in moving toward fulfillment of the American dream.

Higham, Robin, ed. *A Guide to the Sources of United States Military History.* Hamden, Conn.: Archon Books, 1975. 559 pp., bibliog. ◆ Eighteen bibliographic essays, each with sections on general references, background surveys and useful periodicals; information on various applicable archives and suggestions for further research. Concluding chapter, "Museums as Historical Resources."

Lee, Susan Previant, and Peter Passell. *A New Economic View of American History.* New York: W. W. Norton, 1979. 410 pp., charts, bibliog. references. ◆ Covers colonial period to 1930s; each chapter has an annotated bibliography.

Morris, Richard B., ed. *Encyclopedia of American History.* Bicentennial edition. New York: Harper & Row, 1976. 1245 pp., index. ◆ Essential historical facts about American life and institutions; dates, events, achievements and persons stand out, but text designed to be read as a narrative. Comprehensive in coverage; endeavors to incorporate results of latest research.

Poulton, Helen J. *Historian's Handbook: A Descriptive Guide to Reference Works.* Norman: University of Oklahoma Press, c1972, 1973. 304 pp., bibliog. ◆ Surveys wide variety of major reference works in all fields of history and is worldwide in scope; also includes important titles in several allied disciplines and a chapter on organization of a library.

The Reader's Encyclopedia of the American West. Edited by Howard R. Lamar. New York: Thomas Y. Crowell, c1978. 1306 pp., illus. ◆ Arranged alphabetically; topics on frontier stage of development range geographically from coast to coast and Hawaii and Alaska; topics on post-frontier stage . limited to trans-Mississippi West. Includes personalities, ethnic and cultural groups, historians of the West, writers, Indian history, etc.

Reps, John W. *Cities of the American West: A History of Frontier Urban Planning.* Princeton, N.J.: Princeton University Press, c1979. 827 pp., illus., plans, maps, bibliog., index. ◆ Survey of origins and planning of hundreds of cities from Maumee River Valley to Spanish Southwest and Nevada mining camps. Extensively illustrated with plans, surveys and maps.

Schapsmeier, Edward L., and Frederick H. Schapsmeier. *Encyclopedia of American Agricultural History.* Westport, Conn.: Greenwood Press, 1975. 467 pp., indexes. ◆ Includes user's guide; alphabetical entries, and special index groups (Abolitionists to Writers) by subject.

Strunk, William, Jr. *The Elements of Style.* With revisions, an introduction, and a chapter on writing by E. B. White. 3rd ed. New York: Macmillan, c1979. 85 pp. ◆ Rules of usage and principles of composition.

Taylor, George R. *The Transportation Revolution, 1815–1860.* White Plains, N.Y.: M.E. Sharpe, c1951, 1977. 490 pp., illus., maps, bibliog. ◆ Focus on means of transportation and their effect on economy of the U.S.; includes roads and bridges, canal era, steamboats, railroads, merchant marine, changing costs and speed of transportation, domestic and foreign trade, manufacturing, working conditions, financial institutions, role of government, bibliographical essay.

Tyler, Alice Felt. *Freedom's Ferment: Phases of American Social History to 1860.* 1944. Reprint. Freeport, N.Y.: Books for Libraries Press, 1970. 608 pp., illus., bibliog. ◆ Surveys colonial beginnings through Jacksonian period, and evangelical religion; cults and utopias; humanitarian crusades.

Historical Organizations and Periodicals

American Folklife Center, Library of Congress, Washington, D.C. 20540. The Center was established in 1976 to coordinate activities, assistance to the field, research and archival services, model programs and publications. An Archive of American Folk Song, affiliated with the Library of Congress Music Division, was founded in 1928 by Robert Winslow Gordon. It was transferred to the American Folklife Center in 1978, and designated the Archive of Folk Culture in 1981. An index of folksong, subject bibliographies, guides to sources, and other finding aids are available. The Archive of Folk Culture is also compiling a comprehensive directory of folklife resources in the U.S. and Canada. Publications of the Center include *Folklife Center News* (quarterly); monographs and reference aids; craft brochures; posters; calendars.

American Folklore Society, c/o Charles Camp, Executive Secretary-Treasurer, Department of Behavioral Science, College of Medicine, Milton S. Hershey Medical Center, Pennsylvania State University, Hershey, Pennsylvania 17033. Founded in 1888, membership includes individuals and institutions interested in the collection, discussion and publication of folklore throughout the world with emphasis on North America. Publications include *American Folklore Society Newsletter* (quarterly); *Journal of American Folklore* (quarterly); Bibliographical and Special Series (irregular); Memoirs series; Publications of the American Folklore Society, New Series (irregular). The Society also holds an annual meeting.

American Heritage. 1949, bimonthly, subscription. American Heritage Publishing Company, McGraw-Hill, Inc., 10 Rockefeller Plaza, New York, New York 10020. ◆ Cumulative index every 5 years.

American Historical Association, c/o Mack Thompson, Executive Director, 400 A Street, S.E., Washington, D.C. 20003. Founded in 1884, the Association is a membership organization, international in scope, of professional historians, educators and others interested in promoting historical studies and collecting and preserving historical manuscripts. Its activities include professional committees and joint committees with related organizations; awards and honors; annual meeting. It pub-

lishes *American Historical Review* (5/yr.); *Newsletter* (9/yr.); *Employment Information Bulletin* (quarterly); *Recently Published Articles* (3/yr.); *Proceedings,* annual; and a variety of pamphlets on historical subjects.

American Historical Review. 1895, 5/yr., subscription. American Historical Association, 400 A Street, S.E., Washington, D.C. 20003. ◆ Cumulative index every ten years.

American Indian Historical Society, c/o Jeannette Henry Costo, Executive Secretary, 1451 Masonic Avenue, San Francisco, California 94117. Founded in 1964, membership includes American Indians, tribal groups and others supporting its educational and cultural programs. It sponsors classes, forums and lectures on the history of the American Indians. Programs include evaluation and correction of textbooks, development of an Academy for American Indian Studies; scholarships. It founded the Indian Historian Press to publish educational books and periodicals for the general reader and the educational community. Publications include *The Weewish Tree* (children's magazine, 50/yr.); *The Indian Historian* (quarterly); newspaper and books. The Society supersedes the Indian Archives and Library, founded in 1952.

American Quarterly. 1949, 5/yr., membership/subscription. American Studies Association, 4025 Chestnut Street, Philadelphia, Pennsylvania 19174. ◆ Starting with Vol. 6, 1954, a summer supplement carries an annotated selected bibliography of articles in American Studies, a checklist of interdisciplinary dissertations in progress, and grants for graduate study in American Civilization.

American West. 1964, bimonthly, subscription. Western History Association, 20380 Town Center Lane, Suite 160, Cupertino, California 95014.

Center for Southern Folklore, c/o Judy Peiser, Director, 1216 Peabody Avenue, Box 40105, Memphis, Tennessee 38104. Founded in 1972, the Center researches folk traditions of southern U.S. and produces documentary films, records, traveling exhibits, books and slide tape programs. It maintains a library, media and biographical archives, and speakers bureau. Publications include *Center for Southern Folklore Magazine* (1978–1982, semiannual); Southern Folklore Reports (irregular); index of American folklore films and videotapes (1976) with annual supplements (begun 1981); bibliographies, study guides and brochures. Also available, a 7-part Film Series with accompanying study guides, *Southern Experience/American Dream,* with glossary and suggested discussion topics.

Folklife Center News. 1978, quarterly, free. American Folklife Center, U.S. Library of Congress, Washington, D.C. 20540.

Folklore Forum. 1968, 3/yr., subscription. Folklore Forum, Inc., 504 North Fess Street, Bloomington, Indiana 47405. ◆ Accompanied by a Bibliographic and Special Series (begun 1968) of one or two numbers per year.

The Folklore Institute, 504 North Fess, Bloomington, Indiana 47405. Publishes articles and issues on special topics, essay reviews of books central to the study of folklore, which are international in scope. Publications include *Journal* (3/yr); Monograph series, including subject bibliographies and *Folklore Bibliography for the Year* . . . (first one, for 1973).

Folklore Institute. *Journal.* 1964, 3/yr., subscription. The Folklore Institute, Indiana University, 504 North Fess, Bloomington, Indiana 47405.

The History Teacher. 1967, quarterly, subscription. Society for History Education, California State University, Long Beach, California 90840.

Humanities. 1965, bimonthly, free. National Endowment for the Humanities, 806 15th Street, N.W., Washington, D.C. 20506. ◆ Reports on educational programs and scholarly research sponsored by the Endowment.

The Indian Historian. 1964, quarterly, subscription. The American Indian Historical Society, 1451 Masonic Avenue, San Francisco, California 94117.

Institute for Research in History, c/o Marjorie Lightman, Executive Director, 55 West 44th Street, New York, New York 10036. Founded in 1976, the Institute is for scholars engaged in historical research, writing and discussion. It undertakes projects to promote historical understanding, such as lecture services, exhibits, books and compilations of local and regional histories. It publishes *Trends in History* (1979, quarterly), a review of periodical literature; *The Memorandum* (1976, 5/yr.), a newsletter.

Journal of American Folklore. 1888, quarterly, membership/subscription. American Folklore Society, 1703 New Hampshire Avenue, N.W., Washington, D.C. 20009.

Journal of American History. 1914, quarterly, membership. Organization of American Historians, Indiana University, Ballantine Hall, Bloomington, Indiana 47401. Formerly: *Mississippi Valley Historical Review.*

Journal of Cultural Geography. 1980, semiannual, subscription. Popular Culture Association, Bowling Green State University, Bowling Green, Ohio 43403. ◆ Published in cooperation with the Popular Culture Association and American Culture Association.

Journal of Popular Culture. 1967, quarterly, subscription. Popular Culture Association, 100 University Hall, Bowling Green State University, Bowling Green, Ohio 43402. ◆ Cosponsor: Midwest Modern Language Association, Folklore Section.

The Journal of Southern History. 1935, quarterly, subscription. Southern Historical Association, Bennett H. Wall, Secretary-Treasurer, c/o History Department, Tulane University, New Orleans, Louisiana 70118.

Organization of American Historians, c/o Richard S. Kirkendall, Executive Secretary, Indiana University, 112 N. Bryan Street, Bloomington, Indiana 47401. Founded in 1907, membership includes professional historians, college faculty members, secondary school teachers, graduate students and other individuals in related fields, institution subscribers (libraries and historical organizations). Its purpose is to promote historical research and study. It sponsors six prize programs for historical writing, and operates a Professional Register at the annual meeting. Committees include archives, bibliographic needs, historic preservation, history in the schools and colleges, National Coordinating Committee for the Promotion of History, OAH-AHA Committee on the Status of History in the Schools, Status of Women in the Historical Profession, Television, Film and Radio Media, Public History Committee. Publications include *Journal of American History* (quarterly); *Newsletter* (semiannual). Formerly (1965): Mississippi Valley Historical Association.

Pacific Historical Review. 1932, quarterly, subscription. Pacific Coast Branch, American Historical Association, University of California

Press, 2223 Fulton Street, Berkeley, California 94720.

Pioneer America Society, c/o Allen G. Noble, Department of Geography, University of Akron, Akron, Ohio 44325. Founded in 1967, the Society's purposes are to identify, document and promote preservation of our pioneer heritage. It carries out activities related to local history, indigenous architecture, cultural settlement landscape, and oral history, and holds an annual meeting. It publishes *Pioneer America* (semiannual); *Transactions* (cover title: PAST), begun 1977, annual, and supersedes *Proceedings* (1972, 1973).

Pioneer America: *The Journal of American Historic Material Culture.* 1968, semiannual, subscription. M.B. Newton, Jr., Editor, Louisiana State University, Geography-Anthropology Department, Box 22230, Baton Rouge, Louisiana 70893.

The Public Historian. 1979, quarterly, subscription. University of California Press, 2223 Fulton Street, Berkeley, California 94720. ♦ Devoted to academic history and its wider applications in business, state and local history, government, foundations, historical societies and museums, archives and information management, and public history.

Public Works Historical Society, 1313 East 60th Street, Chicago, Illinois 60637. The Society was established in 1976 by action of the Board of Directors of the American Public Works Association. Although functioning under the auspices of the Association, the Society's operations are governed by its own Board of Trustees. Membership is open to anyone interested in the history of public works. Purposes are to promote public appreciation of the historical significance of public works, to encourage scholarly research and publication, and to promote collaboration among historians, educators, and public works professionals. Activities include working for landmark status for historical notable public works structures and facilities; establishing an archive for the collection and preservation of papers of individuals and groups; and supporting research projects by scholars in the field through grants and contracts. It publishes a *Newsletter* (quarterly); "People in Public Works," monthly column in *APWA Reporter;* *Public Works History in the United States: A Guide to the Literature* (1982); *History of Public Works in the United States, 1776–1976* (1976);

Essays in Public Works History series (begun 1976).

Smithsonian. 1970, monthly, subscription. Smithsonian Associates, 900 Jefferson Drive, S.W., Washington, D.C. 20560. Succeeds: *The Smithsonian Journal of History* (1966-1969).

Society for History Education, California State University, Long Beach, California 90840. Founded in 1972, membership includes high school and college history teachers. Its goals are to serve the needs of the historian who is fulfilling the role as a teacher at the university, college, community college, and secondary level. Programs include reprint service to schools; programs and workshops in history education; research. It sponsors Free Book Service for the membership. Publications include *The History Teacher* (quarterly); *Network News Exchange* (2/yr.), a newsletter. The Society is affiliated with the American Historical Association. Supersedes: History Teachers' Association.

Southern Historical Association, c/o Bennett H. Wall, Secretary-Treasurer, History Department, Tulane University, New Orleans, Louisiana 70118. Founded in 1934, membership includes historians of the south who are interested in the preservation of records and in publishing. Its goals are to promote interest and research in southern history; collect and protect historical records of the south; and encourage state and local historical societies in the south. It fosters the teaching of all branches of history in the south; sponsors four awards for publications on southern history; and holds an annual meeting. It publishes the *Journal of Southern History* (quarterly).

Western History Association, Department of History, University of Nevada, Reno, Nevada 89507. Founded in 1962, membership includes professional historians and others interested in the history of the trans-Mississippi west of the United States. It awards prizes for excellence in writing western history, and holds an annual meeting. Publications include *The American West* (bimonthly), and *Western History Quarterly*, a scholarly journal.

Western History Quarterly. 1970, quarterly, subscription. Western History Association, Utah State University of Agriculture and Applied Science, Logan, Utah 84322.

William and Mary Quarterly: *A Magazine of Early American History.* 1892, quarterly, subscription. Institute of Early American History and Culture, Box 220, Williamsburg, Virginia 23185. ◆ 3rd series, begun 1964.

National and International Organizations

American Association for State and Local History (AASLH), 708 Berry Road (P.O. Box 40983), Nashville, Tennessee 37204. Founded in 1940, the Association is a nonprofit, educational organization dedicated to advancing knowledge, understanding and appreciation of local history in the United States and Canada. Membership is open to professionals, institutions, libraries, and individuals. The Association confers prizes and awards in recognition of outstanding achievement in the field, and carries on a broad educational program and other activities designed to help members work more effectively. Professional services include clearinghouse for inquiries about the profession; job placement; consultant service to historical societies and museums; cooperative programs with state and regional organizations; and an annual meeting and joint meetings with related historical organizations. It cosponsors the annual Williamsburg Seminar for Historical Administrators; and sponsors an Independent Study Program (brochure available); regional seminars and workshops; and slide/tape training kits (catalog available). The Association publishes *History News* (monthly), including a Technical Leaflet series; *Directory of Historical Societies and Agencies . . . (biennial); Bicentennial State Histories series; books and booklets (catalog available).*

American Association of Museums (AAM), 1055 Thomas Jefferson Street, N.W., Washington, D.C. 20007. Organized in 1906, the Association is a nonprofit service organization that promotes museums as major cultural resources and represents the interests of the museum profession on a national and international level. Membership includes museums of every size and discipline, museum employees and others concerned with the future of museums. There is a network of six regional affiliate groups to help disperse information and encourage cooperation among institutions, professionals and the public: New England Museums Association; Northeast Museums Conference; Midwest Museums Conference, Mountain-Plains Museums Con-

ference; Western Regional Conference; Southeastern Museums Conference. Programs include a Professional Relations Service; Placement Service; Accreditation; Travel Programs and Tours. It sponsors special seminars and holds an annual meeting. The Association publishes *Museum News* (bimonthly); *AVISO* (monthly); *Official Museum Directory;* books, reports and reprints (brochure available). In 1973, the U.S. Committee of the International Council of Museums (ICOM) became an integral part of the Association as the AAM/ICOM Committee.

National Trust for Historic Preservation (NTHP), 1785 Massachusetts Avenue, N.W., Washington, D.C. 20036. The National Trust was chartered by Congress in 1949 "to further the national policy of preserving for public use America's heritage of historic districts, sites, buildings, structures, and objects; to facilitate public participation in the historic preservation movement and to serve that movement through educational and advisory programs; and to accept and administer for public benefit and use significant historic properties." Membership is open to individuals, organizations and businesses interested in historic preservation.

Trust programs are carried out under five departments: Office of the President; Office of Preservation Programs, including preservation services, historic properties, and regional programs; Office of Development, including membership, merchandising, resources development, public affairs, and The Preservation Press; Office of Finance and Administration; Office of General Counsel. Field services are provided through six regional offices: Mid-Atlantic Regional Office, 1600 H Street, N.W., Washington, D.C. 20006; Midwest Regional Office, 407 South Dearborn Street, Suite 710, Chicago, Ill. 60605; Northeast Regional Office, Old City Hall, 45 School Street, Boston, Mass. 02108; Southern Regional Office, Aiken House, 456 King Street, Charleston, S.C. 29403; Mountain/Plains Regional Office, 1407 Larimer Street, Suite 200, Denver, Colo. 80202; Western Regional Office, 681 Market Street, Suite 859, San Francisco, Calif. 94105.

Its professional services include consultant services, placement service, annual meeting and preservation conference, tours, and annual awards. Its Preservation Library is an invaluable information resource. The Trust maintains two historic house museums and ten museums; and has co-stewardship of six historic properties. Publications include *Preservation News* (monthly); *Historic Preservation* (bimonthly); annual directory and annual report; special reports and information leaflets; property brochures; and publications by The Preservation Press (catalog available).

U.S. National Park Service (NPS), Department of the Interior, Washington, D.C. 20240. The National Park Service was created as a bureau of the Department of the Interior by Congress in 1916 to administer a small number of parks and monuments. The Historic Sites Act of 1935 and the National Historic Preservation Act of 1966 established and expanded the policy for a broad national preservation program. An Office of Archeology and Historic Preservation (OAHP) was organized in 1967 to manage the increased responsibilities of an expanded National Register of Historic Places and a system of matching grants-in-aid to the states and the National Trust for Historic Preservation.

The National Park System is composed of natural, historical, and cultural areas, totaling 333 as of October 1982. Field direction is provided through 10 regional offices: North Atlantic, Boston; Mid-Atlantic, Philadelphia; Southeastern, Atlanta; Midwest, Omaha; Southwest, Santa Fe; Rocky Mountain, Denver; Western, San Francisco; Pacific Northwest, Seattle; Alaska Area, Anchorage; and parks and memorials in Washington, D.C. are administered by the National Capital Region.

NPS publications are as varied as the parks it serves, from archeological studies and architectural records to maps and posters. There are informational folders for most of the parks; interpretive handbooks; and special booklets.

In 1978 a new agency, the Heritage Conservation and Recreation Service (HCRS), was created within the Department of the Interior and combined the natural and historic preservation activities of the NPS Natural Landmarks Program and Office of Archeology and Historic Preservation, and the recreation responsibilities of the Bureau of Outdoor Recreation. The HCRS was abolished in February 1981, and as of June 1981, the Office of Archeology and Historic Preservation was returned to the NPS. It was reorganized and renamed the *National Register Programs* in the summer of 1982. The programs were realigned as follows:

The Interagency Resource Management Division includes the National Registry of Natural Landmarks; the National Register of Historic Places; technical functions of the Interagency Archeological Services Division; and survey and planning of the state grants program.

The Resource Assistance Division includes Technical Preservation Services, and management of grants to the states and National Trust for Historic Preservation.

Historic American Buildings Survey/Historic American Engineering Record (HABS/HAER) Division continues to record historic architecture and engineering sites in America, to preserve the documentation, and to make it accessible to scholars, professionals, and the public.

An office of Department Consulting Archeologist was created at this time, outside the National Register Programs and responsible to the NPS Deputy Director.

Canadian Museums Association (CMA), 331 Cooper Street, Suite 400, Ottawa, Ontario K2P 0G5, Canada. The Canadian Museums Association was incorporated in 1947 to promote the interests of all Canadian museums. Its purposes are to advance public museum and gallery services; act as a clearinghouse of information; promote and support museum training programs; and cooperate with regional, national and international associations. Membership includes the voting categories of individual, association and institution, and nonvoting categories of student and affiliate. The Association sponsors regional meetings and seminars, and holds an annual meeting.

A Museum Documentation Centre was established to provide documentary resources on all aspects of museum operations, to assist in museum research requirements, and to provide the necessary resource materials for the training of museum personnel. The Association also maintains a correspondence training course, a resource center with a library and publications order service, and a resources service program. Publications include *CMA gazette/AMC gazette* (quarterly); *museogramme* (monthly); *Directory of Canadian Museums; CMA Bibliography;* annual report and conference proceedings; books and technical manuals.

Heritage Canada, P. O. Box 1358, Station B, Ottawa, Ontario K1P 5R4, Canada. Heritage Canada is a nonprofit corporation formed in 1973 to promote, preserve and develop articles, buildings and landscapes for the enjoyment of present and future generations. It also holds in trust buildings and landscapes, and works closely with provincial representatives and other voluntary organizations and individuals concerned with preservation. Membership is open to anyone interested in the preservation of buildings and areas of historical and natural value, and members are entitled to voting privileges, periodicals and reports, and use of research services.

Regional Councils, comprised of one representative from each participating organization, were created in 1975 and hold meetings, publish newsletters, initiate local legislation, and sponsor workshops.

Heritage Canada serves as a clearinghouse for exchange of technical information and a communications center for voluntary organizations and individuals; sponsors public information programs; and publishes *Canadian Heritage* (formerly *Heritage Canada*); an annual report and proceedings of symposia; monographs and studies on conservation areas; and bibliography.

National Historic Parks and Sites Branch, Parks Canada, Department of the Environment, 1600 Liverpool Court, Ottawa, Ontario K1A 1G2, Canada. The national park concept was established in Canada in 1885 and expanded as other reserves were added to its first federal park, Rocky Mountain Park. In 1911 a Dominion Forest Reserves and Parks Act was passed and a National Parks Branch created to administer and develop the parks. Today, headquarters for Parks Canada is in Ottawa and its five regional offices are Atlantic, Halifax; Quebec, Quebec City; Ontario, Cornwall; Prairie, Winnipeg; Western, Calgary.

Parks Canada has research programs at the Ottawa headquarters and in the regional offices. The three research divisions at headquarters, under the aegis of the National Historic Parks and Sites Branch, generally focus on broad, Canadian themes. They include archeological research, which focuses on underwater archeology as well as studies in material culture; historical research; and the Canadian Inventory of Historic Building. The regional offices have programs in archeological and historical research that are concerned with more specific, regional topics. Studies from both headquarters and regional programs are published in either of two series: *Canadian Historic Sites: Occasional Papers in Archaeology and History* (1970, quarterly); *History and Archaeology*. These studies also appear in French in the parallel series, *Lieux historiques canadiens: cahiers d'archéologie et d'histoire* and *Histoire et archéologie*.

Methods of Historical Research

Research/Writing/Editing

The American Heritage Dictionary of the English Language. William Morris, ed. New College ed. New York: American Heritage Publishing Co., 1975. 1550 pp., illus.

Bartis, Peter. *Folklife and Fieldwork: A Layman's Introduction to Field Techniques*. Washington, D.C.: American Folklife Center, 1979. 24 pp., illus., bibliog.

Barzun, Jacques, and Henry F. Graff. *The Modern Researcher*. 3rd ed. New York: Harcourt, Brace Jovanovich, c1977. 378 pp., illus., diagrams, bibliog., index.

Black, Henry Campbell. *Black's Law Dictionary: Definitions of the Terms and Phrases of American and English Jurisprudence, Ancient and Modern*. 4th ed. St. Paul, Minn.: West Publishing Co., 1951. 1882 pp. ◆ For working with wills, deeds, contracts, or other legal material.

Bloch, Marc L. B. *The Historian's Craft*. Trans. by Peter Putnam. New York: Vintage Books, 1964. 197 pp.

Brooks, Philip C. *Research in Archives: The Use of Unpublished Primary Sources*. Chicago: University of Chicago Press, 1969. 127 pp., bibliog. ◆ Includes notes on finding sources, limitations on access and use, notes and copies, modern unpublished sources.

Brunvand, Jan H. *Folklore: A Study and Research Guide*. M. Thomas Inge, general editor. New York: St. Martin's Press, 1976. 144 pp., index.

Burnette, O. Lawrence, Jr. *Beneath the Footnote: A Guide to the Use and Preservation of American Historical Sources*. Madison, Wisc.: State Historical Society of Wisconsin, 1969. 450 pp., chart, tables, notes, bibliog., index.

Butterfield, Lyman H., and Julian P. Boyd. "Historical Editing in the United States," American Antiquarian Society *Proceedings,* 72:2 (1962), pp. 283–328.

Cappon, Lester. "The Historian as Editor." In William B. Hesseltine and Donald R. McNeil, eds., *In Support of Clio: Essays in Memory of Herbert A. Kellar* (Madison: State Historical Society of Wisconsin, 1958), pp. 172–193.

Cappon, Lester. "A Rationale for Historical Editing, Past and Present," *William and Mary Quarterly*, XII: 1 (January 1966), pp. 56–75.

Carter, Clarence E. *Historical Editing*. Washington, D.C.: National Archives Division of Information and Publications, 1952. 51 pp. ◆ Bulletin of the National Archives no. 7.

Cartwright, William H., and Richard Watson, Jr., eds. *The Reinterpretation of American History and Culture*. Washington, D.C.: National Council for the Social Studies, 1973. 554 pp., bibliog. references.

Chicago, University Press. *The Chicago Manual of Style*. 13th ed., rev. and expanded. Chicago: University of Chicago Press, 1982. 738 pp., glossary of technical terms, bibliog., index. ◆ Part 1—Bookmaking; Part 2—Style; Part 3—Production and Printing.

Craigie, Sir William A., and James R. Hulbert. *A Dictionary of American English on Historical Principles*. Chicago: University of Chicago Press, 1938–1944. 4 vols.

Cumming, John. *A Guide for the Writing of Local History*. Lansing, Mich.: Bicentennial Commission, c1974. 53 pp., illus., bibliog.

Dundes, Alan. *Interpreting Folklore*. Bloomington: Indiana University Press, c1980. 304 pp., bibliog. notes.

Felt, Thomas E. *Researching, Writing, and Publishing Local History*. 2nd ed. Nashville, Tenn.: American Association for State and Local History, 1981. 165 pp., bibliog., index. ◆ Includes revisions to copyright information and bibliography.

Finberg, H. P. R., and V. H. T. Skipp. *Local History Objective and Pursuit*. North Pomfret, Vt.: David & Charles, 1973. 132 pp., bibliog., index.

Goldstein, Kenneth S. *A Guide for Field Workers in Folklore*. 1964. Reprint. Detroit: Gale Research Co., 1974. 199 pp., bibliog.

Gottschalk, Louis R. *Understanding History: A Primer of Historical Method*. 2nd ed. New York: Alfred A. Knopf, 1969. 310 pp., bibliog. footnotes.

Gray, Wood. *Historian's Handbook: A Key to the Study and Writing of History*. With the collaboration of William Columbus Davis and others. 2nd ed. Boston: Houghton Mifflin, 1964. 88 pp., bibliog. references.

Hale, Richard W., Jr. "Methods of Research for the Amateur Historian," *History News*, 24:9 (September 1969), Technical Leaflet no. 21.

Hexter, Jack H. *Doing History*. Bloomington: Indiana University Press, 1971. 182 pp., bibliog. references.

Hockett, Homer C. *The Critical Method in Historical Research and Writing*. 1955. Reprint. Westport, Conn.: Greenwood Press, 1977. 330 pp., bibliog.

Jones, H. G. *Local Government Records: An Introduction to Their Management, Preservation and Use*. Nashville, Tenn.: American Association for State and Local History, 1980. 208 pp., illus., index.

Jordan, Lewis, ed. *New York Times Manual of Style & Usage: A Desk Book of Guidelines for Writers and Editors*. New and enl. ed. New York: Quadrangle/New York Times Book Co., c1976. 231 pp.

Jordan, Philip D. *The Nature and Practice of State and Local History*. Washington, D.C.: Service Center for Teachers of History, 1958. 45 pp.

Local History Today: Papers Presented at Three 1979 Regional Workshops for Local Historical Organizations in Indiana. David J. Russo, et al., with an introduction by Thomas K. Krasean. Indianapolis: Indiana Historical Society, 1980. 100 pp., map, bibliog. references. ◆ Nine essays on writing, topics, use of physical remains as documents, practical advice, local records resources within Indiana.

McCoy, Florence N. *Researching and Writing in History: A Practical Handbook for Students*. Berkeley: University of California Press, 1974. 100 pp., bibliog.

Metcalf, Fay D., and Matthew T. Downey. *Using Local History in the Classroom*. Nashville, Tenn.: American Association for State and Local History, 1981. 284 pp., illus., appendix.

Miller, Marcia Muth. *How to Collect and Write Local History*. 1st ed. Santa Fe, N.M.: Sunstone Press, 1975. 17 pp. ◆ Techniques for oral and local history.

Murray, Sir James Augustus Henry, ed. *Oxford English Dictionary*. Being a corrected reissue with an introduction, supplement, and bibliography of a new English dictionary on historical principles, founded mainly on the materials collected by the Philological Society. . . . New York: Oxford University Press, 1933. 13 vols. ◆ Vol. 13, "Supplement and Bibliography." Traces changes in the meaning of words.

Nicholson, Margaret. *Practical Style Guide for Authors and Editors.* 1967. Reprint. 1st ed. New York: Holt, Rinehart & Winston, 1971. 143 pp., bibliog. references.

Parker, Donald Dean. *Local History: How to Gather It, Write It, and Publish It.* 1944. Reprint. Westport, Conn.: Greenwood Press, 1979. 186 pp., bibliog., index.

Parton, James. "Popularizing History and Documentary Sources," *The American Archivist,* 22:2 (April 1957), pp. 99–109.

The Past Before Us: Contemporary Historical Writing in the United States. Edited for American Historical Association by Michael G. Kammen. Ithaca, N.Y.: Cornell University Press, 1980. 524 pp. ◆ Three parts: Units of Time and Areas of Study; Expanding Fields of Inquiry; Modes of Gathering and Assessing Historical Materials.

Radin, Max. *Law Dictionary.* Edited by Lawrence G. Greene. 2nd ed. rev. and expanded by Oceana Editorial Staff. Dobbs Ferry, N.Y.: Oceana Publications, 1970. 122, 402, 36 pp.

Russo, David J. *Families and Communities: A New View of American History.* Nashville, Tenn.: American Association for State and Local History, 1974. 322 pp., bibliog., index.

Sahli, Nancy. "Local History Manuscripts: Sources, Uses, and Preservation," *History News,* 34:5 (May 1979), Technical Leaflet no. 115.

Salmon, Lucy M. *The Newspaper and the Historian.* New York: Oxford University Press, 1923. 566 pp., illus., bibliog. notes.

Shafer, Robert Jones, ed. *A Guide to Historical Method.* Rev. ed. Homewood, Ill.: Dorsey, 1974. 255 pp., bibliog.

Skillin, Marjorie E., and Robert M. Gay. *Words Into Type.* 3rd ed. Englewood Cliffs, N.J.: Prentice-Hall, 1974. 585 pp., illus., bibliog.

Steiner, Dale R. *Historical Journals: A Handbook for Writers and Reviewers.* Santa Barbara, Calif.: ABC-Clio Press, 1981. 213 pp., bib-

liogs., index. ◆ Includes advice on articles and book reviewing, directory of journals, and subject index of journal titles.

Strunk, William, Jr. *The Elements of Style.* With revisions, an introduction, and a chapter on writing by E.B. White. 3rd ed. New York: Macmillan, c1979. 85 pp.

Todd, Alden. *Finding Facts Fast: How to Find Out What You Want to Know Immediately.* New York: Morrow, 1972. 108 pp., index.

Tomlinson, Juliette. "Local History in Legal Records," *Old-Time New England,* 58:4 (Spring 1968), pp. 103–109. ◆ Suggests learning legal terminology, guides for the location of records, land, etc.

U.S. Government Printing Office. *Style Manual.* Rev. ed. Washington, D.C.: 1973. 548 pp.

U.S. National Archives and Records Service. *Suggestions for Citing Records in the National Archives of the U.S.* Washington, D.C.: National Archives and Records Service, 1972. 6 pp. ◆ National Archives General Administration Leaflet no. 17.

Van Leunen, Mary Claire. *A Handbook for Scholars.* New York: Knopf, 1978. 354 pp. ◆ Advice on citations, quoting, footnotes, style, references, preparation of manuscripts, composing a vitae.

Van Tassel, David D. *Recording America's Past: An Interpretation of the Development of Historical Studies in America, 1607–1884.* Chicago: University of Chicago Press, 1960. 222 pp., bibliog.

Warner, Sam B., Jr. "Writing Local History: The Use of Social Statistics," rev. ed., *History News,* 25:10 (October 1970), Technical Leaflet no. 7.

Webster's Third New International Dictionary of the English Language, Unabridged. Editor-in-chief, Philip Babcock Gove, and the Merriam-Webster editorial staff. Springfield, Mass.: G. and C. Merriam Co., c1976. 86, 2662 pp., illus. ◆ 1955 unabridged edition lists obsolete words or words no longer in use in present vocabulary.

Weitzman, David L. *Underfoot: An Everyday Guide to Exploring the American Past.* New York: Charles Scribner's Sons, c1976. 192 pp., illus., bibliog., index.

Wilson, John R. M. *Research Guide in His-*

tory. Morristown, N.J.: General Learning Press, c1974. 187 pp., glossary of terms, bibliog. references, subject index.

Wilson, Robert J., III. "Early American Account Books: Interpretation, Cataloguing, and Use," *History News,* 36:9 (September 1981), Technical Leaflet no. 140.

Winks, Robin W., comp. *The Historian as Detective: Essays on Evidence.* 1st ed. New York: Harper & Row, 1969. 543 pp., bibliog. references.

Woolley, Davis C. *Guide for Writing the History of a Church.* Nashville, Tenn.: Broadman Press, 1969. 60 pp.

NOTE

Computers and the Humanities. 1966, bimonthly, subscription. Pergamon Press, Inc., Maxwell House, Fairview Park, Elmsford, New York 10523. ♦ Cumulative index to Vols. 1–6.

Oral History

GENERAL REFERENCE

Church of Jesus Christ of Latter-Day Saints. Historical Department. *A Guide to the Oral History Program of the Historical Department, the Church of Jesus Christ of Latter-Day Saints.* Salt Lake City, Utah: The Church, 1975. 47 pp. ♦ Address: 50 East North Temple, Room 245E, Salt Lake City, Utah 84150.

Columbia University. Oral History Research Office. *The Oral History Collection of Columbia University.* Edited by Elizabeth B. Mason and Louis M. Starr. 4th ed. New York: Oral History Research Office, distr. by Microfilming Corporation of America, Glen Rock, N.J., 1979. 306 pp., illus., index. ♦ Address: Oral History Research Office, Box 20, Butler Library, Columbia University, New York, New York 10027.

Grele, Ronald J., and Gaile A. Grele. *Oral History: An Annotated Bibliography.* Boulder, Colo.: ERIC Clearinghouse for Social Studies/Social Science Education, 1974. 17 pp.

Meckler, Alan, and Ruth McMullin, eds. *Oral History Collections.* New York: R.R. Bowker, 1975. 344 pp. ♦ Includes descriptions of interviews held by 388 different oral history centers.

National Colloquium on Oral History, 1st, Lake Arrowhead, California, 1966. *Oral History at Arrowhead: Proceedings.* Edited by Elizabeth I. Dixon and James B. Mink. 2nd ed. Los Angeles, Calif.: Oral History Association, c1969. 95 pp. ♦ See also: *The Second National Colloquium . . . ,* edited by Louis M. Starr (1968); *The Third National Colloquium . . . ,* edited by Gould P. Colman (1969); *The Fourth National Colloquium . . . ,* edited by Gould Colman (1970); *Selections from the Fifth and Sixth National Colloquia . . . ,* comp. by Peter D. Olch (1972). Succeeded by *Oral History Review.*

"No More Moanin', Voices of Southern Struggle," *Southern Exposure,* 1:3–4 (Winter 1974), entire issue. ♦ Includes bibliography. Available from Institute for Southern Studies, 88 Walton Street, N.W., Atlanta, Georgia 30303.

Shumway, Gary L., comp. *Oral History in the United States: A Directory.* New York: Oral History Association, 1971. 120 pp., index.

Waserman, Manfred J., comp. *Bibliography on Oral History.* Rev. ed. New York: Oral History Association, 1975. 53 pp., index.

NOTES

Archives of American Art Oral History Program, Archives of American Art/Smithsonian Institution, New York Area Center, 41 East 65th Street, New York, New York 10021. The Program began in 1959, and includes tapes of interviews with painters, sculptors, printmakers, craftsmen, dealers, collectors, museum officials and art patrons. Some transcripts are available. Holdings of the Archives are noted in the quarterly reports in the Archives of American Art *Journal,* especially Vol. 11:1–4 (1971), "A Guide to the Archives of American Art Oral History Program"; and in *Archives of American Art: A Directory of Resources,* Garnett McCoy, comp., R.R. Bowker, N.Y., 1972.

Canadian Oral History Association, P. O. Box 301, Station A, Ottawa, Ontario K1N 8V3, Canada. Founded in 1975, the membership organization was formed to help researchers, archivists and others interested in oral history. Its purposes are to develop standards of excellence, to increase competence in the field of oral history through study, education and research, to provide a clearinghouse for information among individual oral history projects across Canada. The Association encourages and supports the creation and preservation of sound recordings which document the history and culture of Canada. In cooperation with the Sound Archives of the Public Archives of Canada, a national inventory of oral history collections will be published. The Sound Archives was established to acquire, preserve, inventory and make available for scholarly research the sound records of historical value to Canada. The National Library of Canada collects commercially marketed sound recordings; the National Museum is concerned with sound recordings which document the folk culture and folk music of Canada. The Sound Archives holdings include recordings of historical events, recordings of radio or television programs, oral history interviews, and other types of sound recordings that have been made to record the present. Publications of the Association include *Bulletin* (1975, biannual); *Journal* (1976, annual); *Manual: Sound Archives* (1975).

Foxfire. 1967, quarterly, subscription. Foxfire Fund, Inc., B. Eliot Wigginton, Editor, Rabun Gap, Georgia 30568. ◆ A bibliographic listing by state of *Foxfire*-type publications appears in *Oral History Review*, 1978, pp. 30–35, at the conclusion of the article "Descendants of *Foxfire*" by Thad Sitton.

International Journal of Oral History. 1980, 3/yr., subscription. Ronald J. Grele, Editor, Meckler Publishing, P.O. Box 405, Saugatuck Station, Westport, Connecticut 06880.

Library Journal. 1876, semimonthly (Sept.-June), monthly (July-Aug.), subscription. R. R. Bowker Company, 1180 Avenue of the Americas, New York, N.Y. 10036. ◆ Frequently gives progress reports on oral history programs, particularly those relating to the public library and local history.

National Union Catalog of Manuscript Collections, Oral History Collections. The *National Union Catalog of Manuscript Collections* includes listings of oral history collections. Participation is open to all public and quasi-public repositories of appropriate material. For instructions on reporting collections and inquiries about the program, write to Editor, NUCMC Descriptive Cataloging Division, U.S. Library of Congress, Washington, D.C. 20540.

The New York Times Oral History Program, Microfilming Corporation of America, 21 Harristown Road, Glen Rock, New Jersey 07452.

Begun in 1972, the program makes available in microform a broad range of oral history transcripts on significant events of the 20th century. Included are collections dealing with the American Indian's view of his history, the social, economic and cultural development of various local regions of the U.S., the civil rights movement of the 1960's, history of the U.S. trucking industry, Louis B. Mayer Oral History Collection of the American Film Institute. Catalog available; also, *Oral History Guide,* no. 1, 1976.

"Oral History," *Journal of Library History,* 2:1 (January 1967–). ◆ Occasional column; authors vary: Elizabeth I. Dixon, Amelia Fry, and others.

Oral History Association, c/o Ronald E. Marcello, Secretary-Treasurer, Box 13734, North Texas Station, North Texas State University, Denton, Texas 76203. The Association was founded in 1966 to foster the growth of oral history; to exchange information, practical and intellectual, on problems connected therewith; to encourage the use of oral history materials; and to improve the techniques of oral history. Membership includes historians, archivists, librarians, editors and directors of oral history programs, and institutions. It sponsors an annual colloquium. Publications include *Newsletter* (quarterly); *Oral History Review* (annual), succeeds *Proceedings;* a directory; bibliography, papers presented at meetings and reprints of papers of special interest.

Oral History Association. *Newsletter.* 1967, quarterly, membership. Oral History Association Newsletter, c/o Thomas Charlton, Editor, Baylor University, Box 228, Waco, Texas 76703.

Oral History Review. 1973, annual, membership. Oral History Association, Ronald E. Marcello, Executive Secretary, Box 13734, North Texas State University, Denton, Texas 76203. Formerly: National Colloquium on Oral History, *Proceedings.*

Provincial Archives of British Columbia, Aural History Program, Victoria, British Columbia V8V 1X4, Canada. The program provides a public aural history for the province, creating, preserving and distributing a wide range of historical sound documents, interviews, speeches, folklore, ethno-musicology and historical sounds. The aural history materials are made available for scholarly research, sound documentaries, museum displays and aural productions. Publications of the Program include *Sound Heritage* (quarterly); *Catalogue; Proceedings of the Centennial Workshop on Ethnomusicology;* and, *A Guide to Aural History Research* (1976).

Sound Heritage. 1974, quarterly, subscription. Provincial Archives of British Columbia, Victoria, British Columbia V8V 1X4, Canada.

U.S. Library of Congress, Oral History Project of Former Members of Congress. The Project was established in 1970 to promote the cause of good government at the national level by strengthening the U.S. Congress as an institution. The Library of Congress is the depository for the tapes and transcripts, and copies are deposited in a library or historical society of the district in which the member of Congress served.

METHODS AND TECHNIQUES

Allen, Barbara, and William Lynwood Montell. *From Memory to History: Using Oral Sources in Local Historical Research.* Nashville, Tenn.: American Association for State and Local History, 1981. 176 pp., bibliog., index.

Baum, Willa K. *Oral History for the Local Historical Society.* 2nd ed., rev. Nashville, Tenn.: American Association for State and Local History, 1971. 62 pp., illus., bibliog.

Baum, Willa K. *Transcribing and Editing Oral History.* Nashville, Tenn.: American Association for State and Local History, 1977. 172 pp., bibliog., record.

Cutler, William W., III. "Accuracy in Oral History Interviewing," *Historical Methods Newsletter,* 3:3 (June 1970), pp. 1–7.

Davis, Cullom; Kathryn Back; and Kay MacLean. *Oral History: From Tape to Type.* New York: American Library Association, 1977. 156 pp., forms, bibliog.

Deering, Mary Jo, and Barbara Pomeroy. *Transcribing Without Tears: A Guide to Transcribing and Editing Oral History Interviews.* Washington, D.C.: George Washington University Library, 1976. 38 pp., sample forms. ◆ Address: Oral History Program, George Washington University Library, 2130 H Street, N.W., Washington, D.C. 20052.

Dexter, Lewis A. *Elite and Specialized Interviewing.* Evanston, Ill.: Northwestern University Press, 1970. 205 pp., bibliog. ◆ Handbooks for Research in Political Behavior series.

Epstein, Ellen Robinson, and Rona Mendelsohn. *Record and Remember: Tracing Your Roots through Oral History.* New York: Sovereign Books, c1978. 119 pp., illus., bibliog.

Envelopes of Sound: Six Practitioners Discuss the Method, Theory, and Practice of Oral History and Oral Testimony. Edited by Ronald J. Grele. Chicago: Precedent Publishing Inc., c1975. 154 pp., bibliog. references.

Fry, Amelia R. "The Nine Commandments of Oral History," *Journal of Library History,* 3:1 (January 1968), pp. 63–73.

Gilb, Corinne L. "Tape-Recorded Interviewing: Some Thoughts from California," *The American Archivist,* 20:4 (October 1957), pp. 335–344.

A Guide for Oral History Programs. Edited by Richard D. Curtiss, Gary L. Shumway, and Shirley E. Stephenson. Fullerton: California State University, Fullerton, Oral History Program, 1973. 347 pp., illus., forms, bibliog.

Hanson, Arthur B. *Libel and Related Torts.* Washington, D.C.: The American Newspaper Publishers Association Foundation, 1969. 2 vols. ◆ Discussion of libel and slander; and various state and Canadian statutes. See also: Supplements to Vols. 1 and 2, 1976.

Hayle, Norman. "Oral History," *Library Trends,* 21:1 (July 1972), pp. 60–82.

Hoopes, James. *Oral History: An Introduction for Students.* Chapel Hill: University of North Carolina Press, c1979. 155 pp., bibliog.

Ives, Edward D. *The Tape-Recorded Interview: A Manual for Field Workers in Folklore and Oral History.* Knoxville: University of Tennessee Press, 1980. 144 pp., illus.

Kelly, Alfred H. "Constitutional Liberty and the Law of Libel," *American Historical Review,* 74:2 (December 1968), pp. 429–452.

McWilliams, Jerry. *The Preservation and Restoration of Sound Recordings.* Nashville, Tenn.: American Association for State and Local History, 1979. 138 pp., illus., bibliog.

Morrissey, Charles T. "Oral History and the Mythmakers," *Historic Preservation,* 16:6 (November-December 1964), pp. 232–237.

Moss, William W. *Oral History Program Manual.* New York: Praeger Publishers, 1974. 110 pp., glossary of terms.

Neuenschwander, John A. *Oral History as a Teaching Approach.* Washington, D.C.: National Education Association, c1976. 46 pp., bibliog.

New York (State). Office of State History. *Localizing Oral History.* Prepared by W. K. McNeil. Albany: 1969. 16 pp., bibliog.

Oblinger, Carl D. *Interviewing the People of Pennsylvania: A Conceptual Guide to Oral History.* Harrisburg: Pennsylvania Historical and Museum Commission, 1978. 84 pp., illus., bibliog. references.

Oral History Evaluation Guidelines: Report of the Wingspread Conference, July 27–28, 1979, Racine, Wisconsin. As amended and approved by the Annual Meeting of the Oral History Association, October 27, 1979, East Lansing, Michigan. Denton, Tex.: Oral History Association, 1980. 14 pp., bibliog. ◆ Evaluation guidelines include information on program or project, ethical and legal, tape and transcript processing, interview content, and interview conduct.

The Practice of Oral History: A Handbook. By Ramon I. Harris, et al. Glen Rock, N.J.: Microfilming Corporation of America, 1975. 98 pp.

Provincial Archives of British Columbia. *Aural History. A Guide to Aural History Research.* Aural History Programme, Provincial Archives of British Columbia; W. J. Langlois, ed. Victoria, B.C.: Provincial Archives of British Columbia, 1976. 58 pp., illus.

Public Archives. Canada. *Manual: Sound Archives.* Ottawa: Public Archives of Canada, 1975. 18 pp.

Shopes, Linda. "Using Oral History for a Family History Project," *History News,* 35:1 (January 1980), Technical Leaflet no. 123.

Shumway, Gary, and William G. Hartley. *An Oral History Primer.* Fullerton: California State University, Fullerton, 1973. 28 pp., illus.

Society of American Archivists. College and University Archives Committee. *Forms Manual.* Madison, Wisc.: 1973. 236 pp. ◆ Forms used in records management, including oral history—legal releases, interview abstracts, application to use tape, etc.

Thompson, Paul R. *The Voice of the Past: Oral History.* New York: Oxford University Press, 1978. 257 pp., bibliog., index.

Tyrrell, William G. "Tape Recording Local History," rev. ed., *History News* (1978), Technical Leaflet no. 35.

Whistler, Nancy. *Oral History Workshop Guide.* Denver, Colo.: Denver Public Library, 1979. 55 pp.

Wigginton, Eliot. "The Foxfire Approach: It Can Work for You," *Media and Methods,* 14:3 (November 1977), pp. 49-52.

Bibliographic Aids

American Catalogue of Books, 1876–1910. 1876–1910. Reprint. New York: P. Smith, by special arrangement with R. R. Bowker & Co., 1941. 8 vols. in 13.

American Civilization: An Introduction to Research and Bibliography. Edited by Lionel B. Wyld. Deland, Fla.: Everett/Edwards, Inc., 1975. 299 pp., bibliog., index.

American Indian Historical Society. *Index to Literature on the American Indian.* San Francisco: Published for the Society by the Indian Historian Press, 1970–. 2 vols.

American Reference Books Annual. Bohden S. Wynar, ed. 1970, annual, subscription. Libraries Unlimited, Inc., Box 263, Littleton, Colorado 80160. ◆ Cumulative index every 5 years. Reviews of new reference books and bibliographies.

Blacks in America: Bibliographic Essays. By James M. McPherson and others. Garden City, N.Y.: Doubleday, 1971. 430 pp.

Books in Print: An Author-Title-Series Index to the Publishers' Trade List Annual. New York: R. R. Bowker Co., 1948–. annual. ◆ Current edition, 1982–1983, 3 author and 3 title vols.; published annually in the fall; supplement published in the spring.

Bradford, Thomas Lindsley. *The Bibliographer's Manual of American History, Containing an Account of All State, Territory, Town and County Histories Relating to the United States* *of North America, with Verbatim Copies of their Titles, and Useful Bibliographical Notes, Together with the Prices at which they have been sold for the Last Forty Years, and with an Exhaustive Index by Titles, and an Index by State.* 1907–1910. Reprint. Detroit: Gale Research Co., 1968. 5 vols.

Bristol, Roger P. *Supplement to Charles Evans' American Bibliography.* Charlottesville: University Press of Virginia for the Bibliographical Society of America and the Bibliographic Society of the University of Virginia, 1970. 636 pp., bibliog. ◆ Lists items printed in America before 1801 which are not listed in Evans. See also: *Index to the Supplement . . .* (1971), 191 pp.

Dundes, Alan, comp. *Folklore Theses and Dissertations in the United States.* Austin: Published for the American Folklore Society by the University of Texas Press, 1976. 610 pp., indexes.

Evans, Charles. *American Bibliography.* Metuchen, N.J.: Mini-Print Corp., 1967. 13 vols. in 1 vol. ◆ A chronological dictionary of all books, pamphlets and periodical publications printed in the U.S., 1639–1800. A volume 14, edited by Roger P. Bristol, is a cumulative author-title index to the whole work. The 14-volume set reprinted by Peter Smith. See also: Bristol, *Supplement . . . ,* cited above.

Fingerhut, Eugene R. *The Fingerhut Guide: Sources in American History.* Santa Barbara, Calif.: American Bibliographic Center-Clio Press, 1973. 148 pp.

"Folklore." In *MLA International Bibliography . . . , Volume I.* New York: Modern Language Association, 1970–. annual.

Griffin, Appleton P. C. *Bibliography of American Historical Societies (the United States and the Dominion of Canada).* 2nd ed., rev. & enl. 1907. Reprint. Detroit: Gale Research Co., 1966. 1374 pp.

Harvard Guide to American History. Rev. ed. Edited by Frank Freidel. Cambridge: The Belknap Press of Harvard University Press, c1974, 1975. 2 vols., index of names.

Haywood, Charles. *A Bibliography of North American Folklore and Folksong.* 2nd rev. ed. New York: Dover Publications, 1961. 2 vols., maps.

Hoornstra, Jean, and Trudy Heath, eds. *American Periodicals, 1741–1900: An Index to the Microfilm Collections—American Periodicals 18th Century, American Periodicals, 1800–1850, American Periodicals, 1850–1900, Civil War and Reconstruction.* Ann Arbor: University Microfilms International, 1979. 341 pp. ◆ Address: Customer Service, Books and Collections, University Microfilms International, 300 North Zeeb Road, Ann Arbor, Michigan 48106.

Jackson, Ellen P. *Subject Guide to Major United States Government Publications.* Chicago: American Library Association, 1968. 175 pp.

Kaplan, Louis. *Bibliography of American Autobiographies.* Prepared in association with James Tyler Cook, Clinton E. Colby, Jr., and Daniel C. Haskell. Madison: University of Wisconsin Press, 1961. 372 pp.

Kelly, James. *American Catalogue of Books; Original and Reprints to be Published in the U.S. from January 1861–January 1871.* 1866–1871. Reprint. New York: John Wiley, 1938. 2 vols. ◆ A publisher's trade catalog; most general list available for the period. Also reprinted by Peter Smith.

Marken, Jack Walter, and Herbert T. Hoover. *Bibliography of the Sioux.* Methuchen, N.J.: Scarecrow Press, 1980. 370 pp., indexes. ◆ First in a series.

Murdock, George P., and Timothy J. O'Leary. *Ethnographic Bibliography of North America.* 4th ed. New Haven, Conn.: Human Relations Area Files Press, 1975. 5 vols., maps. ◆ Systematic assemblage of bibliographical references on primitive and historical cultures; classification by tribal groups showing location of first extensive contacts with Europeans; distinguished 16 areas, and within each area are regional studies, geographical and historical sources, travel accounts.

New York Public Library. Research Libraries. *Dictionary Catalog of the Local History and Genealogy Division.* New York: New York Public Library, 1974. 20 vols.

Peterson, Clarence S. *Consolidated Bibliography of County Histories in Fifty States in 1961.* 2nd ed. Baltimore: The Genealogical Publishing Co., 1963. 186 pp.

Poole's Index to Periodical Literature. By W. F. Poole with the assistance of W. I. Fletcher and the cooperation of the American Library Association and the Library Association of the United Kingdom. 1882–1907. Reprint. Gloucester, Mass.: Peter Smith, 1958–1963. 6 vols. in 7. ◆ See also: *Poole's Index: Date and Volume Key.* By Marion V. Bell and Jean C. Bacon. Chicago: Association of College and Reference Libraries, 1957. 61 pp.

Poulton, Helen J. *Historian's Handbook: A Descriptive Guide to Reference Works.* Norman: University of Oklahoma Press, c1972, 1973. 304 pp., bibliog.

Prucha, Francis Paul. *A Bibliographical Guide to the History of Indian-White Relations in the United States.* Chicago: University of Chicago Press, c1977. 454 pp. ◆ A Publication of the Center for the History of the American Indian of the Newberry Library, 60 West Walton Street, Chicago, Illinois 60610.

Przbienda, Edward, ed. *Monthly Catalog of U.S. Government Publications: Cumulative Personal Author Indexes, 1941–1975.* Cumulative Author Index series no. 2. Ann Arbor, Mich.: Pierian Press, 1971–78. 5 vols.

Roorbach, Orville A. *Bibliotheca Americana: Catalogue of American Publications, including Reprints and Original Works from 1820 to 1852, Inclusive, Together with a list of Periodicals Published in the United States.* 1852. Reprint. New York: P. Smith, 1939. 652 pp. ◆ See also: *Supplement . . . October 1852 to May 1855.* 1855. Reprint, 1939, 220 pp.; *Addenda . . . May 1855 to March 1858.* 1858. Reprint, 1939, 256 pp.; *Volume IV . . . March 1858 to January 1861.* 1861. Reprint, 1939, 162 pp. Current reprint, Peter Smith Publisher, 4 vols. in 2.

Sabin, Joseph. *Bibliotheca Americana: A Dictionary of Books Relating to America from its Discovery to the Present Time (1868).* 1868. Reprint. Amsterdam: N. Israel, 1961. 29 vols. in 15. ◆ Begun by Joseph Sabin, continued by Wilberforce Eames, and completed by R. W. G. Vail. Includes works printed in and published about America from 1492 to the 1870's, and up to the 1890's for the western states. Also available, 29 vols. in 2, reprint set 1966, from Scarecrow Press, Metuchen, N. J., and 29 vols. in 2, photocopy in reduced size, from Mini-Print Corp., New York.

Sealock, Richard B., and Pauline A. Seely. *Bibliography of Place-Name Literature: United States and Canada.* 2nd ed. Chicago: American Library Association, 1967. 352 pp.

Shaw, Ralph R., and Richard H. Shoemaker. *American Bibliography: A Preliminary Checklist for 1801–1819.* Metuchen, N.J.: Scarecrow Press, 1958–1966. 22 vols. ◆ Fills gap between Evans' bibliography and Roorbach's bibliography, both cited above.

Sheehy, Eugene P.; Rita G. Keckeissen; and Eileen McIlvane. *Guide to Reference Books.* 9th ed. New York: American Library Association, 1976. 1050 pp., index. ◆ See also First Supplement, 1965–1966 (1968); Second Supplement, 1967–1968 (1970); Third Supplement, 1969–1978 (1980).

Shipton, Clifford K., and James E. Mooney. *National Index of American Imprints Through 1800; The Short-Title Evans.* Worcester, Mass.: American Antiquarian Society, 1969. 2 vols. (1028 pp.). ◆ Includes works in Evans and those uncovered since, incorporating all corrections found necessary by the American Antiquarian Society in its works on American imprints. Distributed by University Press of Virginia, Charlottesville.

Shoemaker, Richard H., et al. *A Checklist of American Imprints for 1820–1830.* Metuchen, N.J. : Scarecrow Press, 1964–1971. 11 vols., bibliog. of sources.

Spear, Dorothea N. *Bibliography of American Directories through 1860.* 1961. Reprint. Westport, Conn.: Greenwood Press, 1978. 389 pp.

Union List of Serials in Libraries of the U.S. and Canada. Edited by Edna B. Titus. 3rd ed. New York: H. W. Wilson Co., 1965. 5 vols. (4694 pp.), supplements.

U.S. Library of Congress. *U.S. Local Histories in the Library of Congress: A Bibliography.* Edited by Marion J. Kaminkow. Baltimore: Magna Carta Book Co., 1975. 4 vols. ◆ Compiled from a microfilm copy of the Library's shelf list for LC classification F1–975.

U.S. Superintendent of Documents. *Monthly Catalog of United States Government Publications.* No. 1–. Washington, D.C.: U.S. Government Printing Office, January 1895–. indexes. ◆ Title varies; includes both Congressional and the department and bureau publications. Annual index in December issue; decennial indexes for the years beginning 1941–50; February issue contains a list of new serial publications issued by the GPO.

U.S. Work Projects Administration. *W.P.A. Technical Series: Research and Records Bibliography, nos. 1–8.* Washington, D.C.: 1940–43. 8 vols. ◆ Title varies slightly. The Series of "Bibliographies of Research Projects Reports" supplements volumes 1, 2, and 3 of the "Index of Research Projects." Contents: no. 1–3, 5–6, 8—Bibliography of Research Projects Reports; no. 4, 7—Bibliography of Research Projects Reports: Checklist of Historical Records Survey Publications. (No. 7 reprinted by Genealogical Publishing Co., 1969).

Winther, Oscar O., and Richard A. Van Orman. *A Classified Bibliography of the Periodical Literature of the Trans-Mississippi West, 1811–1967.* Westport, Conn.: Greenwood Press, c1970, 1972. 626 pp., 340 pp.

Writings on American History, 1902–. Washington, D.C.: American Historical Association, 1904/1959–. indexes. ◆ Compilers and imprints vary. Vol. for 1961 compiled by James R. Masterson and Joyce E. Eberly for the National Historical Publications and Records Commission is last volume of the original series, published by KTO Press, 1978, 2 vols. *Writings . . . 1962–73,* James J. Dougherty, compiler-editor, et al., 4 vols., published by American Historical Association and KTO Press, 1976. Subsequent volumes annually.

NOTES

America: History and Life: A Guide to Periodical Literature About U.S. and Canadian History, Prehistory to the Present. 1964, quarterly, subscription. American Bibliographic Center-Clio Press, Riviera Campus, 2040 Alameda Padre Serra, Santa Barbara, California 93103. ◆ Part A—Article Abstracts and Citations, with index; Part B—Index to Book Reviews; Part C—American History Bibliography; Part D—Annual Index. Volume 0 of *America: History and Life* contains abstracts of periodical literature, 1954–1963. Cumulative indexes also available.

Art Index: An Author and Subject Index to Domestic and Foreign Art Periodicals and Museum Bulletins Covering Archaeology, Architecture, Art History, Arts and Crafts, City Planning, Fine Arts, Graphic Arts, Industrial Design, etc. 1929, quarterly, service basis. H. W. Wilson Co., 950 University Avenue, Bronx, New York 10452.

Choice. 1964, 11/yr., subscription. Choice, 100 Riverview Center, Middletown, Connecticut 06457. ◆ Association of College and Research Libraries (affiliated with American Library Association).

Clio Bibliography Series, American Bibliographic Center, Eric H. Boehm, Series Editor, Riviera Campus, 2040 Alameda Padre Serra, Santa Barbara, California 93103. Includes: *The American Political Process* (o.p.); *Afro-American History,* 2 vols. (1974–81); *Indians of the United States and Canada,* 2 vols. (1974–81); *Era of the American Revolution* (1975); *Women in American History* (1979); *The American and Canadian West* (1979); *European Immigration and Ethnicity in the United States and Canada* (1982).

Cumulative Book Index: A World List of Books in the English Language. 1928/32, 10/yr., subscription. H. W. Wilson Company, 950 University Avenue, Bronx, New York 10452.

History: Reviews of New Books. 1972, 10/yr., subscription. Heldref Publications, 4000 Albemarle Street, N.W., Washington, D.C. 20016.

Magazine of Bibliographies. 1972, quarterly, subscription. Lalla Campbell Critz, Editor, 1209 Clover Lane, Fort Worth, Texas 76107. ◆ Each issue covers a particular topic for extensive bibliographic coverage.

National Union Catalog. The National Union Catalog represents works cataloged by the Library of Congress and by libraries contributing to its cooperative cataloging program. It constitutes a reference and research tool for a large part of the world's production of significant books as acquired and cataloged by the Library of Congress and other North American libraries. The NUC contains currently issued LC printed card entries for books, maps, pamphlets, atlases, periodicals and other serials, regardless of imprint date, and is regularly printed in nine monthly issues, three quarterly cumulations, and in annual and quinquennial cumulations. The LC catalog publishing program began with *A Catalog of Books Represented by Library of Congress Printed Cards* (1942–1946), and . . . *Supplement* (1948); and continued with *The Library of Congress Author Catalog, 1948–1952* (1953); *The National Union Catalog, A Cumulative List* (quinquennial cumulations, 1958, 1963, 1969, 1973, 1979). Other comprehensive catalogs are published for Register of Additional Locations, Subject, Films, Monographs, Music, Microform Masters, Manuscript Collections and Newspapers. The publication of the NUC Pre-1956 Imprints was begun in 1968 and makes available in book form the total catalog maintained on cards by the Library of Congress since 1901.

Readers' Guide to Periodical Literature: *Author and Subject Index to a Selected List of Periodicals. . . .* 1900/1904, monthly, subscription. H.W. Wilson Company, 950 University Avenue, Bronx, New York 10452. ◆ Issued monthly and cumulated in an annual volume and permanent two-year volumes.

Reviews in American History. 1973, quarterly, subscription. Johns Hopkins University Press, 34th and Charles Streets, Baltimore, Maryland 21218.

Reference Books and Guides to Sources

Aarne, Antti A. *The Types of the Folktale: A Classification and Bibliography.* Trans. and enlarged by Stith Thompson. 1928. Reprint. New York: Burt Franklin, 1971. 279 pp.

American Geographical Society of New York. Map Department. *Index to Maps and Periodicals.* Boston: G. K. Hall, 1968. 10 vols. Boston: G. K. Hall, 1968. 10 vols. ◆ First Supplement, 1971; Second Supplement, 1976.

American Library Directory: *A Classified List of Libraries in the United States and Canada with Personnel and Statistical Data.* New York: R. R. Bowker, 1923–. biennial; current edition, 35th, 1982.

American Newspapers, 1821–1936: *A Union List of Files Available in the United States and Canada.* Edited by Winifred Gregory under the auspices of the Bibliographical Society of America. New York: H. W. Wilson Co., 1943. 791 pp.

Andriot, John L. *Township Atlas of the United States: Named Townships.* McLean, Va.: Andriot Associates, 1977. 724 pp., index. ◆ Contains modern state and county maps, and towns as they exist 1970.

Ash, Lee, comp. *Subject Collections: A Guide to Special Book Collections and Subject*

Emphases as Reported by University, College, Public and Special Libraries and Museums in the United States and Canada. 5th ed., rev. and enl. New York: R. R. Bowker, 1978. 1250 pp.

Bartis, Peter, and Mary Hufford. *Maritime Folklife Resources: A Directory and Index.* Washington, D.C.: American Folklife Center, 1980. 129 pp., glossary, index.

Benton, Mildred, comp. *Federal Library Resources: A User's Guide to Research Collections.* New York: Science Associates/International, Inc., 1973. 111 pp.

Brigham, Clarence S. *History and Bibliography of American Newspapers, 1690–1820.* 1947. Reprint. Westport, Conn.: Greenwood Press, c1975, 1976. 2 vols. (1508 pp.), indexes.

Carman, Harry J., and Arthur W. Thompson. *A Guide to the Principal Sources for American Civilization, 1800–1900, in the City of New York: Manuscripts.* New York: Columbia University Press, 1960. 453 pp.

Carman, Harry J., and Arthur W. Thompson. *A Guide to the Principal Sources for American Civilization, 1800–1900, in the City of New York: Printed Materials.* New York: Columbia University Press, 1962. 630 pp.

Carruth, Gorton, et al., eds. *The Encyclopedia of American Facts and Dates.* 7th rev. ed., with a supplement of the 70s. New York: Thomas Y. Crowell, c1979. 1015 pp., indexes.

Coe, Linda, comp. *Folklife and the Federal Government: A Guide to Activities, Resources, Funds and Services.* Washington, D.C.: American Folklife Center, for sale by U. S. Government Printing Office, 1977. 147 pp., bibliog., index ◆ Publications of the American Folklife Center no. 1.

Crouch, Milton, and Hans Raum, comps. *Directory of State and Local History Periodicals.* Chicago: American Library Association, 1977. 124 pp., index.

Delle Donne, Carmen. *Federal Census Schedules, 1850–1880: Primary Sources for Historical Research.* Washington, D. C.: National Archives and Records Service, 1973. 29 pp., illus. ◆ Reference Information Paper no. 67.

Dictionary of American Biography. Edited by Allen Johnson, Dumas Malone, Harris E. Starr, and Robert Livingston Schuyler. New York: Charles Scribner's Sons, 1946–1980. 26 vols. to date. ◆ Vols. 1–20 original; Vols. 21–26 supplements.

Directory of Historical Societies in the United States and Canada. Nashville, Tenn.: American Association for State and Local History, 1956–. biennial. ◆ Current edition, 12th, 1982.

Directory of State and Provincial Archives. Austin, Tex.: Society of American Archivists, 1975–. 1 vol.

Douglas, George William. *The American Book of Days; A Compendium of Information About Holidays, Festivals, Notable Anniversaries and Christian and Jewish Holy Days with Notes on Other American Anniversaries Worthy of Remembrance.* 2nd ed., rev. by Helen Compton. New York: H. W. Wilson, 1948. 697 pp., illus.

Drake, Milton, comp. *Almanacs of the United States.* New York: Scarecrow Press, 1962. 2 vols. (1397 pp.), bibliog.

Edgar, Neal L. *A History and Bibliography of American Magazines, 1810–1820.* Metuchen, N.J.: Scarecrow Press, 1975. 379 pp., bibliog.

Forbes, Harriette, comp. *New England Diaries, 1602–1800: A Descriptive Catalogue of Diaries, Orderly Books and Sea Journals.* 1923. Reprint. New York: Russell & Russell, 1967. 439 pp.

Funk & Wagnalls Standard Dictionary of Folklore, Mythology and Legend. Maria Leach, editor; Jerome Fried, associate editor. New York: Funk & Wagnalls Co., 1949–50. 2 vols.

Gale Research Company. *Encyclopedia of Associations.* Detroit: 1967–. 3 vols., current edition, 17th, 1983.

Greene, Evarts B., and Richard B. Morris. *A Guide to the Principal Sources for Early American History (1600–1800) in the City of New York.* 2nd ed. New York: Columbia University Press, 1962. 400 pp. ◆ See also: Carman and Thompson, cited above.

Guide to Microforms in Print. Washington, D.C.: Microcard Editions, 1961–. 1 vol., annual. ◆ Cumulative guide in alphabetical order, to books, journals, and other materials available on microfilm and other microforms from U.S.

publications; editors vary, current editor, John J. Walsh. See also: *Subject Guide . . . ,* begun 1962, annual.

Hale, Richard W., Jr., ed. *Guide to Photocopied Historical Materials in the United States and Canada.* Ithaca, N.Y.: Published for the American Historical Association by Cornell University Press, 1961. 241 pp., bibliog. ◆ Updated by U.S. National Historical Publications and Records Commission, *Directory . . .* (1978), cited below.

Historical Periodicals Directory: *An Annotated World List: I—U.S.A. and Canada.* Eric H. Boehm; Barbara H. Pope; and Marie S. Ensign, editors. Santa Barbara, Calif.: ABC-Clio Press, 1981. 300 pp.

Johnson, Thomas Herbert. *The Oxford Companion to American History.* Prepared in consultation with Harvey Wish. New York: Oxford University Press, 1966. 906 pp.

Kane, Joseph Nathan. *The American Counties: Origins of Names, Dates of Creation and Organization, Area, Population, Historical Data, and Published Sources.* 3rd ed. Metuchen, N.J.: Scarecrow Press, 1972. 608 pp.

Kane, Joseph Nathan. *Famous First Facts: A Record of First Happenings, Discoveries and Inventions in the United States.* 4th ed. New York: H. W. Wilson, 1981. 1350 pp., indexes.

Kirkham, E. Kay. *A Handy Guide to Record-Searching in the Larger Cities of the United States.* Logan, Utah: Everton Publishing Co., 1974. 137 pp., illus., maps.

Lathem, Edward Connery, comp. *Chronological Tables of American Newspapers: 1690–1820: Being a Tabular Guide to Holdings of Newspapers Published in America through the Year 1820.* Worcester, Mass.: American Antiquarian Society, c1972. 131 pp. ◆ Companion volume to Brigham, *History and Bibliography of American Newspapers . . . .*

Lord, Clifford, ed. *Localized History Series.* 2nd ed. New York: Columbia University Teachers College Press, 1964–. 1 vol., reading lists, field trip notes. ◆ A paperback series of *Students Guides to Localized History;* includes individual states, cities, regions, and ethnic groups.

Matthews, William. *American Diaries in Manuscript 1580–1954: A Descriptive Bibliogra-*

phy. Athens: University of Georgia Press, 1974. 176 pp.

Matthews, William, and Roy Pearce. *American Diaries: An Annotated Bibliography of American Diaries Written Prior to the Year 1861.* 1945. Reprint. Boston: J. S. Canner & Co., 1959. 383 pp.

Mott, Frank L. *The History of American Magazines.* Cambridge, Mass.: Harvard University Press, 1930–1968. 5 vols., illus., bibliog. footnotes.

The National Union Catalog of Manuscript Collections. Hamden, Conn.: Shoe String Press, 1959/61–. 18 catalog vols. to date, cumulative indexes. ◆ Volumes beginning 1963/64 edited and published by Library of Congress.

Notable American Women, 1607–1950: A Biographical Dictionary. Edward T. James, editor. Janet Wilson, associate editor; Paul S. Boyer, assistant editor. Cambridge, Mass.: Belknap Press of Harvard University Press, 1971. 3 vols. ◆ See also: . . . *The Modern Period: A Biographical Dictionary.* Edited by Barbara Sicherman, et al. Cambridge, Mass.: 1980. 773 pp. Includes women who died between 1951 and 1975.

The Official Museum Directory. Skokie, Ill.: National Register Publishing Co., 1982. 1177 pp. ◆ Biennial; begun 1971, imprint varies.

Peckham, Howard H. *Historical Americana: Books from Which Our History Is Written.* Ann Arbor: University of Michigan Press, 1980. 193 pp., illus.

The Reader's Encyclopedia of the American West. Edited by Howard R. Lamar. New York: Thomas Y. Crowell, c1978. 1306 pp., illus.

Schmeckebier, Lawrence F., and Roy B. Eastin. *Government Publications and Their Use.* 2nd rev. ed. Washington, D.C.: Brookings Institution, 1969. 502 pp.

Smith, Clifford Neal. *Federal Land Series. A Calendar of Archival Materials on Patents Issued by the United States Government with Subject, Tract and Name Indexes.* Chicago: American Library Association, 1974. 2 vols. (338 pp., 349 pp.), maps.

Special Libraries Association. Geography and Map Division. Directory Revision Committee. *Map Collections in the United States and*

Canada: A Directory. 2nd ed. New York: Special Libraries Association, 1970. 159 pp., map.

Special Libraries Association. Picture Division. *Picture Sources 3.* New York: The Association, 1975. 387 pp., indexes.

Stemmons, John D. *The United States Census Compendium; a Directory of Census Records, Tax Lists, Poll Lists, Petitions, Directories, etc. which can be used as a Census.* Logan, Utah: Everton Publishers, 1973. 144 pp., maps, bibliog.

Stevenson, Noel C. *Search and Research. The Researcher's Handbook: A Guide to Official Records and Library Sources for Investigators, Historians, Genealogists, Lawyers, and Librarians.* Rev. ed. Salt Lake City, Utah: Deseret Book Co., 1959. 364 pp.

Stewart, George R. *American Place-Names: A Concise and Selected Dictionary for the Continental United States of America.* New York: Oxford University Press, 1970. 550 pp., bibliog.

Stewart, George R. *Names on the Land: A Historical Account of Place-Naming in the United States.* 3rd ed. Boston: Houghton Mifflin Co., 1967. 511 pp., illus., maps, bibliog., index.

Stowell, Marion Barber. *Early American Almanacs: The Colonial Weekday Bible.* New York: Burt Franklin, c1977. 331 pp., illus., bibliog., appendices, index.

Tallman, Marjorie. *Dictionary of American Folklore.* New York: Philosophical Library, 1960. 324 pp.

Tanselle, George Thomas. *Guide to the Study of United States Imprints.* Cambridge, Mass.: The Belknap Press of Harvard University Press, 1971. 2 vols. (1050 pp.), appendix, index. ◆ Vol. 1 includes basic imprint lists, regional, genre, author; and, related lists, copyright records, catalogues, book-trade directories. Vol. 2 includes individual printers and publishers, general studies, checklists of secondary material.

Thiele, Walter. *Official Map Publications: A Historical Sketch, and a Bibliographic Handbook of Current Maps and Mapping Services in the United States, Canada, Latin America, France, Great Britain, Germany and Certain Other Countries.* Chicago: American Library Association, 1938. 356 pp., bibliog. notes.

Thompson, Stith. *Motif Index of Folk Literature: A Classification of Narrative Elements in Folktales, Ballads, Myths, Fables, Mediaeval Romances, Exampla, Fabliaux, Jest-books, and Local Legends.* Rev. and enl. ed. Bloomington: Indiana University Press, 1955–58. 6 vols.

United States Government Manual. Washington, D.C.: U.S. Government Printing Office, 1940–. 1 vol., annual. ✦ Prepared by the Office of the Federal Register, National Archives and Records Service, General Services Administration. Annual handbook of the federal government.

U.S. Bureau of Labor. *The History and Growth of the United States Census.* 1900. Reprint. Prepared for the Senate Committee on the Census by Carroll D. Wright and William C. Hunt. Washington, D.C.: 1900. 967 pp. ✦ Available from Johnson Reprint Corp., 111 Fifth Avenue, New York, New York 10003. Discusses instructions given to enumerators.

U.S. Bureau of the Census. *Historical Statistics of the United States, Colonial Times to 1970.* Bicentennial Edition. Washington, D.C.: U.S. Government Printing Office, 1976. 2 vols. (1264 pp.).

U.S. Bureau of the Census. *Statistical Abstract of the United States.* Washington, D.C.: U.S. Government Printing Office, 1878–. 1 vol., annual.

U.S. Library of Congress. Catalog Publication Division. *Newspapers in Microform: United States 1948–72.* Washington, D.C.: Library of Congress, 1973. 1056 pp.

U.S. Library of Congress. Census Library Project. *Catalog of U.S. Census Publications, 1790–1945.* Prepared by Henry J. Dubester, Chief. Washington, D.C.: U.S. Government Printing Office, 1950. 320 pp.

U.S. Library of Congress. Census Library Project. *State Censuses; An Annotated Bibliography of Population Taken after the Year 1790 by States and Territories of the United States.* Prepared by Henry J. Dubester, Chief. Washington, D.C.: U.S. Government Printing Office, 1948. 73 pp.

U.S. Library of Congress. General Reference and Bibliography Division. *The National Union Catalog Reference and Related Services.* Compiled by John W. Kimball, Jr. Washington, D.C.: Library of Congress, 1973. 33 pp.

U.S. Library of Congress. Geography and Map Division. *Land Ownership Maps, A Checklist of Nineteenth Century United States County Maps in the Library of Congress.* Compiled by Richard W. Stephenson. Washington, D.C.: U.S. Government Printing Office, 1967. 86 pp., illus., maps, bibliog.

U.S. Library of Congress. Geography and Map Division. *Panoramic Maps of Anglo-American Cities: A Checklist of Maps in the Collections of the Library of Congress, Geography and Map Division.* Compiled by John R. Hébert. Washington, D.C.: Library of Congress; for sale by Supt. of Docs., U.S. Government Printing Office, 1974. 118 pp., bibliog. references.

U.S. Library of Congress. Geography and Map Division. Reference and Bibliography Section. *Fire Insurance Maps in the Library of Congress: Plans of North American Cities and Towns Produced by the Sanborn Map Company: A Checklist.* Intro. by Walter W. Ristow. Washington, D.C.: Library of Congress; for sale by Supt. of Docs., U.S. Government Printing Office, 1981. 773 pp., illus., bibliog. references, indexes.

U.S. Library of Congress. Map Division. *A List of Geographical Atlases in the Library of Congress, with Bibliographical Notes.* Washington, D.C.: U.S. Government Printing Office, 1909–. 6 vols., illus.

U.S. Library of Congress. Map Division. *United States Atlases: A List of National, State, County, City, and Regional Atlases in the Library of Congress.* Clara E. LeGear, comp. Washington, D.C.: U.S. Government Printing Office, 1950–53. 2 vols.

U.S. National Archives. *Guide to Cartographic Records in the National Archives.* By Charlotte M. Ashby and others. Washington, D.C.: National Archives, National Archives and Records Service; for sale by Supt. of Docs., U.S. Government Printing Office, 1971. 444 pp. ✦ Its publication no. 71–16.

U.S. National Archives and Records Service. *Guide to National Archives of the United States.* Washington, D.C.: U.S. Government Printing Office, 1974. 884 pp. ✦ Summary description of all archives as of June 30, 1970; does not include Presidential Libraries.

U.S. National Archives and Records Service. *Federal Population Censuses, 1790–1890:*

A Price List of Microfilm Copies of the Original Schedules. Washington, D.C.: National Archives and Records Service, 1971. 90 pp. ◆ Its publication no. 71–3.

U.S. National Archives and Records Service. *Select List of Publications of the National Archives and Records Service.* Rev. Washington, D.C.: The Service, 1977. 79 pp. ◆ General Information Leaflet, General Services Administration, 3. Revised frequently.

U.S. National Archives and Records Service. Office of Federal Records Centers. *Federal Archives and Records Centers.* Washington, D.C.: Office of Federal Records Centers, National Archives and Records Service, General Services Administration, 1979. 32 pp., illus.

U.S. National Historical Publications and Records Commission. *Directory of Archives and Manuscript Repositories.* 1st ed. Washington, D.C.: National Historical Publications and Records Commission, 1978. 905 pp., bibliog. references, index. ◆ Update of Hamer, *Guide . . .* , cited above.

Who Was Who in America. Chicago: Marquis Who's Who, Inc., 1943–76. 7 vols. ◆ Dictionary of deceased persons; subtitle varies.

Who's Who in America. 41st ed. Chicago: Marquis Who's Who, Inc. 1980–81. 2 vols., biennial. ◆ Biographical dictionary of notable living men and women, begun in 1899.

Women's History Sources: *A Guide to Archives and Manuscript Collections in the United States.* Edited by Andrea Hinding. New York: R. R. Bowker Co., 1979. 2 vols. ◆ Vol. I—Collections; Vol. 2—Index, edited by Suzanna Moody.

World Almanac and Book of Facts. New York: Newspaper Enterprise Association, 1968–. 1 vol., annual, indexes. ◆ First published 1868–1876 annually; revived by Joseph Pulitzer 1886 and published annually. Imprint varies.

Wynar, Lubomyr, and Lois Buttlar. *Guide to Ethnic Museums, Libraries and Archives in the United States.* Kent, Ohio: Kent State University Press, 1978. 378 pp.

Wynar, Lubomyr R.; Lois Buttlar; and Anna T. Wynar. *Encyclopedic Directory of Ethnic Organizations in the United States.* Lit-tleton, Colo.: Libraries Unlimited, 1975. 414 pp., index.

Wynar, Lubomyr R., and Anna T. Wynar, eds. *Encyclopedic Directory of Ethnic Newspapers and Periodicals in the United States.* 2nd ed. Littleton, Colo.: Libraries Unlimited, 1976. 248 pp., index.

Young, Margaret L., et al. *Directory of Special Libraries and Information Centers.* Edited by Margaret Young, Harold Chester Young, Anthony T. Kruzas. 5th ed. Detroit: Gale Research Co., 1979. 2 vols.

NOTES

Annotation. 1973, quarterly, limited circulation. National Historical Publications and Records Commission, National Archives Building, Washington, D.C. 20408.

Biography Index: *A Quarterly Index to Biographical Material in Books and Magazines.* 1946, quarterly, subscription. H. W. Wilson Co., 950 University Avenue, Bronx, New York 10452.

Names: *Journal of the American Name Society.* 1953, quarterly, membership. American Name Society, State University of New York College at Potsdam, Potsdam, New York 13676.

Prologue: *The Journal of the National Archives.* 1969, quarterly, subscription. The National Archives, Washington, D.C. 20408. ◆ Includes historical articles; continuing accounts of the activities of the National Archives; articles of state and local historical significance.

U.S. National Archives and Records Service, General Services Administration, Washington, D.C. 20408. Established by Congress in 1934, the National Archives is responsible for accumulating, appraising, destroying or preserving, and storing all archives and records belonging to the United States government. In 1949, it was renamed the National Archives and Records Service and became part of the General Services Administration. The Archives includes federal records, maps, photographs, and motion picture films. While most materials are available for research, some have restrictions upon their use or publication. Information about material in the Archives is published in *Guide to the National Archives* (cited above); *Prologue,* the quarterly journal;

and, special lists and information papers which are available without charge to scholars and are listed in the . . . *Publications of the National Archives and Records Service* (cited above). Regional archives branches in Federal Records Centers contain materials of regional historical interest. The Centers are located in Atlanta, Boston, Chicago, Denver, Fort Worth, Kansas City, Los Angeles, New York, Philadelphia, San Francisco, Seattle, and Washington, D.C. Presidential Libraries are also operated as part of the National Archives system. Some inventories and guides to materials have been published; for further information write to the appropriate library, or see *Prologue,* for accessions and openings of previously closed papers.

U.S. National Historical Publications and Records Commission, National Archives Building, Washington, D.C. 20408. In 1934, Congress established the National Historical Publications Commission for purposes of promoting the collection and publication of papers of outstanding citizens of the United States and other documents as may be important for an understanding and appreciation of the history of the United States. The Commission cooperates with, and encourages governmental and private bodies in collecting and preserving historical source materials, and plans and recommends historical works and collections of source materials. It has allocated grants to federal, state and local agencies and to nonprofit organizations. In 1974, the Commission was redesignated to include Records. The Commission operates primarily through a national historical publications program, and a national historical records program. Products of the publications program include printed volumes and microfilm of important collections of papers; products of the records program include analytical reports, guides, manuals, finding aids, audiovisual materials, instructional guidelines. There are also publications from projects to improve techniques, address complicated issues, and develop new tools for archival work. The Commission published *Directory of Archives and Manuscript Repositories* (1978), cited above. Brochures outlining guidelines and procedures for grant applications under the publications and/or records programs are available from the Commission.

Surveys of American History

Abernethy, Thomas. *The South in the New Nation, 1789–1819.* Baton Rouge: Louisiana State University Press, 1961. 529 pp., maps, critical essay on authorities. ◆ A History of the South series, vol. 4.

Adams, James T., ed. *Dictionary of American History.* Rev. ed. New York: Charles Scribner's Sons, 1976. 8 vols., index.

American Heritage. *The American Heritage History of the Great West.* Editor in charge: Alvin M. Josephy, Jr., author, David Lavendar. New York: American Heritage Press, 1965. 416 pp., illus., maps.

American Heritage. *The American Heritage Pictorial Atlas of United States History.* By the editors of American Heritage. New York: American Heritage Publishing Co., distr. by McGraw-Hill Book Co., 1966. 424 pp., illus., maps.

American Heritage. *Book of Indians.* By the editors of American Heritage; Editor in charge, Alvin M. Josephy; narrative by William Brandon. New York: American Heritage Publishing Co., distr. by Simon & Schuster, 1961. 424 pp., illus., maps.

The American Heritage History of the 20's and 30's. By the editors of American Heritage, Editor in charge, Ralph K. Andrist. New York: American Heritage Pub. Co., 1970. 416 pp., illus.

Atlas of Early American History: The Revolutionary Era, 1760–1790. Lester J. Cappon, editor-in-chief. Princeton, N.J.: Published for the Newberry Library and the Institute of Early American Culture by Princeton University Press, 1976. 157 pp., maps, bibliog. references, index.

Billington, Ray A. *Westward Expansion: A History of the American Frontier.* 4th ed. New York: Macmillan, 1974. 840 pp., maps, bibliog.

Boorstin, Daniel J. *The Americans: The Colonial Experience.* New York: Random House, 1958. 434 pp., bibliog. references ◆ Trilogy also includes: *The Americans: The National Experience* (1965); *The Americans: The Democratic Experience* (1973).

Bremer, Francis J. *The Puritan Experiment: New England Society from Bradford to Edwards.* New York: St. Martin's Press, c1976. 255 pp., maps, bibliog., index.

Brown, Ralph H. *Historical Geography of the United States.* New York: Harcourt, Brace Jovanovich, 1948. 596 pp., illus., maps, charts.

Brunvand, Jan H. *The Study of American Folklore: An Introduction.* 2nd ed. New York: W. W. Norton, 1978. 460 pp., illus., bibliog. references, appendices, index.

Butterfield, Roger P. *The American Past: A History of the United States from Concord to the Great Society.* 2nd rev. and expanded ed. New York: Simon & Schuster, 1966. 544 pp., illus.

Commager, Henry Steele, ed. *Documents of American History.* 9th ed. Englewood Cliffs, N.J.: Prentice-Hall, 1973. 2 vols. in 1 (634, 815 pp.).

Davidson, Marshall B., ed. *Life in America.* Bicentennial edition with new introduction by the author. Boston: Houghton Mifflin, 1974. 2 vols., illus., bibliog.

Dorson, Richard M. *American Folklore.* Chicago: University of Chicago Press, 1959. 328 pp., table of motifs and tale types, bibliog., index.

Dorson, Richard M., ed. *Folklore and Folklife, An Introduction.* Chicago: University of Chicago Press, 1972, 1982. 561 pp., illus., bibliog.

Driver, Harold E. *The Indians of North America.* 2nd rev. ed. Chicago: University of Chicago Press, 1969. 632 pp., illus., bibliog.

Dundes, Alan. *The Study of Folklore.* Englewood Cliffs, N.J.: Prentice-Hall, 1965. 481 pp., illus., bibliog., music.

Eaton, Clement. *A History of the Old South.* 2nd ed. New York: Macmillan, 1966. 562 pp., illus., maps, bibliog.

The Encyclopedia of Southern History. Edited by David C. Roller and Robert W. Twyman; Avery O. Craven, Dewey W. Grantham, Jr., general consultants. Baton Rouge: Louisiana State University Press, c1979. 1421 pp., illus., bibliog. references, index.

Freidel, Frank B. *America in the Twentieth Century.* 3rd ed. New York: Knopf, 1970. 692 pp., illus., maps, bibliog. references.

Geographic Perspectives on America's Past: *Readings on the Historical Geography of the United States.* Edited by David Ware. New York: Oxford University Press, 1979. 364 pp., illus., bibliog.

Handbook of North American Indians. William C. Sturtevant, general editor. Washington, D.C.: Smithsonian Institution; for sale by Supt. of Docs., U.S. Government Printing Office, 1978–. 20 vols. (proposed), illus., bibliog., index. ◆ Describes history, cultural background and present circumstances of Native Americans; includes scholarly essays on general topics and special subjects and each includes brief discussion of sources.

Hine, Robert V. *The American West: An Interpretive History.* Boston: Little, Brown and Company, c1973. 371 pp., illus., map, bibliog.

A History of the American Colonies. General editors: Milton E. Klein and Jacob E. Cooke. New York: Charles Scribner's Sons, 1973–. 11 vols. to date, illus., maps, bibliog. ◆ Volumes on Georgia, New Hampshire, Pennsylvania, Rhode Island, New York, Massachusetts, Maryland, North Carolina, Delaware, New Jersey, Connecticut; authors vary; volumes since 1979 published by KTO Press.

Horan, James D. *The Great American West: A Pictorial History from Coronado to the Last Frontier.* Rev. and expanded ed. New York: Crown Publishers, c1978. 303 pp., bibliog., index.

John, Elizabeth A. H. *Storms Brewed in Other Men's Worlds: The Confrontation of Indians, Spanish and French in the Southwest, 1540–1795.* College Station: Texas A & M University Press, 1975. 805 pp., plates, illus., bibliog., index.

Josephy, Alvin M., Jr. *The Indian Heritage of America.* New York: Knopf, 1968. 384 pp., illus., maps, bibliog.

Kuykendall, Ralph S. *The Hawaiian Kingdom.* Honolulu: University of Hawaii Press, 1938–1967. 3 vols., illus., maps, bibliog. references. ◆ Vol. 1—*1778-1854 Foundation and Transformation,* new ed, 1969; Vol. 2—*1854-1874 Twenty Critical Years,* new ed, 1966; Vol. 3—*1874-1893 The Kalakaua Dynasty,* completed by Charles H. Hunter, 1967.

Laing, Alexander K. *The American Heritage History of Seafaring America.* New York: American Heritage Publishing Co., distr. by McGraw-Hill Co., 1974. 344 pp., illus.

Levine, Lawrence W. *Black Culture and Black Consciousness: Patterns of Afro-American Folk Thought from Slavery to Freedom.* New York: Oxford University Press, c1977, 1978. 522 pp., bibliog. references, index.

Lord, Clifford, and Elizabeth H. Lord. *Historical Atlas of the United States.* Rev. ed. New York: Holt, 1953. 238 pp., maps, sources.

McManis, Douglas R. *Colonial New England: A Historical Geography.* New York: Oxford University Press, 1975. 159 pp., illus., bibliog.

Morison, Samuel Eliot. *The Oxford History of the American People.* New York: Oxford University Press, 1965. 1150 pp., illus., maps.

Morris, Richard B., ed. *Encyclopedia of American History.* Bicentennial Edition. New York: Harper & Row, 1976. 1245 pp., index.

The National Experience: *A History of the United States.* By John M. Blum and others. 4th ed. New York: Harcourt, Brace Jovanovich, c1977. 905 pp., illus., maps, bibliog. references, index.

New American Nation Series. Henry Steele Commager and Richard B. Morris, eds. New York: Harper & Row, 1954–. 40 vols., illus., maps, bibliog. notes, index. ◆ Covers the whole course of the nation's development. Some volumes cited in the topical sections that follow this section.

Paullin, Charles O. *Atlas of the Historical Geography of the United States.* Edited by John K. Wright. Washington, D.C. and New York: Published jointly by Carnegie Institution of Washington and the American Geographical Society of New York, 1932. 162 pp., 688 maps. ◆ Maps, cartograms and reproductions of early maps on many different scales, illustrating the natural environment of the U.S. and its demographic, economic, political and military history. Includes bibliographical discussions of special topics and map sources.

Pessen, Edward. *Jacksonian America: Society, Personality, and Politics.* Rev. ed. Homewood, Ill.: Dorsey Press, 1978. 379 pp., bibliog., index.

Potter, David M. *The Impending Crisis, 1848–1861.* Completed and edited by Don E. Fehrenbacher. New York: Harper & Row, 1976. 638 pp., plates, illus., bibliog., index. ◆ New American Nation Series.

Quinn, David B. *North America from Earliest Discovery to First Settlements: The Norse Voyages to 1612.* New York: Harper & Row, c1977. 612 pp., illus., bibliog., index. ◆ New American Nation Series.

Risjord, Norman K. *Forging the American Republic, 1760–1815.* Reading, Mass.: Addison-Wesley Pub. Co., 1973. 400 pp., maps, bibliog.

Robinson, W. Stitt. *The Southern Colonial Frontier, 1607–1763.* Albuquerque: University of New Mexico Press, c1979. 293 pp., illus., bibliog., index.

Rohrbough, Malcolm J. *The Trans-Appalachian Frontier: People, Societies and Institutions, 1775–1850.* New York: Oxford University Press, 1978. 444 pp., maps, bibliog., index.

Russell, Francis. *The American Heritage History of the Confident Years.* New York: American Heritage Pub. Co., 1969. 400 pp., illus. ◆ From 1865.

Russell, Francis. *The American Heritage History of the Making of the Nation.* New York: American Heritage Publishing Co., distr. by Simon & Schuster, 1968. 416 pp., illus., maps. ◆ Survey, 1783–1865.

Simmons, R. C. *The American Colonies: From Settlement to Independence.* New York: D. McKay Co., c1976. 438 pp., maps, bibliog. references, index.

Stampp, Kenneth M. *The Era of Reconstruction, 1865–1877.* New York: Knopf, c1965, 1970. 228 pp., bibliog. note.

Underhill, Ruth M. *Red Man's America: A History of Indians in the United States.* Rev. ed. Chicago: University of Chicago Press, 1971. 395 pp., illus., bibliog.

U. S. Geological Survey. *The National Atlas of the United States of America.* Arch C. Gerlach, ed. Washington, D.C.: U.S. Geological Survey, 1970. 417 pp., maps.

Unruh, John D., Jr. *The Plains Across: The Overland Immigrants and the Trans-Mississippi West, 1840–1860.* Urbana: University of Illinois Press, 1979. 565 pp., illus., maps, bibliog.

Washburn, Wilcomb E. *The Indian in America.* New York: Harper & Row, c1975. 296 pp., illus., bibliog. ◆ New American Nation Series.

Webster's Guide to American History: *A Chronological, Geographical and Biographical Survey and Compendium.* Edited by Charles Van Doren and Robert McHenry. Springfield, Mass.: G. and C. Merriam Co., 1971. 1428 pp., illus., maps, index.

NOTE

The States and the Nation. A 51-volume Bicentennial History series, co-published by W. W. Norton and Company, Inc. and the American Association for State and Local History (1976–1980), and sponsored by the National Endowment for the Humanities. Each book is an interpretive portrait of the state, with photographic essay, maps, bibliography and index. Available as a set or individually from W. W. Norton and Company, 500 Fifth Avenue, New York, New York 10060.

Topical Histories

Political

Bassett, Margaret. *Profiles and Portraits of American Presidents and their Wives.* New and updated ed. New York: McKay, c1976. 306 pp., illus., bibliog.

Bemis, Samuel F., and Grace Gardner Griffin. *Guide to the Diplomatic History of the United States, 1775–1921.* 1935. Reprint. Gloucester, Mass.: Peter Smith, 1975. 979 pp.

Congressional Quarterly, Inc. *Guide to U.S. Elections.* Washington, D.C.: Congressional Quarterly, Inc., 1975. 1103 pp. ◆ See also: Supplement, 1976. Sections on political parties, presidential, gubernatorial, senate, and house contests; and Southern primaries.

Cunliffe, Marcus, and the Editors of American Heritage. *The American Heritage History of the Presidency.* New York: American Heritage Publishing Co., distr. by Simon & Schuster, 1968. 384 pp., illus., bibliog.

The Documentary History of the Ratification of the Constitution. Edited by Merrill Jensen. Madison: State Historical Society of Wisconsin, 1976–. 15 vols. (proposed), indexes. ◆ Vol. 1—*Constitutional Documents and Records, 1776–1787;* Vol. 2—*Ratification of the Constitution by States: Pennsylvania,* with microfiche supplement.

Eliot, Thomas H., et al., eds. *American Government: Problems and Readings in Political Analysis.* 2nd ed. New York: Dodd Mead, 1965. 332 pp., bibliog. footnotes.

Friedman, Lawrence M. *A History of American Law.* New York: Simon & Schuster, c1973. 655 pp., bibliog. essay, bibliog.

Governmental Affairs Institute, Washington, D.C. Elections Research Center. *America at the Polls: A Handbook of American Presidential Election Statistics, 1920–1964.* Compiled and edited by Richard M. Scammon. Pittsburgh: University of Pittsburgh Press, 1965. 521 pp.

Jensen, Merrill. *The Founding of a Nation: A History of the American Revolution, 1763–1776.* New York: Oxford University Press, 1968. 735 pp., bibliog. footnotes.

Keller, Morton. *Affairs of State: Public Life in Late Nineteenth Century America.* Cambridge, Mass.: Belknap Press of Harvard University Press, 1977. 631 pp., bibliog. references, index.

Labaree, Leonard W. *Royal Government in America: A Study of the British Colonial System Before 1783.* New Haven, Conn.: Yale University Press, 1930. 491 pp., bibliog. note.

McKee, Thomas H. *The National Conventions and Platforms of All Political Parties, 1789–1905; Convention, Popular and Electoral Vote, also, the Political Complexion of Both Houses of Congress at Each Biennial Period.* 6th ed., rev. and enl. 1906. Reprint. New York: AMS Press, 1971. 418 pp., illus.

Main, Jackson Turner. *The Sovereign States, 1775–1783.* New York: New Viewpoints, 1973. 502 pp., maps, bibliog.

Millett, Stephen M. *A Selected Bibliography of American Constitutional History.* Santa Barbara, Calif.: Clio Press, 1975. 116 pp., index. ◆ Arranged topically to follow chronological order, antecedents, drafting the constitution, organization of government, history of the court, the justices and landmark cases.

Morgan, Edmund S. *Birth of the Republic, 1763–1789.* Chicago: University of Chicago Press, c1956, 1977. 202 pp., bibliog., index.

Morris, Dan, and Inez Morris. *Who Was Who in American Politics.* New York: Hawthorn Books, c1974. 637 pp. ◆ Subtitle: Biographical Dictionary of Over 4,000 Men and Women Who Contributed to the United States Political Scene from Colonial Days Up to and Including the Immediate Past.

Plano, Jack C., and Milton Greenberg. *The American Political Dictionary.* 5th ed. New York: Holt, Rinehart & Winston, 1979. 488 pp., index. ◆ Topics include legislative process, labor, foreign policy, state and local government.

Schlesinger, Arthur M., Jr. *History of American Presidential Elections.* Fred L. Israel, associate editor. New York: Chelsea House, 1971. 4 vols. (3959 pp.), bibliog. references.

Schlesinger, Arthur M., Jr., ed. *A History of U.S. Political Parties.* New York: R. R. Bowker, 1973. 4 vols. (3544 pp.). ◆ Vol. 1—*1789–1860, from Factions to Parties;* Vol. 2—*1860–1910, the Gilded Age of Politics;* Vol. 3—*1910–1945, from Square Deal to New Deal;* Vol. 4—*1945–1972, the Politics of Change.*

Schwartz, Bernard. *The American Heritage History of the Law in America.* Editor, Alvin M. Josephy, Jr. New York: American Heritage Publishing Co., distr. by McGraw-Hill Co., 1974. 379 pp., illus., bibliog.

Smith, James Morton, and Paul L. Murphy, eds. *Liberty and Justice.* Rev. ed. New York: Knopf, 1965–68. 2 vols. (626 pp.). ◆ Vol. 1—*Forging the Federal Union: American Constitutional Development to 1869;* Vol. 2—*The Modern Constitution: American Constitutional Development Since 1865.*

Sperber, Hans, and Travis Trittschuh. *American Political Terms: An Historical Dictionary.* Detroit: Wayne State University Press, 1962. 516 pp., bibliog.

Town and County: Essays on the Structure of Local Government in the American Colonies. Edited by Bruce C. Daniels. Middletown, Conn.: Wesleyan University Press, c1978. 279 pp., bibliog. references, index.

Walker, Samuel. *Popular Justice: A History of American Criminal Justice.* New York: Oxford University Press, 1980. 287 pp.

Williamson, Chilton. *American Suffrage; from Property to Democracy, 1760–1860.* Princeton, N.J.: Princeton University Press, 1960. 316 pp., bibliog.

NOTES

American Academy of Political and Social Science, Ingeborg Hessler, Business Manager, 3937 Chestnut Street, Philadelphia, Pennsylvania 19104. Founded in 1889, membership includes professionals and laymen concerned with the political and social sciences and related fields. Its purpose is to promote the progress of political and social science through publications and meetings. The Academy does not take sides in controversial issues, but seeks to gather and present reliable information to assist the public in forming an intelligent and accurate judgement. It holds an annual meeting and publishes *Annals* (1890, bimonthly).

The Book of the States. Council of State Governments, Iron Works Pike, Lexington, Kentucky 40511. Since 1935 this biennial publication has provided authoritative information on the structures, working methods, financing and functional activities of state governments. The legislative, executive and judicial branches are surveyed along with intergovernmental relations and the major areas of public service performed by the states. Emphasis is given to the development of the two years preceding the biennial publication. Supplements: *State Administrative Officials; State Elective Officials and the Legislatures.*

Military

Albion, Robert G. *Naval and Maritime History: An Annotated Bibliography.* 4th ed., rev. and enl. Mystic, Conn.: American Munson Institute of Marine History, 1972. 370 pp.

Allard, Dean C.; Martha L. Crawley; and Mary W. Edmison. *U.S. Naval History Sources in the United States.* Washington, D.C.: Department of the Navy, Naval History Division, 1979. 235 pp.

American Heritage. *The American Heritage Book of the Revolution.* By the editors of

American Heritage. Editor in charge: Richard M. Ketchum; narrative by Bruce Lancaster. New York: American Heritage Publishing Co., distr. by Simon & Schuster, 1958. 384 pp., illus., maps.

American Heritage. *The American Heritage History of World War I.* By the editors of American Heritage; narrative by Samuel L. A. Marshall. New York: American Heritage Publishing Co., distr. by Simon & Schuster, 1964. 384 pp., illus.

American Heritage. *The American Heritage Picture History of the Civil War.* Editor in charge: Richard M. Ketchum. New York: American Heritage Publishing Co., distr. by Doubleday, 1960. 630 pp., illus., maps. ◆ See also: *American Heritage Civil War Chronology, with Notes on the Leading Participants . . .* , special supplement (1960).

Boatner, Mark M. *The Civil War Dictionary.* New York: D. McKay Co., 1959. 974 pp., illus., maps, diagrams, bibliog.

Boatner, Mark M. *Encyclopedia of the American Revolution.* Rev. ed. New York: David McKay Company, Inc., 1974. 1287 pp., maps, bibliog., index.

Cunliffe, Marcus. *Soldiers and Civilians: Martial Spirit in America, 1775–1865.* Boston: Little, Brown and Company, 1968. 499 pp., illus., bibliog. references.

Gephart, Ronald M. *Periodical Literature on the American Revolution: Historical Research and Changing Interpretations, 1895–1970; A Selective Bibliography.* Washington, D.C.: Library of Congress; for sale by Supt. of Docs., U.S. Government Printing Office, 1971. 93 pp.

Goldberg, Alfred, ed. *History of the United States Air Force, 1907–1957.* New York: Arno Press, c1957, 1972. 277 pp., illus., bibliog.

A Guide to the Study and Use of Military History. Edited by John E. Jessup, Jr., and Robert W. Coakley. Washington, D.C.: Center of Military History, United States Army; for sale by Supt. of Docs., U.S. Government Printing Office, 1979. 507 pp., illus., bibliogs., index.

Gurney, Gene. *A Pictorial History of the United States Army in War and Peace, from Colonial Times to Vietnam.* New York: Crown Publishing, c1966, 1978. 815 pp., illus., maps.

Heinl, Robert D., Jr. *Soldiers of the Sea: The U.S. Marine Corps, 1775–1962.* Annapolis: United States Naval Institute, 1962. 692 pp., illus., bibliog.

Higginbotham, Don. *The War of American Independence: Military Attitudes, Policies, and Practice, 1763–1789.* New York: Macmillan, 1971. 509 pp., maps, bibliog. essay.

Higham, Robin, ed. *A Guide to the Sources of United States Military History.* Hamden, Conn.: Archon Books, 1975. 559 pp., bibliog.

Kaminkow, Marion J., and Jack Kaminkow, comps. *Mariners of the American Revolution; With an Appendix of American Ships Captured by the British during the Revolutionary War.* Baltimore, Md.: Magna Carta Book Co., 1967. 248 pp., illus., bibliog.

Knox, Dudley W. *A History of the United States Navy.* Rev. ed. New York: G. P. Putnam's Sons, 1948. 704 pp., illus., maps, bibliog.

Lane, Jack C. *America's Military Past: A Guide to Information Sources.* Detroit: Gale Research Co., c1980. 280 pp., indexes.

Life. *Picture History of World War II.* New York: Time, Inc., 1950. 368 pp., illus., maps.

Matloff, Maurice, ed. *American Military History.* Washington, D.C.: U.S. Government Printing Office, 1969. 701 pp., illus., maps, bibliog. ◆ U.S. Army Historical Series.

Millis, Walter. *Arms and Men: A Study in American Military History.* New York: Putnam, 1956. 382 pp., bibliog.

Nevins, Allan; James I. Robertson, Jr.; and Bell I. Wiley, eds. *Civil War Books: A Critical Bibliography.* Baton Rouge, La.: Published for the U.S. Civil War Centennial Commission by Louisiana State University Press, 1967–69. 2 vols. (278, 326 pp.), index.

Parish, Peter J. *The American Civil War.* New York: Holmes & Meier Publishers, 1975. 750 pp., illus., maps, bibliog., index.

Sulzberger, Cyrus L. *The American Heritage Picture History of World War II.* New York: American Heritage Publishing Co., distr. by Simon & Schuster, 1966. 640 pp., illus., maps.

U.S. War Department. *War of the Rebellion . . . Official Records of the Union and Confed-*

erate Armies. Published under the direction of the Secretary of War. Washington, D.C.: U.S. Government Printing Office, 1880–1901. 70 vols.

Weigley, Russell F. *History of the United States Army*. New York: Macmillan, 1967. 688 pp., bibliog. references.

NOTES

Civil War History: *A Journal of the Middle Period*. 1955, quarterly, subscription. Kent State University Press, Kent, Ohio 44242.

Company of Military Historians, North Main Street, Westbrook, Connecticut 06498. Founded in 1951, the Company is a professional society of military historians, museologists, artists, writers and private collectors interested in the history of American military units, organization, tactics, uniforms, arms, and equipment. It holds an annual meeting. Publications include *Military Collector and Historian* (quarterly); *Military Uniforms in America* (quarterly); *Military Music in America* (records).

Council on America's Military Past (CAMP), c/o Col. Herbert M. Hart, National Secretary, P. O. Box 1151, Fort Myer, Virginia 22211. Founded in 1966, the Council is a nonprofit corporation whose members are interested in the identification, location, restoration, preservation, and memorialization of old military installations and units. It actively works for the cause of historic preservation and endorses efforts to prevent treasure and souvenir hunters from destroying artifacts at historic sites. Membership is open to individuals and local groups. It publishes *Periodical* (quarterly); *Headquarters Heliogram* (monthly newspaper); *Brief Guide to Research on Army Posts* (1971). It also holds an annual meeting.

Council on America's Military Past. *Periodical*. 1967, quarterly, membership/subscription. c/o Secretary, P. O. Box 1151, Fort Myer, Virginia 22211. ♦ Subscription includes *Headquarters Heliogram,* monthly, tabloid format.

Military Collector and Historian. 1951, quarterly, membership/subscription. Company of Military Historians, North Main Street, Westbrook, Connecticut 06498.

U.S. Army Military History Research Collection, c/o Dr. Richard J. Sommers, Archivist-Historian, U.S. Army Military History Research Collection, Carlisle Barracks, Pennsylvania 17013. Includes an extensive collection of published and unpublished materials relating exclusively to the role of the military in the development of the U.S.; and dedicated solely to perpetuating the history and traditions of the Army, the contributions of the Army to the development of the U.S.; and the lives and experiences of the men and women who participated in its development. The nucleus of the collection is from the U.S. Army War College, National War College, and U.S. Army Command and General Staff College. It makes available original source material and oral history materials.

Economic

Bishop, John L. *History of American Manufactures from 1608 to 1860.* 3rd ed., rev. and enl. 1868. Reprint. New York: A. M. Kelley, 1966. 3 vols., bibliog. footnotes.

Brownlee, W. Eliot. *Dynamics of Ascent: A History of the American Economy.* 2nd ed. New York: Knopf, c1979. 534 pp., illus., bibliogs., index.

Bruchey, Stuart. *The Roots of American Economic Growth, 1607–1861: An Essay in Social Causation.* New York: Harper & Row, 1965. 234 pp., bibliog.

Cahn, William *A Pictorial History of American Labor: The Contributions of the Working Man and America's Growth from Colonial Times to the Present.* New York: Crown Publishing, 1972. 341 pp., illus., bibliog.

Chamberlain, John. *The Enterprising Americans: A Business History of the United States.* New and updated ed. New York: Harper & Row, 1974. 282 pp., illus., bibliog.

Clemens, Paul G. E. *The Atlantic Economy and Colonial Maryland's Eastern Shore: From Tobacco to Grain.* Ithaca, N.Y.: Cornell University Press, 1980. 249 pp., illus., bibliog., index.

Cochran, Thomas G. *Business in American Life: A History.* New York: McGraw-Hill, 1972. 401 pp., bibliog. references.

Cochran, Thomas C. *200 Years of American Business.* New York: Basic Books, c1977. 288 pp., bibliog., index.

Commons, John Rogers. *History of Labour in*

the United States. 1918–1935. Reprint. New York: A.M. Kelley, 1966. 4 vols., illus., bibliog.

Conference on American Agriculture, Washington, D.C., 1977. *Farmers, Bureaucrats and Middlemen: Historical Perspectives on American Agriculture.* Edited by Trudy Huskamp Peterson. Special ed. Washington, D.C.: Howard University Press, 1980. 357 pp., illus., bibliog. references, index. ◆ National Archives Conferences, vol. 17.

Connor, Seymour V., and Jimmy M. Skaggs. *Broadcloth and Britches: The Santa Fe Trade.* 1st ed. College Station: Texas A & M University Press, c1977. 225 pp., plates, illus., bibliog., index.

Degler, Carl N., ed. *The Age of the Economic Revolution, 1876–1900.* 2nd ed. Glenview, Ill.: Scott, Foresman, c1977. 197 pp., illus., bibliog. references, index.

Dewey, Davis R. *Financial History of the United States.* 12th ed. 1934. Reprint. New York: A.M. Kelley, 1968. 600 pp., illus., bibliog.

Dunbar, Seymour. *A History of Travel in America.* 1915. Reprint. Westport, Conn.: Greenwood Press, 1968. 4 vols. (1529 pp.), illus., facsims, maps, bibliog. ◆ Subtitle: Showing the Development of Travel and Transportation from the Crude Methods of the Canoe and the Dog-Sled to the Highly Organized Railway Systems of the Present, Together with a Narrative of the Human Experiences and Changing Social Conditions that Accompanied this Economic Conquest of the Continent.

Encyclopedia of American Economic History: Studies of the Principal Movements and Ideas. Glenn Porter, ed. New York: Charles Scribner's Sons, 1968. 3 vols., bibliogs.

Fite, Gilbert C. *The Farmer's Frontier, 1865–1900.* New York: Holt, Rinehart & Winston, 1966. 272 pp., illus., maps, bibliogs.

Fite, Gilbert C., and Jim E. Reese. *An Economic History of the United States.* 3rd ed. Boston: Houghton Mifflin, 1973. 684 pp., illus., bibliog., index.

Friedman, Milton, and Anna J. Schwartz. *A Monetary History of the United States, 1867–1960.* Princeton, N.J.: University of Princeton Press, 1963. 860 pp., diagrams, tables, bibliog. footnotes. ◆ National Bureau of Economic Research, Studies in Business Cycles, 12.

Fusonie, Alan M., comp. *Heritage of American Agriculture: A Bibliography of Pre-1860 Imprints.* Beltsville, Md.: National Agricultural Library, U.S. Department of Agriculture, 1975. 71 pp. ◆ Library List no. 98. Selected monographs, periodicals and publications of agricultural societies prior to the Civil War.

Gates, Paul W. *The Farmer's Age: Agriculture, 1815–1860.* New York: Holt, Rinehart & Winston, 1960. 460 pp., illus., maps, tables, bibliog. ◆ Economic History of the United States series.

Groner, Alex, and the Editors of American Heritage and Business Week. *The American Heritage History of American Business and Industry.* New York: American Heritage Publishing Co., 1972. 384 pp., illus., bibliog.

Hayter, Earl W. *The Troubled Farmer, 1850–1900: Rural Adjustment to Industrialism.* De Kalb: Northern Illinois University Press, 1968. 349 pp., bibliog.

Higgs, Robert. *The Transformation of the American Economy, 1865–1914: An Essay in Interpretation.* New York: Wiley, 1971. 143 pp., illus., bibliog.

Jackson, William Turrentine. *Wagon Roads West: A Study of Federal Road Surveys and Construction in the Trans-Mississippi West, 1846–1869.* Lincoln: University of Nebraska Press, c1964, 1979. 422 pp., illus., plates, bibliog., index. ◆ Reprint of edition published by Yale University Press, New Haven, which was issued as no. 9 of Yale Western Americana series.

Jensen, Oliver O. *The American Heritage History of Railroads in America.* New York: American Heritage, distr. by McGraw-Hill, 1975. 320 pp., illus., maps, bibliog.

Johnson, Laurence A. *Over the Counter and On the Shelf: Country Storekeeping in America, 1620–1920.* Edited by Marcia Ray. New York: Bonanza Books, c1961, 1970. 140 pp., illus., bibliog.

Lee, Susan Previant, and Peter Passell. *A New Economic View of American History.* New York: W.W. Norton, 1979. 410 pp., charts, bibliog. references.

Lovett, Robert W. *American Economic and Business History Information Sources: An Annotated Bibliography of Recent Works Pertaining to Economics, Business, Agricultural and*

Labor History and the History of Science and Technology for the United States and Canada. Detroit: Gale Research Co., 1971. 323 pp.

McBrearty, James C. *American Labor History and Comparative Labor Movements: A Selected Bibliography.* Tucson: University of Arizona Press, 1973. 262 pp.

Morris, Richard B. *Government and Labor in Early America.* 1946. Reprint. New York: Octagon Books, 1965. 557 pp., bibliog. footnotes.

Myers, Margaret G. *A Financial History of the United States.* New York: Columbia University Press, 1970. 451 pp., bibliog.

Neufeld, Maurice J. *A Representative Bibliography of American Labor History.* Ithaca, N.Y.: New York State School of Industrial and Labor Relations, Cornell University, 1964. 146 pp., bibliog.

North, Douglass Cecil. *Growth & Welfare in the American Past: A New Economic History.* 2nd ed. Englewood Cliffs, N.J.: Prentice-Hall, 1974. 207 pp., illus., bibliog.

Orsagh, Thomas. *The Economic History of the United States Prior to 1860: An Annotated Bibliography.* Santa Barbara, Calif.: American Bibliographical Center-Clio Press, 1975. 100 pp., indexes.

Rasmussen, Wayne D., ed. *Agriculture in the United States: A Documentary History.* New York: Random House, c1975. 4 vols. (3652 pp.).

Russell, Howard S. *A Long, Deep Furrow: Three Centuries of Farming in New England.* Hanover, N.H.: University Press of New England, 1976. 672 pp., illus., maps, bibliog. ◆ See also: abridged edition: Mark Lapping, ed., 1982, 400 pp.

Schapsmeier, Edward L., and Frederick H. Schapsmeier. *Encyclopedia of American Agricultural History.* Westport, Conn.: Greenwood Press, 1975. 467 pp., indexes.

Schlebecker, John T., ed. *Bibliography of Books and Pamphlets on History of Agriculture in the United States, 1607–1967.* Santa Barbara, Calif.: American Bibliographic Center-Clio Press, 1969. 183 pp.

Schlebecker, John T. *Whereby We Thrive: A History of American Farming, 1607–1972.* Ames: Iowa State University Press, 1975. 342 pp., illus., bibliog., index.

Schob, David E. *Hired Hands and Plowboys: Farm Labor in the Midwest, 1815–1860.* Urbana: University of Illinois Press, 1975. 329 pp., bibliog.

Shannon, Fred A. *The Farmer's Last Frontier: Agriculture, 1860–1897.* 1945. Reprint. White Plains, N.Y.: M.E. Sharpe, 1977. 434 pp., illus., bibliog., index. ◆ Originally issued as Vol. 5 of Economic History of the United States.

Society of American Archivists. Committee on Business Archives. *Directory of Business Archives in the United States and Canada.* Chicago: Society of American Archivists, 1975. 38 pp.

Stover, John F. *The Life and Decline of the American Railroad.* New York: Oxford University Press, 1970. 324 pp., illus., maps, bibliog.

Taft, Philip. *Organized Labor in American History.* New York: Harper & Row, 1964. 818 pp., bibliog. references.

Taylor, George R. *The Transportation Revolution, 1815–1860.* White Plains, N.Y.: M.E. Sharpe, c1951, 1977. 490 pp., illus., maps, bibliog.

U.S. Bureau of Labor Statistics. *Publications of the Bureau of Labor Statistics 1886–1967: Numerical Listings, Annotations, Subject Index.* Washington, D.C.: U.S. Government Printing Office, 1968. 156 pp. ◆ Bulletin no. 1567.

U.S. Department of Agriculture. Economics, Statistics, and Cooperative Services. *Chronological Landmarks in American Agriculture.* Maryanna S. Smith, comp. Washington, D.C.: U.S. Department of Agriculture, May 1979. 103 pp.

U.S. National Archives and Records Service. *Agricultural Maps in the National Archives of the United States, ca.1860–1930.* Compiled by William J. Heynen. Washington, D.C.: National Archives and Records Service, General Services Administration, 1976. 25 pp. ◆ Reference Information Leaflet no. 75.

Wood, James P. *The Story of Advertising.* New York: Ronald Press Co., 1958. 512 pp., illus., bibliog.

NOTES

Agricultural History. 1927, quarterly, subscription. Agricultural History Society, James

Shideler, Editor, University of California Press, 2223 Fulton Street, Berkeley, California 94720.
• Includes annual bibliography, begun Vol. 29, no. 4, 1955 (issue number varies); 1955–66 by E. M. Pittenger; 1968–74 by Earl M. Rogers; 1975–, by Earl M. Rogers and Susan H. Rogers.

Agricultural History Society, c/o Wayne D. Rasmussen, Executive Secretary, Economic Research Service, U.S. Department of Agriculture, Washington, D.C. 20250. Founded in 1919, membership includes historians, geographers, agricultural economists, farmers, agricultural scientists and others promoting the study and publication of research in the history of agriculture. The Society sponsors annual symposiums on major areas of agricultural history and publishes the proceedings. It also publishes *Agricultural History* (quarterly), and *Symposium Proceedings* (annual).

Bibliography on the History of Agriculture in the United States. Begun in 1963, the Agricultural History Group of the U.S. Department of Agriculture in cooperation with the Agricultural History Center of the University of California at Davis is compiling and publishing, in sections, a new comprehensive bibliography of American agricultural history, drawing upon the original work of Everett E. Edwards (1930) and the bibliographical card index maintained by the Agricultural History Group, and carrying out a further search through scholarly journals and catalogs. The first section of the revised bibliography was published in 1966. Subjects covered to date include: Fruits and Vegetables; Science and Technology; Agriculture in California; History of the Granger Movement; Agriculture in the Pacific Northwest and Alaska; During the New Deal Period; in the United States 1790–1840; in the Southern States, 1865–1900; Farmer and the Revolution, 1763–1790; in the Mountain States; in the Midwest, 1840–1900; in the Southwest; History of the Farmers' Alliance and the Populist Party; History of the U.S. Department of Agriculture; History of Black Americans in Agriculture; History of Apiculture and Sericulture; George Washington's Interest in Agriculture; in the Great Plains; U.S. Forest Service; History of Grapes, Wines and Raisins. Address: Agricultural History Center, University of California, Davis, California 95616.

Business History Conference, School of Business–254, Indiana University, Blooming-ton, Indiana 47401. Founded in 1955, membership includes business historians and economic historians; most are from the academic community but a number of business firms are represented through their corporate historians. Its purpose is to bring together persons who are active historians of American business with interests ranging from writing biographies of businessmen and histories of firms to the application of mathematics and economic theory to the analysis of the evolution of American business. It awards a biannual prize in business history, and holds an annual meeting. The Conference publishes *Conference Newsletter* (semiannual); and *Economic and Business History,* annual.

Economic History Association, P. O. Box 3630, Wilmington, Delaware 19807. Founded in 1941, membership includes teachers and students of economic history. Prizes are given for a journal article and a doctoral dissertation in American economic history. It has a special committee on research in economic history, publishes *Journal of Economic History* (quarterly), and holds an annual meeting

The Journal of Economic History. 1941, quarterly, membership. Economic History Association, P. O. Box 3630, Wilmington, Delaware 19807.

Regional Economic History Research Center, Eleutherian Mills-Hagley Foundation, P. O. Box 3630, Greenville, Wilmington, Delaware 19807. Established in 1975, the Center sponsors an interdisciplinary research program in the economic history of the Mid-Atlantic states, 1750–1850. The project focuses on the transition from the rural, agrarian, settlement era to the early phase of an industrial, urban society, paying particular attention to the social context and consequences of that transition. The Center invites the participation of economic, social, and intellectual historians of science and technology, agriculture, labor, and others. Researchers are in residence at the Eleutherian Mills Historical Library; stipends are awarded in the spring and fall of each year. Publications include *Working Papers,* an annual series which includes contributions from the Center's spring and fall conferences, essays by researchers at the Center, occasional bibliographies and finding aids; Monograph series, scholarly books published in cooperation with Johns Hopkins University Press.

Social

American Public Works Association. *History of Public Works in the United States, 1776–1976.* Editor: Ellis L. Armstrong; associate editors, Michael C. Robinson, Suellen M. Hoy. Chicago, Ill.: The Association, 1976. 736 pp., illus., bibliogs., index.

Bartlett, Richard A. *The New Country: A Social History of the American Frontier, 1776–1890.* New York: Oxford University Press, 1974. 487 pp., illus., maps, bibliog. essay, index.

Berthoff, Rowland T. *An Unsettled People: Social Order and Disorder in American History.* New York: Harper & Row, 1971. 528 pp., illus., maps, bibliog. references.

Boyer, Paul, and Stephen Nissenbaum. *Salem Possessed: The Social Origins of Witchcraft.* Cambridge, Mass.: Harvard University Press, 1974. 231 pp., illus., tables, maps.

Bremner, Robert H., et al., eds. *Children and Youth in America: A Documentary History, 1600–1932.* Cambridge Mass.: Harvard University Press, 1970. 2 vols., illus., facsims., music.

Buenker, John D., and Nicholas Burckel. *Immigration and Ethnicity: A Guide to Information Sources.* Detroit: Gale Research Co., c1977. 305 pp., indexes.

Clark, Norman H. *Deliver Us From Evil: An Interpretation of American Prohibition.* New York: Norton, 1976. 246 pp., bibliog.

Curti, Merle; Robert Daniel; et al. *Making of an American Community: Democracy in a Frontier County.* Stanford, Calif.: Stanford University Press, 1959. 483 pp., maps, diagrams, bibliog. footnotes.

Degler, Carl N. *At Odds: Women and Family in America from the Revolution to the Present.* New York: Oxford University Press, 1980. 527 pp., bibliog. references.

Demos, John. *A Little Commonwealth: Family Life in Plymouth Colony.* New York: Oxford University Press, 1970. 201 pp., facsims., illus.

De Pauw, Linda Grant; Conover Hunt; and Miriam Schneir. *"Remember the Ladies": Women in America, 1750–1815.* New York: Viking Press, in association with The Pilgrim Society, 1976. 168 pp., illus., bibliog.

Dinnerstein, Leonard; Roger L. Nichols; and David M. Reimers. *Natives and Strangers: Ethnic Groups and the Building of America.* New York: Oxford University Press, 1979. 333 pp., illus., bibliog., index.

Fishel, Leslie H., Jr., and Benjamin Quarles. *The Black American: A Documentary History.* 3rd ed. Glenview, Ill.: Scott, Foresman & Co., 1976. 624 pp., illus., bibliog., index.

Fogarty, Robert S. *Dictionary of American Communal and Utopian History.* Westport, Conn.: Greenwood Press, 1980. 271 pp., bibliog., index.

Franklin, John Hope. *From Slavery to Freedom: A History of Negro Americans.* 5th ed. New York: Knopf, 1980. 554 pp., illus., bibliog., index.

Furnas, Joseph C. *The Americans: A Social History of the United States, 1587–1914.* New York: G. P. Putnam's, 1969. 1015 pp., illus., bibliog. references.

Glaab, Charles N., and A. Theodore Brown. *A History of Urban America.* 2nd ed. Revision prepared by Charles N. Glaab. New York: Macmillan Co., 1976. 350 pp., bibliog., index.

Gutman, Herbert G. *The Black Family in Slavery and Freedom, 1750–1925.* New York: Pantheon Books, c1976. 664 pp., genealogy tables, bibliog. references.

Handlin, Oscar. *The Uprooted: The Epic Story of the Great Migrations that Made the American People.* 2nd enl. ed. Boston: Little, Brown and Co., 1973. 333 pp., bibliog.

Hansen, Marcus L. *The Atlantic Migration, 1607–1860: A History of the Continuing Settlement of the United States.* Edited by Arthur M. Schlesinger. New York: Harper, c1940, 1961. 386 pp., illus., bibliog.

Hansen, Marcus L. *The Mingling of the Canadian and American Peoples. Vol. 1: Historical.* Completed and prepared for publication by John B. Brebner. 1940. Reprint. New Haven, Conn.: Yale University Press, 1970. 274 pp., maps, bibliog. footnotes.

Harvard Encyclopedia of American Ethnic Groups. Stephan Thernstrom, ed. Cambridge, Mass.: Harvard University Press, 1980. 1076 pp., bibliogs.

Hechinger, Fred M., and Grace Hechinger.

Growing Up in America. New York: McGraw-Hill, 1975. 451 pp., bibliog., index.

Hippler, Arthur E., and John R. Wood. *The Alaska Eskimos: A Selected Bibliography*. Fairbanks, Alaska: Institute of Social and Economic Research, University of Alaska, 1977. 328 pp., index.

Holloway, Mark. *Heavens on Earth: Utopian Communities in America, 1680–1880*. 2nd ed. rev. New York: Dover Publications, 1966. 246 pp., illus., map, bibliog.

Hoover, Dwight W. *Cities*. New York: R. R. Bowker Co., 1976. 231 pp., indexes. ♦ Bibliography on the history and sociology of cities.

Jones, Maldwyn Allen. *American Immigration*. Chicago: University of Chicago Press, 1960. 359 pp., illus., bibliog.

Kammen, Michael G. *A Season of Youth: The American Revolution and the Historical Imagination*. New York: Knopf, 1978. 384 pp., illus., bibliog. references, index.

Kerber, Linda K. *Women of the Republic: Intellect and Ideology in Revolutionary America*. Chapel Hill: Published for the Institute of Early American History and Culture by the University of North Carolina Press, c1980. 304 pp., illus., bibliog., index.

Kett, Joseph F. *Rites of Passage: Adolescence in America, 1790 to the Present*. New York: Basic Books, c1977. 327 pp., bibliog. references.

Krichmar, Albert, et al. *The Women's Rights Movement in the United States, 1848–1970: A Bibliography and Sourcebook*. Metuchen, N.J.: Scarecrow Press, 1972. 436 pp., bibliog.

Lingeman, Richard R. *Don't You Know There's a War On? The American Home Front, 1941–1945*. New York: Putnam, 1970. 400 pp., bibliog.

Lingeman, Richard R. *Small Town America: A Narrative History, 1620 to The Present*. New York: G.P. Putnam's Sons, c1980. 547 pp., bibliog.

McKelvey, Blake. *The Emergence of Metropolitan America, 1915–1966*. New Brunswick, N.J.: Rutgers University Press, 1968. 311 pp., illus., maps, bibliog. references.

McKelvey, Blake. *The Urbanization of America, 1860–1915*. New Brunswick, N.J.:

Rutgers University Press, c1963, 1969. 370 pp., illus., chapter notes, bibliog., index.

Milden, James W. *The Family in Past Time: A Guide to the Literature*. New York: Garland Publishing, 1977. 200 pp., index. ♦ Annotated bibliography of books, articles and dissertations in English.

Miller, Wayne C., et al., comps. *A Comprehensive Bibliography for the Study of American Minorities*. New York: New York University Press, 1976. 2 vols. ♦ See also: *Handbook*. 225 pp.

Moquin, Wayne, comp. *Makers of America*. General Editors: Mortimer J. Adler and Charles Van Doren; assistant editor, Dorothy Anderson. Chicago: Encyclopedia Britannica Educational Corp., 1971. 10 vols., illus., maps, bibliog. ♦ Contains 731 documents, in the broadest sense, reflecting the ethnic diversity of the U.S. Vol. 10 includes indexes and bibliographies.

Morgan, Edmund S. *American Slavery, American Freedom: The Ordeal of Colonial Virginia*. New York: W. W. Norton & Co., 1975. 454 pp., map, bibliog.

Morgan, Edmund. *The Puritan Family: Religion and Domestic Relations in Seventeenth-Century New England*. New ed., rev. and enl. Westport, Conn.: Greenwood Press, c1966, 1980. 196 pp., bibliog. references, index.

Quaife, Milo Milton, et al. *The History of the United States Flag from the Revolution to the Present including a Guide to Its Use and Display*. 2nd ed. New York: Harper & Row, 1964. 190 pp., illus., bibliog. references.

Reps, John W. *Cities of the American West: A History of Frontier Urban Planning*. Princeton, N.J.: Princeton University Press, c1979. 827 pp., illus., plans, maps, bibliog., index.

Rothman, David J., and Sheila M. Rothman, eds. *Sources of the American Social Tradition*. New York: Basic Books, 1975. 549 pp., illus., bibliogs. ♦ Collection of diaries, letters, speeches and reports documenting American social life from Puritan colonies to immigrant ghettos to student communes.

Sears, Stephen W. *Hometown, U.S.A.* New York: American Heritage Publishing Co., distr. by Simon & Schuster, 1975. 224 pp., illus. ♦ Photographs and essay on life, 1865–1918.

Seller, Maxine. *To Seek America: A History of Ethnic Life in the United States.* Englewood Cliffs, N.J.: Jerome S. Ozer, c1977. 328 pp., bibliog., index.

Senungetuk, Joseph E. *Give or Take a Century: An Eskimo Chronicle.* San Francisco: Indian Historian Press, 1971. 206 pp., illus., chronology, special lists.

Spruill, Julia Cherry. *Women's Life and Work in the Southern Colonies.* 1938. Reprint. New York: W. W. Norton Co., 1972. 426 pp., illus., bibliog.

Still, Bayrd. *Urban America: A History with Documents.* Boston: Little, Brown and Company, 1974. 566 pp., illus., bibliog. references.

Tyler, Alice Felt. *Freedom's Ferment: Phases of American Social History to 1860.* 1944. Reprint. Freeport, N.Y.: Books for Libraries Press, 1970. 608 pp., illus., bibliog.

Wade, Richard C. *The Urban Frontier: The Rise of Western Cities, 1790–1830.* Cambridge, Mass.: Harvard University Press, 1959. 362 pp., bibliog. footnotes, and "note."

Walters, Ronald G. *American Reformers, 1815–1860.* New York: Hill & Wang, 1978. 235 pp., bibliog.

Ward, David. *Cities and Immigrants: A Geography of Change in Nineteenth-Century America.* New York: Oxford University Press, 1971. 164 pp., illus., maps, bibliog.

Wasserman, Paul, and Jean Morgan, eds. *Ethnic Information Sources of the United States: A Guide to Organizations, Agencies, Foundations, Institutions, Media, Commercial and Trade Bodies, Government Programs.* Detroit: Gale Research Co., 1976. 751 pp., indexes.

Weisenberger, Bernard A., and the editors of American Heritage. *The American Heritage History of the American People.* New York: American Heritage Publishing Co., 1971. 396 pp., illus.

NOTES

Immigration History Society, c/o Professor Carlton C. Qualey, Minnesota Historical Society, 690 Cedar Street, St. Paul, Minnesota 55101. Founded in 1965, membership includes scholars, students and individuals interested in the study of human migration, particularly immigration to the U.S. It serves as a means of communication for historians, sociologists, economists and others engaged in the interdisciplinary quantitative and comparative approaches to the study of America's ethnic groups. It meets annually with the Organization of American Historians; and holds joint sessions at annual meetings of related organizations. Publications include *Journal of American Ethnic History* (semiannual); and, *Immigration History Newsletter* (1968, semiannual).

Journal of American Ethnic History. 1981, semiannual, membership/subscription. Immigration History Society, c/o Minnesota Historical Society, 690 Cedar Street, St. Paul, Minnesota 55101.

Journal of Social History. 1967, quarterly, subscription. Carnegie-Mellon University Press, Schenley Park, Pittsburgh, Pennsylvania 15213.

Journal of Urban History. 1974, quarterly, subscription. Sage Publications, Inc., 275 South Beverly Drive, Beverly Hills, California 90212.

Cultural/Intellectual

Ahlstrom, Sydney E. *A Religious History of the American People.* New Haven, Conn.: Yale University Press, 1973. 1158 pp., bibliog.

American Heritage. *The American Heritage Cookbook and Illustrated History of American Eating and Drinking.* With chapters by Cleveland Amory, and others. Rev. ed. New York: American Heritage Publishing Co., distr. by Simon & Schuster, 1964. 629 pp., illus.

Andrist, Ralph. *American Century: 100 Years of Changing Life Style in America.* New York: McGraw-Hill for American Heritage Press, 1972. 351 pp., illus.

Arts in America: A Bibliography. Edited by Bernard Karpel. Washington, D.C.: Smithsonian, 1979–80. 4 vols.

The Arts in America: The Nineteenth Century. By Wendell Garrett and others. New York: Charles Scribner's Sons, 1969. 412 pp., illus., bibliog.

Bailey, Thomas A. *Voices of America: The Nation's Story in Slogans, Sayings and Songs.* With the assistance of Stephen M. Dobbs. New

York: Free Press, c1976. 520 pp., illus., bibliog., index.

Barnouw, Erik. *A History of Broadcasting in the United States.* New York: Oxford University Press, 1966–1970. 3 vols., illus., bibliogs.

Beach, Mark. *A Bibliographic Guide to American Colleges and Universities: From Colonial Times to the Present.* Westport, Conn.: Greenwood Press, 1975. 314 pp., index.

Bell, Whitfield J., Jr. *The Colonial Physician & Other Essays.* 1st ed. New York: Science History Publications, 1975. 229 pp., illus., bibliog. references.

Betts, John Rickards. *America's Sporting Heritage: 1850–1950.* Reading, Mass.: Addison-Wesley Publishing Co., 1974. 428 pp., bibliog., index.

Bobbit, Mary Read. *A Bibliography of Etiquette Books Published in America Before 1900.* New York: New York Public Library, 1947. 35 pp. ◆ Reprinted form the Bulletin of the New York Public Library of December 1947.

Burr, Nelson R. *A Critical Bibliography of Religion in America.* Princeton, N.J.: Princeton University Press, 1961. 2 vols.

Cable, Mary, and the editors of American Heritage. *American Manners and Morals: A Picture History of How We Behaved and Misbehaved.* New York: American Heritage Publishing Co., 1969. 399 pp., illus.

Carson, Gerald. *The Polite Americans: A Wide Angle View of Our More or Less Good Manners Over 300 Years.* New York: Morrow, 1966. 346 pp., illus., bibliog.

Chase, Gilbert, ed. *America's Music, from the Pilgrims to the Present.* 2nd rev. ed. New York: McGraw-Hill Book Co., 1966. 759 pp., music, bibliog.

Church, Robert L., and Michael W. Sedlak. *Education in the United States: An Interpretive History.* New York: The Free Press, c1976. 489 pp., illus., bibliogs.

Commager, Henry S. *The American Mind: An Interpretation of American Thought and Character Since the 1880's.* New Haven, Conn.: Yale University Press, 1950. 476 pp., bibliog.

Cremin, Lawrence A. *American Education: The Colonial Experience 1607–1783.* 1st ed. New York: Harper & Row, 1970. 688 pp., bibliog. references.

Cremin, Lawrence A. *American Education: The National Experience, 1783–1876.* New York: Harper & Row, 1980. 607 pp., bibliog. essay.

Daniels, George H. *Science in American Society: A Social History.* New York: Knopf, 1971. 390 pp., bibliog.

Davidson, Marshall B., and the editors of American Heritage. *The American Heritage History of the Writer's America.* New York: American Heritage, distr. by McGraw-Hill, 1973. 403 pp., illus.

Davis, Richard Beale. *Intellectual Life in the Colonial South, 1585–1763.* Knoxville: University of Tennessee Press, 1978. 3 vols., plates, illus., bibliogs., index.

Duffy, John. *The Healers: The Rise of the Medical Establishment.* New York: McGraw-Hill, c1976. 385 pp., bibliog., index.

Dulles, Foster Rhea. *A History of Recreation: America Learns to Play.* 2nd ed. New York: Appleton-Century-Crofts, 1965. 446 pp., illus., bibliog. references.

Earle, Alice M. *Stage-Coach and Tavern Days.* New York: Macmillan Company, 1900. 449 pp., illus.

Elson, Ruth M. *Guardians of Tradition: American Schoolbooks of the Nineteenth Century.* Lincoln: University of Nebraska Press, 1964. 424 pp., illus.

Foster, Stephen. *Their Solitary Way: The Puritan Social Ethic in the First Century of Settlement in New England.* New Haven, Conn.: Yale University Press, 1971. 214 pp., bibliog.

Garrett, Wendell D., and Jane N. Garrett, comps. *The Arts in Early American History.* Introductory essay by Walter M. Whitehill; A Bibliography by Wendell D. and Jane N. Garrett. Chapel Hill: University of North Carolina Press, 1965. 170 pp., bibliog.

Gaustad, Edwin Scott. *Historical Atlas of Religion in America.* Rev. ed. New York: Harper & Row, c1976. 189 pp., maps, illus., tables, bibliog., appendix.

Gohdes, Clarence L. F., comp. *Literature and Theatre of the States and Regions of the*

U.S.A.: An Historical Bibliography. Durham, N.C.: Duke University Press, 1967. 276 pp.

Hall, Ben M. *The Best Remaining Seats: The Story of the Golden Age of the Movie Palace.* 1st ed. New York: C. N. Potter, 1961. 266 pp., illus., drawings, index.

Handbook of American Popular Culture. Edited by M. Thomas Inge. Westport, Conn.: Greenwood Press, 1978–1981. 3 vols., bibliog., index. ◆ Vol. 1—Popular; Vol. 2—Sources; Vol. 3—Bibliography.

Hindle, Brooke. *The Pursuit of Science in Revolutionary America, 1735–1789.* Chapel Hill: Published for the Institute of Early American History and Culture, Williamsburg, Va. by the University of North Carolina Press, 1956. 410 pp., illus., bibliog. footnotes, bibliog. note.

Hofstadter, Richard. *America at 1750: A Social Portrait.* New York: Knopf, 1971. 293 pp., bibliog. references.

Horn, David. *The Literature of American Music in Books and Folk Music Collections: A Fully Annotated Bibliography.* Metuchen, N.J.: Scarecrow Press, 1977. 556 pp.

Hudson, Winthrop Sill. *Religion in America: An Historical Account of the Development of American Religious Life.* 3rd ed. New York: Charles Scribner's Sons, 1981. 486 pp., bibliog.

Jones, Howard Mumford. *The Age of Energy: Varieties of American Experience, 1865–1915.* New York: Viking Press, 1970. 545 pp., illus., bibliog. references.

Jones, Howard M. *O Strange New World: American Culture, The Formative Years.* New York: Viking Press, 1964. 464 pp., illus.

Larkin, Oliver. *Art and Life in America.* Rev. and enl. ed. New York: Holt, Rinehart & Winston, 1960. 559 pp., illus., bibliog. notes.

Lathrop, Elise L. *Early American Inns and Taverns.* 1935. Reprint. New York: Benjamin Blom, 1968. 365 pp., illus., bibliog.

Leventhal, Herbert. *In the Shadow of the Enlightenment: Occultism and Renaissance Science in Eighteenth-Century America.* New York: New York University Press, 1976. 330 pp., illus., bibliog.

Lowenstein, Eleanor. *Bibliography of American Cookery Books, 1742–1860.* Worcester, Mass.: American Antiquarian Society; New York: Corner Book Shop, 1972. 132 pp.

McLanathan, Richard. *The American Tradition in the Arts.* New York: Harcourt, Brace & World, 1968. 492 pp., illus., bibliog.

Mitterling, Philip I. *U.S. Cultural History: A Guide to Information Sources.* Detroit: Gale Research Co., c1980. 581 pp., indexes.

Moody, Richard. *America Takes the Stage: Romanticism in American Drama and Theatre, 1750–1900.* 1955. Reprint. New York: Kraus Reprint Co., 1969. 322 pp., illus., music, bibliog. ◆ Indiana University Publications, Humanities series no. 34.

Morgan, Howard Wayne. *Victorian Culture in America, 1865–1914.* Itasca, Ill.: F.E. Peacock Publishing, 1973. 126 pp., illus., bibliog.

Mott, Frank Luther. *American Journalism: A History, 1690–1960.* 3rd ed. New York: Macmillan, 1962. 901 pp., illus.

Nye, Russel Blaine. *The Cultural Life of the New Nation, 1776–1830.* New York: Harper & Row, 1963. 324 pp., bibliog. footnotes, index.

Nye, Russel Blaine. *The Unembarrassed Muse: The Popular Arts in America.* New York: Dial Press, 1970. 497 pp., illus., bibliog. references. ◆ Two Centuries of America, A Bicentennial Series.

The Pursuit of Knowledge in the Early American Republic: *American Scientific and Learned Societies from Colonial Times to the Civil War.* Edited by Alexandra Oleson and Sanborn C. Brown. Baltimore: Johns Hopkins University Press, c1976. 372 pp., bibliog. references, index. ◆ See also: *The Organization of Knowledge in Modern America, 1860–1920.* Edited by Alexandra Oleson and John Voss. c1979. 478 pp., bibliog. references, index.

Quinn, Arthur H. *A History of the American Drama from the Beginnings to the Civil War.* 2nd ed. New York: Appleton-Century-Crofts, c1951. 530 pp., bibliog., list of American plays.

Root, Waverly L., and Richard de Rochemont. *Eating in America, A History.* New York: William Morrow and Co., 1976. 512 pp., bibliog.

Sandeen, Ernest R., and Frederick Hale. *American Religion and Philosophy: A Guide to Information Sources.* Detroit: Gale Research Co., 1978. 377 pp., indexes.

Saum, Lewis O. *The Popular Mood of Pre-Civil War America.* Westport, Conn.: Greenwood Press, 1980. 336 pp., bibliog., index.

Savelle, Max. *Seeds of Liberty: The Genesis of the American Mind.* Westport, Conn.: Greenwood Press, c1948, 1981. 618 pp., illus., bibliog. references, index.

Schudson, Michael. *Discovering the News: A Social History of American Newspapers.* New York: Basic Books, c1978. 228 pp., bibliog. references, index.

Shryock, Richard H. *Medicine and Society in America, 1660–1860.* New York: New York University Press, 1960. 182 pp., bibliog.

Stearns, Raymond P. *Science in the British Colonies of America.* Urbana: University of Illinois Press, 1970. 766 pp., illus., bibliog.

Tyack, David B. *The One Best System: A History of American Urban Education.* Cambridge, Mass.: Harvard University Press, 1974. 353 pp., illus., bibliog., index.

Van Orman, Richard A. *A Room for the Night: Hotels of the Old West.* Bloomington: Indiana University Press, 1966. 162 pp., illus., bibliog. references.

Wilmeth, Don B. *American and English Popular Entertainment: A Guide to Information Sources.* Detroit: Gale Research Co., c1980. 465 pp., indexes.

Wish, Harvey. *Society and Thought in America.* New York: Longmans, Green, 1950–52. 2 vols., illus., bibliog. ◆ Vol. 2: Modern America, 2nd ed., rev., and enl., published by D. McKay Co., New York, 1962.

Wright, Louis B. *Culture on the Moving Frontier.* New York: Harper, 1961. 275 pp., bibliog. references.

Genealogy and Family History

Genealogical Research Methods

American Genealogical Research Institute. *How to Trace Your Family Tree: A Complete and Easy to Understand Guide for the Beginner.* Garden City, N.Y.: Doubleday, 1975. 197 pp., bibliog.

American Society of Genealogists. *Genealogical Research.* Edited by Milton Rubincam, et al. Washington, D.C.: The Society, 1960–. 2 vols. ◆ Vol. 1—Methods and Sources; Vol. 2—(no subtitle), edited by Kenn Stryker-Rodda, covers regional genealogy and special studies.

Beard, Timothy F., and Denise Demong. *How to Find Your Family Roots.* New York: McGraw-Hill, c1977. 1007 pp., index.

Bell, James B. *Family History Record Book.* Minneapolis: University of Minnesota Press, 1980. 160 pp., charts.

Daughters of the American Revolution. Genealogical Advisory Committee to the Registrar General. *Is That Lineage Right? A Training Manual for the Examiner of Lineage Papers with Helpful Hints for the Beginner in Genealogical Research.* Washington, D.C.: National Society of the Daughters of the American Revolution, 1965. 55 pp., bibliog.

Doane, Gilbert H., and James B. Bell. *Searching for Your Ancestors: The How and Why of Genealogy.* 5th ed. Minneapolis: University of Minnesota Press, 1980. 208 pp., bibliogs., appendices, index.

Draznin, Yaffa. *The Family Historian's Handbook: A Complete How-to Guide for Tracing Your Roots—Whatever Your Ethnic Background.* New York: Jove Publications, Inc., 1978. 256 pp., appendices, bibliog., index.

Everton, George B. *The How Book for Genealogists.* 7th ed. Logan, Utah: Deseret Book Co., 1973. 237 pp., illus.

Gobble, John R. *What to Say in Your Genealogical Letters: Do's and Don'ts in Genealogical Correspondence.* Logan, Utah: Everton Publishers, 1967. 25 pp., illus.

Greenwood, Val D. *The Researcher's Guide to American Genealogy.* Baltimore: Genealogical Publishing Co., 1978. 535 pp., illus., bibliog.

Helmbold, F. Wilbur. *Tracing Your Ancestry: A Step-by-Step Guide to Researching Your Family History.* Birmingham, Ala.: Oxmoor House, 1976. 210 pp., illus., bibliog., index. ◆ See also, companion publication: *Tracing Your Ancestry: Logbook* (128 pp.), a supply of lineage charts, family group records, census and search control forms, annotated bibliography.

Jones, Vincent L.; Arlene H. Eakle; and Mildred H. Christensen. *Genealogical Research: A Jurisdictional Approach.* Rev. ed. Woods Cross, Utah: Genealogical Copy Service, 1972. 326 pp., bibliog., illus., appendices, index.

Kirkham, E. Kay. *Simplified Genealogy for Americans.* Salt Lake City, Utah: Deseret Book Co., c1968, 1977. 172 pp., glossary, maps, index.

Lichtman, Allan J. *Your Family History: How to Use Oral History, Personal Family Archives, and Public Documents to Discover Your Heritage.* 1st ed. New York: Vintage Books, 1978. 205 pp., bibliog., index.

Linder, Bill R. "Black Genealogy: Basic Steps to Research," *History News,* 36:2 (February 1981), Technical Leaflet no. 135.

Linder, Bill R. *How to Trace Your Family History.* New York: Everest House, c1978. 187 pp.

Miller, Carolynne L. "Genealogical Research: A Basic Guide," rev. ed., *History News,* 24:3 (March 1969), Technical Leaflet no. 14.

Myrick, Shelby, Jr. "Glossary of Legal Terminology: An Aid to Genealogists," *History News,* 25:7 (July 1970), Technical Leaflet no. 55.

Nichols, Elizabeth L. *Help is Available: A Simplified Step-by-Step Instruction Book for the Beginner in Genealogy.* Logan, Utah: Everton Pub., 1972. 168 pp., illus.

Rottenberg, Dan. *Finding Our Fathers: A Guidebook to Jewish Genealogy.* 1st ed. New York: Random House, c1977. 401 pp., illus., bibliog.

Stryker-Rodda, Harriet M. *How to Climb Your Family Tree: Genealogy for Beginners.* Philadephia and New York: J.B. Lippincott Co., c1977. 144 pp., bibliog.

Watts, Jim, and Allen F. Davis. *Generations: Your Family in Modern American History.* 2nd ed. New York: Knopf, distr. by Random House, c1978. 288 pp., illus., bibliogs.

Westin, Jeane Eddy. *Finding Your Roots: How Every American Can Trace His Ancestors at Home and Abroad.* Los Angeles: J.P. Tarcher, distr. by St. Martin's Press, New York, 1977. 243 pp., figures, appendices, bibliog., index.

Wright, Norman Edgar. *Building an American Pedigree: A Study of Genealogy.* Provo, Utah: Brigham Young University Press, 1974. 639 pp., maps, appendices.

Guides to Sources

The American Genealogical-Biographical Index to American Genealogical-Biographical and Local History Materials. Edited by Fremont Rider. Middletown, Conn.: Godfrey Memorial Library, 1952–. 116 vols. to date. ♦ Supersedes *American Genealogical Index,* 1942–52, 48 vols., begun in 1936 as a surname index printed on cards.

Blockson, Charles L., and Ron Fry. *Black Genealogy.* Englewood Cliffs, N.J.: Prentice-Hall, c1977. 232 pp., illus., appendices, bibliog., index. ♦ Appendix is directory of libraries and archives in U.S. and other countries, mostly African.

Brooke-Little, John P. *An Heraldic Alphabet.* London: Macdonald, 1973. 224 pp., illus.

Camp, Anthony J. *Everyone Has Roots: An Introduction to English Genealogy.* Baltimore: Genealogical Publishing Co., 1978. 189 pp., bibliog.

Canada. Public Archives. *Tracing Your Ancestors in Canada.* Ottawa: Public Archives, 1966. 31 pp.

Cappon, Lester J. *American Genealogical Periodicals: A Bibliography With a Chronological Finding List.* Second printing with additions. New York: New York Public Library, 1964. 32 pp. ♦ Descriptions of national and local genealogical periodicals; geographical finding list by state.

Colket, Meredith B., and Frank E. Bridgers. *Guide to Genealogical Records in the National Archives.* Washington, D.C.: National Archives and Records Service, General Services Administration, 1964. 145 pp., tables. ♦ National Archives Publication no. 64–8. A guide to the use of such sources as population and mortality census schedules, passenger arrival lists, military, naval and marine records, etc.

Crowther, George R. *Surname Index to Sixty-five Volumes of Colonial and Revolutionary Pedigrees.* Washington, D.C.: National Genealogical Society, 1964. 143 pp. ♦ Special Publication no. 27.

Cunningham, Ronald, and Evan Evans. *A Handy Guide to the Genealogical Library and Church Historical Departments.* 5th ed. Logan, Utah: Everton Publishing, 1980. 268 pp., illus.

Daughters of the American Revolution. *DAR Patriot Index.* Washington, D.C.: Daughters of the American Revolution, 1966. 771 pp. ◆ See also: First Supplement (1969); Second Supplement (1973); Third Supplement (1976).

Everton, George B., ed. *The Handy Book for Genealogists.* 7th ed., rev. and enl. Logan, Utah: Deseret Book Co., 1981. 392 pp., bibliog., general dictionary, index.

Filby, P. William, comp. *American and British Genealogy and Heraldry: A Selected List of Books.* 2nd ed. Chicago: American Library Association, 1975. 467 pp., index. ◆ Sections on U.S., Latin America, Canada, England, Ireland, Scotland, Wales, British Island area, British dominions and former dominions; heraldry; addresses of small publishers and authors who publish privately.

Genealogical and Local History Books in Print. 3rd ed. Netti Schreiner Yantis, ed. Springfield, Va.: Genealogical Books in Print, 1980. 900 pp. ◆ Address: 6818 Lois Drive, Springfield, Virginia 22150.

Gibson, Jeremy W. S. *Wills and Where to Find Them.* Baltimore: Genealogical Publishing Co., 1974. 210 pp., maps, glossary, index.

Glenn, Thomas Allen, comp. *A List of Some American Genealogies Which Have Been Printed in Book Form.* 1897. Reprint. Baltimore: Genealogical Publishing Co., 1969. 71 pp., appendices.

Haigh, Roger M. *Finding Aids to the Microfilmed Manuscript Collection of the Genealogical Society of Utah.* Salt Lake City: University of Utah Press, 1978–. 5 vols. ◆ Various authors; covers preliminary surveys, descriptive inventories and bibliographic guides to Mexican, German, English, French, New York, and other manuscripts in the genealogical archives of the Mormon Church.

Hamilton-Edwards, Gerald K. S. *In Search of British Ancestry.* 3rd ed. Baltimore: Genealogical Publishing Co., 1974. 293 pp., illus., bibliog., index.

Hotten, John Camden. *The Original Lists of Persons of ˜Quality: Emigrants, Religious Exiles, Political Rebels, Serving Men Sold For a Term of Years, Apprentices, Maidens Pressed and Others Who Went from Great Britain to the American Plantations, 1600–1700. . . .* 1874. Reprint. Baltimore: Genealogical Publishing Co., 1968. 580 pp. ◆ One of the earliest compilations of lists of ship passengers.

Index to American Genealogies, and *Genealogical Material Contained in All Works such as Town Histories, County Histories, Local Histories, Historical Society Publications, Biographies, Historical Periodicals, and Kindred Works, Alphabetically Arranged, with Supplement 1900 to 1908.* 5th ed., rev. 1908. Reprint. Baltimore: Genealogical Publishing Co., c1967, 1979. 2 vols. in 1 (352, 107 pp.). ◆ Original cover title: *Munsell's Genealogical Index.*

Jacobus, Donald Lines. *Index to Genealogical Periodicals.* 1932–1953. Reprint. Baltimore: Genealogical Publishing Co., 1978. 3 vols. in 1 (365 pp.).

Kirkham, E. Kay. *A Genealogical and Historical Atlas of the United States.* Logan, Utah: The Everton Publishers, c1976, 1980. 328 pp., maps, bibliog., index.

Kirkham, E. Kay. *A Handy Guide to Record-Searching in the Larger Cities of the United States.* Logan, Utah: Everton Publishing Co., 1974. 137 pp., illus., maps. ◆ Guide to vital records in major U.S. cities, such as censuses, directories, early newspapers, maps; birth, marriages, and death records; how and where to find them.

Kirkham, E. Kay. *Our Native Americans: Their Records of Genealogical Value.* Logan, Utah: Everton Publishers, 1980. 235 pp. ◆ First volume; federal government records, Oklahoma Historical Society records, Genealogical Society of Utah listings.

Kirkham, E. Kay. *Survey of American Church Records: For the Period Before the Civil War, East of the Mississippi River.* 4th ed., rev. and enl. Logan, Utah: Everton Publishers, 1978. 344 pp., glossary, bibliog. ◆ This edition includes Vol. 1, major denominations, and Vol. 2, minor denominations.

Lancour, Harold, comp. *A Bibliography of Ship Passenger Lists 1538–1825: A Guide to Published Lists of Immigrants to North America.* 3rd ed., rev. and enl. by Richard J.

Wolfe. New York: New York Public Library, 1978. 137 pp. ♦ Includes a list of passenger arrival records in the National Archives, by Frank E. Bridgers.

Mander, Meda. *Tracing Your Ancestors.* North Pomfret, Vt.: David & Charles, 1976. 148 pp., bibliog., appendices, index. ♦ Guide for British genealogical research.

Meyer, Mary Keysor, ed. *Directory of Genealogical Societies in the U.S.A. and Canada.* 2nd ed. Pasadena, Md.: Libra Publications, 1980. 109 pp., index. ♦ Address: author, 297 Cove Road, Pasadena, Maryland 21122.

Miller, Olga K. *Migration, Emigration, Immigration.* Logan, Utah: Everton Publishers, Inc., 1974–81. 2 vols., maps, bibliogs., index. ♦ Vol. 1—principally to the U.S. and in the U.S., 2nd ed.; Vol. 2—religious, political and refugee groups; U.S.; foreign countries; maps; conclusion; index to authors.

The Morton Allan Directory of European Passenger Steamship Arrivals for the Years *1890–1930 at the Port of New York, and For the Years 1904–1926 at the Ports of New York, Philadelphia, Boston and Baltimore.* 1931. Reprint. Baltimore: Genealogical Publishing Co., 1979. 268 pp.

National Genealogical Society. *Index of Revolutionary War Pension Applications in the National Archives.* Rev. and enl. Washington, D.C.: The Society, 1976. 658 pp. ♦ Special Publication no. 40.

Neagles, James, and Lila L. Neagles. *Locating Your Immigrant Ancestor: A Guide to Naturalization Records.* Logan, Utah: Everton Publishing, 1975. 153 pp.

New England Historical and Genealogical Register: *Index of Persons, Subjects, Places.* 1906–1911. Reprint. Edited by Josephine E. Rayne and Effie L. Chapman. Baltimore: Genealogical Publishing Co., 1972. 4 vols. (1750 pp.).

New York Public Library. Research Libraries. *Dictionary Catalog of the Local History and Genealogy Division.* New York: New York Public Library, 1974. 20 vols.

Passenger and Immigration Lists Index: *A Guide to Published Arrival Records of 300,000 Passengers Who Came to the United States and Canada in the Seventeenth, Eighteenth and Nineteenth Centuries.* Edited by P. William Filby, with Mary K. Meyer. Detroit: Gale Research Co., 1979, c1980. 3 vols., bibliog. references.

Smith, Elsdon C. *New Dictionary of American Family Names.* New York: Harper & Row, c1973. 570 pp.

Sperry, Kip. *A Survey of American Genealogical Periodicals and Periodical Indexes.* Detroit: Gale Research Co., 1978. 199 pp., appendices, index. ♦ Gale Genealogy and Local History Series vol. 3.

Stephenson, Jean. *Heraldry for the American Genealogist.* Washington, D.C.: National Genealogical Society, 1959. 44 pp., illus. ♦ Special Publication no. 25.

Stern, Malcolm H., comp. *First American Jewish Families: 600 Genealogies 1654–1977.* Cincinnati: American Jewish Archives, 1978. 419 pp., bibliog., index.

Stern, Malcolm H. "Jewish Genealogy: An Annotated Bibliography," *History News,* 36:5 (May 1981), Technical Leaflet no. 138.

U.S. Bureau of the Census. *Heads of Families at the First Census of the United States Taken in the Year 1790.* 1908. Reprint. Baltimore: Genealogical Publishing Co., 1973–1980. 12 vols.

U.S. Library of Congress. *Genealogies in the Library of Congress: A Bibliography.* Edited by Marion J. Kaminkow. Baltimore: Magna Carta Book Co., 1972. 2 vols. ♦ See also: *Supplement, 1972–1976.* 1977. 285 pp.; and, *A Complement to Genealogies in the Library of Congress.* 1981. 118 pp., indexes. Includes listings not in previous three volumes, corrections, supplements, new editions.

U.S. National Archives and Records Service. *Genealogical Sources Outside the National Archives.* Washington, D.C.: General Services Administration, 1972. 8 pp. ♦ Information Leaflet no. 6.

U.S. National Archives and Records Service. *Guide to Genealogical Records in the National Archives.* Washington, D.C.: for sale by Supt. of Docs., U.S. Government Printing Office, c1972. 145 pp.

Where to Write for Birth and Death Records. Rev. ed. Washington, D.C.: U.S. Government Printing Office, 1976. 8 pp.

Where to Write for Divorce Records. Washington, D.C.: U.S. Government Printing Office, 1976. 5 pp.

Where to Write for Marriage Records. Washington, D.C.: U.S. Government Printing Office, 1976. 6 pp.

Zieber, Eugene. *Heraldry in America.* 2nd ed. 1909. Reprint. Baltimore: Genealogical Publishing Co., 1977. 427 pp., illus., bibliog. references, index.

NOTES

American Family Records Association, 311 East 12th Street, Kansas City, Missouri 64106. Founded in 1978, the Association is a not for profit educational organization dedicated to increasing the education and knowledge of members and the public in family history and genealogical records. Membership includes individuals, organizations, affiliated and associated societies, and chapters. Its programs include legislative affairs, youth programs, microfilm program, AFRA DATA BASE/computerized listing of names of persons with related genealogical data, adult adoptee organizations program. It publishes *Family Records Today* (quarterly), which incorporates some features from *National Genealogical Inquirer* which ceased publication, Winter 1981.

American Society of Genealogists, c/o Mrs. Bert Hagler, 3812 Flagler Avenue, Key West, Florida 33040. Founded in 1940, the Society is a nonprofit organization dedicated to improving the quality of genealogical research and to providing education in this field. Membership consists of specialists in genealogy and heraldry chosen on the basis of their published work in these fields, limited to 50 fellows. The Society promotes scientific methods of genealogical research through publication of articles in genealogical and historical periodicals and participation in various genealogical courses. Fellows of the Society have participated in the incorporation of the Board of Certified Genealogists. It also publishes *Genealogical Research: Methods and Sources* (2 vols.), cited above.

Board for Certification of Genealogists, c/o Mrs. Donna R. Hotaling, Executive Secretary, 1307 New Hampshire Avenue, N. W., Washington, D.C. 20036. The Board will refer inquiries to certified genealogists and record searchers who undertake for a fee research in the Library of Congress, the National Archives, and other information centers in Washington, as well as in local record repositories throughout the nation.

Family Records Today: *The Journal of the American Family Records Association.* 1980, quarterly, membership/subscription. American Family Records Association, 311 East Twelfth Street, Kansas City, Missouri 64106.

The Genealogical Helper. 1947, bimonthly, subscription. Everton Publishers, P. O. Box 368, Logan, Utah 84321. ◆ The July/August issue includes an annual directory of genealogical societies, libraries, periodicals, and professionals.

Genealogical Journal. 1972, quarterly, subscription. Utah Genealogical Association, Box 1144, Salt Lake City, Utah 84110.

Journal of Family History: *Studies in Family, Kinship, and Demography.* 1976, quarterly, subscription. National Council on Family Relations, 1219 University Avenue, S.E., Minneapolis, Minnesota 55414. ◆ Supersedes: *Family in Historical Perspective.*

Local History and Genealogy Room, General Reference and Bibliography Division, U.S. Library of Congress, Washington, D.C. 20540. In addition to the local history and genealogy publications in the Library's general collection, there is a reference collection of 5,000 volumes in the Local History and Genealogy Room. It contains various indexes, guides, and other works conveniently arranged for reader's usage. The staff will aid in locating material, but cannot undertake research in family history and heraldry. These helpful leaflets are available from the Division: *Reference Service and Facilities of the Local History and Genealogy Room; Guide to Genealogical Research: A Selected List;* and, *Surnames: A Selected List of Books.*

National Genealogical Society, 1921 Sunderland Place, N.W., Washington, D.C. 20036. Founded in 1903, membership includes individuals, libraries and societies. Its purposes are to promote interest in genealogical research, to stimulate and foster the preservation and publication of official records of genealogical interest of all kinds, national, state, county, township, city and town, church and cemetery, bible and family resources. Members list with the Society the families on which they are working and on which they can exchange data with others interested in the same families. It maintains a library of approximately 10,000 volumes on genealogy, local history and source material. It publishes *National Genealogical Society Quarterly;* and, *Newsletter* (bimonthly).

National Genealogical Society Quarterly. 1912, quarterly, membership. National Genealogical Society, 1921 Sunderland Place, N.W., Washington, D.C. 20036.

National Society Daughters of the American Revolution, Library, 1776 D Street, N.W., Washington, D.C. 20006. The library has a large collection of genealogical materials in printed, processed, and typewritten form. Included are entries in family bibles and inscriptions on tombstones, abstracts of court records, lineage books, abstracts of Revolutionary War pension and bounty land warrant application files in the National Archives and copies of church records. The Society does not do original research but will furnish the names of genealogists who will do research in its holdings for a fee. The library is closed to nonmembers during April.

U.S. Immigration and Naturalization Service, Washington, D.C. 20536. The Service has records of all naturalizations that occurred after September 26, 1906. A form can be obtained from any of the Service's district offices; the form is used for inquiries about citizenship after that date.

U.S. National Archives and Records Service, General Services Administration, Washington, D.C. 20408. Inquiries for information on census and military service records may be sent to the National Archives; forms are available to facilitate the record search. Also available is an information leaflet, no. 5, on genealogical records in the National Archives.

2

Archeology

Historical archeology is a return to basics—from the ground up, as it were. Not too many years ago—50, perhaps—little thought was given to the significance of archeology in the restoration process. It probably would not have occurred to William Sumner Appleton, the doughty doyen who headed the great effort of the Society for the Preservation of New England Antiquities to preserve the American heritage, to take too seriously the evidence that archeological procedures might adduce. What was above ground was complex enough.

And yet even in his time historical archeology was becoming a scientific procedure. It was developing the techniques that today help materially in the recovery, study, and reconstruction of man's past. As Dr. John Cotter has pointed out, "The field of historical archeology, in contrast to pre-historical archeology, deals with those periods which have written records." Thus it complements historical and architectural research. It must be taken seriously, especially by those who have not been exposed to the role it can play in solving preservation problems. Unbelievers should consult the often-sprightly works of J. C. Harrington, Ivor Noel Hume, and James Deetz, whose studies often read like detective stories without a villain.

In this chapter there is a combination of scholarly and technical references and readings and introductory works for the nonprofessional. The latter may well be for the education of the illiterate in archeology, so that he/she will not be tempted to go out and joyously (and recklessly) dig. Nothing is in greater need of supervision of trained scientists than an historical archeological project. The amateur too quickly reaches the point of no return, destroying forever evidence that might have thrown significant light on a small dark spot on the past. The star role of the nonprofessional may well be to be so well grounded in the importance of archeological remains that he/she performs the rescue and assures the saving of the ground so that the professional may later conduct a scientific exploration.

In any event, here are listed the important organizations and journals, the significant bibliographies and reference books, the surveys, the new studies on investigation and methods, and the regional studies. There is even a section on marine archeology and another on the rapidly developing field of cultural resources management.

Out of it all comes one clear message: Ponder long, hard, and wisely before launching an archeological dig, for once the ground is disturbed, there is no second chance. Remember too that our children or children's children may develop new and better techniques for unearthing and interpreting our past.

Basic Reference Shelf

Bass, George F. *Archaeology Beneath the Sea.* New York: Walker & Co., 1975. 238 pp., illus., maps, plans, index. ◆ Describes methods used, dangers and difficulties, and rewards of underwater research. Also discusses the problems of looting which have destroyed sites. Some chapters have appeared in other publications in previous years.

Bibliography of Historical Archaeology, c/o John L. Cotter, Associate Curator Emeritus and Editor, American Historical Archaeology, The University Museum, University of Pennsylvania, 33rd and Spruce Streets, Philadelphia, Pennsylvania 19104. ◆ A basic reference for the address file; source for computerized bibliography of published monographs, journal articles and unpublished manuscripts relating to American historical archaeology. See full description in reference section.

Conservation Archaeology: A Guide for Cultural Resource Management Studies. Edited by Michael B. Schiffer and George J. Gumerman. New York: Academic Press, c1977. 495 pp., illus., bibliog., index. ◆ State-of-the-art survey of the aspect of American archeology that is funded through contracts with government agencies. Contributors cover a variety of issues including how resources should be conserved, legal mandates, definition of conservation archeology, steps in contracted research and examples of resource surveys.

Deetz, James. *In Small Things Forgotten: The Archaeology of Early American Life.* 1st ed. Garden City, N.Y.: Anchor Press/Doubleday, 1977. 184 pp., illus., bibliog. references, index. ◆ Synthesis of previous research and current views on the theoretical position of historic site archeology as illustrated by a social-scientific approach to explaining changes observed in Anglo-American culture in New England from the early 17th century to the present. Companion volume to Deetz, *Invitation to Archaeology.*

Deetz, James. *Invitation to Archaeology.* Garden City, N.Y.: Natural History Press for the American Museum of Natural History, 1967. 150 pp., illus., bibliog. ◆ Explores principles, methods and problems of the present-day archeologist. Includes excavation techniques, radiocarbon dating, form analysis and space-time patterns; appendix; and selected readings.

Hester, Thomas R.; Robert F. Heizer; and John A. Graham. *Field Methods in Archaeology.* 6th ed. Palo Alto, Calif: Mayfield Pub. Co., c1975. 408 pp., illus., diagrams, maps, bibliog., indexes. ◆ Covers planning, excavating, and recording results of all kinds of archeological digs. Illustrated with maps, data, photographs of sites, diagrams of methods for recording depth of an object encountered in excavation. Instructions on how to lay out a grid system; basic equipment; appendices with tables of equivalents and conversion factors; extensive bibliography for further research.

Historical Archaeology: A Guide to Substantive and Theoretical Contributions. Edited by Robert L. Schuyler. Farmingdale, N.Y.: Baywood Publishing, 1978. 286 pp., illus., bibliogs. ◆ A source book of 35 reprinted articles for practitioners or introductory text for the general reader. Part I—Emergence and Definition of a New Discipline; Part 2—Subfields of Historical Archaeology; Part 3—Substantive Contributions; Part 4—Theoretical Positions; Part 5—Future Trends.

Joukowsky, Martha. *A Complete Manual of Field Archaeology: Tools and Techniques of Field Work for Archaeologists.* Englewood Cliffs, N.J.: Prentice-Hall, c1980. 630 pp., illus., bibliog., index. ◆ Advice on procedures of archeological fieldwork; sources of materials and equipment; opportunities for novices to participate in excavations; general guideline for the first dig; state-by-state listing of liaison officers, archeologists and agencies; listing of common abbreviations and equivalents; sample site forms; and summary of relevant federal legislation.

McGimsey, Charles R., III. *Public Archeology.* New York: Seminar Press, 1972. 265 pp. ◆ A guide to encouraging and enlisting support for archeology programs, techniques for ensuring legislative protection of endangered sites; describes financial support, administrative arrangements, legal bases that characterize current state and federal archeological programs.

Noel Hume, Ivor. *A Guide to Artifacts of Colonial America.* 1st ed. New York: Alfred A. Knopf, 1970. 323 pp., illus., bibliog. ◆ An alphabetical guide to artifacts from British-American sites of the 17th and 18th centuries, from armour to wig curlers. Illustrated with drawings and photographs. Bibliography follows each section.

Noel Hume, Ivor. *Historical Archaeology.* 1969. Reprint. New York: Norton, 1975. 362 pp., illus., diagrams, charts, bibliog., index. ◆ Covers preparation for digging, how to proceed, different types of sites, recording and presenting the story, treatment, study and storage of artifacts. Emphasis on analysis and interpretation based on historical, architectural and archeological evidence. Includes a topical bibliography.

Schiffer, Michael B. *Behavioral Archeology.* New York: Academic Press, c1976. 222 pp., illus., bibliog., index. ◆ An essay on the nature and methods of archeological inference in a fundamental way. Presents a synthetic model of archeological inference; then amplification and application of the behavioral approach and synthetic model.

Sharer, Robert J., and Wendy Ashmore. *Fundamentals of Archaeology.* Menlo Park, Calif.: Benjamin/Cummings Pub., Co., c1979. 614 pp., illus., glossary, bibliog. references, index. ◆ Surveys techniques, methods and theoretical framework of contemporary prehistoric archeology. Chapters include nature and history of the discipline; overview of the nature of archeological research with emphasis on design and planning; individual sections on particular aspects of the conduct of research from data acquisition through analysis.

South, Stanley A. *Method and Theory in Historical Archeology.* New York: Academic Press, c1977. 345 pp., illus., bibliogs., index. ◆ A systematic comparative study of archeological data relative to the historic period in North America. Based on use of empirical material, and concerned with building a sound research foundation for progress in science. References follow each section.

Archeological Organizations and Periodicals

American Anthropological Association, 1793 New Hampshire Avenue, N.W., Washington, D.C. 20009. The Association is a non-profit membership organization founded in 1902. It is a professional society of anthropologists, educators, students and others interested in the biological and cultural origin and development of mankind. It sponsors visiting lecturers, and Congressional Fellowship and Departmental Services Programs; maintains a speakers bureau, consultants bureau, and placement service; bestows awards; sponsors competitions; conducts research programs and compiles statistics. There are special committees on the profession, ethics, status of women in anthropology. Publications include *Anthropology Newsletter* (9/yr.), *American Anthropologist* (quarterly), *Guide to Departments of Anthropology* (annual), and special publications. The Association holds an annual meeting.

American Anthropologist. 1898, quarterly, membership. American Anthropological Association, 1703 New Hampshire Avenue, N.W., Washington, D.C. 20009.

American Antiquity. 1935, quarterly, membership. Society for American Archaeology, 1703 New Hampshire Avenue, N.W., Washington, D.C. 20009.

American Society for Conservation Archaeology, Sarah Bridges, Secretary, c/o Program Development, Wildlife Office, U.S. Fish and Wildlife Service, Department of the Interior, Washington, D.C. 20240. Founded in 1974, membership includes individuals and institutions. The Society promotes and coordinates activities, including public education, which aid in the preservation and protection of historic and prehistoric archaeological resources. It sponsors an annual meeting. Publications include *Proceedings* (annual), which contains papers presented at the symposium; *Report* (1974, bimonthly).

Archaeological Institute of America, 53 Park Place, Room 802, New York, New York 10007.

Founded in 1879, the Institute is a scientific society of archeologists and others interested in archeological study and research. It founded five schools of archeology: American School of Classical Studies in Athens (1881), School of Classical Studies of the American Academy in Rome (1895), American Schools of Oriental Research (Jerusalem, 1900 and Baghdad, 1921), School of American Research (1907) headquartered in Santa Fe, New Mexico. Publications include *Archaeology* (bimonthly); *American Journal of Archaeology* (quarterly); monographs (irregular); *Bulletin* (annual).

Archaeology. 1948, bimonthly, subscription. Archaeological Institute of America, 53 Park Place, Room 802, New York, New York 10007.

Association for Field Archaeology, Boston University, 745 Commonwealth Avenue, Boston, Massachusetts 02215. Founded in 1970, membership includes students and professionals involved in primary analysis of excavated archeological materials. It is concerned with disseminating information relating to archeological field techniques, excavations, preservation and interpretation. It seeks to prevent illegal acquisition of archeological material via the art market. The Association conducts seminars; and an annual meeting in conjunction with the Society for American Archaeology or Archaeological Institute of America. It publishes *Journal of Field Archaeology* (quarterly).

Canadian Historic Sites: *Occasional Papers in Archaeology and History.* 1970, irregular. Canadian Government Publishing Centre, Supply and Services Canada, Hull, Quebec K1A 0S9, Canada. Also in French: *Lieux historiques canadiens: cahiers d'archéologie et d'histoire.* Complete list of titles available; nos. 1–26 to date.

Conference on Historic Site Archaeology, Stanley South, Chairman, The Institute of Archeology and Anthropology, University of South Carolina, Columbia, South Carolina 29208. The Conference was organized in 1959 to present papers emphasizing artifact analysis. Since 1960 the papers presented at the annual Conference have been published with participants being urged to emphasize analysis and synthesis in their presentations. Members of the Conference are eligible to submit a manuscript for judging for the John M. Goggin Award for method and theory in historical archeology. Membership in the Conference is open to archeologists, historians, architects, students and others interested in historical archeology. Members receive the current volume of the *Papers,* and meeting announcements.

Council for Northeast Historical Archaeology, c/o Jo Ann Cotz, 179 Park Avenue, Midland Park, New Jersey 07432. Founded in 1971, membership is open to interested individuals and institutions. The Council is a nonprofit educational organization which aims to stimulate and to encourage the collection, preservation, advancement and dissemination of knowledge and information concerning the study and practice of historical archeology in northeastern North America (U.S. and Canada). Temporally, the Council is concerned with the entire historic period ranging from initial contact between Europeans and Native Americans to and through the Industrial Revolution. It publishes *Northeast Historical Archaeology* (2/yr).

Early Man. 1979, quarterly, membership/subscription. Center for American Archeology, 1911 Ridge Avenue, Evanston, Illinois 60201. The Center for American Archeology conducts a program of archeological teaching and research jointly sponsored by Northwestern University.

Historical Archaeology. 1967, annual, membership. Society for Historical Archaeology, 1703 New Hampshire Avenue, N.W., Washington, D.C. 20009.

History and Archaeology. 1975, occasional. Canadian Government Publishing Centre, Supply and Services Canada, Hull, Quebec K1A 0S9, Canada. Also in French: *Histoire et archéologie.* List of titles available; nos. 1–60 to date.

Journal of Field Archaeology. 1974, quarterly, membership. Association for Field Archaeology, Boston University, 745 Commonwealth Avenue, Boston, Massachusetts 02215.

The London Archaeologist. 1968, quarterly, subscription. London Archaeologist Association, 7, Coalecroft Road, S.W. 15, London, England.

Man In The Northeast. 1971, semiannual, subscription. Man In The Northeast, Inc., Department of Anthropology, Franklin Pierce College, Rindge, New Hampshire 03461. Board of associate editors represent states and provinces in the northeastern U.S. and eastern Canada; also specialists covering Algonkian and Iroquoian linguistics, historic site archeology, ethnohistory, and physical anthropology.

MASCA Journal. 1965, 1–2/yr., free. Applied Science Center for Archaeology, University of Pennsylvania, The University Museum, 33rd and Spruce Streets, Philadelphia, Pennsylvania 19104. Formerly: *ASCA Newsletter; MASCA Newsletter.*

Mid-Continental Journal of Archaeology. 1976, 2/yr., subscription. Kent State University Press, Kent, Ohio 44242. Cover title *MCJA.* Devoted to prehistoric archeology in the area bounded by the Appalachian mountains on the east and the great plains on the west.

North American Archaeologist. 1979, quarterly, subscription. Baywood Publishing Co., Inc., 120 Marine Street, Box D, Farmingdale, New York 11735.

Northeast Historical Archaeology. 1971, 2/yr., membership/subscription. Council for Northeast Historical Archaeology, c/o Jo Ann Cotz, 179 Park Avenue, Midland Park, New Jersey 07432.

Northwest Anthropological Research Notes. 1967, semiannual, subscription. Roderick Sprague, Editor, Laboratory of Anthropology, University of Idaho, Moscow, Idaho 83843.

Pacific Coast Archaeological Society Quarterly. 1965, quarterly, subscription. Pacific Coast Archaeological Society, Inc., Box 10926, Costa Mesa, California 92627. Includes: *PCAS Newsletter.*

Popular Archaeology. 1972, bimonthly, subscription. Life and Lettres Publishers, Inc., P. O. Box 4211, Arlington, Virginia 22204. Includes: *American Archaeologist.*

SEHA Newsletter and Proceedings. 1951, 6/yr., membership. Ross T. Christensen, Editor, Department of Anthropology and Archaeology, 140 Maeser Building, Brigham Young University, Provo, Utah 84602. Cosponsor: Society for Early Historic Archaeology. Formerly: *UAS Newsletter.*

Society for American Archaeology, 1703 New Hampshire Avenue, N.W., Washington, D.C. 20009. Founded in 1935, the Society's purpose is to stimulate scientific research in the archeology of the New World by creating closer professional relations among archeologists; by guiding, on request, the research work of amateurs; by advocating the conservation of archeological data, and furthering the control or elimination of commercialization of archeological objects; and by promoting a more rational public appreciation of the aims and limitations of archeological research. Membership is open to professionals, nonprofessionals, and students interested in archeology. It publishes *American Antiquity* (quarterly); Special Publications (irregular).

Society for Historical Archaeology, 1703 New Hampshire Avenue, N.W., Washington, D.C. 20009. Founded in 1967, the Society is a nonprofit scientific-educational organization which aims to promote scholarly research in, and the dissemination of knowledge concerning historical archaeology; to exchange information in this field; to hold periodic conferences to discuss problems of mutual interest relating to the study of historical archaeology; and to obtain the cooperation of the concerned disciplines for projects of research. Main focus is the era since the beginning of the exploration of the non-European world by Europeans, with prime concern in the Western Hemisphere. Membership is open to professionals, historians, anthropologists, ethnohistorians, and other individuals and institutions who share an interest in history as it emerges from archeological research and the study of the written records. The Society publishes a *Newsletter* (quarterly), and *Historical Archaeology* (annual).

Society for Historical Archaeology. *Newsletter.* 1968, quarterly, subscription. 1703 New Hampshire Avenue, N.W., Washington, D.C. 20009. Includes subscription to *Historical Archaeology.*

Society for Post-Medieval Archaeology, c/o Rosemary Weinstein, Secretary, The Museum of London, London Wall, London EC2Y 5HN, England. Publications include *Post-Medieval Archaeology* (1966), and *Post-Medieval Newssheet.*

Society of Professional Archeologists, J. Ned Woodall, Secretary-Treasurer, Box 7808, Wake Forest University, Winston-Salem, North Carolina 27109. The Society publishes a *Directory of Professional Archeologists* (1st ed., 1979, 31 pp.), a listing of accredited professional archeologists, and a newsletter.

Southwestern Anthropological Association Newsletter. 1960, quarterly, membership/subscription. American Anthropological Association, 1703 New Hampshire Avenue, N.W., Washington, D.C. 20009.

Methods of Archeological Research

Advances in Obsidian Glass Studies: *Archaeological and Geochemical Perspectives.* Edited by R. E. Taylor. Park Ridge, N.J.: Noyes Press, c1976. 360 pp., illus., bibliog. references, index.

Aerial Remote Sensing Techniques in Archeology. Edited by Thomas R. Lyons and Robert K. Hitchcock. Albuquerque: Chaco Center, National Park Service, U.S. Department of the Interior, 1977. 201 pp., illus., bibliogs. ◆ Papers chiefly resulting from a symposium held May 4, 1972, at the 37th annual meeting of the Society for American Archaeology, Bal Harbour, Florida.

The Archaeology of the Clay Tobacco Pipe. Edited by Peter Davey. Oxford, Eng.: B.A.R., 1979–. illus., bibliogs. ◆ B.A.R. British series, 63–.

The Archaeology of Us: Modern Material Culture. Edited by Richard A. Gould and Michael B. Schiffer. New York: Academic Press, 1981. 368 pp., bibliog., index.

Atkinson, Richard J. C. *Field Archaeology.* 2nd ed. 1953. Reprint. Westport, Conn.: Hyperion Press, 1979. 233 pp., illus., bibliog., index.

Barker, Philip A. *The Techniques of Archaeological Excavation.* New York: Universe Books, 1977. 279 pp., illus., bibliog., index.

Biek, Leo. *Archaeology and the Microscope: The Scientific Examination of Archaeological Evidence.* New York: Praeger, 1963. 287 pp., illus., tables, bibliog.

Binford, Lewis R. *An Archaeological Perspective.* New York: Seminar Press, 1972. 464 pp., illus., maps, tables, index.

Binford, Lewis R. *Bones: Ancient Men and Modern Myths.* New York: Academic Press, c1981. 320 pp., illus., bibliog., index.

Bodey, Hugh, and Michael Hallas. *Elementary Surveying for Industrial Archaeologists.* Aylesbury: Shire Publications, 1977. 64 pp., illus., plans, glossary, bibliog., index.

Bracegirdle, Brian. *Photography as Illustration: The Use of the Camera for Books and Reports.* South Brunswick, N.J.: A.S. Barnes, c1970, 1972. 247 pp., illus., bibliog. references.

Bradford, John. *Ancient Landscapes: Studies in Field Archaeology.* 1957. Reprint. Westport, Conn.: Greenwood Press, 1980. 297 pp., illus., maps, bibliog. references, index.

Brodribb, Arthur Charles Conant. *Drawing Archaeological Finds.* 1st American ed. New York: Association Press, c1970, 1971. 96 pp., illus.

Brothwell, Don R. *Digging Up Bones: The Excavation, Treatment and Study of Human Skeletal Remains.* 3rd ed., rev. and updated. Ithaca, N.Y.: Cornell University Press, 1981. 208 pp., illus., bibliog., index.

Brothwell, Don R., and Eric Higgs, eds. *Science in Archaeology: A Survey of Progress and Research.* With a foreword by Grahame Clark. New York: Praeger, 1970. 720 pp., illus., maps, bibliogs. ◆ Describes scientific methods used in archeology; sections include dating, environment, man, microscopy and radiography, artifacts, statistics, and prospecting.

Chaplin, Raymond E. *The Study of Animal Bones from Archeological Sites.* London and New York: Seminar Press, 1971. 170 pp., illus., map, bibliog. references.

Chronologies in New World Archaeology. Edited by R. E. Taylor and Clement W. Meighan. New York: Academic Press, c1978. 587 pp., illus., bibliogs., index.

Clarke, David L. *Analytical Archaeology.* 2nd ed., revised by Bob Chapman. New York: Columbia University Press, 1978. 526 pp., illus., bibliog., maps, index.

Coles, John M. *Experimental Archaeology.* New York: Academic Press, 1979. 274 pp., illus., bibliog., index.

Coles, John M. *Field Archaeology in Britain.* London: Methuen; distr. in U.S. by Harper & Row, N.Y., 1972. 267 pp., illus., maps, bibliog., index.

Collier, John, Jr. *Visual Anthropology: Photography as a Research Method.* New York:

Holt, Rinehart & Winston, 1967. 138 pp., illus., bibliog.

Computer Graphics in Archaeology: *Statistical Cartographic Applications to Spatial Analysis in Archaeological Contexts.* Steadman Upham, editor; contributions by Frank Aldrich, et al. Tempe: Arizona State University, 1979. 156 pp., illus., bibliogs. ◆ Based on papers from a symposium held at the 41st annual meeting of the Society for American Archaeology, St. Louis, 1976.

Crawford, Osbert G. S. *Archaeology in the Field.* London: Phoenix House, 1960. 280 pp., illus., maps, bibliog.

Dancey, William S. *Archaeological Field Methods: An Introduction.* Minneapolis, Minn.: Burgess Pub. Co., c1981. 186 pp., illus., bibliog., index.

Daniel, Glyn E. *Man Discovers His Past.* New York: Crowell, c1966, 1968. 95 pp., illus., maps, bibliog. references.

Data Bank Applications in Archaeology. Sylvia W. Gaines, editor; contributors, Louis Bourrelly, et al. Tucson, Ariz.: University of Arizona Press, c1981. 152 pp., index.

Dating Techniques for the Archaeologist. Co-edited by Henry N. Michael and Elizabeth K. Ralph. Cambridge, Mass.: MIT Press, 1971. 226 pp., illus., bibliog. references.

Deetz, James. *Invitation to Archaeology.* Garden City, N.Y.: Natural History Press for the American Museum of Natural History, 1967. 150 pp., illus., bibliog.

Driesch, Angela von den. *A Guide to the Measurement of Animal Bones from Archaeological Sites: As Developed by the Institute für Palaeoanatomie, Domestikationsforschung und Geschichte der Tiermedizin of the University of Munich.* Cambridge, Mass.: Peabody Museum of Archaeology and Ethnology, Harvard University, 1976. 136 pp., illus., bibliog. references. ◆ Peabody Museum Bulletin 1. For complete list: Publications Department, Peabody Museum of Archaeology and Ethnology, Harvard University, 11 Divinity Avenue, Cambridge, Massachusetts 02138.

Eidt, Robert C., and William I. Weeks. *Abandoned Settlement Analysis: Theory and Practice.* Shorewood, Wisc.: Field Test Associates, 1974. 159 pp., illus., bibliogs., index.

Eighmy, Jeffrey L. *Archeomagnetism: A Handbook for the Archeologist.* Washington, D.C.: U.S. Department of the Interior, Heritage Conservation and Recreation Service, 1980. 104 pp., illus., bibliog. ◆ Cultural Resource Management series.

Experimental Archeology. Edited by Daniel Ingersoll, John E. Yellen, and William Macdonald. New York: Columbia University Press, 1977. 423 pp., illus., bibliogs., index.

Fagan, Brian M. *In the Beginning: An Introduction to Archaeology.* 4th ed. Boston: Little, Brown and Company, c1981. 548 pp., illus., maps, bibliog., index. ◆ Covers survey, excavation, analysis, dating techniques, preservation of materials, history of archeology, recent federal legislation designed to protect.

Fleming, Stuart J. *Dating in Archaeology: A Guide to Scientific Techniques.* New York: St. Martin's Press, c1976, 1977. 272 pp., illus., maps, bibliog., index.

Fleming, Stuart J. *Thermoluminescence Techniques in Archaeology.* New York: Oxford University Press, 1979. 233 pp., illus., bibliog. references, index.

For Theory Building in Archaeology: *Essays on Faunal Remains, Aquatic Resources, Spatial Analysis and Systemic Modeling.* Edited by Lewis R. Binford. New York: Academic Press, c1977. 419 pp., illus., bibliogs., index.

Fowler, Peter J. *Approaches to Archaeology.* New York: St. Martin's Press, 1977. 203 pp., illus., bibliog., index.

Geoarchaeology: *Earth Science and the Past:* [*Papers.*] Edited by D. A. Davidson and M. L. Shackley. Boulder, Colo.: Westview Press, 1976. 408 pp., illus., bibliog., indexes. ◆ Presented at a symposium on the theme "Sediments in Archaeology" held at the University of Southampton, December 15–16, 1973.

Glassie, Henry H. *Pattern in the Material Folk Culture of the Eastern United States.* Philadelphia: University of Pennsylvania Press, c1968, 1969. 316 pp., illus., bibliog. ◆ University of Pennsylvania Monographs in Folklore and Folklife no. 1.

Goffer, Zvi. *Archaeological Chemistry: A Sourcebook on the Applications of Chemistry to Archaeology.* New York: Wiley, c1980. 376 pp., illus., bibliog. references, index.

Gorenstein, Shirley. *Introduction to Archaeology.* New York: Basic Books, 1965. 165 pp., illus., bibliog.

Greenhood, David. *Mapping.* Revised with the assistance of Gerard L. Alexander. Chicago: University of Chicago Press, 1964. 289 pp., illus., maps, charts, diagrams, bibliog.

Grinsell, Leslie; Philip Rahtz; and David P. Williams. *The Preparation of Archaeological Reports.* 2nd ed. New York: St. Martin's Press, 1974. 105 pp., illus., bibliog., index.

Harrington, Jean Carl. *Archaeology and the Historical Society.* Nashville, Tenn.: American Association for State and Local History, c1965. 48 pp., illus., bibliog.

Harris, Edward C. *Principles of Archaeological Stratigraphy.* New York: Academic Press, 1979. 136 pp., illus., bibliog., index.

Hester, Thomas R.; Robert F. Heizer; and John A. Graham. *Field Methods in Archaeology.* 6th ed. Palo Alto, Calif.: Mayfield Pub. Co., c1975. 408 pp., illus., diagrams, maps, bibliog., indexes. ♦ Includes planning, excavating, and recording results of all kinds of archeological digs; heavily illustrated; appendices with tables of equivalents and conversion factors; extensive bibliography. First edition by R. F. Heizer, *A Manual of Archaeological Field Methods* (1949).

Hogg, Alexander, H. A. *Surveying for Archaeologists and Other Fieldworkers.* New York: St. Martin's Press, 1980. 315 pp., illus., index.

International Symposium on Photogrammetric Surveys of Monuments and Sites, 1st, Athens, 1974. *Photogrammetric Surveys of Monuments and Sites: Proceedings.* Edited by John Badekas. Amsterdam: North Holland Publ.; New York: American Elsevier, 1975. 176 pp., plates, illus., bibliogs.

Jennings, Sarah, et al. *East Anglian Archaeology, Report no. 13: Eighteen Centuries of Pottery from Norwich.* Norwich, Eng.: Norwich Survey in collaboration with Norfolk Museums Service, 1981. 281 pp., illus., maps, glossary, bibliog. ♦ Series begun in 1975 on Suffolk, Norfolk, East Anglia, Norwich; for publishing final reports on archaeology excavations and surveys of the region. The Norwich Survey, Centre of East Anglian Studies, Earl-

ham Hall, University of East Anglia, Norwich, NR4 7TJ, England.

Joukowsky, Martha. *A Complete Manual of Field Archaeology: Tools and Techniques of Field Work for Archaeologists.* Englewood Cliffs, N.J.: Prentice-Hall, c1980. 630 pp., illus., bibliog., index.

Keisch, Bernard. *Secrets of the Past: Nuclear Energy Applications in Art and Archaeology.* Washington, D.C.: U.S. Atomic Energy Commission, Office of Information Services, 1972. 119 pp., illus., charts, bibliog.

Kenyon, Kathleen M. *Beginning in Archaeology.* Rev. ed with sections on American archaeology by Saul S. and Gladys D. Weinberg. New York: Frederick A. Praeger, c1961, 1966. 228 pp., illus., diagrams, charts, bibliog., index.

King, Thomas F. *The Archeological Survey: Method and Uses.* Washington, D.C.: Heritage Conservation and Recreation Service, U.S. Department of the Interior, for sale by Supt. of Docs., U.S. Government Printing Office, 1978. 134 pp., illus., bibliog. ♦ Cultural Resource Management series.

Lagacé, Robert O. *Nature and Use of the HRAF Files: A Search and Teaching Guide.* New Haven: Human Relations Area Files, c1974. 49 pp., illus., bibliog.

Limbrey, Susan. *Soil Science and Archaeology.* New York: Academic Press, 1975. 384 pp., illus., bibliog., index.

Lister, Florence C., and Robert H. Lister. *A Descriptive Dictionary for 500 Years of Spanish-Tradition Ceramics (13th Through 18th Centuries).* Lansing, Mich.: Society for Historical Archaeology, 1976. 100 pp., illus, bibliog.

Lyons, Thomas R., and Thomas Eugene Avery. *Remote Sensing: A Handbook for Archaeologists and Cultural Resource Managers.* Washington, D.C.: Cultural Resources Management Division, National Park Service, U.S. Department of the Interior; for sale by Supt. of Docs., U.S. Government Printing Office, 1977. 109 pp., illus., bibliog., index. ♦ See also Supplements: 1—*Practical Exercises on Remote Sensing in Archeology* (1978); 2—*Remote Sensing: Instrumentation for Nondestructive Exploration of Cultural Resources* (1978); 3—*Aerial Anthropological Perspec-*

tives: A Bibliography of Cultural Resource Studies (1980); 4—Remote Sensing: A Handbook: Basic Manual Supplement: Oregon (1980); 5—Multispectral Analyses of Cultural Resources: Chaco Canyon and Bandelier National Monument (1981); 6—Archeological Applications of Remote Sensing in the North Carolina Lowlands (1981); 7—Aerial and Terrestrial Photography for Archeologists (1981).

McHargue, Georgess, and Michael Roberts. A Field Guide to Conservation Archaeology in North America. Philadelphia: Lippincott, c1977. 319 pp., illus., drawings, charts, maps, bibliog., references, index.

Matthews, Sydney K. Photography in Archaeology and Art. New York: Humanities Press, 1968. 161 pp., illus., bibliog.

Michaels, Joseph W. Dating Methods in Archaeology. New York: Seminar Press, 1973. 230 pp., illus., bibliogs.

Newlands, David L., and Claus Breede. An Introduction to Canadian Archaeology. Toronto and New York: McGraw-Hill Ryerson, c1976. 151 pp., illus., bibliog., index.

Noel Hume, Ivor. Historical Archaeology. 1969. Reprint. New York: Norton, 1975. 362 pp., illus., diagrams, charts, bibliog., index. ◆ Covers preparation for digging, how to proceed, different types of sites, recording and presenting the story, treatment, study and storage of artifacts.

Olsen, Stanley J. Mammal Remains from Archaeological Sites: Part I–Southeastern and Southwestern United States. Cambridge, Mass.: Peabody Museum, 1964. 162 pp., illus., maps, bibliog. ◆ Papers of the Peabody Museum of Archaeology and Ethnology, vol. 56, no. 1.

Oswald, Adrian. Clay Pipes for the Archaeologist. Oxford, Eng.: British Archaeological Reports, 1975. 207 pp., illus., maps, bibliog., appendix. ◆ British Archaeological Reports, 14.

Photography in Archaeological Research. Edited by Elmer Harp, Jr. 1st ed. Albuquerque: University of New Mexico Press, c1975. 380 pp., illus., bibliog., index. ◆ School of American Advanced Seminar series.

Plenderleith, Harold J., and A. E. A. Werner. The Conservation of Antiquities and Works of Art: Treatment, Repair, and Restoration. 2nd ed. London and New York: Oxford University Press, 1971. 394 pp., illus., diagrams, tables, formulae, bibliog. footnotes, index. ◆ Includes data on the nature of the materials in museum collections, the causes of their deterioration and detailed information on methods of preservation, repair and restoration; intended as a handbook for the collector, the archeologist, and the museum curator, and as a workshop guide for the technician.

Pyddoke, Edward, ed. The Scientist and Archaeology. New York: Roy Publishers, c1963, 1964. 208 pp., illus., maps, bibliog.

Pyddoke, Edward. Stratification for the Archaeologist. London: Phoenix House, 1961. 124 pp., illus.

Reed, R. Ancient Skins, Parchments and Leathers. London and New York: Seminar Press, 1972. 342 pp., illus., bibliog., references.

Remote Sensing Experiments in Cultural Resource Studies: Nondestructive Methods of Archaeological Exploration, Survey, and Analysis. Assembled by Thomas R. Lyons. Albuquerque: Chaco Center, 1977. 186 pp., illus., bibliogs.

Research Strategies in Historical Archeology. Edited by Stanley South. New York: Academic Press, c1977. 345 pp., illus., bibliogs., index. ◆ Twelve studies to illustrate methods.

Robbins, Maurice, and Mary B. Irving. The Amateur Archaeologist's Handbook. 3rd ed. New York: Harper & Row, 1981. 304 pp., illus., drawings, tables, glossary, appendices, bibliog., index.

Ryder, Michael L. Animal Bones in Archaeology: A Book of Notes and Drawings for Beginners. 2nd ed. Oxford: Published for the Mammal Society by Blackwell Scientific, 1969. 65 pp., illus., bibliog.

St. Joseph, John K. S. The Uses of Air Photography. New ed. With contributions by D. E. Coombe, et al. London: J. Baker, 1977. 196 pp., illus., maps.

Sampling in Archaeology. Collaborating editors, David L. Asch, et al.; James W. Mueller, editor. Tucson: University of Arizona Press, c1975. 300 pp., illus., bibliog., indexes. ◆ Based on papers presented at a symposium held at the 38th annual meeting of the Society for American Archaeology, San Francisco, 1973.

Schiffer, Michael B. *Behavioral Archeology.* New York: Academic Press, c1976. 222 pp., illus., bibliog., index.

Shackley, Myra L. *Archaeological Sediments: A Survey of Analytical Methods.* New York: Wiley, 1975. 159 pp., illus., bibliog., indexes.

Shepard, Anna O. *Ceramics for the Archaeologist.* Washington, D.C.: Carnegie Institute, c1956, 1980. 414 pp., illus., drawings, tables, bibliog., appendices, index. ◆ Carnegie Institute of Washington Publication no. 609.

Simulation Studies in Archaeology. Edited by Ian Hodder. Cambridge and New York: Cambridge University Press, 1978. 139 pp., illus., bibliogs., index.

Simulations in Archaeology. Edited by Jeremy A. Sabloff. 1st ed. Albuquerque: University of New Mexico Press, c1981. 39 pp., illus., bibliog., index.

Social Archeology: Beyond Subsistence and Dating. Edited by Charles L. Redman, et al. New York: Academic Press, c1978. 417 pp., illus., bibliogs., index.

South, Stanley A. *Method and Theory in Historical Archeology.* New York: Academic Press, c1977. 345 pp., illus., bibliogs., index.

Spatial Archaeology. Edited by David L. Clarke. New York: Academic Press, 1977. 386 pp., illus., bibliogs., index.

Sullivan, George. *Discover Archaeology: An Introduction to the Tools and Techniques of Archaeological Fieldwork.* Garden City, N.Y.: Doubleday, 1980. 273 pp., illus., bibliog., index.

Symposium on Archaeological Chemistry, 5th, Dallas, 1973. *Archaeological Chemistry: A Symposium sponsored by the Division of the History of Chemistry at the 165th Meeting of the American Chemical Society, Dallas, Tex., April 9–10, 1970.* Curt W. Beck, ed. Washington, D.C.: American Chemical Society, 1974. 254 pp., illus., bibliog. references, index. ◆ Advances in Chemistry series no. 138. American Chemical Society, 1155 Sixteenth Street, N.W., Washington, D.C. 20036.

Symposium on Archaeological Chemistry, 6th, Chicago, 1977. *Archaeological Chemistry II: Proceedings.* Giles F. Carter, ed. Washington, D.C.: American Chemical Society, 1978. 389 pp., illus. ◆ Focus on understanding the origin and distribution of archeological specimens composed of pottery, glass, metal, bone and pitch through new and established analytical techniques.

Symposium on Cultural Resources Management and Remote Sensing, Tucson, Ariz., 1978. *Remote Sensing and Non-Destructive Archeology.* Edited by Thomas R. Lyon and James I. Ebert; Remote Sensing Division, Southwest Cultural Resources Center, National Park Service, and University of New Mexico. Washington, D.C.: Cultural Resources Management Division, National Park Service, 1978. 71 pp., illus., bibliogs.

Talmadge, Valerie; Olga Chesler; and the staff of Interagency Archeological Services. *Importance of Small, Surface, and Disturbed Sites as Sources of Significant Archeological Data.* Washington, D.C.: National Park Service, U.S. Department of the Interior, 1977. 35 pp., bibliog.

Tite, M. S. *Methods of Physical Examination in Archaeology.* London and New York: Seminar Press, 1972. 389 pp., illus., bibliogs.

United Nations Educational, Scientific and Cultural Organization. *Field Manual for Museums.* Museums and Monuments No. XII. Paris: UNESCO, 1970. 171 pp., illus., diagrams, drawings, forms, bibliogs.

U.S. National Park Service. *Field Manual for Museums.* 1941. Reprint. Ann Arbor, Mich.: Finch Press, 1974. 426 pp., illus., plans, bibliog.

U.S. National Park Service. *Using the UTM Grid System to Record Historic Sites.* By Wilford T. Cole. Washington, D.C.: for sale by Supt. of Docs., U.S. Government Printing Office, 1980. 42 pp. ◆ UTM is the Universal Transverse Mercator/Grid System and its application to mapping historic and archeological sites.

Walker, Iain C. *Clay Tobacco-Pipes, with Particular Reference to the Bristol Industry.* Ottawa: Parks Canada; available from Printing and Publishing, Supply and Services Canada, 1977. 4 vols. (1839 pp.), illus., maps, bibliog. ◆ In series, History and Archaeology, 11a, b, c, d.

Webster, Graham. *Practical Archaeology: An Introduction to Archaeological Fieldwork and Excavation.* 2nd ed. New York: St. Martin's Press, 1974. 164 pp., illus., bibliog. references, index.

Wood, Eric Stuart. *Collins Field Guide to Archaeology.* With an introduction by Sir Mortimer Wheeler. 2nd rev. ed. London: Collins, 1968. 384 pp., illus., maps, plans, bibliog.

Zeuner, Friedrich E. *Dating the Past: An Introduction to Geochronology.* 4th ed., rev. and enl. Darien, Conn.: Hafner Pub. Co., c1958, 1970. 516 pp., illus., maps, bibliog.

Reference Books and Guides to Sources

Advances in Archeological Method and Theory. Michael B. Schiffer, ed. New York: Academic Press, 1978–. 1 vol. annual. ◆ 4 vols. to date; vol. 5, 1982, in press.

Archaeological Survey of Canada. *Annual Review.* Ottawa; 1972 –. 1 vol., illus., annual. ◆ See also: *Research Report.* No. 1–. Ottawa: National Museum of Man, 1971–.

Bailey, Lynn Robison. *From Adze to Vermilion: A Guide to the Hardware of History, and the Literature of Historic Sites Archaeology.* Pasadena, Calif.: Socio-Technical Books, 1971. 237 pp., illus., bibliog., index.

Bray, Warwick, and David Trump. *The Penguin Dictionary of Archaeology.* New York: Penguin, 1972. 269 pp., illus., maps, plans. ◆ Originally published as *A Dictionary of Archaeology,* London, 1970.

The Cambridge Encyclopedia of Archaeology. Andrew Sherratt, ed.: foreword by Grahame Clark. New York: Crown Publishers, 1980. 495 pp., illus., bibliog., index.

Champion, Sara. *Dictionary of Terms and Techniques in Archaeology.* New York: Facts on File, 1980. 144 pp., bibliog.

The Concise Encyclopedia of Archaeology. Edited by Leonard Cottrell. 2nd ed. New York: Hawthorn Books, 1971. 430 pp., illus., maps, bibliog.

Conference on Historic Site Archaeology. *Papers.* Vol. 1–, May 1967–. Edited by Stanley South. Raleigh, N.C.: The Conference, 1967–. 1 vol., annual. ◆ 12 vols. to date.

Deetz, James, ed. *Man's Imprint from the Past: Readings in the Methods of Archaeology.* Boston: Little, Brown, and Company, 1971. 396 pp., illus., maps, bibliogs.

Folsom, Franklin. *America's Ancient Treasures; A Guide to Archeological Sites and Museums.* New York: Rand McNally, 1971. 202 pp., illus., bibliog., index.

Gettens, Rutherford J., and Bertha M. Usilton, comps. *Abstracts of Technical Studies in Art and Archaeology, 1943–1952.* Smithsonian Institution, Freer Gallery of Art, Occasional Papers, vol. 2, no. 2. Publication 4176. Washington, D.C.: Smithsonian Institution, 1955. 408 pp., index.

Gomme, George L. *Index of Archaeological Papers, 1665–1890.* 1907. Reprint. New York: Burt Franklin, 1965. 2 vols (910 pp.).

Harvard University. Peabody Museum of Archaeology and Ethnology. Library. *Catalogue: Authors.* Boston: G. K. Hall, 1963. 26 vols. ◆ Card catalogue includes journal articles and compilations such as Festschriften and the proceedings of congresses. See also: *Supplement 1–2.* Boston: 1970–71. 6 vols., 2 vols. (No. 1 covers items added 1963–69; No. 2 covers 1969–71.); *Catalogue: Subjects.* Boston: 1963. 27 vols.; *Catalogue: Subjects, Supplement 1–2.* Boston: 1970–71. 2 vols.; *Catalogue: Index to Subject Headings.* Rev. ed. Boston: 1971. 237 pp.; *Supplement 3.* Boston: 1975. 7 vols.

Heizer, Robert F.; Thomas R. Hester; and, Carol Graves. *Archaeology: A Bibliographic Guide to the Basic Literature.* New York: Garland Pub., 1980. 400 pp., index.

Hulan, Richard, and Stephen S. Laurence. *A Guide to the Reading and Study of Historic Site Archaeology.* Museum Brief no. 5. Columbia: Published for the Conference on Historic Site Archaeology by the Museum of Anthropology, University of Missouri, 1970. 127 pp.

The Illustrated Encyclopedia of Archaeology. Glyn Daniel, consultant editor. New York: Crowell, 1977. 224 pp., illus., maps, index.

Keller, Jana; Kathleen H. Quinn; and Stephanie H. Rodeffer. *A Bibliography of Archeological Reports Relating to the Eastern*

United States on File at Interagency Archeological Services Division, Atlanta, Georgia. Washington, D.C.: Department of the Interior, Heritage Conservation and Recreation Service, 1979. 250 leaves, maps, indexes.

Murdock, George P., et al. *Outline of Cultural Materials.* 4th rev. ed., 3rd printing with modifications. New Haven, Conn.: Human Relations Area Files, c1961, 1967. 164 pp. ◆ Used to classify information on modern complex societies; originally developed as a tool for the Cross-Cultural Survey.

Noel Hume, Ivor. *A Guide to Artifacts of Colonial America.* 1st ed. New York: Alfred A. Knopf, 1970. 323 pp., illus., bibliog.

Readings in Archaeological Method and Technique. Edited by Robert Kautz. Davis, Calif.: Center for Archaeological Research at Davis, University of California, 1974. 98 pp., illus., bibliog. ◆ Publication no. 4

U.S. National Park Service *Archeological Research Series.* Washington, D.C.: available from Supt. of Docs., U.S. Government Printing Office, 1951–. illus., maps. ◆ Nos. 1–4 available from National Technical Information Service, Springfield, Virginia; Nos. 6–7D available from Government Printing Office

NOTES

Art and Archaeology Technical Abstracts. 1955, irregular (approx. 2/yr.). Circulation Department, AATA, c/o New York University, Conservation Center, Institute of Fine Arts, 1 East 78th Street, New York, New York 10021. ◆ Formerly *IIC Abstracts.* Analytical bibliography of world literature relating to conservation technology.

Bibliography of Historical Archaeology, John L. Cotter, Associate Curator Emeritus and Editor, American Historical Archaeology, and William G. Hershey, Co-editor and Computer Program Designer, The University Museum, University of Pennsylvania, 33rd and Spruce Streets, Philadelphia, Pennsylvania 19104. Initiated in 1965, the Bibliography includes published monographs, journal articles, and unpublished manuscripts relating to American Historical Archaeology. Items are compiled on entry forms which include bibliographic data, illustrations and special materials, subject, archaeological discipline, cul-

tural information, scientific techniques/theoretical discussions, annotations. Entries are then coded and entered into a computer. There are prefix codes for subject taxonomy: General Methodology and Techniques; Supportive Historical Documentation; Excavation Reports; Studies and Analyses; Studies of Cultures; Architecture; Artifacts. In addition there are 92 entry codes for author, title, imprint, format, availability, annotation, etc., for indexing purposes. The items are then edited and tested.

In 1972 University Microfilms made available a microfilm/xerographic copy of the entry forms, totaling about 900 items, which was indexed by author. Then the Bibliography was kept updated with annual increments published in *Historical Archaeology* (1968 to 1975) and the Historical Archaeology *Newsletter* (1979). Since 1980 the Bibliography has been revised for computerization with the aid of National Endowment for the Humanities and other grants. With computerization, the Bibliography will ultimately be made available through printouts and a published work, and a continuing Bibliographic Center will be established at The University Museum, Philadelphia.

Human Relations Area Files, Inc., 755 Prospect Street, New Haven, Connecticut 06511. The Files constitute a collection of data on approximately 300 primitive, historical and contemporary cultures. Each culture is assigned a "Cultural File" within which source materials (books, articles, manuscripts, plus translations done especially for the files) were developed for the study of specific cultures or areas, and also for the study of particular topics cross-culturally. Key to cultural groups is George P. Murdock's *Outline of World Cultures;* and the companion volume *HRAF Outline of Cultural Materials,* groups the subject categories into 79 major and 619 minor subject divisions. See also: Lagacé, *Nature and Use of the HRAF Files: A Research and Teaching Guide* (cited in Methods section).

Studies in Conservation/Etudes de Conservation. 1952, quarterly, membership/subscription. International Institute for Conservation of Historic and Artistic Works, 6 Buckingham Street, London WC2N 6BA, England.

U.S. National Park Service, Archeological Programs. The National Park Service conducts a national program to identify, protect, preserve, or recover significant archeological remains outside of National Park Service areas that are threatened by federal construction or federally sponsored activities. It is able to provide technical assistance nationwide, and to coordinate federally sponsored archeological activities and to help other federal agencies. Programs of the Washington office include: developing for the Secretary of the Interior national goals and objectives, policies, standards, guidelines and procedures for all federal agencies to follow in the administration of the archeological and historic data recovery program; managing the Federal Antiquities Program (P.L. 59–209) which regulates archeological and paleontological investigations on most federally owned or controlled lands; assisting federal agencies in fulfillment of Executive Order 11593 responsibilities by helping them locate, identify, and evaluate historic properties under their jurisdiction or control; consulting with the Advisory Council on Historic Preservation; and reporting annually to Congress. Some archeological activities are in the Interagency Resource Management Division of National Register Programs. Other archeological activities are conducted in the Office of the Departmental Consulting Archeologist, created in June 1982 as part of the reorganization.

Programs of the archeological field offices, now located in the NPS Regional Offices in Atlanta, Denver, San Francisco, include: maintaining liaison with other federal agencies at the regional level in order to identify and plan for needed data recovery projects; identifying firms or institutions capable of performing data recovery; establishing the scope of archeological services required for projects, negotiating contracts, and reviewing data recovery proposals; monitoring field and laboratory work; reviewing and approving final reports submitted following completion of data recovery

Publications: *Cultural Resource Management Studies,* a series of exceptional reports on various aspects of cultural resources management for distribution to the profession and to the public; *Final Reports on Archeological Investigations,* a list of titles and descriptive abstracts of final reports on archeological investigations administered by Interagency Archeological Services. Studies and Reports are available from IAS, or the National Technical Information Service, Department of Commerce, 5285 Port Royal Road, Springfield, Virginia 22161.

Archeology: General Works

Archaeological Perspectives on Ethnicity in America: *Afro-American and Asian American Culture History.* Edited by Robert L. Schuyler. Farmingdale, N.Y.: Baywood Publishing Co., 1980. 147 pp., bibliogs. ◆ Baywood Monographs in Archaeology, vol. 1.

Binford, Sally R., and Lewis R. Binford. *New Perspectives in Archeology.* Chicago: Aldine Pub., Co., 1968. 373 pp., illus., bibliog., index. ◆ Covers system theory, cultural ecology, and the materialist-oriented evolution thesis of how objects function within a cultural context.

Campbell, John M., ed. *Prehistoric Cultural Relations Between the Arctic and Temperate Zones of North America.* 1962. Reprint. New York: Johnson Reprint Corp., 1972. 181 pp., illus., maps, bibliog.

Chang, Kwang-Chih, ed. *Settlement Archaeology.* Palo Alto, Calif.: National Press Books, 1968. 229 pp., illus., maps, bibliogs.

Childe, V. Gordon. *Piecing Together the Past: The Interpretation of Archaeological Data.* 1956. Reprint. New York: Praeger, 1969. 176 pp., illus. ◆ Based on author's lectures on the principles of archaeological classification, current terminology, and the implicit interpretive concepts.

Childe, V. Gordon. *A Short Introduction to Archaeology.* New York: Collier, 1962. 127 pp., bibliogs.

Clark, John Grahame Douglas. *Archaeology and Society: Reconstructing the Prehistoric Past.* 3rd ed., rev. and reset. New York: Barnes and Noble, 1960. 272 pp., illus., maps.

Daniel, Glyn. *The Origins and Growth of Archaeology.* New York: Thomas Y. Crowell, c1967, 1968. 298 pp., illus., bibliog. references.

Deetz, James. *In Small Things Forgotten: The Archaeology of Early American Life.* 1st ed. Garden City, N.Y.: Anchor Press/Doubleday, 1977. 184 pp., illus., bibliog. references, index.

Evans, John G. *An Introduction to Environmental Archaeology.* Ithaca, N.Y.: Cornell University Press, 1978. 154 pp., illus., maps, bibliog., index.

Fagan, Brian M. *Archaeology: A Brief Introduction.* Boston: Little, Brown and Company, c1978. 194 pp., illus., bibliog., index.

Forde-Johnston, James L. *History from the Earth: An Introduction to Archaeology.* Greenwich, Conn.: New York Graphic Society, 1974. 256 pp., illus., maps, plans, bibliog., index.

Fowler, P. J., ed. *Recent Work in Rural Archaeology.* Totowa, N.J.: Rowman and Littlefield, 1975. 160 pp., illus., bibliog.

Griffin, James Bennett. *Archeology of Eastern United States.* Chicago: University of Chicago Press, 1952. 392 pp., illus, maps, bibliog.

Grimm, Jacob L. *Archaeological Investigation of Fort Ligonier, 1960–1965.* Pittsburgh: Carnegie Museum, 1970. 186 pp., illus., bibliog. references. ◆ With Appendix: Animal Remains from Archaeological Excavations at Fort Ligonier, by John E. Guilday. Annals of Carnegie Museum, vol. 42.

Hassan, Fekri A. *Demographic Archaeology.* New York: Academic Press, c1981. 298 pp., illus., bibliog., index.

Haven, Samuel F. *Archaeology of the United States; or, Sketches, Historical and Bibliographical, of the Progress of Information and Opinion Respecting Vestiges of Antiquity in the United States.* 1856. Reprint. With a new introduction by Gordon R. Willey. New York: Published by AMS Press for Peabody Museum of Archaeology and Ethnology, Harvard University, Cambridge, 1973. 168 pp., bibliog. references. ◆ Harvard University, Peabody Museum of Archaeology and Ethnology, Antiquities of the New World, no. 3.

Heizer, Robert F. *Man's Discovery of His Past: Literary Landmarks in Archaeology.* Englewood Cliffs, N.J.: Prentice-Hall, 1962. 179 pp., illus., bibliog.

Hester, James J., and James Grady. *Introduction to Archaeology.* 2nd ed. New York: Holt, Rinehart & Winston, c1982. 496 pp., illus., bibliogs., index.

Historical Archaeology: A Guide to Substantive and Theoretical Contributions. Edited by Robert L. Schuyler. Farmingdale, N.Y.: Baywood Publishing, 1978. 286 pp., illus., bibliogs.

Hole, Frank, and Robert F. Heizer. *Prehistoric Archeology: A Brief Introduction.* New York: Holt, Rinehart & Winston, c1977. 477 pp., illus., bibliog., index.

Jennings, Jesse D. *Prehistory of North America.* 2nd ed. New York: McGraw-Hill, 1974. 436 pp., illus., bibliog.

Kidd, Kenneth E. *Historic Site Archaeology in Canada.* Ottawa: National Museums of Canada, 1969. 47 pp. ◆ Anthropology Papers, no. 22.

King, Thomas F.; Patricia P. Hickman; and Gary Berg. *Anthropology in Historic Preservation: Caring for Culture's Clutter.* New York: Academic Press, 1977. 344 pp., illus., bibliog., index.

Knudson, S. J. *Culture in Retrospect: An Introduction to Archaeology.* Chicago: Rand McNally College Publishing Company, c1978. 555 pp., illus., bibliogs., indexes.

Leone, Mark P., ed. *Contemporary Archaeology: A Guide to Theory and Contributions.* Carbondale: Southern Illinois University Press, 1972. 460 pp., illus., maps, bibliog., index.

McGimsey, Charles R., III. *Public Archeology.* New York: Seminar Press, 1972. 265 pp.

Noel Hume, Ivor. *All the Best Rubbish.* 1st ed. New York: Harper & Row, 1974. 320 pp., illus., bibliog.

Orme, Bryony. *Anthropology for Archaeologists: An Introduction.* Ithaca, N.Y.: Cornell University Press, 1981. 300 pp., illus., bibliog., index.

Patterson, Thomas C. *America's Past: A New World Archaeology.* Glenview, Ill.: Scott, Foresman, 1973. 156 pp., illus., maps, bibliog. essay, index.

Piggott, Stuart. *Approach to Archaeology.* 1959. Reprint. New York: McGraw-Hill Company, 1965. 134 pp., illus.

Place, Robin. *Introduction to Archaeology.* New York: Philosophical Library, 1968. 168 pp., illus., drawings, diagrams, charts, bibliog. references, index.

Pyddoke, Edward. *What Is Archaeology?* New York: Roy Publishers, c1964, 1965. 64 pp., illus., maps, bibliog.

Redman, Charles L., ed. *Research and Theory in Current Archeology.* Huntington,

N.Y.: R. E. Krieger Pub. Co., c1973, 1980. 390 pp., bibliog., index. ◆ An expansion of the symposium, "Archeology's Future: Roles and Relevance," presented at the 1971 meetings of the American Anthropological Association.

Shackley, Myra L. *Environmental Archaeology.* Boston: Allen & Unwin, c1981. 256 pp., illus., bibliog. references, index.

Sharer, Robert J., and Wendy Ashmore. *Fundamentals of Archaeology.* Menlo Park, Calif.: Benjamin-Cummings Pub. Co., c1979.

Society for Historical Archaeology. *Historical Archaeology and the Importance of Material Things: Papers of the Thematic Symposium, Eighth Annual Meeting of the Society for Historical Archaeology, Charleston, South Carolina, January 7–11, 1975.* Edited by Leland Ferguson. Lansing, Mich.: Society for Historical Archaeology, c1977. 68 pp., illus., bibliog. ◆ Special Publication series no. 2

Thomas, David Hurst. *Archaeology.* New York: Holt, Rinehart & Winston, c1979. 510 pp., illus., bibliog., index.

Thomas, David Hurst. *Predicting the Past: An Introduction to Anthropological Archaeology.* New York: Holt, Rinehart & Winston, 1974. 84 pp., illus., table, bibliog.

Wainwright, Frederick T. *Archaeology and Place Names and History: An Essay on the Problems of Co-ordination.* London: Routledge and Paul, 1962. 135 pp., illus.

Watson, Patty Jo; Steven A. LeBlanc; and Charles L. Redman. *Explanation in Archaeology, An Explicitly Scientific Approach.* New York: Columbia University Press, 1971. 191 pp., illus., bibliog.

Willey, Gordon R. *An Introduction to American Archaeology: Vol. 1. North and Middle America.* Englewood Cliffs, N.J.: Prentice-Hall, 1966. 530 pp., illus., glossary, bibliog.

Willey, Gordon, and Philip Phillips. *Method and Theory in American Archaeology.* Chicago: University of Chicago Press, c1958, 1962. 269 pp., illus., bibliog.

Willey, Gordon R., and Jeremy A. Sabloff. *A History of American Archaeology.* San Francisco: W. H. Freeman, 1974. 252 pp., illus., bibliog.

William Marsh Rice University, Houston, Tex. *Prehistoric Man in the New World.* Contributors: Pedro Armillas and others. Editors: Jesse D. Jennings and Edward Norbeck. Chicago: Published for William Marsh Rice University by the University of Chicago Press, c1964, 1971. 633 pp., illus., maps, tables, bibliogs.

Wilson, David. *The New Archaeology.* 1st American ed. New York: Knopf, distr. by Random House, c1974, 1975. 349 pp., bibliog., index.

Woodall, J. Ned. *An Introduction to Modern Archaeology.* Cambridge, Mass.: Schenkman Publishing Co., 1972. 96 pp., bibliog.

Woolley, Charles Leonard. *Digging Up the Past.* 2nd ed. 1954. Reprint. Westport, Conn.: Greenwood Press, 1977. 125 pp., plates, illus., index.

Yellen, John E. *Archaeological Approaches to the Present: Models for Reconstructing the Past.* New York: Academic Press, c1977. 259 pp., illus., bibliog.

Regional Archeological Studies

Adams, William H. *Silcott, Washington: Ethnoarchaeology of a Rural American Community.* Pullman: Laboratory of Anthropology, Washington State University, 1977. 169 pp., illus., bibliog. ◆ Report of Investigations no. 54.

Adams, William H.; Linda P. Gaw; and Frank C. Leonhardy. *Archaeological Excavations at Silcott, Washington: The Data Inventory.* Pullman: Laboratory of Anthropology, Washington State University, 1975. 280 pp., illus., charts, bibliog. ◆ Reports of Investigations no. 53.

Alex, Lynn M. *Exploring Iowa's Past: A Guide to Prehistoric Archaeology.* Iowa City: University of Iowa Press, 1980. 169 pp., illus., maps.

Archaeology at Hatchery West. Lewis R. Binford, et al. Washington, D.C.: Society for American Archaeology, 1970. 91 pp., illus., bibliog.

Archeological Research Associates. *A Preliminary Archeological Assessment of the Central Oklahoma Project Area.* Annetta

Cheek, principal investigator and editor; Charles Cheek, editor. Tulsa, Okla.: Archeological Research Associates, 1975. 210 pp., illus., graphs, maps, bibliog.

Archeological Resources of the Proposed Cuero I Reservoir, DeWitt and Gonzales Counties, Texas. By Daniel E. Fox, et al. Austin: Texas Historical Commission, 1974. 311 pp., illus., bibliog. ◆ Archeology Survey Report no. 12.

Archeological Salvage and Survey in Nebraska: Highway Archeological and Historical Salvage Investigations in Nebraska, 1965–1968, by Gayle F. Carson. A Preliminary Report of the Point of Rocks Archeological Survey, 1971, by Richard E. Jensen. Lincoln: Nebraska State Historical Society, 1973. 240 pp., illus. ◆ Nebraska State Historical Society Publications in Anthropology no. 5.

Bell, Robert E. Oklahoma Archaeology; An Annotated Bibliography. 2nd ed. Norman: University of Oklahoma Press, c 1978. 155 pp., index.

Benchley, Elizabeth. An Overview of the Prehistoric Resources of the Metropolitan St. Louis Area. Washington, D.C.: U.S. Department of the Interior, National Park Service, 1976. 93 pp., illus., bibliog.

Benes, Peter, ed. New England Historical Archeology. Proceedings of The Dublin Seminar for New England Folklife, 1977. Boston: Boston University Scholarly Publications, 1977. 160 pp., illus., maps, bibliog.

Binford, Lewis R. Nunamuit Ethnoarchaeology. New York: Academic Press, 1978. 509 pp., illus., bibliog., index.

Butler, B. Robert. A Guide to Understanding Idaho Archaeology: The Upper Snake and Salmon River Country. 3rd ed. Pocatello: Idaho Museum of Natural History, 1978. 97 pp., illus., bibliog.

Calver, William L., and Reginald P. Bolton. History Written with a Pick and Shovel: Military Buttons, Belt-Plates, Badges, and Other Relics Excavated from Colonial, Revolutionary, and War of 1812 Camp Sites by the Field Exploration Committee of the New-York Historical Society. Charlottesville: University Press of Virginia, c1950, 1970. 320 pp., illus., maps, bibliog.

Chapman, Carl H. The Archaeology of Missouri, Vol. I. Columbia: University of Missouri Press, 1975. 320 pp., illus., tables, bibliog. ◆ University of Missouri Studies, 12. See also: Vol. II. 1980. 336 pp., illus., maps, tables, bibliog.

Cotter, John L. Archaeological Excavations at Jamestown Colonial National Historic Site, Virginia. Washington, D.C.: National Park Service, U.S. Department of the Interior, 1959. 299 pp., illus., maps, bibliog. ◆ Archeological Research series no. 4.

Dincauze, Dena F. The Neville Site: 8,000 Years of Amoskeag, Manchester, New Hampshire. Cambridge, Mass.: Peabody Museum of Archaeology and Ethnology, Harvard University, 1976. 150 pp., illus., bibliog. ◆ Peabody Museum Monographs no. 4.

Dincauze, Dena F., and Judith Meyer. Prehistoric Resources of East-Central New England: A Preliminary Predictive Study. Washington, D.C.: National Park Service, U.S. Department of the Interior, 1977. 55 pp., maps, bibliog. ◆ Cultural Resource Management Studies.

Dow, Richard Alan, ed. "Fortifications." In Northeast Historical Archaeology, 2:1 (Spring 1972), special issue. ◆ Includes illus., drawings, maps, table, formulas, bibliog. notes.

Fitting, James E. The Archaeology of Michigan: A Guide to the Prehistory of the Great Lakes Region. 2nd rev. ed. Bloomfield Hills, Mich.: Cranbrook Institute of Science, 1975. 274 pp., illus., bibliog., index. ◆ Bulletin Series no. 56.

Five Artifact Studies. By Audrey Noel Hume, et al. Charlottesville, Va.: University Press of Virginia, c1973. 116 pp., illus., appendices, bibliog. ◆ Colonial Williamsburg Occasional Papers in Archaeology, vol. 1. Subjects covered are artifacts from an eighteenth century well; shoe buckles, window glass, bayonets, and horseshoes.

Funkhouser, William D., and William S. Webb. Archaeological Survey of Kentucky. Lexington: University of Kentucky, Department of Anthropology and Archaeology, 1932. 463 pp., illus., maps, bibliog. ◆ Reports on Archaeology and Anthropology, University of Kentucky, vol. 2.

Hanson, Lee, and Dick Ping Hsu. Casemates and Cannonballs: Archaeological Investigations at Fort Stanwix, Rome, New York. Washington, D.C.: U.S. Department of the Interior, National Park Service; for sale by Supt. of Docs., U.S. Government Printing Office, 1975. 177 pp., illus., maps, appendix, bibliog., index. ✦ Publications in Archeology, 14.

Harrington, Jean Carl. *Search for the Cittie of Ralegh: Archeological Excavations at Fort Raleigh National Historic Site, North Carolina.* Washington, D.C.: National Park Service, U.S. Department of the Interior, 1962. 63 pp., illus., maps. ✦ Archeological Research series no. 6.

Harrington, Virginia S., and J. C. Harrington. *Rediscovery of The Nauvoo Temple, Report on the Archeological Excavations.* Salt Lake City, Utah: Nauvoo Restoration, 1971. 54 pp., illus., bibliog., index.

Holland, Charlton G. *An Archeological Survey of Southwest Virginia.* Washington, D.C.: Smithsonian Institution Press; for sale by Supt. of Docs., U.S. Government Printing Office, 1970. 194 pp., illus., maps, bibliog. ✦ Smithsonian Contributions to Anthropology, no. 12.

Kinsey, W. Fred. *Archeology in the Upper Delaware Valley: A Study of the Cultural Chronology of the Tocks Island Reservoir.* Harrisburg: Pennsylvania Historical and Museum Commission, 1972. 499 pp., illus., charts, bibliog., appendix, index. ✦ Anthropological Series no. 2.

Kirk, Ruth, and Richard D. Daugherty. *Exploring Washington Archaeology.* Seattle: University of Washington Press, c1978. 112 pp., illus., index.

Lehmer, Donald J. *Introduction to Middle Missouri Archeology.* Washington, D.C.: Supt. of Docs., U.S. Government Printing Office, 1971. 206 pp., illus., maps, bibliog. ✦ Anthropological Papers no. 1.

Longace, William A. *Archaeology as Anthropology: A Case Study.* Tucson: University of Arizona Press, 1970. 57 pp., illus., maps, bibliog. ✦ Anthropological Papers of the University of Arizona no. 17.

McGimsey, Charles R., III; Hester A. Davis; and Carl Chapman. *These Are the Stewards of the Past.* Columbia: University of Missouri, Extension Division, 1970. 23 pp., illus. ✦ Issued by the Steering Committee of the Mississippi Alluvial Valley Archaeological Program. Includes directory of state archeologists and anthropologists, and agencies that can assist.

McGregor, John C. *Southwestern Archaeology.* 2nd ed. Urbana: University of Illinois Press, 1965. 511 pp., illus., bibliogs.

Mason, Ronald J. *Great Lakes Archaeology.* New York: Academic Press, c1981. 426 pp., illus., bibliog., index.

Maxwell, Moreau S., and Lewis R. Binford. *Excavations at Fort Michilimackinac, Mackinac City, Michigan: 1959 Season.* East Lansing: Michigan State University, 1961. 130 pp., illus., bibliog. references.

Miller, J. Jefferson, II, and Lyle M. Stone. *Eighteenth-Century Ceramics from Fort Michilimackinac, A Study in Historical Archeology.* Washington, D.C.: Smithsonian Institution Press, for sale by Supt. of Docs., U.S. Government Printing Office, 1970. 130 pp., illus., maps, bibliog. ✦ Smithsonian Studies in History and Technology no. 4.

Noble, David Grant. *Ancient Ruins of the Southwest: An Archaeological Guide.* Flagstaff, Ariz.: Northland Press, 1981. 156 pp., illus., bibliog. references.

Noel Hume, Ivor. *Early English Delftware from London and Virginia.* Williamsburg, Va.: Colonial Williamsburg Foundation; Charlottesville, distr. by University Press of Virginia, c1977. 125 pp., illus., bibliog., index. ✦ Colonial Williamsburg Occasional Papers in Archaeology, vol. 2.

Noel Hume, Ivor. *Excavations at Rosewell in Gloucester County, Virginia, 1957–1959.* Washington, D.C.: Smithsonian Institution, 1962. 154–227 pp., illus., maps, bibliog., footnotes. ✦ U.S. National Museum Bulletin 225, Paper 18.

Noel Hume, Ivor. *Here Lies Virginia: An Archaeologist's View of Colonial Life and History.* New York: Knopf, 1963. 316 pp., illus., maps, bibliog.

North Carolina Statewide Archaeological Survey: *An Introduction and Application to Three Highway Projects in Hertford, Wilkes, and Ashe Counties.* By Thomas E. Sheitlin, et al. Raleigh: North Carolina Archaeological Council and Archaeology Branch, Division of Archives and History, Department of Cultural Resources, 1979. 311 pp., illus., maps, bibliog. ✦ North Carolina Archaeological Council Publication no. 11.

Quimby, G. I., Jr. *Indian Life in the Upper*

Great Lakes 11,000 B.C. to A.D. 1800. Chicago: University of Chicago Press, c1960, 1971. 182 pp., illus., bibliog.

Quimby, George I. *Indian Culture and European Trade Goods: The Archaeology of the Historic Period in the Western Great Lakes Region.* 1966. Reprint. Westport, Conn.: Greenwood Press, 1978. 217 pp., illus., bibliog., index.

Readings in Long Island Archaeology and Ethnohistory. Volume I–. Stony Brook, N.Y.: Suffolk County Archaeological Association; reproduced by Xerox Corporation, 1977–. illus., charts, diagrams, maps, bibliog. references. ◆ Vol. 1—*Early Papers in Long Island Archaeology* (1977); Vol. 2—*The Coastal Archaeology Reader: Selections from the New York State Archaeological Association Bulletin, 1954–1977* (1978); Vol. 3—*The History and Archaeology of the Montauk Indians* (1979).

Rockwell, Tim O. *Belle Grove Excavations: Middletown, Va.* Washington, D.C.: Preservation Press, 1974. 110 pp., illus., bibliog., appendix.

Snow, Dean R. *Archaeology of New England.* New York: Academic Press, 1980. 379 pp., illus.

Teague, George A., and Lynnette O. Shenk. *Excavations at Harmony Borax Works: Historical Archaeology at Death Valley National Monument.* Washington, D.C.: National Park Service, U.S. Department of the Interior, 1977. 238 pp. ◆ Western Archaeological Center Publications in Anthropology, no. 6.

Texas Archaeology: *Essays Honoring R. King Harris.* Edited by Kurt D. House. Dallas: SMU Press, c1978. 178 pp., illus., maps, bibliogs. ◆ Institute for the Study of Earth and Man, Reports of Investigations, no. 3.

Tuck, James A. *Onondaga Iroquois Prehistory: A Study in Settlement Archaeology.* 1st ed. Syracuse, N.Y.: Syracuse University Press, 1971. 255 pp., illus., diagrams, charts, bibliog., appendices, index.

Tuohy, Donald R. *Archaeological Survey in Southwestern Idaho and Northern Nevada.* Carson City: Nevada State Museum, 1963. 136 pp., illus., maps. ◆ Anthropology Papers, no. 8.

Witthoft, John, and Fred W. Kinsey, III, eds. *Susquehannock Miscellany.* Harrisburg:

Pennsylvania Historical and Museum Commission, 1959. 167 pp., illus., maps, bibliog.

Yager Conference on Archaeology and Geochronology, Hartwick College, 1976. *Archaeology and Geochronology of the Susquehanna and Schoharie Regions: Proceedings of the Yager Conference at Hartwick College, 6 November 1976.* Edited by John R. Cole and Laurie R. Godfrey. Oneonta, N.Y.: Hartwick College, 1977. 143 pp., illus., bibliogs.

NOTE

Colonial Williamsburg, Archaeological Series. Begun in 1969, the series presents results of archeological excavations and research carried out in Williamsburg and its environs from the earliest days of the restoration. Titles to date include: glass; pottery and porcelain; Wetherburn's Tavern; the wells of Williamsburg; James Geddy & Son, Craftsmen; colonial gardener; Carter's Grove; food.

Marine Archeology

Archeology Under Water: *An Atlas of the World's Submerged Sites.* General editor, Keith Muckelroy. New York: McGraw-Hill, 1980. 192 pp., illus., bibliog., index.

Arnold, J. Barto, III. *1977 Underwater Site Test Excavations off Padre Island, Texas.* Austin: Texas Antiquities Committee, c1978. 23 pp., illus., bibliog. ◆ Texas Antiquities Committee Publication, no. 5.

Arnold, J. Barto, III, and Robert S. Weddle. *The Nautical Archeology of Padre Island: The Spanish Shipwrecks of 1554.* New York: Academic Press, c1978. 462 pp., illus., bibliog., index. ◆ Texas Antiquities Committee Publication, no. 9

Bass, George F. *Archaeology Beneath the Sea.* New York: Walker & Co., 1975. 238 pp., illus., maps, plans, index.

Bass, George F., ed. *A History of Seafaring: Based on Underwater Archaeology.* New York: Walker and Company, 1972. 320 pp., illus., bibliog.

Cleator, Philip Ellaby. *Underwater Archaeol-*

ogy. New York: St. Martin's Press, 1973. 224 pp., illus., diagrams, maps, bibliog.

Conference on Underwater Archaeology, St. Paul, 1963. *Diving Into the Past: Theories, Techniques, and Application of Underwater Archaeology.* The Proceedings of a Conference on Underwater Archaeology, sponsored by the Minnesota Historical Society, St. Paul, April 26–27, 1963. Edited by June D. Holmquist and Ardis H. Wheeler. St. Paul: Minnesota Historical Society, 1964. 111 pp., illus., drawings, diagrams, bibliog., index.

Conference on Underwater Archaeology, 9th, San Antonio, 1978. *Beneath the Waters of Time: The Proceedings of the Ninth Conference on Underwater Archaeology.* Edited by J. Barto Arnold, III. Austin: Texas Antiquities Committee, c1978. 244 pp., illus., bibliogs. • Texas Antiquities Committee Publication, no. 6.

Dumas, Frédéric. *Deepwater Archaeology.* Trans. from French by Honor Frost. London: Routledge and K. Paul, 1962. 71 pp., illus., bibliog.

Durgess, Robert F. *Man: 12,000 Years Under the Sea: A Story of Underwater Archaeology.* New York: Dodd, Mead, c1980. 331 pp., illus., bibliog., index.

Fischer, George R., and Marion J. Riggs. *Prospectus for Underwater Archeology.* Washington, D.C.: U.S. National Park Service, Office of Archeology and Historic Preservation, 1969. 23 pp., illus.

Marx, Robert F. *Into the Deep: The History of Man's Underwater Exploration.* New York: Van Nostrand Reinhold, c1978. 198 pp., plates, illus., bibliog., index.

Muckelroy, Keith. *Maritime Archaeology.* Cambridge and New York: Cambridge University Press, 1978. 270 pp., illus., maps, bibliog., index.

New World Underwater Archeology 1971. Washington, D.C.: Division of Archeology and Anthropology, Office of Archeology and Historic Preservation, 1972. 32 pp.

New York (State) University. State Education Department. Office of State History. *Diving Into History: A Manual of Underwater Archeology for Divers in New York State.* By Paul J. Scudiere. Albany, N.Y.: The University, 1969. 33 pp., illus., drawings, diagrams, bibliog.

Peterson, Mendel. *History Under the Sea: A Manual for Underwater Exploration.* Rev. ed. Washington, D.C.: Smithsonian Institution Press, 1969. 208 pp., illus., maps, bibliog.

Petsche, Jerome E. *The Steamboat "Bertrand": History, Excavation, and Architecture.* Washington, D.C.: National Park Service; for sale by Supt. of Docs., U.S. Government Printing Office, 1974. 177 pp., illus., bibliog.

Rackl, Hanns-Wolf. *Diving Into the Past: Archaeology Under Water.* Trans. by Ronald J. Floyd. New York: Charles Scribner's Sons, 1968. 292 pp., illus., drawings, diagrams, maps, bibliog., index.

Schulke, Flip. *Underwater Photography for Everyone.* Englewood Cliffs, N.J.: Prentice-Hall, c1978. 220 pp., illus., bibliog., index.

Scudiere, Paul J. "Underwater Archaeology: Guidelines for the Amateur Explorer," *History News,* 27:5 (May 1972), Technical Leaflet no. 61.

Silverberg, Robert. *Sunken History: The Story of Underwater Archaeology.* Philadelphia: Chilton Books, 1963. 177 pp.

Spence, Edward Lee. *A Look at South Carolina's Underwater Heritage.* Charleston, S.C.: Nelsons' Southern Printing Co., c1974. 22 pp., illus.

Surveying in Archaeology Underwater. By P. Throckmorton and others. London: Quaritch; Atlantic Highlands, N.J.: Humanities Press, 1969. 94 pp.

Throckmorton, Peter. *Shipwrecks and Archaeology: The Unharvested Sea.* Boston: Little, Brown and Company, 1970. 270 pp., illus., maps, plans, bibliog. references.

United Nations Educational, Scientific and Cultural Organization. *Underwater Archaeology: A Nascent Discipline.* Museums and Monuments No. XIII. Paris: UNESCO, 1972. 306 pp., figures, illus., maps.

NOTES

CEDAM International, P. O. Box 24725, Dallas, Texas 75224. Founded in 1967, the acronym stands for Conservation, Exploration, Diving, Archeology, Museums. Membership includes individuals and regional groups. Professional and lay persons actively pursue underwater exploration and study of maritime history and archeology. The organization's purposes are to promote the preservation of underwater maritime history sites that include sunken ships, and promote scientific development of maritime history and archeological facts from underwater sites. It bestows honorary membership for outstanding and distinguished service to underwater archeology. It maintains two museums in Mexico, and a library of 350 volumes. It publishes a *Bulletin* (quarterly); a special bulletin as needed; and holds an annual meeting.

Council for Nautical Archaeology. The Council was formed in 1964 to promote legislation for the protection of nautical archaeological sites. Museums, academic institutions, and the British Sub-Aqua Club are among the bodies represented on the Council which has no office location, only officers. It publishes the *International Journal of Nautical Archaeology and Underwater Exploration* (1972, quarterly). The CNA established the Nautical Archaeological Trust in Britain in 1972 to further research and education in nautical archaeology. It also sponsors the Nautical Archaeological Society to further research and education in nautical archaeology and to ensure publication of the results. The Society publishes a newsletter and is located at 1 Old Hall, South Grove, Highgate, London N6, England.

International Journal of Nautical Archaeology and Underwater Exploration. 1972, quarterly, subscription. Council for Nautical Archaeology, Academic Press, Inc., 111 Fifth Avenue, New York, New York 10003.

Cultural Resources Management

Advisory Council on Historic Preservation. "Issues in Archeology," *Report,* 5:2–3 (March-April-May 1977), special issue. ◆ Report of a meeting of specialists; includes identification, techniques, legislation; federal project planning—the Corps of Engineers, the Bureau of Reclamation; the U.S. Forest Service Cultural Resources Program; regional programs; managing archeological resources at all levels; problems in protection and preservation of archeological resources.

Archeology and Archeological Resources: *A Guide for those Planning to Use, Affect, or Alter the Land's Surface.* Prepared by the Committee on the Public Understanding of Archaeology of the Society for American Archaeology; principal author, Charles R. McGimsey. Washington, D.C.: Society for American Archaeology, 1975. 24 pp., illus.

Brew, J. O. "Salvage Archaeology and History Preservation." American Council of Learned Societies *Newsletter,* 20:4 (May 1969), reprinted in *Museum News,* 48:2 (October 1969), pp. 20–26.

Coastal Environments, Inc. *Cultural Resources Evaluation of the Northern Gulf of Mexico Continental Shelf.* Prepared for the Interagency Archeological Services, Office of Archeology and Historic Preservation, National Park Service, U.S. Department of the Interior. Baton Rouge, La.: CEI, 1977. 3 vols., illus., bibliogs. ◆ Cultural Resource Management Studies.

Conservation Archaeology: *A Guide for Cultural Resource Management Studies.* Edited by Michael B. Schiffer and George J. Gumerman. New York: Academic Press, c1977. 495 pp., illus., bibliog., index.

DeJarnett, David L. *Archaeological Salvage in the Walter F. George Basin of the Chattahoochee River in Alabama.* University: University of Alabama Press, 1975. 237 pp., illus., bibliog., index.

Lindsay, Alexander J.; Glenna Williams-Dean; and Jonathan Haas. *The Curation and Management of Archeological Collections: A Pilot Study.* Washington, D.C.: Anthropological Research Services, American Anthropological Association, 1979. 2 vols (560 pp.). ◆ Prepared for Heritage Conservation and Recreation Service, Interagency Archeological Services Division. Examines curation practices in the nation's museums and repositories housing federally owned archeological collections.

McGuire, Randall H. *Rancho Punta de Agua: Excavations at a Historic Ranch Near Tucson, Arizona.* Tucson: Arizona State Museum, 1979. 113 pp., illus., charts, tables, bibliog., appendix. ◆ Arizona State Museum, Contributions to Highway Salvage Archeology in Arizona, no. 57.

Management of Archaeological Resources: *The Airlie House Report.* Edited by Charles R. McGimsey, III, and Hester A. Davis. Lawrence,

Kans.: Society for American Archaeology, 1977. 124 pp., illus., bibliogs. ◆ Covers such topics as law in archeology, cultural resources, guidelines for preparation and evaluation of archeological reports, crisis in communication, archeology and native Americans, certification and accreditation.

Nickerson, Gifford S. *Considerations of the Problems of Vandalism and Pot-Hunting in American Archaeology.* Missoula: Montana State University, 1962. 15 pp., map. ◆ Anthropology and Sociology Papers, no. 22.

Petsche, Jerome. *Bibliography of Salvage Archaeology in the United States.* With a foreword by Joan M. Brew. Lincoln, Neb.: 1968. 168 pp. ◆ Publications in Salvage Archaeology no. 10. Missouri Basin Project, River Basin Surveys, Museum of Natural History, Smithsonian Institution.

Scholars as Contractors: *Report of a Workshop on the Contract Archeology Process.* William J. Mayer-Oakes and Alice W. Portnoy, eds. Washington, D.C.: U.S. Department of the Interior, Heritage Conservation and Recreation Service, Interagency Archeological Services Division; for sale by Supt. of Docs., U.S. Government Printing Office, 1979. 265 pp., in various pagings, illus., bibliogs.

Scholars as Managers: *or, How Can the Managers Do It Better: Report of a Workshop on Management Techniques in Archeology.* Alice W. Portnoy, ed. Washington, D.C.: U.S. Department of the Interior, Cultural Resource Management Studies, Office of Archeology and Historic Preservation, Heritage Conservation and Recreation Service, Interagency Archeological Services, 1978. 211 pp., illus.

Silverberg, Robert. *Men Against Time: Salvage Archaeology in the United States.* New York: Macmillan, 1967. 202 pp., illus., bibliog.

Wasley, William W., and Alfred E. Johnson. *Salvage Archaeology in Painted Rocks Reservoir, Western Arizona.* Tucson: University of Arizona Press, 1965. 123 pp., illus., maps, plans, bibliog., appendices. ◆ Anthropological Papers, no. 9

NOTE

U.S. Department of Agriculture, Forest Service, and U.S. Department of the Interior, Bureau of Land Management. *Cultural Resource Management Overviews.* Begun in 1979, the Forest Service and Bureau of Land Management have a joint agreement to produce a series of volumes which are designed to provide baseline data for land use planning. Eighteen overviews are planned, covering most of Arizona and New Mexico. Each describes what is known about the history and prehistory of its study area, what archeological research has been done, what kinds of research questions might be pursued in the future, and what the general condition of the resource base appears to be today. Available from Supt. of Docs., U.S. Government Printing Office.

3

Architecture

"It is the solidity of the frame that pleaseth the builder," said an 18th century New England divine. Equally pleasing to the architectural historian and the restoration architect is the framework provided by research, for other than careful scrutiny and analysis of the structure itself and the land under and around it, only the study of the written and graphic record will offer the clues needed to assure historical accuracy.

This chapter greatly expands and updates a brief section in Volume 1: Historic Preservation in this series. It reflects the renewed and heightened interest of the American people in their heritage, the growth of the historic preservation movement, the surge in tourism, and even the greater availability of funds for architectural surveys and research. It is probably a truism, as well, to say that more Americans are now seeing what they only looked at before. As a result, more are willing to invest in old houses, an investment of time, money, and effort that offers rich rewards.

Since there is no standard handbook on architectural research, it is not inappropriate to consult again the handbooks for historical research and then follow the general principles. Differences in research method will be learned as the sources are uncovered. One can start with this chapter, however, to build one's own bibliography, for here are listed the major works that will speed the research process. It even includes the many new pioneering studies in the field, the books for readers as well as for scholars. But not, it should be added, the so-called "coffee-table" books. Of making many of those books there has been no end.

The chapter deals extensively with reference books and guides and even lists many of those fine old builder's guides and pattern books that Henry-Russell Hitchcock singled out for special attention in his *American Architectural Books*. . . . To which should be added that the architectural historian, whether amateur or professional, would also be well advised to track down the early descriptive guides that are listed in Frank J. Roos's *Bibliography of Early American Architecture*. . . .

Sections on architectural surveys, architects, period styles, and building types complete the references directly relating to architecture. The reader-user should be alerted to one fact, however. For references to building construction, building materials, and metal components in buildings, one should consult the following chapter, on technology. This chapter then concludes with sections on the necessary concomitants to architectural study, landscape architecture, and urban design and planning. The final offering is on regional architectural studies, since it has always been the editors' hope that this bibliography could be made valuable locally as well as nationally.

Only a few more introductory words. It is quite probable that only membership in one or more architectural organizations, national, state, or special interest, will enable the researcher to keep up with information programs and publications. Note especially the National Trust for Historic Preservation, with its excellent library, its information services, its workshops and seminars, and its publications. And finally, the office of the State Historic Preservation Officer should be consulted: many states (not all) can offer technical advice and assistance that can't be found elsewhere.

Basic Reference Shelf

Andrews, Wayne. *Architecture, Ambition and Americans: A Social History of American Architecture.* Rev. ed. New York: Free Press of Glencoe, c1978. 332 pp., illus., bibliog., index. ◆ Survey of architecture as a fine art, with emphasis on architectural taste. Chapters on southern colonies, northern colonies, federal period, romantic era, age of elegance, Chicago story, and modern times.

Ellsworth, Linda. "The History of a House: How to Trace It," *History News,* 31:9 (September 1976), Technical Leaflet no. 89. ◆ How to find information in sources such as property abstract, legal records, prints and photographs, newspapers, city directories, manuscript collections, and builder's catalogs.

Fitch, James Marston. *American Building, 1: The Historical Forces That Shaped It.* 2nd ed., rev. and enl. Boston: Houghton Mifflin Co., c1947, 1966. 350 pp., illus., drawings, diagrams, bibliog. notes, index. ◆ Comprehensive view of architecture in the U.S.; accounts for materials, needs, technical equipment, esthetic theory and creative genius that shaped saltbox and skyscraper.

Hamlin, Talbot Faulkner. *Greek Revival Architecture in America: Being an Account of Important Trends in American Architecture and American Life Prior to the War Between the States.* 1944. Reprint. New York: Dover Publications, 1964. 439 pp., diagrams, appendices, bibliog. footnotes, bibliog., index. ◆ Surveys the decades between 1820–1860; considers expression "Middle American" more appropriate term than strict Greek Revival. Analyzes general characteristics and local variations throughout the country.

Historic American Buildings Survey. *Recording Historic Buildings: The Historic American Buildings Survey.* Compiled by Harley J. McKee. Washington, D.C.: U.S. National Park Service, 1970. 165 pp., illus., drawings, diagrams, tables, bibliog., index. ◆ Basic text on various techniques for recording buildings by drawing, photography, documentation. Out-of-print; revised edition in preparation for fall 1983 by the Preservation Press, National Trust for Historic Preservation.

Hitchcock, Henry-Russell. *American Architectural Books: A List of Books, Portfolios, and Pamphlets on Architecture and Related Subjects Published in America Before 1895.* New expanded ed.; intro. by Adolf K. Placzek. New York: DaCapo Press, 1976. 150 pp. ◆ Listing of architectural periodicals by the author, and a chronological short-title list compiled under the direction of William H. Jordy, which was originally publication no. 4 (October 1955) of the American Association of Architectural Bibliographers.

Hitchcock, Henry-Russell. *Architecture: Nineteenth and Twentieth Centuries.* 4th ed. New York: Penguin Books, 1977. 688 pp., illus., drawings, diagrams, bibliog., index. ◆ Presents viewpoint of art history, i.e., exterior appearance, style, and social background.

Hunt, William Dudley, Jr. *Encyclopedia of American Architecture.* New York: McGraw-Hill, c1980. 612 pp., illus., index. ◆ Includes biographies of major architects, technical definitions, examinations of periods and genre, and other useful details.

Isham, Norman Morrison. *Early American Houses;* and, *A Glossary of Colonial Architectural Terms.* 1928; 1939. Reprint. New York: DaCapo Press, 1967. 61, 37 pp., illus., drawings, diagrams, index. ◆ Two volumes in one; detailed technical description of a number of early American homes, and a glossary of terms.

Jacobs, Jane. *The Death and Life of Great American Cities.* New York: Random House, Vintage Books, 1961. 458 pp., index. ◆ Analyzes aspects of city life; sidewalks, parks, buildings, slums, planning; emphasizes critical need for different approach to city planning.

Marshall, Howard W. *American Folk Architecture: A Selected Bibliography.* Washington, D.C.: American Folklife Center, 1981. 79 pp. ◆ Articles and books on theory and general topics, antecedent references from the British Isles, and resources on specific regions of the country.

Newton, Norman T. *Design on the Land: The Development of Landscape Architecture.* Cambridge, Mass.: Belknap Press of Harvard University Press, 1971. 714 pp., illus., map, plans, bibliog. ◆ History of landscape architecture as an art and as a profession, from ancient times to the present. Includes European precedents, development of parks, biography, planning, National Park System, and conservation of natural resources.

Olmsted, Frederick Law. *Frederick Law Olmsted, Landscape Architect, 1822–1903.* Edited by Frederick Law Olmstead, Jr., and Theodora Kimball. 1922–28. Reprint. New York: Benjamin Blom, 1970. 2 vols. in 1 (131, 575 pp.), illus., maps, bibliog. ◆ Half title: *Forty Years of Landscape Architecture,* 1922 edition. Volume 2 on Central Park, also reprinted by MIT Press, Cambridge, Mass., 1973.

Reps, John W. *The Making of Urban America: A History of City Planning in the United States.* Princeton, N.J.: Princeton University Press, 1965. 574 pp., maps, plans, illus. ◆ Basic survey; well-illustrated history of city planning from colonial period through the nineteenth century.

Rifkind, Carole. *A Field Guide to American Architecture.* New York: New American Library, 1980. 322 pp., illus., line drawings, bibliog., index. ◆ Includes historical background, construction materials, and basic structure and styles of all types of buildings. Four categories: ecclesiastical, residential, commercial, utilitarian.

Roth, Leland M. *A Concise History of American Architecture.* New York: Harper & Row, c1979. 400 pp., illus., bibliog., index. ◆ Introductory survey to major developments that have shaped the American-built environment from the arrival of the Europeans to the present. Includes style chronology and glossary.

Scully, Vincent J. *The Shingle Style and the Stick Style: Architectural Theory and Design from Richardson to the Origins of Wright.* Rev. ed. New Haven, Conn.: Yale University Press, c1955, 1971. 184 pp., illus., diagrams, bibliog., index. ◆ Concerned with a process in growth in architectural thought and design of American domestic architecture, 1872–1889, and with the buildings, projects, and writings of the architects. Additions to footnotes, and updated bibliography.

Sharp, Dennis. *Sources of Modern Architecture: A Bibliography.* New York: George Wittenborn, 1967. 56 pp., illus. ◆ Architectural Association (London) Papers, vol. 2. Contents list and subject headings in English, French and German; sections for bio-bibliography and for subject bibliography.

Webber, Joan. *How Old Is Your House?: A Guide to Research.* Chester, Conn.: Pequot Press, c1978. 101 pp., illus., plans, bibliog.

Whiffen, Marcus. *American Architecture Since 1780: A Guide to the Styles.* Cambridge, Mass.: MIT Press, 1969. 313 pp., illus., glossary, bibliog., index. ◆ Chronological arrangement; each style includes note on its characteristics, a brief history, and a few illustrations. Does not consider factors such as construction, function and plan.

Withey, Henry F., and Elsie Rathburn Withey. *Biographical Dictionary of American Architects (Deceased).* 1956. Reprint. Los Angeles: Hennessey & Ingalls, 1970. 678 pp. ◆ Brief biographical sketches of men and women, working ca.1740–1952, now deceased. Usually indicates best-known works; references cited at end of articles.

Architectural Organizations and Periodicals

AIA Journal. 1944, monthly, subscription. American Institute of Architects, Octagon,

1735 New York Avenue, N.W., Washington, D.C. 20006.

American Association of Architectural Bibliographers, Campbell Hall, University of Virginia, Charlottesville, Virginia 22903. Founded in 1954, the purpose of the Association is to further interest in, knowledge of, and research for architectural bibliography. It sponsors research for publications. The Association publishes *Papers,* devoted to writings by and about the world's foremost architects and the work of eminent writers on architecture. Membership is limited to those individuals who have a professional association with architectural history.

American Institute of Architects, Octagon, 1735 New York Avenue, N.W., Washington, D.C. 20006. Founded in 1857, the Institute serves the needs of and improves the capability of the nation's architects. It conducts "War on Community Ugliness," sponsors education programs; maintains a library and a comprehensive architectural slide collection. Its publications include *AIA Journal* (monthly); *AIA Memo* (monthly, organization news); a directory; and special leaflets.

Antiques. 1922, monthly, subscription. Straight Enterprises, Inc., 551 Fifth Avenue, New York, New York 10017.

Architectural Record. 1891, monthly, subscription. Walter F. Wagner, Jr., 1221 Avenue of the Americas, New York, New York 10020. ♦ Published studies, between 1951–1961, include apartments and dormitories, industry, offices, religious buildings, commercial, in addition to those cited in appropriate sections below.

Blueprints. 1981, quarterly, membership. National Building Museum, Pension Building, 440 G Street, N.W., Washington, D.C. 20001. ♦ The NBM is a privately funded organization mandated by Congress in 1980 to commemorate and encourage the American building arts.

Classical America. 1972, 2/yr., membership. Society for a Classical America, 10–41 51st Avenue, Long Island City, New York 11101.

Friends of Cast Iron Architecture, c/o Julia Hullar, Secretary, 235 East 87th Street, 6C, New York, New York 10028. Founded in 1970, membership includes preservationists, architectural historians, architects and laymen interested in history, interesting buildings and urban amenities. Its major objective is to promote the preservation of worthwhile examples of cast iron architecture throughout the country. It conducts walking tours and public lectures to arouse public interest and appreciation of this uniquely American form. The Friends urge owners to maintain these historic buildings and to avoid making inappropriate renovation. It sponsors an annual lecture and a library; and, holds an annual meeting. It publishes *Report Letters* (quarterly).

Journal of the Society of Architectural Historians. 1941, quarterly, membership. Society of Architectural Historians, Suite 716, 1700 Walnut Street, Philadelphia, Pennsylvania 19103.

Newsletter of the Society of Architectural Historians. 1957, bimonthly, membership. Society of Architectural Historians, Suite 716, 1700 Walnut Street, Philadelphia, Pennsylvania 19103.

Old House Journal: *Renovation and Maintenance Ideas for the Antique House.* 1973, monthly, subscription. Old House Journal, 69A Seventh Avenue, Brooklyn, New York 11217.

Progressive Architecture. 1920, monthly, subscription. John Morris Dixon, Editor. Penton–IPC, Box 95759, Cleveland, Ohio 44101.

Society for a Classical America, 10–41 51st Avenue, Long Island City, New York 11101. Founded in 1968, membership includes individuals interested in promoting the Classical tradition in American art. Its goal is to make it possible for America "to enjoy new interpretations of classical architecture, classical painting and sculpture, classical public monuments and classical cities, and to see that the classical tradition finds its way into all aspects of American life." The Society plans lectures, tours, and publications and cosponsors with W. W. Norton and Company the Classical Series in Art in Architecture. It publishes *Classical America* (2/yr.), and holds an annual meeting.

Society of Architectural Historians, Suite 716, 1700 Walnut Street, Philadelphia, Pennsylvania 19103. Founded in 1940, the Society's members and chapters include architects, city planners, educators, scholars, libraries, historical organizations, interior designers, museum personnel, students and others interested in architecture and the preservation of buildings of historical and aesthetic significance. It sponsors tours of the U.S. and Europe, and makes an annual book award. Publications include *Journal of the Society of Architectural Historians* (quarterly); *Newsletter* (6/yr.); *Architectural Preservation Forum* (1979, 3/yr.), a news sheet of the SAH Committee on Architectural Preservation, to supplement the *Newsletter* as an exchange of ideas and viewpoints on the many preservation issues which concern the Society; *Placement Service Bulletin* (3/yr.); and, tour guides.

Vernacular Architecture Forum, c/o Ellen Coxe, Secretary-Treasurer, 406 Second Street, Annapolis, Maryland 21403. Begun in 1980, the organization is designed to encourage the study and preservation of all aspects of vernacular architecture and landscapes through interdisciplinary methods. Members are drawn from a variety of fields including anthropology, architectural history, folklore, geography, history, American studies and historic preservation. It maintains a bibliography of source materials and sponsors conferences and tours. It publishes *Vernacular Architecture Newsletter* (quarterly).

Vernacular Architecture Newsletter. 1979, quarterly, membership/subscription. Vernacular Architecture Forum, c/o Ellen Coxe, Secretary-Treasurer, 406 Second Street, Annapolis, Maryland 21403.

The Victorian Society in America, c/o Kristina Butvydas, Executive Director, The Athenaeum of Philadelphia, East Washington Square, Philadelphia, Pennsylvania 19106. Founded in 1966, the Society is dedicated to the preservation and enjoyment of 19th century heritage. Membership includes local, state and regional chapters. It sponsors an annual meeting, autumn symposium, study tours and summer courses, slide programs and exhibits, and maintains a library of slides. The Society publishes *The Victorian* (1973, monthly except July and August); *Nineteenth Century* (1975, quarterly).

Methods of Architectural Research

Bullock, Orin M., Jr. "Architectural Research." In *The Restoration Manual . . .* (Nor-

walk, Conn.: Silvermine Publishing Co., 1966), pp. 33–77.

Dean, Jeff. *Architectural Photography: Techniques for Architects, Preservationists, Historians, Photographers, and Urban Planners.* Nashville, Tenn.: American Association for State and Local History, 1981. 132 pp., illus., bibliog. ♦ How to take photographs of buildings with a 35 mm single-lens-reflex camera; recommends equipment, lighting; section on photography related to historic building surveys.

Ellsworth, Linda. "The History of a House: How to Trace It," *History News,* 31:9 (September 1976), Technical Leaflet no. 89.

Greater Portland Landmarks, Inc. *Researching the Old House.* Portland, Me.: Greater Portland Landmarks, Inc., 1981. 72 pp.

Guidelines for Local Surveys: A Basis for Preservation. By Anne Derry, H. Ward Jandl, Carol D. Shull, Jan Thorman. Washington, D.C.: National Register of Historic Places, Office of Archeology and Historic Preservation, U.S. Department of the Interior; for sale by Supt. of Docs., U.S. Government Printing Office, 1977. 83 pp., illus., bibliog., index. ♦ NPS Publication no. 189.

Historic American Buildings Survey. *Recording Historic Buildings: The Historic American Buildings Survey.* Compiled by Harley J. McKee. Washington, D.C.: U.S. National Park Service, 1970. 165 pp., illus., drawings, diagrams, tables, bibliog., index.

Little, Nina Fletcher. "Finding the Records of an Old House," *Old-Time New England,* 40:2 (October 1949), pp. 145–148.

Little, Nina Fletcher. "On Dating New England Houses: Part I—The Seventeenth Century, Floor Plans and Framing," *Antiques,* 47:3 (March 1945), pp. 155–157. ♦ See also: "Part II—Interiors, Seventeenth Century and Transitional Period," *Antiques,* 47:4 (April 1945), pp. 228–231; "Part III—The Great Georgian Period, 1735–1780," *Antiques,* 47:5 (May 1945), pp. 273–275; Part IV—The Adam Period, 1780–1820," *Antiques,* 47:6 (June 1945), pp. 334–336.

Mercer, Henry C. *The Dating of Old Houses.* 1923. Reprint. Doylestown, Pa.: The Bucks County Historical Society, 1973? 23 pp., illus.,

♦ See also: *Old-Time New England,* 14:4 (April 1924), pp. 170–190.

Nelson, Lee H. "Nail Chronology as an Aid to Dating Old Buildings," rev. ed., *History News,* 24:11 (November 1968), Technical Leaflet no. 48.

Pawlett, Nathaniel M., and K. Edward Lay. *Early Road Location: The Key to Discovering Historic Resources?* Charlottesville: Virginia Highway and Transportation Research Council, 1980. various pagings, illus., bibliog. ♦ Describes methodology used in surveying and documenting architecture along 18th century road systems in Virginia. Publication no. VHTRC80–R44.

Schlereth, Thomas J. "Historic Houses as Learning Laboratories: Seven Teaching Strategies," *History News,* 33:4 (April 1978), Technical Leaflet no. 105.

U.S. National Park Service. *Using the UTM Grid System to Record Historic Sites.* By Wilford T. Cole. Washington, D.C.: U.S. Government Printing Office, 1980. 42 pp. ♦ UTM, the Universal Transverse Mercator/Grid System and its application to mapping historic and archeological sites. Preservation Planning Series.

U.S. Office of Archeology and Historic Preservation. National Register Division. *How to Complete National Register Forms.* By H. Ward Jandl and Katherine H. Cole. Washington, D.C.: U.S. Government Printing Office, 1977. 74 pp., illus., maps. ♦ NPS Publication no. 171.

Webber, Joan. *How Old Is Your House?: A Guide to Research.* Chester, Conn.: Pequot Press, c1978. 101 pp., illus., plans, bibliog.

NOTE

U.S. Office of Archeology and Historic Preservation, National Register Division. *How To* pamphlet series, begun in 1979. Titles include "Establish Boundaries for National Register Properties," "Evaluate and Nominate Potential National Register Properties that have Achieved Significance within the Last 50 Years," "Improve Quality of Photos for National Register Nominations," "Apply for Certification of Significance under section 2124 of the Tax Reform Act of 1976." Authors vary.

Reference Books and Guides to Sources

General Reference

American Association of Architectural Bibliographers. *Index of Drawings Before 1900.* Compiled by James H. Grady, Frederick D. Nichols, and William B. O'Neal. Charlottesville, Va.: 1957. 24 pp.

American Association of Architectural Bibliographers. *Papers.* Vol. I–, 1965–. Charlottesville, Va.: University Press of Virginia, 1965–. 14 vols. to date, annual. ♦ Supersedes the Association's *Publications* (nos. 1–27, 1954–64. Vol. II is Index to Papers, I–X.

Architectural Index. Vol. 1, no. 1–. Boulder, Colo.: Ervin J. Bell, Publisher, 1950–. 1 vol., annual. ♦ Indexes articles from the major architectural magazines and journals. Address: P.O. Box 1168, Boulder, Colorado 80302.

Bibliographic Guide to Art and Architecture. Boston: G. K. Hall and Co., 1976–. 1 vol., annual. ♦ Formerly: *Art and Architecture Book Guide.*

Briggs, Martin Shaw. *Everyman's Concise Encyclopedia of Architecture.* 1959. Reprint. Totowa, New Jersey: Biblio Distribution Center, 1974. 372 pp., illus., bibliog. references. ♦ Alphabetically arranged dictionary of terms and biographies.

Chicago. Art Institute. Ryerson Library. *Index to Art Periodicals.* Boston: G.K. Hall, 1962. 11 vols.

Columbia University. Libraries. Avery Architectural Library. *Avery Index to Architectural Periodicals.* 2nd ed. Boston: G. K. Hall, 1973. 15 vols. with supplements. ♦ Photographic reproduction of Library's card file; indexes articles on architecture in its broadest sense, including archeology, decorative arts, interior decoration, furniture, landscape architecture, city planning, and housing. See also: 1st Supplement to new edition, 1 vol., 1975; 3rd Supplement, 1979.

Columbia University. Libraries. Avery Architectural Library. *Catalog of the Avery Memorial Architectural Library of Columbia University.* Rev. and enl. ed. Boston: G. K. Hall, 1968. 19 vols. with supplements. ♦ See also:

1973 Supplement, 4 vols.; 1975 Supplement, 4 vols.; 1980 Supplement, 2nd ed.

Ellison, Julie K., comp. *Index to the Microfilm Edition of American Architectural Books, Based on the Henry-Russell Hitchcock Bibliography of the Same Title and "A List of Architectural Books Available in America Before the Revolution" by Helen Park.* New Haven, Conn.: Research Publications, 1973. 20 pp.

Garrett, Wendell D., and Jane N. Garrett, comps. *The Arts in Early American History.* Introductory essay by Walter M. Whitehill; A Bibliography by Wendell D. and Jane N. Garrett. Chapel Hill: University of North Carolina Press, 1965. 170 pp. ◆ Section III of the bibliography covers architecture: general, architects, French Canada and Maritime, regional (U.S.).

Gebhard, David, and Deborah Nevins. *200 Years of American Architectural Drawings.* New York: Whitney Library of Design for the Architectural League of New York and the American Federation of Arts, 1977. 301 pp., illus., bibliog., index.

Harris, Cyril M., ed. *Dictionary of Architecture and Construction.* New York: McGraw-Hill Book Co., 1975. 553 pp., illus. ◆ Definitions and illustrations for the nonspecialist; includes terms used by urban planners, landscape architects and art historians.

Harris, John. *Catalogue of British Drawings for Architecture, Decoration, Sculpture and Landscape Gardening, 1550–1900, in American Collections.* Introduction by Henry-Russell Hitchcock. Upper Saddle River, N.J.: Gregg Press, 1971. 355 pp., illus.

Harris, John, and Jill Lever. *Illustrated Glossary of Architecture, 850–1830.* London: Faber and Faber, 1979. 79 pp., illus., plans. ◆ Defines and illustrates the terms of architecture in general use for the study of British architecture until about 1830. Available from Merrimack Book Service, Salem, New Hampshire 03079.

Hatje, Gerd. *Encyclopedia of Modern Architecture.* Translations by Irene and Harold Meek, et al. London: Thames & Hudson, 1963. 336 pp., illus., plans, bibliog. ◆ Articles on architects, schools, styles, associations, countries, construction terms, and materials which, since the mid-19th century, have contributed to the development of modern architecture.

Henry Francis duPont Winterthur Museum. Libraries. *The Winterthur Museum Libraries Collection of Printed Books and Periodicals.* Wilmington, Del.: Scholarly Resources, Inc., c1974. 9 vols.

Historic American Buildings Survey. *Catalog of the Measured Drawings and Photographs of the Survey in the Library of Congress, March 1, 1941.* New York: Burt Franklin, Publisher, c1941, 1971. 470 pp. ◆ See also: *Supplement* (1959); *Check List of Subjects, Additions to the Survey Material Deposited in the Library of Congress Since Publication of the Supplement, January 1959 to January 1963* (1963).

Historic Architecture Sourcebook. Edited by Cyril M. Harris. New York: McGraw-Hill, c1977. 581 pp., illus. ◆ Illustrated dictionary of terms.

Hitchcock, Henry-Russell. *American Architectural Books: A List of Books, Portfolios, and Pamphlets on Architecture and Related Subjects Published in America Before 1895.* New expanded ed.; introduction by Adolf K. Placzek. New York: DaCapo Press, 1976. 150 pp. ◆ Reprint of 1962 edition with a listing of architectural periodicals by the author and a chronological short-title list compiled under the direction of W. H. Jordy, which was originally Publication no. 4 (October 1955) of the American Association of Architectural Bibliographers.

Hunt, William Dudley, Jr. *Encyclopedia of American Architecture.* New York: McGraw-Hill, c1980. 612 pp., illus., index. ◆ Includes biographies of major architects, technical definitions, examinations of periods and genre.

Johns Hopkins University. John Work Garrett Library. *The Fowler Architectural Collection of the Johns Hopkins University.* Catalog compiled by Laurence Hall Fowler and Elizabeth Baer. Baltimore: Evergreen House Foundation, 1961. 383 pp., plates, bibliog.

Koyl, George S., ed. *American Architectural Drawings: A Catalog of Original and Measured Drawings of the United States of America to December 31, 1917.* Compiled and edited by George S. Koyl. Philadelphia: American Institute of Architects, Philadelphia Chapter, 1969. 5 vols., drawings.

Massey, James C. *Sources for American Architectural Drawings in Foreign Collections: A Preliminary Survey Carried Out Under a Grant* *from the Ford Foundation.* Washington, D.C.: Historic American Buildings Survey, 1969. 140 pp., illus., plans.

Miller, William C. *Architectural Research Centers: An Annotated Directory.* Monticello, Ill.: Council of Planning Librarians, 1971. 29 pp. ◆ Exchange Bibliography no. 199. See also: Volume 2, 1972. Exchange Bibliography no. 333.

The National Register of Historic Places. Washington, D.C.: National Park Service, for sale by Supt. of Docs., U.S. Government Printing Office, 1969. 352 pp., illus. ◆ See also: *1972.* 603 pp., illus., index; *Supplement, 1974.* 664 pp., illus., index; *1976.* 961 pp., illus., index. ◆ A cumulative listing of all National Register properties is published each February in the *Federal Register,* and additions to the list are printed usually on the first Tuesday of each month.

National Trust for Historic Preservation. *Library Resources in Washington, D.C. Relating to Historic Preservation.* Compiled by Lelahvon Lugo. Washington, D.C.: The Preservation Press, 1977. 55 pp., index.

Nevins, Deborah, and Robert A. M. Stern. *Architect's Eye: American Architectural Drawings from 1799 to 1978.* New York: Pantheon Books, c1979. 173 pp.

Park, Helen O'Brien. *A List of Architectural Books Available in America Before the Revolution.* Los Angeles: Hennessey & Ingalls, Inc., 1973. 80 pp., illus. ◆ Art and Architecture Bibliographic Series no. 1. See also: *Journal of the Society of Architectural Historians,* 20 (October 1961), pp. 115–130.

Peterson, Charles E. "The Technology of Early American Building (TEAB)," *Newsletter of APT,* 1:1 (April 1961), entire issue.

Pevsner, Nikolaus; John Fleming; and Hugh Honour. *A Dictionary of Architecture.* Rev. and enl. Woodstock, N.Y.: Overlook Press, 1976. 554 pp., illus., diagrams. ◆ Biographical notes on leading architects and definitions of terms.

Phillips, Margaret. *Guide to Architectural Information.* Lansdale, Pa.: Design Data Center, 1971. 89 pp. ◆ Arranged by type of reference work: indexes, bibliographies, dictionaries, directories, handbooks, etc.

Putnam, Robert E., and G. E. Carlson. *Architectural and Building Trades Dictionary.* 3rd ed. Chicago: American Technical Society, 1974. 510 pp. ◆ Legal terms and building material sizes as well as definition of terms.

Roos, Frank J., Jr. *Bibliography of Early American Architecture: Writings on Architecture Constructed Before 1860 in Eastern and Central United States.* Rev. ed. Urbana: University of Illinois Press, 1968. 389 pp.

Saylor, Henry H. *Dictionary of Architecture.* New York: John Wiley & Sons, Inc., c1952, 1967. 221 pp., drawings.

Sokol, David M. *American Architecture and Art: A Guide to Information Sources.* Detroit: Gale Research Co., c1976. 341 pp., indexes.

Stafford, Maureen, and Dora Ware. *An Illustrated Dictionary of Ornament.* New York: St. Martin's Press, c1974, 1975. 246 pp., illus., bibliog., index. ◆ Illustrations and definitions of terms and motifs used in architectural, furniture and other designs.

Sturgis, Russell, ed. *A Dictionary of Architecture and Building: Biographical and Descriptive.* By Russell Sturgis and many architects, painters, engineers, and other expert writers, American and Foreign. 1901–02. Reprint. Detroit: Gale Research Co., 1966. 3 vols., illus., drawings, diagrams, bibliog.

Summerson, John. *The Classical Language of Architecture.* Cambridge, Mass.: MIT Press, c1963, 1966. 56 pp., illus., bibliog. references.

U.S. Library of Congress. Geography and Map Division. Reference and Bibliography Section. *Fire Insurance Maps in the Library of Congress: Plans of North American Cities and Towns Produced by the Sanborn Map Company: A Checklist.* Introduction by Walter W. Ristow. Washington, D.C.: Library of Congress; for sale by the Supt. of Docs., U.S. Government Printing Office, 1981. 773 pp., illus., bibliog. references, indexes.

Ware, Dora, and Betty Beatty. *A Short Dictionary of Architecture.* 3rd rev. and enl. ed. New York: Fernhill House, Ltd., c1953, 1961. 135 pp., illus., bibliog.

White, Norval. *The Architecture Book.* 1st ed. New York: Knopf, 1976. 343 pp., illus.

Winterthur Portfolio. Winterthur, Del.: Henry

Francis duPont Winterthur Museum, 1964–. 1 vol., annual. ◆ Articles include interiors, decorative arts, architects and architecture, gardens and landscape.

Wodehouse, Lawrence. *Indigenous Architecture Worldwide: A Guide to Information Sources.* Detroit: Gale Research Co., c1980. 392 pp., indexes.

Wood, Charles B. *American Architectural Books, 1775–c1899: Including Architecture and the Building Trades; . . . With an Important Unpublished Note on the Works of Asher Benjamin by Abbott Lowell Cummings.* South Woodstock, Conn.: Charles B. Wood II, Inc., 1970. 71 pp., bibliog. ◆ Catalogue XIII, Winter 1970/71.

Wood, Charles B. *A Selection of Architectural Books Published Between c1900–1960: Catalogue.* South Woodstock, Conn.: Charles B. Wood III, Inc., 1973. 41 pp. ◆ Part I— Architectural books published during the 20th century (nos. 1–385); Part II—International fairs and expositions, 1851–1933 (nos. 386–443).

Wood, Charles B. *A Survey and Bibliography of Writings on English and American Architectural Books Published Before 1895.* Reprinted from the *Winterthur Portfolio,* II (1965), pp. 127–137.

NOTES

Architectural Periodicals Index. 1972, quarterly, subscription. Royal Institute of British Architects, 66 Portland Place, London W1N 4AD, England. ◆ Supersedes: Sir Banister Fletcher Library, *RIBA Library Bulletin,* vols. 1–26 (1946–1972) and Royal Institute of British Architects, London, *RIBA Annual Review of Periodical Articles,* vols. 1–17 (1965–1972). Last issue of the year cumulative.

Architectural Series: Bibliography. Vance Bibliographies, P. O. Box 229, Monticello, Illinois 61856. Series begun July 1978; indexes available. Subjects covered include city planning and urban design; current literature and periodicals; construction and building materials; energy uses; historic preservation; landscape architecture; architects; styles and ornamentation; architecture of various communities, cities, states; research sources; historical society architectural publications, compiled by state and Canada; bibliographies cover U.S. and foreign countries.

Art Index: *An Author and Subject Index to Domestic and Foreign Art Periodicals and Museum Bulletins Covering Archeology, Architecture, Art History, Arts and Crafts, Fine Arts, Graphic Arts, Industrial Design, Etc.* 1929, quarterly, service basis. H. W. Wilson Company, 950 University Avenue, Bronx, New York 10452.

Committee for the Preservation of Architectural Records, Inc., 15 Grammercy Park South, New York, New York 10003. Organized in 1973 by a group of architectural historians, librarians, preservationists, architects, archivists, and museum curators, the Committee was sponsored initially by the Architectural League of New York and New York State Council on the Arts. The national scope of the project has been assumed by the Prints and Photographs Division, Library of Congress, Washington, D.C. 20540 (Attention: Ford Peatross or Mary Ison). The Committee serves as a national clearinghouse of information, encouraging the preservation of records of architecture and the building arts. It locates, records and indexes the contents of such records including written and graphic material, and works toward the formation of a nationwide information system and a union catalog of collections of architectural records. It also publishes a quarterly newsletter.

Federal Writers' Project, Works Progress Administration. *American Guidebook Series.* The series consists of 49 state guides, 10 city guides, 26 travel guides and several ethnic studies. They contain much valuable information and many excellent views of buildings and communities, and usually contain a special section on architecture. Many works of this series have been reprinted. Available from: Somerset Publishers, Division of Scholarly Press, Inc., 22929 Industrial Drive East, St. Clair Shores, Michigan 48080.

U.S. National Park Service, Historic American Buildings Survey. National Register Programs, Washington, D.C. 20240. The Historic American Buildings Survey was established to record, as completely as possible, American building art, including all construction types, all use types, and all periods and regions throughout the country and the territories. Architectural merit and historical association constitute the basic criteria. The National Park Service began the Survey in 1933 with architects, draftsmen, and photographers employed under several federal relief programs.

In 1934, the National Park Service entered into an agreement with the American Institute of Architects and the Library of Congress to conduct the Survey on a permanent basis. The National Park Service administers the planning and operation of the Survey with funds appropriated by Congress and supplemented by gifts from individuals, foundations, and associations; sets up qualitative standards; organizes projects, directs the preparation of records and places them with the Library of Congress. The Library preserves the records, makes them available for study, and supplies reproductions through its Prints and Photographs Division. The American Institute of Architects provides professional counsel through its national membership. The Survey became a long-range program under the Historic Sites Act of 1935.

Currently, the National Park Service, through the National Register Programs office, conducts a broad national program of intensive architectural surveys on a shared-fund basis in cooperation with state and local governments, preservation groups, and historical societies. The program includes annual measured drawing projects done by student architects and university faculty supervisors; inventory recording projects conducted to evaluate large areas; architectural photogrammetry of skyscrapers and buildings of complex design; projects in industrial archeology undertaken in cooperation with the Smithsonian Institution; historic district studies; landscape architecture recordings; and civil engineering projects in cooperation with the American Society of Civil Engineers.

Several detailed catalogs listing HABS records are available, including the old national series and a new series of revised and expanded state and regional publications. Reprints may be ordered from the National Technical Information Service, 5283 Port Royal Road, Springfield, Virginia 22151. The new series of revised catalogs of the records by individual state and urban areas are done generally in cooperation with state organizations.

The University Prints. 15 Brattle Street, Harvard Square, Cambridge, Massachusetts 02138. "Special Study Set—Comprehensive Survey of American Architecture." Scholarly collection of architecture available both as slides and as prints. Individual study sets in spiral binding; brochures available on special sets; catalog on all sets available.

Builder's Guides/Pattern Books

Badger, Daniel D. *Badger's Illustrated Catalogue of Cast-Iron Architecture.* 1865. Reprint. New introduction by Margot Gayle. New York: Dover Publications, 1981. 140 pp., illus. ◆ Documents the cast-iron facades of 19th century New York City; lists the location, proprietor and architect of principal works erected.

Beecher, Catharine E., and Harriet Beecher Stowe. *The American Woman's Home: or, Principles of Domestic Science: being a Guide to the Formation and Maintenance of Economical, Healthful, Beautiful and Christian Homes.* With a new intro. by Joseph Van Why. 1869. Reprint. Watkins Glen, N.Y.: American Life Foundation and Study Institute, 1979. 25, 500 pp., illus., bibliog.

Benjamin, Asher. *The Works of Asher Benjamin.* 1806–1843. Reprint. New York: DaCapo Press, 1973–74. 7 vols., plates, drawings, diagrams.

Bicknell, Amos Jackson. *Bicknell's Village Builder; A Victorian Architectural Guidebook.* 1872. Reprint. New introduction by Paul Goeldner. Watkins Glen, N.Y.: American Life Foundation and Study Institute, 1976. 144 pp., illus. ◆ Combines *Bicknell's Village Builder,* rev. ed., 1872, and *Supplement,* 1st ed., 1871. Plans, elevations, details of 23 architects from 15 cities from Massachusetts to Wyoming.

Bicknell, Amos Jackson. *Wooden and Brick Buildings with Details.* 1875. Reprint. New York: DaCapo Press, 1977. 2 vols. (118, 113 pp.), illus.

Bicknell's Victorian Buildings: *Floor Plans and Elevations for 45 Houses and Other Structures.* By A. J. Bicknell & Co., New York. 1878. Reprint. New York: Dover Publications, 1979. 130 pp., illus., supplementary plates at the end. ◆ Reprint of 5th edition, 1878, published by A. J. Bicknell (later W. T. Comstock Co.), New York, under title *Bicknell's Village Builder.*

Biddle, Owen. *An Improved and Enlarged Edition of Biddle's Young Carpenter's Assistant; Being a Complete System of Architecture for Carpenters, Joiners and Workmen in General, Adapted to the Style of Building in the United States.* Revised and corrected with several additional articles, by John Haviland. Ann Arbor, Mich.: University Microfilms, 1970. 52 pp., plates, photocopy.

The Builder's Dictionary: *or Gentleman and Architects Companion.* 1734. Reprint. Washington, D.C.: Foundation for Preservation Technology for the Association for Preservation Technology, 1981. 2 vols. (1017 pp.), 33 plates, illus.

Cleaveland, Henry W.; William Backus; and Samuel D. Backus. *Village and Farm Cottages.* 1856. Reprint. Watkins Glen, N.Y.: American Life Foundation and Study Institute, 1976. 189 pp., illus. ◆ Treatise on Victorian town planning, building materials, construction, landscaping, interiors, house painting, gardening and ventilation.

Cummings, Marcus F., and Charles C. Miller. *Victorian Architectural Details: Two Pattern Books.* Watkins Glen, N.Y.: American Life Foundation and Study Institute, 1978. [106], [116] pp., 52, 56 plates, plans. ◆ Facsimile copy of two books published 1868 and 1873.

Exterior Decoration; *A Treatise on the Artistic Use of Colors in the Ornamentation of Buildings, and a Series of Designs....* 1885. Reprint. Philadelphia: The Athenaeum of Philadelphia, c1975, 1976. 95 pp., illus., color chips, color keys, bibliog. ◆ Originally a counter-top display book for the sale of ready-mixed paints, published by DeVoe Paint Company. New foreword by Roger Moss, Jr.; new introduction and bibliography by Samuel J. Dornsife.

Fowler, Orson S. *The Octagon House; A Home for All.* 1853. Reprint. New York: Dover Publications, 1973. 192 pp., illus., bibliog.

Halsted, Byron David. *Barns, Sheds and Outbuildings.* 1881. Reprint. Brattleboro, Vt.: Stephen Greene Press, c1977. 240 pp., illus., bibliog. ◆ Originally published by Orange Judd, New York, under title *Barn Plans and Outbuildings.*

Hussey, Elisha Charles. *Victorian Home Building: A Transcontinental View.* 1876. Reprint. Watkins Glen, N.Y.: American Life Foundation and Study Institute, 1976. 416 pp., illus., plans. ◆ A New York City architect provides designs for middle and upper class villas in the Italianate and Second Empire styles, one church, two stables, and a bank.

Knight, Frederick. *Scroll Ornaments of Early Victorian Period.* 1825–30. Reprint. New York: Dover Publications, c1978. 47 pp., chiefly illus.

Lafever, Minard. *The Beauties of Modern Ar-*

chitecture. 3rd ed. 1835. Reprint. New York: DaCapo Press, 1968. 176 pp., 48 plates, bibliog.

Lafever, Minard. *The Modern Builder's Guide.* 1833. Reprint. New York: Dover Publications, 1969. 146 pp., plates, prints, drawings, diagrams, bibliog. footnotes, glossary.

Late Victorian Architectural Details. Watkins Glen, N.Y.: American Life Foundation and Study Institute, 1978. 300 pp., illus., plates. ◆ An abridged facsimile of *Combined Book of Sash, Doors, Blinds, Mouldings, Stair Work, Mantels, and All Kinds of Interior and Exterior Finish,* a pattern book first published in 1871 and enlarged to this facsimile of the 1898 edition published by Rand, McNally & Co., Chicago.

Meyer, Franz Sales. *Handbook of Ornament; A Grammar of Art, Industrial and Architectural Designing in all its Branches for Practical as well as Theoretical Use.* 1928. Reprint. New York: Dover Publications, 1957. 548 pp., illus. ◆ First published in German in 1888; unabridged and unaltered republication of the English translation of the last revised edition.

Newsom, Samuel, and Joseph C. Newsom. *Picturesque California Homes: A Volume of Forty Plates, Plans, Details and Specifications of Houses Costing from $700 to $15,000 and Adapted to Families Having Good Taste and Moderate Means: City and Country Homes.* 1884/1885. Reprint. Introduction by David Gebhard. Los Angeles: Hennessey & Ingalls, 1978. 6 pp., 35 leaves of plates, illus.

The Origins of Cast Iron Architecture in America: *Including, Illustrations of Iron Architecture Made by the Architectural Iron Works of the City of New York (c.1865); and Cast Iron Buildings, Their Construction and Advantages (c.1856).* By D. D. Badger, and James Bogardus. New York: DaCapo Press, c1961, 1970. 2 vols. in 1, prints, drawings, charts.

Palliser, Palliser & Co., Firm, Architects. *Palliser's Model Homes: Showing a Variety of Designs for Modern Dwellings.* 1878. Reprint. Felton, Calif.: Glenwood Publishers, c1972. 96 pp., illus. ◆ Also available from American Life Foundation, Watkins Glen, N.Y.

Palliser, Palliser & Co., Firm, Architects. *Palliser's New Cottage Homes and Details...* 1887. Reprint. New York: DaCapo Press, 1975. 150 pp., illus. ◆ Contains more than 1500 detailed drawings of homes of the 1880s of the Queen Anne, Stick, Shingle, and early Elizabethan/Tudor styles. Also, available from Old House Journal, and American Life Foundation.

Radford, William A. *Practical Plans for Barns, Carriage Houses, Stables & Other Country Buildings.* 1908. Reprint. David and Joan Loveless. Stockbridge, Mass.: Berkshire Traveller Press, c1978. 206 pp., illus.

Ranlett, William H. *The Architect: A Series of Original Designs, for Domestic and Ornamental Cottages and Villas, Connected with Landscape Gardening, Adapted to the United States.* 1849, 1851. Reprint. New York: DaCapo Press, 1976. 2 vols. (82, 87 pp.), 60, 60 plates, illus.

Sloan, Samuel. *City and Suburban Architecture: Containing Numerous Designs and Details for Edifices, Private Residences, and Mercantile Buildings.* 1859. Reprint. New York: DaCapo Press, 1976. 104 pp., 136 plates.

Sloan, Samuel. *The Model Architect: A Series of Original Designs for Cottages, Villas, Suburban Residences, etc., Accompanied by Explanations, Specifications, and Elaborate Details, Prepared Expressly for the Use of Projectors and Artisans Throughout the United States.* 1852. Reprint. New York: DaCapo Press, 1975. 2 vols. (100, 102 pp.), 91, 92 plates. ◆ Available also from Dover Publications, N.Y., 1980, 2 vols. in 1, under title *Sloan's Victorian Buildings: Illustrations and Floor Plans for 56 Residences and Other Structures.* Intro. by Harold N. Cooledge, Jr.

Vaux, Calvert. *Villas and Cottages: A Series of Designs Prepared for Execution in the United States.* 1857. Reprint. New York: DaCapo Press, 1968. 318 pp., drawings, diagrams. ◆ Also available, 1864 reprint by Dover Publications, N.Y., 1970.

Victorian Architecture, Two Pattern Books. By A. J. Bicknell and William T. Comstock. 2nd printing corrected. 1873, 1881. Reprint, with a new introduction by John Maass. Watkins Glen, N.Y.: American Life Foundation, c1975, 1976. 86, 85 pp., 75, 80 plates, illus.

Wheeler, Gervase. *Homes for the People, in Suburb and Country: The Villa, the Mansion, and the Cottage.* 1855. Reprint. New York: Arno Press, 1972. 443 pp., illus.

Woodward, George E. *Woodward's Country*
Homes. 1868. Reprint. Watkins Glen, N.Y.: American Life Foundation and Study Institute, 1977. 188 pp., illus. ◆ Designs for cottages, stables, carriage houses, churches, school houses, ice houses, fences, gates and remodeling old houses.

Woodward, George E. *Woodward's Victorian Architecture and Rural Art.* 1867, 1868. Reprint. Watkins Glen, N.Y.: American Life Foundation and Study Institute, 1978. 2 vols. (144, 156 pp.), illus. ◆ Companion volume to *Woodward's Country Homes.*

Woodward, George E., and Edward G. Thompson. *Woodward's National Architect: Containing 1000 Original Designs, Plans, and Details, to Working Scale, for the Practical Construction of Dwelling Houses for the Country, Suburb and Village, with Full and Complete Sets of Specifications and an Estimate of the Cost of Each Design.* 1869. Reprint. New York: DaCapo Press, 1975. 200 pp., illus.

Surveys of Architecture

History of Architecture

Fletcher, Banister Flight, Sir. *Sir Banister Fletcher's A History of Architecture.* 18th ed., rev. by J. C. Palmes. New York: Scribner, 1975. 1390 pp., illus. ◆ 6th–16th eds. published under title: A History of Architecture on the Comparative Method, for Students, Craftsmen, and Amateurs; 17th ed. published under title: A History of Architecture on the Comparative Method.

Gardner, Helen. *Gardner's Art Through the Ages.* Rev. by Horst de La Croix and Richard G. Tansey. 6th ed. New York: Harcourt, Brace Jovanovich, 1975. 959 pp., illus., maps, plans, bibliog.

Giedion, Siegfried. *Space, Time and Architecture: The Growth of a New Tradition.* 5th rev. and enl. ed. Cambridge, Mass.: Harvard University Press, 1967. 897 pp., illus., bibliog., index.

Hamlin, Talbot F. *Architecture Through the Ages.* Rev. ed. New York: Putnam, 1953. 684 pp., illus., bibliog.

Hitchcock, Henry-Russell. *Architecture: Nineteenth and Twentieth Centuries.* 4th ed. New York: Penguin Books, 1977. 688 pp., illus., drawings, diagrams, bibliog., index.

Jordan, Robert Furneaux. *A Concise History of Western Architecture.* New York: Harcourt, Brace and World, 1970. 359 pp., illus., bibliog.

Kimball, Sidney Fiske, and George Harold Edgell. *A History of Architecture.* 2nd ed. Westport, Conn.: Greenwood Press, c1946, 1972. 621 pp., illus., glossary, index.

Millon, Henry A., ed. *Key Monuments in the History of Architecture.* Essays by Alfred Frazer. New York: Abrams, 1965. 536 pp., illus., maps, plans, glossary.

Pevsner, Nikolaus. *A History of Building Types.* Princeton, N.J.: Princeton University Press, c1976. 352 pp., illus., drawings, bibliog., index. ◆ Arranged by use of building; includes American and Continental buildings.

Pevsner, Nikolaus. *Outline of European Architecture.* 7th ed. reprinted (with revised bibliography). Harmondsworth, Eng. and Baltimore: Penguin Books, c1943, 1963, 1974. 496 pp., illus., plans, bibliog., index.

Pevsner, Nikolaus. *Pioneers of Modern Design: From William Morris to Walter Gropius.* Rev. ed. Baltimore: Penguin Books, c1936, 1964. 253 pp., illus., diagrams, tables, bibliog., notes, index.

Pevsner, Nikolaus. *The Sources of Modern Architecture and Design.* New York: Frederick A. Praeger, 1968. 216 pp., plates, illus., drawings, notes, bibliog. notes, bibliog., index.

Summerson, John. *Architecture in Britain, 1530–1830.* 6th rev. ed. Harmondsworth and New York: Penguin, 1977. 611 pp., illus., maps, plans, bibliog., index.

American Architecture

Andrews, Wayne. *Architecture, Ambition and Americans: A Social History of American Architecture.* Rev. ed. New York: Free Press of Glencoe, c1978. 332 pp., illus., bibliog., index.

Andrews, Wayne. *Architecture in America: A Photographic History from the Colonial Period to the Present.* Rev. ed. New York: Atheneum Publishers, 1977. 179 pp., illus., bibliog., index.

Burchard, John, and Albert Bush-Brown. *The Architecture of America: A Social and Cultural History.* Boston: Little, Brown and Com-

pany, 1961. 595 pp., illus., bibliog., index. ◆ Covers the period 1600–1960.

Fitch, James Marston. *American Building, 1: The Historical Forces That Shaped It.* 2nd ed., rev. and enl. Boston: Houghton Mifflin Co., c1947, 1966. 350 pp., illus., drawings, diagrams, bibliog. notes, index.

Fitch, James Marston. *American Building, 2: The Environmental Forces That Shape It.* 2nd ed., rev. and enl. Boston: Houghton Mifflin Co., 1972. 349 pp., illus., drawings, diagrams, charts, graphs, tables, bibliog., index.

Gifford, Don, ed. *The Literature of Architecture: The Evolution of Architectural Theory and Practice in Nineteenth-Century America.* New York: E.P. Dutton & Co., 1966. 640 pp., illus., bibliog.

Gowans, Alan. *Images of American Living: Four Centuries of Architecture and Furniture as Cultural Expression.* Philadelphia: J.B. Lippincott, 1964. 498 pp., illus., bibliog.

Gutheim, Frederick A. *One Hundred Years of Architecture in America, 1857–1957: Celebrating the Centennial of the American Institute of Architects.* New York: Reinhold Publishing Co., 1957. 96 pp., illus.

Hamlin, Talbot F. *The American Spirit in Architecture.* New Haven, Conn.: Yale University Press, 1926. 353 pp. ◆ Pageant of America, vol. 13.

Hitchcock, Henry-Russell. "Art of the United States: Architecture," *Encyclopedia of World Art* (New York: McGraw-Hill, 1959–1968), Vol. I, pp. 246–278.

Kimball, Sidney Fiske. *American Architecture.* 1928. Reprint. New York: AMS Press, 1970. 262 pp., illus., bibliog.

Lynes, Russell. *The Domesticated Americans.* New York: Harper & Row, 1963. 308 pp., illus. ◆ History of developments in houses, based on social and functional factors which includes equipment.

Lynes, Russell. *The Tastemakers.* New York: Grossett and Dunlap, 1972. 362 pp., illus., bibliog. ◆ Includes substantial references to architecture.

Mumford, Lewis, ed. *Roots of Contemporary American Architecture.* 2nd ed. New York: Dover Publications, 1972. 452 pp., illus.

Mumford, Lewis. *Sticks and Stones: A Study of American Architecture and Civilization.* 2nd rev. ed. New York: Dover Publications, c1924, 1955. 238 pp., illus., prints, diagrams. ◆ Series of critical essays.

National Trust for Historic Preservation. *America's Forgotten Architecture.* The Trust, Tony P. Wrenn, and Elizabeth D. Mulloy. New York: Pantheon Books, c1976. 311 pp., illus., bibliog., index.

The Rise of an American Architecture. By Henry-Russell Hitchcock and others. Edited with an introduction and exhibition notes by Edgar Kaufmann, Jr. New York: Praeger Publishers in association with the Metropolitan Museum of Art, 1970. 241 pp., illus., bibliog., index. ◆ Includes essays by four eminent architectural historians and texts from the exhibition.

Robinson, Willard B. *American Forts: Architectural Form and Function.* Urbana: Published for the Amon Carter Museum of Western Art, Fort Worth, by the University of Illinois Press, c1977. 229 pp., illus., bibliog. ◆ Architectural-engineering exposition of fortification design.

Roth, Leland M. *A Concise History of American Architecture.* New York: Harper & Row, c1979. 400 pp., illus., bibliog., index.

Schuyler, Montgomery. *American Architecture, and Other Writings.* Edited by William H. Jordy and Ralph Coe. Cambridge, Mass.: Belknap Press of Harvard University Press, 1961. 2 vols., illus., plans, bibliog. ◆ Essays written c1870–1914, revealing views at that time by a perceptive and respected critic.

Scully, Vincent. *American Architecture and Urbanism.* New York: Praeger Publishers, 1969. 257 pp., illus., prints, drawings, diagrams, bibliog. notes, index.

Sky, Alison, and Michelle Stone. *Unbuilt America: Forgotten Architecture in the United States from Thomas Jefferson to the Space Age: A Book.* New York: McGraw-Hill, c1976. 308 pp., illus., bibliog., index.

Tallmadge, Thomas Eddy. *The Story of Architecture in America.* Rev. and enl. ed. New York: W. W. Norton, 1936. 332 pp., illus., plans. ◆ By a practicing architect; describes the period 1890–1915 in the Chicago area.

Whiffen, Marcus, and Frederick Koeper. *American Architecture, 1607–1976.* Cambridge, Mass.: MIT Press, 1981. 495 pp., illus., bibliog., index.

Whitehill, Walter Muir, and Frederick D. Nichols. *Palladio in America.* Milan: Electa Editrice, c1976. 127 pp., illus., bibliog. ◆ Guide for exhibition at University of Virginia; scholarly discussion on the life and works of Palladio and his influence on American architecture.

American Architects

GENERAL WORKS

Architectural Record. *Great American Architects Series.* Nos. 1–6; May 1895–July 1899. Reprint. New York: DaCapo, 1977. 6 nos. in 1 vol. (approx. 650 pp.), illus. ◆ Unabridged republication of a compilation of essays, critiques, interviews and reviews by Russell Sturgis and Montgomery Schuyler.

Cole, Doris. *From Tipi to Skyscraper: A History of Women in Architecture.* Boston: i Press, distr. by G. Braziller, 1973. 135 pp., illus., bibliog.

Columbia University. Libraries. Avery Architectural Library. *Avery Obituary Index of Architects and Artists.* Boston: G. K. Hall, 1963. 338 pp.

Cook, John W., and Heinrich Klotz. *Conversations with Architects: Philip Johnson, Kevin Roche, Paul Rudolph, Bertrand Goldberg, Morris Lapidus, Louis Kahn, Charles Moore, Robert Venturi, and Denise Scott Brown.* New York: Praeger, 1973. 272 pp., illus.

Diamonstein, Barbaralee, ed. *American Architecture Now.* Intro. by Paul Goldberger. New York: Rizzoli, c1980. 253 pp., illus. ◆ Interviews with I. M. Pei, Hugh Hardy, Cesar Pelli, Richard Meier, John Portman, Frank O. Gehry, Charles Moore, Michael Graves, Richard Weinstein, Jonathan Barnett, Robert A. M. Stern, Charles Gwathmey, James Stewart Polshek, Edward Larrabee Barnes.

Heyer, Paul. *Architects on Architecture: New Directions in America.* New York: Walker & Co., 1966. 415 pp., illus., drawings, plans, elevations, building index. ◆ Includes Frank Lloyd Wright, Gropius, Le Corbusier, Saarinen, Neutra, Edward D. Stone, Philip Johnson, et al.

Hoag, Edwin, and Joy Hoag. *Masters of Modern Architecture: Frank Lloyd Wright, Le Corbusier, Mies van der Rohe, and Walter Gropius.* Indianapolis: Bobbs-Merrill, c1977. 209 pp., illus., bibliog., index.

McCoy, Esther. *Five California Architects.* New York: Praeger Publishers, c1960, 1975. 200 pp., illus., index. ◆ Irving Gill, the Greene Brothers, Bernard Maybeck, R. M. Schindler.

Norton, Paul F. *Latrobe, Jefferson and the National Capitol.* New York: Garland Publishing, 1977. 362 pp., illus., plans, bibliog.

Ravenel, Beatrice St. Julien. *Architects of Charleston.* 2nd ed., rev. Charleston, S.C.: Carolina Art Association, c1945, 1964. 329 pp., illus., reference notes, bibliog., index.

Withey, Henry F., and Elsie Rathburn Withey. *Biographical Dictionary of American Architects (Deceased).* 1956. Reprint. Los Angeles: Hennessey & Ingalls, 1970. 678 pp. ◆ Brief biographical sketches of men and women working ca. 1740–1952, now deceased; references at end of articles.

Wodehouse, Lawrence. *American Architects From the Civil War to the First World War: A Guide to Information Sources.* Detroit: Gale Research Co., 1976. 343 pp., indexes.

Wodehouse, Lawrence. *American Architects from the First World War to the Present: A Guide to Information Sources.* Detroit: Gale Research Co., c1977. 305 pp., bibliog. notes, appendix, index.

Wodehouse, Lawrence. *American Architects from the First World War to the Present: A Guide to Information Sources.* Detroit: Gale Research Co., c1977. 305 pp., bibliog. notes, appendix, index.

WILLIAM BUCKLAND

Beirne, Rosamond Randall, and John Henry Scarff. *William Buckland, 1734–1774: Architect of Virginia and Maryland.* Baltimore: The Maryland Historical Society, 1958. 175 pp., illus., plans, bibliog. appendices, index.

CHARLES BULFINCH

Kirker, Harold. *The Architecture of Charles Bulfinch.* Cambridge, Mass.: Harvard University Press, 1977. 398 pp., illus., drawings, diagrams, bibliog., footnotes, appendices, index.

Place, Charles A. *Charles Bulfinch, Architect and Citizen.* 1925. Reprint. New York: DaCapo Press, 1968. 294 pp., illus., maps, plans.

DANIEL H. BURNHAM

Hines, Thomas S. *Burnham of Chicago: Architect and Planner.* New York: Oxford University Press, 1974. 445 pp., illus., bibliog., index.

Moore, Charles. *Daniel H. Burnham: Architect, Planner of Cities.* 1921. Reprint. New York: DaCapo Press, 1968. 2 vols. in 1, illus., bibliog. footnotes.

RALPH ADAMS CRAM

Tucci, Douglass S. *Ralph Adams Cram: American Medievalist.* Boston: Boston Public Library, 1975. 49 pp., illus., plates, bibliog. ◆ Catalog of an exhibition.

JAMES DAKIN

Scully, Arthur. *James Dakin, Architect: His Career in New York and the South.* Baton Rouge: Louisiana State University Press, 1973. 209 pp., illus., plans, bibliog.

ALEXANDER JACKSON DAVIS

Donnell, Edna. *A. J. Davis and the Gothic Revival.* Reprinted from *Metropolitan Museum Studies,* vol. V, Part 2 (September 1936), pp. 183–233, illus., bibliog.

HUGH FERRISS

Leich, Jean Ferriss. *Architectural Visions: The Drawings of Hugh Ferriss.* With an essay by Paul Goldberger. New York: Whitney Library of Design, 1980. 143 pp., illus., bibliog.

R. BUCKMINSTER FULLER

Marks, Robert W., and R. Buckminster Fuller. *The Dymaxion World of Buckminster Fuller.* Garden City, N.Y.: Doubleday, c1960, 1973. 246 pp., illus.

FRANK FURNESS

O'Gorman, James F. *The Architecture of Frank Furness.* Catalogue of Selected Buildings by George E. Thomas and James F. O'Gorman; Checklist of the Architecture and Projects of Frank Furness by George E. Thomas and Hyman Myers. Philadelphia: Philadelphia Museum of Art, 1973. 211 pp., illus., plates.

MAXIMILIAN GODEFROY

Alexander, Robert L. *The Architecture of Maximilian Godefroy.* Baltimore: Johns Hopkins University Press, 1975. 246 pp., illus., bibliog. references.

BRUCE GOFF

Cook, Jeffrey. *The Architecture of Bruce Goff.* New York: Harper & Row, c1978. 135 pp., illus., index.

JONATHAN GOLDSMITH

Hitchcock, Elizabeth G. *Jonathan Goldsmith: Pioneer Master Builder of the Western Reserve.* Cleveland: Western Reserve Historical Society, 1980. 131 pp., illus., bibliog. notes.

BERTRAM GROSVENOR GOODHUE

Whitaker, Charles Harris, ed. *Bertram Grosvenor Goodhue: Architect and Master of Many Arts.* Text by Harley Burr Alexander, et al. 1925. Reprint. New York: DaCapo Press, 1976. 50 pp., 277 illus., index.

GREENE AND GREENE

Current, William R., and Karen Current. *Greene and Greene: Architects in the Residential Style.* Fort Worth, Tex.: Amon Carter Museum of Western Art, 1974. 128 pp., illus.

PETER HARRISON

Bridenbaugh, Carl, ed. *Peter Harrison, First American Architect.* Chapel Hill: University of North Carolina Press, 1949. 195 pp., illus., diagrams, bibliog. footnotes, appendices, index.

PHILIP HOOKER

Root, Edward W. *Philip Hooker: A Contribution to the Study of the Renaissance in America.* New York: C. Scribner's Sons, 1929. 242 pp., illus., plans, bibliog.

HORNBLOWER & MARSHALL

Peterson, Anne E. *Hornblower & Marshall: Architects.* Washington, D.C.: The Preservation Press, 1978. 40 pp., illus., bibliog.

GEORGE HOWE

Stern, Robert A. M. *George Howe: Toward a Modern American Architecture.* New Haven, Conn.: Yale University Press, 1975. 273 pp., illus., plans, bibliog.

THOMAS JEFFERSON

The Eye of Thomas Jefferson: *[Exhibition].* William Howard Adams, ed. Washington, D.C.: National Gallery of Art, 1976. 411 pp., illus., plans. ◆ See also: *Jefferson and the Arts: An Extended View.* Edited with introductions by William Howard Adams. 1976. 283 pp., illus., bibliog. references. Seven essays.

Guinness, Desmond, and Julius Trousdale Sadler, Jr. *Mr. Jefferson, Architect.* New York: Viking Press, 1973. 177 pp., illus.

Jefferson, Thomas. *Thomas Jefferson, Architect: Original Designs in the Coolidge Collection of the Massachusetts Historical Society.* 1916. Reprint. With an essay and notes by Fiske Kimball. New York: DaCapo Press, 1968. 205 pp., illus., drawings, bibliog. references, index. ◆ First published 1916, not definitive. New introduction by F. D. Nichols provides additional information.

PHILIP JOHNSON

Johnson, Philip Cortelyou. *Philip Johnson.* Introduction and notes by Charles Noble; photographs by Yukio Futagawa. New York: Simon & Schuster, 1972. 130 pp., chiefly illus., plans, bibliog.

ALBERT KAHN

Hildebrand, Grant. *Designing for Industry: The Architecture of Albert Kahn.* Cambridge, Mass.: MIT Press, 1974. 232 pp., illus., bibliog. references.

MINARD LAFEVER

Landy, Jacob. *The Architecture of Minard Lafever.* New York: Columbia University Press, 1970. 313 pp., illus., bibliog., index.

BENJAMIN HENRY LATROBE

Hamlin, Talbot Faulkner. *Benjamin Henry Latrobe.* New York: Oxford University Press, 1955. 633 pp., illus., drawings, bibliog. footnotes, bibliog., index.

SAMUEL MCINTIRE

Cousins, Frank, and Phil M. Riley. *The Wood Carver of Salem: Samuel McIntire, His Life and Work.* 1916. Reprint. New York: AMS Press, 1970. 168 pp., illus., index.

Kimball, Sidney Fiske. *Mr. Samuel McIntire, Carver: The Architect of Salem.* Portland, Me.:

The Southworth-Anthoensen Press for the Essex Institute, 1940. 157 pp., illus., appendices, index. ◆ Reprinted by Peter Smith, Gloucester, Mass., 1966.

MCKIM, MEAD AND WHITE

McKim, Mead and White. *A Monograph of the Works of McKim, Mead and White, 1879–1915.* New ed., 4 vols. in 1. New York: B. Blom, 1973; Arno Press, 1977. 73 pp., 399 pp., plates, bibliog. ◆ Critical essay by Leland Roth surveys history of the firm and gives reasons for inclusions of the various buildings.

Roth, Leland M. *The Architecture of McKim, Mead and White, 1870–1920: A Building List.* New York: Garland Publishing, 1978. 213 pp., illus., bibliog., index.

BERNARD MAYBECK

Cardwell, Kenneth H. *Bernard Maybeck: Artisan, Architect, Artist.* Santa Barbara, Calif.: Peregrine Smith, 1977. 255 pp., illus., bibliog., index.

LUDWIG MIES VAN DER ROHE

Spaeth, David. *Ludwig Mies van der Rohe: An Annotated Bibliography and Chronology.* New York: Garland Publishing, 1979. 280 pp., index. ◆ Papers of the American Association of Architectural Bibliographers no. 13.

ROBERT MILLS

Gallagher, H. M. Pierce. *Robert Mills, Architect of the Washington Monument, 1781–1855.* New York: AMS Press, c1935, 1966. 233 pp., illus., bibliog.

RICHARD HUNT MORRIS

Baker, Paul R. *Richard Hunt Morris.* Cambridge, Mass.: MIT Press, c1980. 588 pp., illus., bibliog., index.

SAMUEL AND JOSEPH CATHER NEWSOM

Samuel and Joseph Cather Newsom: *Victorian Architectural Imagery in California 1878–1908. . . . David Gebhard, Harriett Von Breton, Robert W. Winter. Santa Barbara, Calif.: Art Museum, University of California at Santa Barbara, c1979. 105 pp., illus., bibliogs. ◆ Catalog of architectural exhibition, documented text, selected list of works of Newsoms, two bibliographies.

JOHN NOTMAN

Greiff, Constance M. *John Notman, Architect, 1810–1865.* 1st ed. Philadelphia: Athenaeum of Philadelphia, c1979. 253 pp., illus., plans, bibliog., index.

EDWARD T. AND WILLIAM A. POTTER

Landau, Sarah B. *Edward T. and William A. Potter: American Victorian Architects.* New York: Garland Publishing, 1979. 490 pp., illus., bibliog.

HENRY HOBSON RICHARDSON

Hitchcock, Henry-Russell. *The Architecture of H. H. Richardson and His Times.* Rev. ed. Cambridge, Mass.: MIT Press, c1936, 1966. 343 pp., illus., diagrams, notes, bibliog., index.

O'Gorman, James F. *H. H. Richardson and His Office, A Centennial of His Move to Boston, 1874: Selected Drawings.* Cambridge, Mass.: Department of Printing and Graphic Arts, Harvard College Library, 1974. 220 pp., plates, illus., bibliog. references, index.

JOHN WELLBORN ROOT

Hoffman, Donald. *The Architecture of John Wellborn Root.* Baltimore: Johns Hopkins University Press, 1973. 263 pp., illus., bibliog.

Monroe, Harriet. *John Wellborn Root: A Study of His Life and Work.* 1896. Reprint. Park Forest, Ill.: Prairie School Press, 1966. 291 pp., illus., drawings, diagrams, appendices, index.

PAUL RUDOLPH

Rudolph, Paul. *The Architecture of Paul Rudolph.* Introduction by Sibyl Moholy-Nagy; commentaries to the work by Paul Rudolph; captions by Gerhard Schwab. New York: Praeger Press, 1970. 239 pp., illus., drawings, maps, plans.

EERO SAARINEN

Saarinen, Eero. *Eero Saarinen on His Work: A Selection of Buildings 1947 to 1964 with Statements by the Architect.* Edited by Aline B. Saarinen. Rev. ed. New Haven, Conn.: Yale University Press, 1968. 117 pp., illus., plans.

ELIEL SAARINEN

Christ-Janer, Albert. *Eliel Saarinen: Finnish-American Architect and Educator.* Chicago:

University of Chicago Press, 1979. 169 pp., illus., bibliogs., index.

R. M. SCHINDLER

Gebhard, David. *Schindler.* New York: Viking Press, c1971, 1972. 216 pp., illus., plans, bibliog.

Schindler, Rudolph M. *R. M. Schindler: An Exhibition of the Architecture of R. M. Schindler, 1887–1953.* Catalogue designed by David Gebhard. Santa Barbara?: 1967. 111 pp., illus., plans, bibliog. references.

SKIDMORE, OWINGS & MERRILL

Skidmore, Owings & Merrill. *Skidmore, Owings and Merrill, 1963–1973.* Introduction by Arthur Drexler. New York: Architectural Book Publishing Company, c1974. 283 pp., illus.

SMITH, HINCHMAN & GRYLLS

Holleman, Thomas J., and James P. Gallacher. *Smith, Hinchman & Grylls: 125 Years of Architecture and Engineering.* Detroit: Published for Smith, Hinchman & Grylls, Inc., by Wayne State University Press, 1978. 239 pp., illus., bibliog., index.

JOHN F. STAUB

Barnstone, Howard. *The Architecture of John F. Staub: Houston and the South.* With the assistance of Stephen Fox, Jerome Iowa, and David Courtwright. Austin: Published in cooperation with the Museum of Fine Arts, Houston by University of Texas Press, c1979. 363 pp., illus., bibliog., index.

WILLIAM STRICKLAND

Gilchrist, Agnes Addison. *William Strickland, Architect and Engineer, 1788–1854.* Enl. ed. 1950. Reprint. New York: DaCapo Press, 1969. 1 vol. (145 pp.), various pagings, illus., plans, bibliog. references.

LOUIS SULLIVAN

Morrison, Hugh. *Louis Sullivan: Prophet of Modern Architecture.* 1935. Reprint. Westport, Conn.: Greenwood Press, 1971. 391 pp., illus., diagrams, building list, bibliog., index. ◆ Appendix: "Dankmar Adler, A Biographical Sketch."

Sullivan, Louis H. *The Drawings of Louis*

Henry Sullivan. A Catalogue of the Frank Lloyd Wright Collection at the Avery Architectural Library. By Paul Edward Sprague; with a foreword by Adolf K. Placzek. Princeton, N.J.: Princeton University Press, c1979. 72 pp., 72 leaves of plates, bibliog., index.

WILLIAM TINSLEY

Forbes, John Douglas. *Victorian Architect: The Life and Work of William Tinsley.* Bloomington: Indiana University Press, 1953. 153 pp., illus., map, bibliog. note.

TOWN & DAVIS

Newton, Roger Hale. *Town & Davis, Architects: Pioneers in American Revivalist Architecture, 1812–1870, including a Glimpse of Their Times and Their Contemporaries.* New York: Columbia University Press, 1942. 135 pp., plates.

HENRY C. TROST

Engelbrecht, Lloyd C., and June-Marie Engelbrecht. *Henry C. Trost: Architect of the Southwest.* El Paso, Tex.: El Paso Public Library Association, 1981. 154 pp., illus., bibliog., index.

RICHARD UPJOHN

Upjohn, Everard M. *Richard Upjohn: Architect and Churchman.* 1939. Reprint. New York: DaCapo Press, 1968. 243 pp., illus., bibliog., appendices, index.

STANFORD WHITE

Baldwin, Charles C. *Stanford White.* 1931. Reprint. New York: DaCapo Press, 1971. 399 pp., illus., appendix, index.

FREDERICK CLARKE WITHERS

Kowsky, Francis R. *The Architecture of Frederick Clarke Withers and the Progress of the Gothic Revival after 1850.* Middletown, Conn.: Wesleyan University Press, distr. by Columbia University Press, N.Y., c1980. 225 pp., illus., drawings, maps, bibliog.

FRANK LLOYD WRIGHT

Brooks, Harold Allen. *The Prairie School: Frank Lloyd Wright and His Midwest Contemporaries.* New York: W. W. Norton, 1976. 373 pp., illus., bibliog., index.

Hitchcock, Henry-Russell. *In the Nature of Materials, 1887–1941: The Buildings of Frank Lloyd Wright.* New York: DaCapo Press, c1942, 1973. 143 pp., plates, illus., bibliog., index.

Manson, Grant C. *Frank Lloyd Wright to 1910: The First Golden Age.* 1958. Reprint. New York: Van Nostrand Reinhold, 1979. 228 pp., illus., plans, bibliog. ♦ Reprint of Vol. 1 of 1958 edition.

Smith, Norris Kelly. *Frank Lloyd Wright: A Study in Architectural Content.* Englewood Cliffs, N.J.: Prentice-Hall, 1966. 178 pp., illus., bibliog. footnotes.

Storrer, William Allin. *The Architecture of Frank Lloyd Wright: A Complete Catalog.* Cambridge, Mass.: MIT Press, 1978. 1 vol. (500 pp.), illus., plans, indexes.

Sweeney, Robert L. *Frank Lloyd Wright: An Annotated Bibliography.* Los Angeles: Hennessey & Ingalls, 1978. 303 pp., illus., indexes.

Twombly, Robert C. *Frank Lloyd Wright: An Interpretive Biography.* New York: Harper & Row, 1973. 373 pp., illus., plans.

Wright, Frank Lloyd. *In the Cause of Architecture, Frank Lloyd Wright: Essays.* By Frank Lloyd Wright for Architectural Record, 1908–1952; with a Symposium on Architecture with and without Wright by Eight Who Knew Him, Andrew Devane. . . et al.; edited by Frederick Gutheim. New York: Architectural Record, c1975. 246 pp., illus., index.

NOTES

Makers of Contemporary Architecture Series. George Braziller, Inc., Publishers, One Park Avenue, New York, New York 10016. Five monographs published in 1962 on the greats of modern architecture: R. Buckminster Fuller, Philip Johnson, Louis I. Kahn, and Eero Saarinen. Each volume includes illustrations and bibliography.

Masters of World Architecture Series. George Braziller, Inc., Publishers, One Park Avenue, New York, New York 10016. Series of monographs published in 1960; seven are on American architects, Walter Gropius, Le Corbusier, Eric Mendelsohn, Richard Neutra, Louis Sullivan, Ludwig Mies van der Rohe, and Frank Lloyd Wright. Each volume contains illustrations and bibliography.

Period Styles

Guides to Styles

Blumenson, John J.-G. *Identifying American Architecture: A Pictorial Guide to Styles and Terms, 1600–1945.* Nashville, Tenn.: American Association for State and Local History, 1977. 118 pp., illus., bibliog., index.

Hammett, Ralph W. *Architecture in the United States: A Survey of Architectural Style Since 1776.* New York: John Wiley & Sons, c1976. 409 pp., illus., bibliog., index.

Panek, Roger T. *American Architectural Styles, 1600–1940.* Dover, Mass.: Architectural Styles, 1976. 30" x 40" wall chart. ♦ Shows with a bar graph 43 major styles in the 4 major geographic areas, each style illustrated with a drawing. Supplemental text to chart with summaries and in-depth discussions of each style available from Architectural Styles, Box 272, Dover, Mass. 02030.

Poppeliers, John; S. Allen Chambers; and Nancy B. Schwartz. *What Style Is It?* Washington, D.C.: Preservation Press, National Trust for Historic Preservation, 1977. 48 pp., illus., diagrams, glossary, bibliog.

Pothorn, Herbert. *Architectural Styles.* New York: Viking Press, 1971. 187 pp., illus., drawings, glossary, charts.

Rifkind, Carole. *A Field Guide to American Architecture.* New York: New American Library, 1980. 322 pp., illus., line drawings, bibliog., index.

Whiffen, Marcus. *American Architecture Since 1780: A Guide to the Styles.* Cambridge, Mass.: MIT Press, 1969. 313 pp., illus., glossary, bibliog., index.

Vernacular

Brunskill, R. W. *Illustrated Handbook of Vernacular Architecture.* Rev. and expanded ed. London and Boston: Faber and Faber, 1978. 249 pp., illus., drawings, diagrams, charts, maps, glossary, appendices, bibliog., index.

Built in Texas. Edited by Francis E. Abernethy. Waco, Tex.: E. Heart Press, 1979. 276 pp., illus., bibliog. references.

Carolina Dwelling: *Towards Preservation of Place: In Celebration of the North Carolina*

Vernacular Landscape. Edited by Doug Swaim. Raleigh: North Carolina State University, c1978. 257 pp., illus., bibliog. references.

Fishwick, Marshall, and Neil J. Meredith, eds. *Popular Architecture.* Bowling Green, Ohio: Bowling Green Popular Press, 1974? 120 pp., illus., bibliog. references.

Glassie, Henry H. *Folk Housing in Middle Virginia: Structural Analysis of Historic Artifacts.* Knoxville: University of Tennessee Press, c1975, 1979. 231 pp., illus., drawings, bibliog., index.

Glassie, Henry H. *Pattern in the Material Folk Culture of the Eastern United States.* Philadelphia: University of Pennsylvania Press, c1968, 1969. 316 pp., illus., bibliog. ◆ University of Pennsylvania Monographs in Folklore and Folklife no. 1.

Jakle, John A.; Douglas K. Meyer; and Robert W. Bastian. *American Common Houses: A Selected Bibliography of Vernacular Architecture.* Monticello, Ill.: Vance Bibliographies, 1981. 28 pp.

Jordan, Terry G. *Texas Log Buildings: A Folk Architecture.* Austin: University of Texas Press, c1978. 230 pp., illus., bibliog., index.

Long, Amos, Jr. *The Pennsylvania German Family Farm: A Regional Architecture and Folk Cultural Study of an American Agricultural Community.* Breinigsville, Pa.: The Pennsylvania German Society, 1972. 518 pp., illus., bibliog. references. ◆ History of the regional, vernacular architecture and folk culture. Publications of the Pennsylvania German Society vol. 6.

Marshall, Howard W. *American Folk Architecture: A Selected Bibliography.* Washington, D.C.: American Folklife Center, 1981. 79 pp.

Marshall, Howard W. *Folk Architecture in Little Dixie: A Regional Culture in Missouri.* Columbia: University of Missouri Press, 1981. 146 pp., illus., bibliog., index.

Moholy-Nagy, Sibyl. *Native Genius in Anonymous Architecture in North America.* New York: Schocken Books, c1957, 1976. 190 pp., illus.

Oliver, Paul, ed. *Shelter and Society.* New York: Praeger Publishers, 1969. 167 pp., illus., bibliog.

Pillsbury, Richard, and Andrew Kardos. *A Field Guide to the Folk Architecture of the Northeastern United States.* Hanover, N.H.: Dartmouth College, Department of Geography, 1970. 99 pp., illus., bibliog. ◆ Geography Publications at Dartmouth no. 8.

Rapoport, Amos. *House Form and Culture.* Englewood Cliffs, N.J.: Prentice-Hall, 1969. 146 pp., illus., bibliog.

Shelter, Sign and Symbol. Edited by Paul Oliver. 1975. Reprint. Woodstock, N.Y.: Overlook Press, 1980. 228 pp., illus., bibliogs.

Upton, Dell. "Ordinary Buildings: A Bibliographical Essay on American Vernacular Architecture." In *American Studies International,* XIX:2 (Winter 1981), pp. 57-75.

Wampler, Jan. *All Their Own: People and the Places They Build.* Cambridge, Mass.: Schenkman Publishing Co.; New York, distr. solely by Halsted Press, c1977. 201 pp., illus., bibliog. references.

Wilson, Eugene M. *Alabama Folk Houses.* Montgomery: Alabama Historical Commission, 1975. 115 pp., illus., tables, bibliog.

Wilson, Richard Guy. "Popular Architecture." In *Handbook of American Popular Culture,* edited by M. Thomas Inge (Westport, Conn.: Greenwood Press, 1979), Vol. 2, pp. 265–285.

NOTE

"Folklore: Material Culture—Architecture (North America)." In *MLA International Bibliography. . . , Volume I.* 1970–. ◆ Section under Folklore Chapter includes references on vernacular architecture. Beginning in 1978, compiled by Gerald L. Pocius, Memorial University of Newfoundland.

Colonial/Georgian/Federal

Architects' Emergency Committee. *Great Georgian Houses of America.* 1933–1937. Reprint. New York: Dover Publications, 1970. 2 vols., illus., prints, diagrams.

Building Early America: *Contributions Toward the History of a Great Industry.* The Carpenter's Company of the City and County of Philadelphia; Charles E. Peterson, ed. Radnor, Pa.: Chilton Book Co., c1976. 407 pp., illus., bibliog. references, index.

Bunting, Bainbridge. *Early Architecture in New Mexico.* 1st ed. Albuquerque: University of New Mexico Press, c1976. 122 pp., bibliog., index.

Cummings, Abbott Lowell. *The Framed Houses of Massachusetts Bay, 1625–1725.* Cambridge, Mass.: Belknap Press, 1979. 261 pp., illus., bibliog. references, index.

Eberlein, Harold D. *The Architecture of Colonial America.* 1915. Reprint. New York: Johnson Reprint Co., 1968. 289 pp., plates.

Eberlein, Harold D., and Cortlandt Van Dyke Hubbard. *American Georgian Architecture.* 1952. Reprint. New York: DaCapo Press, 1976. 64 plates, drawings.

Eberlein, Harold D., and Cortlandt Van Dyke Hubbard. *Colonial Interiors, Federal and Greek Revival.* 3rd series. New York: W. Helburn, c1938, 1968. 153 pp., illus.

French, Leigh, Jr. *Colonial Interiors: Photographs and Measured Drawings of the Colonial and Federal Periods.* New York: W. Helburn, 1923. unpaged, 125 plates, illus., diagrams.

The Georgian Period: *Being Photographs and Measured Drawings of Colonial Work with Text.* By William Rotch Ware. 1923 ed. with new classification and indexes. New York: U.P.C. Co., 1923. 6 vols., illus., prints, drawings, diagrams. ◆ Reprinted by Dover Publications, N.Y., 1970, 3 vols.

Howells, John Mead. *Lost Examples of Colonial Architecture: Buildings that have Disappeared or Been so Altered as to be Denatured.* New York: Dover Publications, 1963. 244 pp., illus., index.

Isham, Norman Morrison. *Early American Houses;* and, *A Glossary of Colonial Architectural Terms.* 1928, 1939. Reprint. New York: DaCapo Press, 1967. 61, 37 pp., drawings, diagrams, glossary, index.

Jackson, Joseph. *American Colonial Architecture, Its Origin and Development.* 1924. Reprint. New York: Johnson Reprint Co., 1969. 228 pp., illus., bibliog., index.

Kelly, John Frederick. *Early Domestic Architecture of Connecticut.* 1924. Reprint. New York: Dover Publications, 1963. 210 pp., illus., drawings, diagrams, index.

Kimball, Sidney Fiske. *Domestic Architecture of the American Colonies and of the Early Republic.* New York: Dover Publications, c1922, 1966. 314 pp., illus., prints, drawings, diagrams, notes on individual houses, chronological chart, index.

Kubler, George, and Martin Soria. *Art and Architecture in Spain and Portugal and Their American Dominions, 1500–1800.* Baltimore: Penguin Books, 1959. 445 pp., illus.

Millar, Donald. *Measured Drawings of Some Colonial and Georgian Houses.* New York: Architectural Book Publishing Co., 1916. 3 vols. in portfolios, plates.

Millar, John Fitzhugh. *The Architects of the American Colonies: Or, Vitruvius Americanus.* Barre, Mass.: Barre Publishers, 1968. 205 pp., drawings, bibliog., index.

The Monograph Series, *Records of Early American Architecture.* New York: n.p., 1915–1940. 26 vols. in 21 vols., illus., plans. ◆ White Pine Series of Architectural Monographs, edited by Russell F. Whitehead. Monographs dated bimonthly from 1915–1924 at the expense of the White Pine Bureau, an association formed by a group of white pine producers, for the purpose of promoting architectural uses of white pine. The series recorded data on colonial frame structures. 3 nos./yr., 1915; 6 nos./yr., 1916–40; Vol. 5, no. 6 never published. Title varies: v.1–14 The White Pine Series. . . ; v. 15–17 The Monograph Series. . . . Also available as reprints by Arno Press, N.Y., 1977, monographs on early homes of Massachusetts, Rhode Island, New England, and survey of early American design.

Morrison, Hugh S. *Early American Architecture from the First Colonial Settlements to the National Period.* New York: Oxford University Press, 1952. 619 pp., illus., prints, drawings, diagrams, maps, bibliog. notes, index.

Murtagh, William J. *Moravian Architecture and Town Planning; Bethlehem, Pa., and other Eighteenth-century American Settlements.* Chapel Hill: University of North Carolina Press, 1967. 145 pp., illus., map, bibliog.

Newcomb, Rexford. *Spanish Colonial Architecture in the United States.* New York: J. J. Augustin, 1937. 29 pp., illus.

Pierson, William H. *American Buildings and Their Architects: Vol. I–The Colonial and*

Neo-Classical Styles. Garden City, N.Y.: Doubleday & Co., 1970. 503 pp., illus., prints, diagrams, maps, glossary, bibliog. notes, index.

Schmidt, Carl F. *Colonial and Post-Colonial Details*. Scottsville, N.Y.: The Author, 1969. 61 pp., 103 plates, drawings, glossary.

Swann, Don, Jr. *Colonial and Historic Homes of Maryland: One Hundred Etchings*. 1939. Reprint. Baltimore: Johns Hopkins University Press, 1975. 211 pp., illus., map.

Tatum, George B. *Philadelphia Georgian: The City House of Samuel Powel and Some of Its Eighteenth-Century Neighbors*. Middletown, Conn.: Wesleyan University Press, 1976. 187 pp., illus., bibliog., index.

Waterman, Thomas T. *The Dwellings of Colonial America*. With an introduction by Nancy Halverson Schless. New York: W. W. Norton & Co., c1950, 1980. 312 pp., illus., diagrams, bibliog., glossary, index.

19th Century

American Victorian Architecture: A Survey of the '70's and '80's in Contemporary Photographs. With a new introduction by Arnold Lewis and notes on the plates by Keith Morgan. New York: Dover Publications, c1975. 152 pp., illus.

American Victoriana: Floor Plans and Renderings from the Gilded Age. Being a gallery of color plates with descriptive text and black and white facsimile pages from the Scientific American, architects and builders editions, 1880 through 1905. Compiled by Eugene Mitchell; edited by Judith Lynch Waldron; introduction by William J. Murtagh. San Francisco: Chronicle Books, c1979. 103 pp., illus., index.

Andrews, Wayne. *American Gothic: Its Origins, Its Trials, Its Triumphs*. New York: Vintage Books, 1975. 154 pp., illus., bibliog., index.

Artistic Country-Seats: Types of Recent American Villa and Cottage Architecture, with Instances of Country Club-houses. Edited by George William Sheldon. 1886. Reprint. New York: DaCapo Press, 1978. 2 vols., illus. ◆ Reprint of Vol. 1–2 of 5-volume edition published by D. Appleton, N.Y., 1886.

Brooklyn Institute of Arts and Sciences. Museum. *The American Renaissance, 1876–1917*. Brooklyn, N.Y.: Brooklyn Museum, distr. by Pantheon Books, c1979. 232 pp., illus., bibliog., index.

Carrott, Richard G. *The Egyptian Revival; Its Sources, Monuments, and Meaning, 1808–1858*. Berkeley, Calif.: University of California Press, c1978. 221 pp., illus., plans, bibliog.

Condit, Carl W. *The Chicago School of Architecture: A History of Commercial and Public Building in the Chicago Area, 1875–1925*. Chicago: University of Chicago Press, 1969. 238 pp., illus., bibliog., index. ◆ Revised and enlarged from "The Rise of the Skyscraper . . .", 1952.

Davis, Alexander Jackson. *Rural Residences*. 1838. Reprint. New Introduction by Jane B. Davies. New York: DaCapo Press, 1979. 48 pp., illus. ◆ Styles illustrated include villas and cottages, farmhouse, church, schoolhouse; and, Gothic, Oriental, bracketed, Tuscan, and "American."

Downing, Andrew Jackson. *The Architecture of Country Houses: Including Designs for Cottages, and Farmhouses, and Villas, with Remarks on Interiors, Furniture, and the Best Modes of Warming and Ventilating*. 1850. Reprint. New York: Dover Publications, 1969. 484 pp., illus., drawings, diagrams. ◆ Also available from DaCapo Press, N.Y., 1968.

Downing, Andrew Jackson. *Cottage Residences, Rural Architecture and Landscape Gardening*. Edited by Hugh Guthrie. Watkins Glen, N.Y.: Library of Victorian Culture, 1967. 220 pp., illus., plans, bibliog.

Early, James. *Romanticism and American Architecture*. New York: A. S. Barnes, 1965. 171 pp., illus., index. ◆ Chapters devoted to concepts of Associationism, the Picturesque, Nature, Functionalism, and Nationalism.

Eidlitz, Leopold. *The Nature and Function of Art, More Especially of Architecture*. 1881. Reprint. New York: DaCapo Press, 1977. 493 pp., index. ◆ On the artistic and architectural theories of the High Victorian school.

Gillon, Edmund V., Jr., and Clay Lancaster. *Victorian Houses: A Treasury of Lesser-Known Examples*. New York: Dover Publications, c1973. 117 pp., illus.

Girouard, Mark. *Sweetness and Light: The Queen Anne Movement, 1860–1900.* Oxford, Eng.: Clarendon Press, 1977. 250 pp., illus. ◆ Includes a chapter on the style in the U.S.

Hamlin, Talbot F. *Greek Revival Architecture in America: Being an Account of Important Trends in American Architecture and American Life Prior to the War Between the States.* 1944. Reprint. New York: Dover Publications, 1964. 439 pp., illus., diagrams, appendices, bibliog. footnotes, bibliog., index.

Handlin, David P. *The American Home: Architecture and Society, 1815–1915.* 1st ed. Boston: Little, Brown and Company, c1979. 545 pp., bibliog. references, index.

Hansen, Hans Jürgen, ed. *Late Nineteenth Century Art: The Art, Architecture and Applied Art of the "Pompous Age."* New York: McGraw-Hill Book Co., c1970, 1972. 264 pp., illus., bibliog.

Holly, Henry Hudson. *Country Seats and Modern Dwellings: Two Victorian Domestic Architectural Stylebooks.* 1866, 1878. Reprint. Watkins Glen, N.Y.: American Life Foundation, 1977. 2 vols. in 1 (424 pp.), illus., index. ◆ Includes *Country Seats; Modern Dwellings.*

Jordy, William H. *American Buildings and Their Architects: Vol. III—Progressive and Academic Ideals at the Turn of the 20th Century.* Garden City, N.Y.: Doubleday & Co., 1972. 420 pp., illus., notes, glossary, index.

Kidney, Walter C. *The Architecture of Choice: Eclecticism in America, 1880–1930.* New York: G. Braziller, 1974. 178 pp., illus., bibliog., references.

Kirker, Harold. *California's Architectural Frontier: Style and Tradition in the Nineteenth Century.* 1960. Reprint. New York: Russell & Russell, 1970. 224 pp., illus., bibliog., index.

Lancaster, Clay. *The Japanese Influence in America.* Intro. by Alan Priest. New York: W. H. Rawls, distr. by Twayne Publishers, 1963. 292 pp., illus., plans, bibliog. references.

Loth, Calder, and Julius Trousdale Sadler, Jr. *The Only Proper Style: Gothic Architecture in America.* Boston, Mass.: New York Graphic Society, c1975. 184 pp., illus., bibliog., index.

Maass, John. *The Gingerbread Age: A View of Victorian America.* New York: Rinehart, 1957. 212 pp., illus., prints, drawings, bibliog., index.

Maass, John. *The Victorian Home in America.* New York: Hawthorn Books, 1972. 235 pp., illus., appendix, bibliog., index.

Mumford, Lewis. *The Brown Decades: A Study of the Arts in America, 1865–1895.* New York: Dover Publications, c1955, 1959. 266 pp., illus., bibliog.

Owen, Robert Dale. *Hints on Public Architecture, Containing Among Other Illustrations, Views and Plans of the Smithsonian Institution; Together with an Appendix Relative to Building Materials.* 1849. Reprint. New York: DaCapo Press, 1978. 176 pp., illus. ◆ Reprint of 1849 edition published by Putnam, N.Y.; issued as Publications P of Smithsonian Institution.

Pierson, William H. *American Buildings and Their Architects: Vol. IIA—Technology and the Picturesque, the Corporate and the Early Gothic Styles.* Garden City, N.Y.: Doubleday & Co., l978. 500 pp., illus.

Rhoads, William B. *The Colonial Revival.* New York: Garland Publishing, 1977. 2 vols. (1134 pp.), illus., bibliog.

Schmidt, Carl F. *Greek Revival Details.* Scottsville, N.Y.: The Author, 1968. 144 pp., illus., drawings, diagrams, glossary.

Scully, Vincent J. *The Shingle Style and the Stick Style: Architectural Theory and Design from Richardson to the Origins of Wright.* Rev. ed. New Haven, Conn.: Yale University Press, c1955, 1971. 184 pp., illus., prints, diagrams, bibliog., index.

Stanton, Phoebe B. *The Gothic Revival and American Church Architecture; An Episode in Taste, 1840–1856.* Baltimore: Johns Hopkins University Press, 1968. 350 pp., illus., prints, diagrams, tables, bibliog. footnotes, index.

Stevens, John Calvin, and Albert Winslow Cobb. *Examples of American Domestic Architecture.* 1889. Reprint. Watkins Glen, N.Y.: American Life Foundation, 1979. 40 pp., illus., plates.

Upjohn, Richard. *Upjohn's Rural Architecture; Designs, Working Drawings and Specifications for a Wooden Church and Other Rural Structures.* 1852. Reprint. New York: DaCapo Press, 1975. [13] pp., 25 plates.

Ware, William R. *The American Vignola; A Guide to the Making of Classical Architecture.* Introductory notes by John Barrington Bayley and Henry Hope Reed. New York: W. W. Norton and Co., c1977. 124 pp., illus. ◆ New edition of 1905–06 work, including measured drawings of ancient, Renaissance, and Baroque architectural details; instructions on designing doors, vaults, etc.

Wright, Gwendolyn. *Moralism and the Model Home: Domestic Architecture and Cultural Conflict in Chicago, 1873–1913.* Chicago: University of Chicago Press, 1980. 382 pp., illus., bibliog., index.

20th Century

American Institute of Architects. *Mid-Century Architecture in America: Honor Awards of the American Institute of Architects 1949–1961.* Baltimore: Johns Hopkins University Press, 1961. 254 pp., illus. ◆ Edited with an introduction by Wolf Von Eckardt.

Banham, Reyner. *The Age of the Masters: A Personal View of Modern Architecture.* New York: Harper & Row, c1975. 170 pp., illus.

Banham, Reyner. *The Architecture of the Well-Tempered Environment.* Chicago: University of Chicago Press, 1969. 295 pp., illus., plans, bibliog.

Bush, Donald J. *The Streamlined Decade.* New York: George Braziller, c1975. 214 pp., illus., bibliog., index.

Edgell, George H. *The American Architecture of Today.* 1928. Reprint. New York: AMS Press, 1970. 401 pp., illus., bibliog.

Ford, James, and Katherine Morrow Ford. *The Modern House in America.* New York: Architectural Book Publishing Co., 1940. 134 pp., illus., index.

Greif, Martin. *Depression Modern: The Thirties Style in America.* New York: Universe Books, 1975. 192 pp., illus., index.

Hamlin, Talbot. *Forms and Functions of Twentieth-Century Architecture.* New York: Columbia University Press, 1952. 4 vols., illus., bibliogs. ◆ Includes elements of building, principles of composition, building types.

Hitchcock, Henry-Russell. *Modern Architecture: Romanticism and Reintegration.* 1929. Reprint. New York: Hacker Art Books, 1970. 252 pp., illus., bibliog. references.

Hitchcock, Henry-Russell, and Philip

Johnson. *The International Style.* 1932. Reprint. New York: W. W. Norton, 1966. 260 pp., illus.

Jacobus, John. *Twentieth-Century Architecture: The Middle Years, 1940 to 1965.* New York: Praeger Publishers, 1966. 215 pp., illus.

Jencks, Charles. *Modern Movements in Architecture.* Garden City, N.Y.: Anchor Press, 1973. 432 pp., illus., tables, bibliog.

Joedicke, Jurgen. *Architecture Since 1945: Sources and Directions.* New York: Praeger Publishers, 1969. 179 pp., illus., bibliog.

Jordy, William H. *American Buildings and Their Architects: Vol. IV—The Impact of European Modernism in the Mid-Twentieth Century.* Garden City, N.Y.: Doubleday & Co., 1972. 469 pp., illus., notes, glossary, index.

McCallum, Ian Robert More. *Architecture U.S.A.* New York: Reinhold Publishing Corp., 1959. 216 pp., illus., bibliog.

McCoy, Esther. *Case Study Houses, 1945–1962.* 2nd ed. Los Angeles: Hennessey & Ingalls, 1977. 217 pp., illus., bibliog., index. ◆ Published in 1962 under title *Modern California Homes.* Originally from "The Case Study House Program" of Arts & Architecture magazine.

Mujica, Francisco. *History of the Skyscraper.* 1929. Reprint. New York: DaCapo Press, 1977. 72 pp., illus.

New York (City). Museum of Modern Art. *Built in USA: 1932–1944,* edited by Elizabeth Mock; *Post-War Architecture,* edited by Henry-Russell Hitchcock and Arthur Drexler. 1944, 1952. Reprints. New York: Arno Press for the Museum of Modern Art, 1968. 127, 128 pp., illus., plans.

Peisch, Mark L. *The Chicago School of Architecture: Early Followers of Sullivan and Wright.* New York: Random House, 1964. 177 pp., 42 plates, bibliog. ◆ Columbia University Studies in Art History and Archaeology no. 5.

Robinson, Cervin, and Rosemarie H. Bletter. *Skyscraper Style: Art Deco New York.* New York: Oxford University Press, 1975. 88 pp., illus., bibliog. references.

Scully, Vincent, Jr. *Modern Architecture: The Architecture of Democracy.* Rev. ed. New York: G. Braziller, 1974. 158 pp., illus., bibliog.

Scully, Vincent. *The Shingle Style Today; or, the Historian's Revenge.* New York: G. Braziller, 1974. 118 pp., illus., bibliog. references, index.

Sharp, Dennis. *Sources of Modern Architecture: A Bibliography.* New York: George Wittenborn, 1967. 56 pp., illus. ◆ Architectural Association (London) Papers, Vol. 2.

Stern, Robert A. M. *New Directions in American Architecture.* 2nd ed., enl. New York: George Braziller, c1969, 1977. 152 pp., illus., plans, bibliog. references.

Stickley, Gustav. *Craftsman Homes: Architecture and Furnishings of the American Arts and Crafts Movement.* 2nd ed. 1909. Reprint. New York: Dover Publications, 1979. 205 pp.

Todd, Dorothy, and Raymond Mortimer. *The New Interior Decoration: An Introduction to Its Principles, and International Survey of Its Methods.* 1929. Reprint. New York: DaCapo Press, 1977. 42 pp., illus., plates, index.

Wingler, Hans M. *The Bauhaus: Weimer, Dessau, Berlin, Chicago.* Translated by Wolfgang Jabs and Basil Gilbert. Edited by Joseph Stein. Cambridge, Mass.: MIT Press, 1969. 653 pp., illus., bibliog. ◆ Extensive supplementary material, paperback edition, 1978.

Building Types

Domestic/Residential

Alpern, Andrew. *Apartments for the Affluent: A Historical Survey of Buildings in New York.* New York: McGraw-Hill, 1975. 159 pp., illus., index. ◆ History and examples, from 1869 to the present.

Apps, Jerry, and Allen Strang. *Barns of Wisconsin.* Madison, Wisc.: Tamarack Press, c1977. 143 pp., illus., bibliog., index.

Arthur, Eric. *The Barn: A Vanishing Landmark in North America.* New York: A & W Visual Library, 1975. 256 pp., illus., measured drawings, diagrams, bibliog., index.

Ball, Berenice M. *Barns of Chester County, Pennsylvania.* West Chester, Pa.: Chester County Day Committee of the Womens' Auxil-

iary, Chester County Hospital, 1974. 241 pp., illus., bibliog., index.

Bealer, Alex W. *The Log Cabin: Homes of the North American Wilderness.* Barre, Mass.: Barre Publishing, distr. by Crown Publishers, N.Y., c1978. 191 pp., illus., bibliog., index.

Cohn, Jan. *The Palace or the Poorhouse: The American House as a Cultural Symbol.* East Lansing, Mich.: Michigan State University, 1979. 267 pp., bibliog. references.

Ekblaw, Karl J. T. *Farm Structures.* New York: Macmillan, 1914. 347 pp., illus., tables. ◆ See also, author's series of farm bulletins for National Lumber Manufacturers Association, Trade Extension Department, Chicago, which include hog houses, implement sheds, grain storage buildings, poultry houses, 1916–1917.

Fitchen, John. *The New World Dutch Barn: A Study of Its Characteristics, Its Structural System, and Its Probable Erectional Procedures.* Syracuse, N.Y.: Syracuse University Press, c1968, 1977. 178 pp., illus., diagrams, maps, pictorial glossary, bibliog., index.

Foley, Mary Mix. *The American House.* New York: Harper & Row, c1979. 298 pp., drawings. ◆ Guide to style and history of the American house from colonial period to the present.

Grow, Lawrence. *Old House Plans: Two Centuries of American Domestic Architecture.* New York: Universe Books, 1978. 127 pp., illus., plans, measured drawings.

Handlin, David P. *The American Home: Architecture and Society, 1815–1915.* 1st ed. Boston: Little, Brown and Company, c1979. 545 pp., bibliog. references, index.

Historic American Buildings Survey. *Shaker Built: A Catalog of Shaker Architectural Records from the Historic American Buildings Survey.* Edited by John Poppeliers with the assistance of Deborah Stephens. Washington, D.C.: Historic American Buildings Survey, 1974. 87 pp., illus., drawings, bibliog.

Kauffman, Henry J. *The American Farmhouse.* New York: Hawthorn Books, c1975. 265 pp., plates, bibliog., index. ◆ 17th–19th century farmhouses through photographs and floor plans. Also available in paperback, Bonanza Books, 1979.

Keeler, Charles A. *The Simple Home.* 1904. Reprint. With a new introduction by Dimitri

Shipounoff. Santa Barbara, Calif.: Peregrine Smith, 1979. 55 pp., plates, bibliog. references.

Klamkin, Charles. *Barns: Their History, Preservation and Restoration.* New York: Hawthorn Books, 1973. 162 pp., illus., index. ◆ Also available in paperback, Bonanza Books, 1979.

Lassiter, William L. *Shaker Architecture: Descriptions with Photographs and Drawings of Shaker Buildings at Mount Lebanon, New York, and Watervliet, New York, and West Pittsfield, Massachusetts.* New York: Vantage Press, 1966. 127 pp., illus., drawings, plans, bibliog.

Lockwood, Charles. *Bricks and Brownstone: The New York Row House, 1783–1929: An Architectural and Social History.* New York: McGraw-Hill Book Co., c1972, 1982. 262 pp., illus., plans, bibliog., index.

Mercer, Henry C. *The Origin of Log Houses in the United States.* 1924. Reprint. Doylestown, Pa.: Bucks County Historical Society, 1976. 31 pp., illus., bibliog. references.

Schmidt, Carl F. *The Octagon Fad.* Scottsville, N.Y.: The Author, 1958. 207 pp., illus., bibliog.

Shurtleff, Harold R. *The Log Cabin Myth: A Study of the Early Dwellings of the English Colonists of North America.* Edited by Samuel Eliot Morison. 1939. Reprint. Gloucester, Mass.: Peter Smith, 1967. 243 pp., illus., drawings, bibliog. footnotes.

Thollander, Earl. *Barns of California: A Collection.* San Francisco, Calif.: California Historical Society, 1974. 150 pp., illus. ◆ Pen and ink drawings with accompanying text.

U.S. Office of Archeology and Historic Preservation. *Selected Bibliography on Cottages and Cabins.* David W. Look, comp. Washington, D.C.: U.S. Department of the Interior, National Park Service, August 1975. 3 pp. ◆ Technical Preservation Services Reading List.

U.S. Office of Archeology and Historic Preservation. *Selected Bibliography on Log Structures.* David W. Look, comp. Washington, D.C.: U.S. Department of the Interior, National Park Service, August 1975. 4 pp. ◆ Technical Preservation Services Reading List.

Walker, Lester. *American Shelter: An Illus-*

trated Encyclopedia of the American Home. Woodstock, N.Y.: Overlook Press, 1981. 320 pp., bibliog.

Weslager, C.A. *The Log Cabin in America From Pioneer Days to the Present.* New Brunswick, N.J.: Rutgers University Press, 1969. 382 pp., illus., diagrams, maps, bibliog., notes, index.

Wright, Gwendolyn. *Moralism and the Model Home: Domestic Architecture and Cultural Conflict in Chicago, 1873–1913.* Chicago: University of Chicago Press, 1980. 382 pp., illus., bibliog., index.

Religious

Adams, Robert H. *White Churches of the Plains: Examples from Colorado.* Boulder: Colorado Associated University Press, 1970. 84 pp., illus.

Andrew, Laurel B. *The Early Temples of the Mormons: The Architecture of the Millenial Kingdom in the American West.* Albany, N.Y.: State University of New York Press, 1978. 218 pp., illus., bibliog. references.

Architectural Record. *Religious Buildings.* New York: McGraw-Hill, c1979. 177 pp.

Black, Linda Perlis. *Synagogue Architecture and Planning: An Annotated Bibliography.* Monticello, Ill.: Council of Planning Librarians, 1978. 24 pp. ◆ Exchange Bibliography no. 1469.

Chambers, George W., and C. L. Sonnichsen. *San Augustin, First Cathedral Church in Arizona.* Tucson: Arizona Historical Society, 1974. 55 pp., illus.

De Breffny, Brian. *The Synagogue.* 1st American ed. New York: Macmillan, 1978. 215 pp., illus., bibliog. references, index.

De Visser, John, and Harold Kalman. *Pioneer Churches.* New York: W. W. Norton and Co., 1976. 192 pp., illus., bibliog., index. ◆ Photo essay on historic North American churches, ca.1600–1775.

Donnelly, Marian Card. *The New England Meeting Houses of the Seventeenth Century.* Middletown, Conn.: Wesleyan University Press, 1968. 165 pp., bibliog.

Dorsey, Stephen Palmer. *Early English*

Churches in America, 1607–1807. New York: Oxford University Press, 1952. 206 pp., illus., prints, charts, bibliog., index.

Kampf, Avram. *Contemporary Synagogue Art: Developments in the United States, 1945–1965.* New York: Union of American Hebrew Congregations, c1966, 1976. 276 pp., illus., bibliog.

Kelly, John Frederick. *Early Connecticut Meetinghouses: Being an Account of the Church Edifices Built Before 1830, Based Chiefly Upon Town and Parish Records.* New York: Columbia University Press, 1948. 2 vols., illus., bibliog.

Kervick, Francis William Wynn. *Architects in America of Catholic Tradition.* 1st ed. Rutland, Vt.: C.E. Tuttle, 1962. 140 pp., illus.

Kubler, George. *The Religious Architecture of New Mexico: In the Colonial Period and Since the American Occupation.* 4th ed. Albuquerque: University of New Mexico Press for the School of American Research, c1940, 1973. 232 pp., illus., maps, tables, bibliog.

Lane, George A. *Chicago Churches and Synagogues: An Architecural Pilgrimage.* Chicago: Loyola University Press, 1981. 254 pp., illus., index.

Mazmanian, Arthur B. *The Structure of Praise: A Design Study, Architecture for Religion in New England from the Seventeenth Century to the Present.* Rev. ed. Boston: Beacon Press, 1970. 151 pp., illus.

Newcomb, Rexford. *The Franciscan Mission Architecture of Alta California.* 1916. Reprint. New York: Dover Publications, 1973. 74 pp. of plates.

Pearson, Arnold. *Early Churches of Washington State.* Seattle: University of Washington Press, c1980. 182 pp., bibliog., index.

Rose, Harold Wickliffe. *The Colonial Houses of Worship in America: Built in the English Colonies Before the Republic, 1607–1789, and Still Standing.* New York: Hastings House, c1963, 1964. 574 pp., illus., maps, bibliog.

Sinnott, Edmund W. *Meetinghouse and Church in Early New England.* New York: McGraw-Hill, 1963. 243 pp., illus., bibliog. references.

Tucci, Douglass S. *Church Building in Boston, 1720–1970: With an Introduction to the Work of Ralph Adams Cram and the Boston Gothicists.* Concord, Mass.: Rumford Press, 1974. 134 pp., illus., bibliog. references.

Wischnitzer, Rachel. *Synagogue Architecture in the United States: History and Interpretation.* Philadelphia: Jewish Publication Society of America, 1955. 204 pp., illus., bibliogs.

Educational

Architectural Record. *Schools for the New Needs: Educational, Social, Economic.* New York: F. W. Dodge Corp., c1956. 312 pp., illus., plans. ◆ From articles originally in *Architectural Record.*

Barnard, Henry. *School Architecture.* 1848. Reprint. Edited by Jean and Robert McClintock. New York: Teachers College Press, 1970. 338 pp., illus., plans. ◆ Classics in Education no. 42. Includes school designs of A. J. Davis, James Renwick, etc., documentary compilation of the state of school architecture in lower New England near mid-century.

Bryan, John Morrill. *An Architectural History of the South Carolina College, 1801–1855.* Columbia: University of South Carolina Press, 1976. 133 pp., illus., bibliog., index.

Gerold, William. *College Hill: A Photographic Study of Brown University in its Two Hundredth Year.* Providence, R.I.: Brown University Press, 1965. 1 vol., chiefly illus.

Johannesen, Eric. *Ohio College Architecture Before 1870.* Columbus: Ohio Historical Society, 1969. 56 pp., illus., bibliog.

Klauder, Charles Z., and Herbert C. Wise. *College Architecture in America and its Part in the Development of the Campus.* New York: Charles Scribner's Sons, 1929. 301 pp., illus., diagrams, charts, index.

LaChance, Walter W. *Schoolhouses and their Equipment, with Plans and Illustrations of the Newest Schoolhouse Architecture.* Buffalo, N.Y.: Baker, Jones, Hausauer, 1925. 207 pp., illus., index.

O'Neal, William B. *Jefferson's Buildings at the University of Virginia: The Rotunda.* Charlottesville, Va.: University Press of Virginia, 1960. 88 pp., illus., bibliog. references, index.

Parsons, Kermit Carlyle. *The Cornell Campus: A History of its Planning and Develop-*

ment. Ithaca, N.Y.: Cornell University Press, 1968. 336 pp., illus., maps, bibliog. footnotes.

Partridge, Loren W. *John Galen Howard and the Berkeley Campus: Beaux-Arts Architecture in the "Athens of the West."* Berkeley, Calif.: Berkeley Architectural Heritage Association, 1978. 65 pp., illus., bibliog.

Powell, William S. *The First State University: A Pictorial History of the University of North Carolina.* Chapel Hill: University of North Carolina Press, 1972. 309 pp., illus.

Schlereth, Thomas J. *The University of Notre Dame: A Portrait of Its History and Campus.* Notre Dame, Ind.: University of Notre Dame, c1976. 252 pp., illus., bibliog., index.

Turner, Paul V.; Marcia E. Vetrocq; and Karen Weitze. *The Founders and the Architects: The Design of Stanford University.* Stanford, Calif.: Department of Art, Stanford University, 1976. 96 pp., bibliog. references.

Wriston, Barbara. "The Use of Architectural Handbooks in the Design of Schoolhouses from 1840–1860," *Journal of the Society of Architectural Historians,* 22:3 (October 1973), pp. 155–160.

Public/Government

Architectural Record. *Hospitals, Clinics and Health Centers.* New York: F. W. Dodge Corp., 1960. 264 pp., illus., plans. ◆ From articles originally in *Architectural Record.*

Braithwaite, David. *Fairground Architecture: The World of Amusement Parks, Carnivals and Fairs.* New York: Praeger Publishers, 1968. 195 pp., illus., bibliog.

Court House: A Photographic Document. Edited by Richard Pare; Phyllis Lambert; et al. New York: Horizon Press, c1978. 255 pp., bibliog., index.

A Courthouse Conservation Handbook. Washington, D.C.: Preservation Press, 1976. 75 pp., illus., bibliog. ◆ A project of the National Trust in cooperation with the National Clearinghouse for Criminal Justice Planning and Architecture; includes architectural history, design considerations, current use of courthouses.

Craig, Lois. *The Federal Presence: Architecture, Politics, and Symbols in United States Government Building.* By Lois Craig and the staff of the Federal Architecture Project. Cambridge, Mass.: MIT Press, c1978. 580 pp., bibliog., index.

Daniel, Jean Houston, and Price Daniel. *Executive Mansions and Capitols of America.* Waukesha, Wisc.: Country Beautiful, distr. by G. P. Putnam, N.Y., 1969. 290 pp., illus., bibliog.

Davis, Julia Finette, comp. "International Exposition 1851–1900." In *Papers* of the American Association of Architectural Bibliographers (Charlottesville, Va.: University Press of Virginia, 1968), vol. 4, pp. 47–130.

Hitchcock, Henry-Russell, and William Seale. *Temples of Democracy: The State Capitols of the U.S.A.* New York: Harcourt, Brace Jovanovich, c1976. 333 pp., illus., bibliog., index.

Hopkins, Alfred. *Prisons and Prison Building.* New York: Architectural Book Publishing Co., c1930. 140 pp., illus., plans.

Johnson, Herbert Alan, and Ralph K. Andrist. *Historic Courthouses of New York State: 18th and 19th Century Halls of Justice Across the Empire State.* New York: Columbia University Press, 1977. 175 pp., illus.

Johnston, Norman B. *The Human Cage: A Brief History of Prison Architecture.* New York: Published for the American Foundation, Institute of Corrections by Walker, 1973. 68 pp., illus., bibliog.

Maass, John. *The Glorious Enterprise: The Centennial Exposition of 1876 and H. J. Schwarzmann, Architect-in-Chief.* New ed. Watkins Glen, N.Y.: American Life Foundation, 1973. 156 pp., illus., bibliog.

Radoff, Morris L. *Buildings of the State of Maryland at Annapolis.* Annapolis: Hall of Records Commission of the State of Maryland, 1954. 140 pp., illus., maps. ◆ Publication no. 9.

Radoff, Morris L. *The County Courthouses and Records of Maryland.* Annapolis: Hall of Records Commission of the State of Maryland, 1960–. illus. ◆ Part 1—The Courthouses (1960), 175 pp., illus., bibliog. footnotes.

Robinson, Willard B., and Todd Webb. *Texas Public Buildings of the Nineteenth Century.* Austin: University of Texas Press for the Amon Carter Museum of Western Art, 1974.

290 pp., illus. ◆ Texas Architectural Survey Publication no. 2.

Stanek, Edward, and Jacqueline Stanek. *Iowa's Magnificent County Courthouses.* Des Moines, Ia.: Wallace-Homestead Book Co., 1976. 312 pp., illus., bibliog. references.

U.S. Office of Archeology and Historic Preservation. *The Old St. Louis Post Office: Summary Report for the Advisory Council on Historic Preservation.* Prepared by S. Allen Chambers, Jr. with the assistance of Nancy Beinke. Washington, D.C.: 1970. 40 pp., illus., map, plans.

U.S. Public Works Administration. *Public Buildings: A Survey of Architecture of Projects Constructed by Federal and Other Governmental Bodies Between the Years 1933 and 1939 with the Assistance of the Public Works Administration.* C. W. Short, Public Works Administration; R. Stanley-Brown, Public Buildings Administration. Washington, D.C.: U.S. Government Printing Office, 1939. 2, 697 pp., illus., maps, plans, tables, diagrams.

Whiffen, Marcus. *The Public Buildings of Williamsburg, Colonial Capital of Virginia: An Architectural History.* Williamsburg, Va.: Colonial Williamsburg, distr. by Holt, Rinehart & Winston, 1958. 269 pp., illus., prints, drawings, diagrams, maps, bibliog., index. ◆ Williamsburg Architecture Studies no. 1.

Wortman, Julie A. *Legacies: Kansas' Older County Courthouses.* Topeka: Kansas State Historical Society, 1981. 63 pp., illus.

Commercial/Utilitarian

Alaska. Office of Statewide Cultural Programs. *Alaska's Historic Roadhouses.* Prepared by Office of Statewide Cultural Programs, Alaska Division of Parks, Department of Natural Resources. Principal investigator, Michael E. Smith. Boulder, Colo.: Western Interstate Commission for Higher Education, 1974. 101 pp., illus., bibliog. ◆ History and Archaeology series no. 6. Inventory and selected examples of inns and taverns.

Andrews, Peter. *Inns of New England and the Maritimes.* Los Angeles: Knapp Press; New York, distr. by Holt, Rinehart & Winston, 1978. 154 pp., illus. ◆ Classic Country Inns of America series; An Architectural Digest Book. See also: *Inns of the Mid-Atlantic and the South*

(1978), and *Inns of the Pacific Coast and the Southwest* (1978).

Architectural Record. *Motels, Hotels, Restaurants and Bars.* 2nd ed. New York: McGraw-Hill, c1960. 327 pp., illus. ◆ From articles originally published in *Architectural Record.*

Architectural Record. *Stores and Shopping Centers.* Edited by James S. Hornbeck. New York: McGraw-Hill, 1962. 181 pp., illus., diagrams. ◆ From articles originally published in *Architectural Record.*

Berg, Walter G. *Buildings and Structures of American Railroads.* 1893. Reprint. New Haven, Conn.: Research Publications, Inc., 1972. 500 pp., plans, illus., bibliog. references, appendix. ◆ Subtitle: A Reference Book for Railroad Managers, Superintendents, Master Mechanics, Engineers, Architects, and Students.

Cavalier, Julian. *Classic American Railroad Stations.* San Diego, Calif.: A.S. Barnes & Co., 1980. 212 pp., illus., index.

Droege, John A. *Passenger Terminals and Trains.* 1916. Reprint. Milwaukee: Kalmbach Publishing Co., 1969. 410 pp., illus., diagrams, schedules, tables, index.

Grant, H. Roger, and Charles W. Bohi. *The Country Railroad Station in America.* 1st ed. Boulder, Colo.: Pruett Publ. Co., c1978. 183 pp., illus., bibliog., index.

Gutman, Richard; Elliott Kaufman; and David Slovic. *American Diner.* New York: Harper & Row, 1979. 154 pp., illus. ◆ Photo essay.

Haas, Irvin. *America's Historic Inns and Taverns.* New York: Arco Publishing Co., c1972. 182 pp., illus.

Hendrickson, Robert. *The Grand Emporiums: The Illustrated History of America's Great Department Stores.* New York: Stein and Day, c1979. 488 pp., plates, index.

Hix, John. *The Glass House.* Cambridge, Mass.: MIT Press, 1974. 208 pp., illus., bibliog. ◆ Construction of greenhouses and other glass and metal structures.

Kramer, Jack J., and Matthew Barr. *The Last of the Grand Hotels.* New York: Van Nostrand Reinhold, 1978. 156 pp., illus., bibliog., index.

Limerick, Jeffrey; Nancy Ferguson; and Richard Oliver. *America's Grand Resort Hotels.* New York: Pantheon Books, c1979. 304 pp., illus., bibliog., index.

McGinty, Brian. *The Palace Inns: A Connoisseur's Guide to Historic American Hotels.* Harrisburg, Pa.: Stackpole Books, c1978. 191 pp., illus., bibliog., index.

McNamara, Brooks. *The American Playhouse in the Eighteenth Century.* Cambridge, Mass.: Harvard University Press, 1969. 174 pp., illus., bibliog. references, index.

Marcus, Leonard S. *The American Store Window.* New York: Whitney Library of Design, 1978. 208 pp., illus., bibliog., index.

Meeks, Carroll Louis Vanderslice. *The Railroad Station: An Architectural History.* New Haven, Conn.: Yale University Press, 1956. 203 pp., illus., table of trainsheds, drawings, maps, diagrams, bibliog.

National Register of Historic Places. *Historic Railroad Stations: A Selected Inventory.* Prepared by the National Register of Historic Places, Office of Archeology and Historic Preservation, National Park Service, U.S. Department of the Interior. Washington, D.C.: The Register, 1974. 120 pp., illus. ◆ Catalog of 600 stations, includes those on the National Register, state inventories, HABS, and HAER; inventory organized and compiled by H. Ward Jandl, Jan Thorman and Katherine H. Cole.

Naylor, David. *American Picture Palaces: The Architecture of Fantasy.* New York: Van Nostrand Reinhold, c1981. 224 pp., illus., bibliog., index.

Sexton, Randolph W., and Benjamin F. Betts. *American Theatres of Today: Illustrated with Plans, Sections, and Photographs of Exterior and Interior Details of Modern Motion Picture Theatres Throughout the United States.* 1927–30. Reprint. Vestal, N.Y.: Vestal Press, c1977. 175, 167 pp., illus.

Sharp, Dennis. *The Picture Palace and Other Buildings for the Movies.* New York: Praeger Publishers, 1969. 224 pp., illus., bibliog.

Smith, Lucinda, and Ave Pildas. *Movie Palaces: Survivors of an Elegant Era.* New York: Clarkson N. Potter, 1980. 112 pp., illus., index. ◆ Theaters of the 20's and 30's.

Stoddard, Richard. *Theatre and Cinema Architecture: A Guide to Information Sources.* Detroit: Gale Research Co., 1978. 368 pp., indexes. ◆ Performing Arts Information Guide series vol. 5.

Sulzby, James F., Jr. *Historic Alabama Hotels and Resorts.* University: University of Alabama Press, 1960. 294 pp., illus., bibliog.

Tidworth, Simon. *Theatres: An Architectural and Cultural History.* New York: Praeger Publishers, 1973. 224 pp., illus., bibliog.

Vieyra, Daniel I. *"Fill 'er up": An Architectural History of America's Gas Stations.* New York: Macmillan, c1979. 111 pp., illus., bibliog. references, index.

NOTES

League of Historic American Theatres, Andrea Rounds, Executive Director, c/o The National Theatre, 1321 E Street, N. W., Washington, D. C. 20004. Formed in 1977, the League is a nonprofit association of historic theatres, dedicated to promoting the preservation and use of America's historic theatres. Membership includes theatre professionals, organizations, suppliers and individuals in both historic preservation and the performing arts. An historic theatre is defined as one built prior to 1940; is architecturally significant and deemed worthy of preservation; has played an important role in the history of the American stage; and/or can be used as a performing arts facility. The League identifies and documents historic theatres; distributes a National List of Historic Theatre Buildings (rev. ed. in prep. for 1983); conducts tours of historic theatres; promotes the solution of common problems through conferences and workshops; publishes a quarterly newsletter and membership directory; and facilitates the exchange of information among members.

Railroad Station Historical Society, 430 Ivy Avenue, Crete, Nebraska 68333. Founded in 1967, membership includes persons interested in railroad stations and other railroad buildings and structures from the historical and architectural point of view. It preserves photographs and data on railroad stations and conducts research on the care and maintenance of depots of historical interest. It has an Archives Committee, and holds an annual meeting. Publications include *The Bulletin* (monthly); *Railway History Monographs* (annual); *List of Members* (annual).

Society for Commercial Archeology, c/o Museum of Transportation, 300 Congress Street, Boston, Massachusetts 02210. Founded in 1976, membership includes individuals and organizations in fields ranging from art, architecture, historic preservation, business and engineering. The Society is concerned with artifacts and structures, signs and symbols of the American commercial process. Its goals are to promote public awareness and exchange of information and to encourage the selective conservation of the commercial landscape. Features of the commercial environment include transportation facilities; roadside development; components of the traditional business district; and recreation facilities. Its focus also encompasses both the celebrated and anonymous work of many of America's best designers, the mass-produced forms of the machine age, and the vernacular conception of local builders.

Theatre Historical Society, P. O. Box 767, San Francisco, California 94101. Founded in 1969, membership includes individual hobbyists, college and public libraries, historical societies and architects. Its purpose is to preserve the history of popular theatre in the U.S.; to make available information relating to American theatres; to encourage study in the field; to promote the preservation of important theatre buildings. Emphasis is placed on theatre architecture, management, advertising and publicity, and includes movie houses, legitimate, vaudeville and stock company houses. The Society collects archive materials, and holds an annual meeting. It publishes *Marquee* (begun 1969, quarterly); *Annual; Directory;* and special materials.

Landscape Architecture

Barlow, Elizabeth. *Frederick Law Olmsted's New York.* Illustrative portfolio by William Alex. New York: Praeger in association with Whitney Museum of American Art, 1972. 173 pp., illus., bibliog., index.

Bush-Brown, James, and Louise Bush-Brown. *America's Garden Book.* Rev. ed. by the New York Botanical Garden. New York: Scribner's Sons, 1980. 819 pp., illus.

Cleveland, H. W. S. *Landscape Architecture as Applied to the Wants of the West.* 1873. Reprint. Pittsburgh: University of Pittsburgh

Press, 1965. 59 pp. ◆ With an introduction by Roy Lubove, ed.

Clifford, Derek P. *A History of Garden Design.* London: Faber & Faber, 1962. 232 pp., illus.

Cook, Clarence C. *A Description of the New York Central Park.* 1968. Reprint. New York: Benjamin Blom, 1972. 206 pp., illus., map. ◆ First comprehensive guide and history of the park.

Downing, Andrew Jackson. *Treatise on the Theory and Practice of Landscape Gardening.* 1875. Reprint. Little Compton, R.I.: Theophrastus Publishers, 1977. 576 pp., index. ◆ Reprint contains supplement (1859), and a second supplement (1875) by H. W. Sargent.

Eaton, Leonard K. *Landscape Artist in America: The Life and Work of Jens Jensen.* Chicago: University of Chicago Press, 1964. 240 pp., illus., bibliog. ◆ Landscape architect, 1860–1951.

Eliot, Charles William. *Charles Eliot, Landscape Architect.* 1902. Reprint. Freeport, N.Y.: Books for Libraries Press, 1971. 770 pp., illus., plans.

Fabos, Julius G.; Gordon T. Milde; and V. Michael Weinmayr. *Frederick Law Olmsted, Sr.; Founder of Landscape Architecture in America.* Amherst: University of Massachusetts Press, 1968. 114 pp., illus., maps, plans, appendix, bibliog.

Fairbrother, Nan. *The Nature of Landscape Design: An Art Form, a Craft, a Social Necessity.* New York: Knopf, 1974. 252 pp., illus.

Favretti, Rudy J., and Joy P. Favretti. *For Every House a Garden: A Guide for Reproducing Period Gardens.* Chester, Conn.: The Pequot Press, 1977. 137 pp., illus., glossary.

Favretti, Rudy J., and Joy P. Favretti. *Landscapes and Gardens for Historic Buildings: Reproducing and Recreating Authentic Settings.* Nashville, Tenn.: American Association for State and Local History, 1978. 202 pp., illus., plans, bibliog.

Fein, Albert. *Frederick Law Olmsted and the American Environmental Tradition.* New York: George Braziller, Inc., 1972. 180 pp., illus., diagrams, maps, bibliog., index.

Ferguson, Bruce K. *Landscape Architecture of the Midwestern, Rocky Mountain and Southwestern States: Articles in "Landscape*

Architecture" Magazine, 1910–1979. Monticello, Ill.: Vance Bibliographies, October 1980. 11 pp. ◆ Architecture Series, Bibliography A344. See also: *Middle Atlantic and New England States.* October 1980, 17 pp., no. A345; *Southern States.* October 1980, 8 pp., no. A346; *Pacific States.* October 1980, 10 pp., no. A347.

French, Jere Stuart. *Urban Green: City Parks of the Western World.* Dubuque, Iowa: Hunt Pub. Co., 1973. 129 pp., illus., bibliog.

Garden Club of America. *Gardens of Colony and State: Gardens and Gardeners of the American Colonies and of the Republic before 1840.* Compiled and edited for the Garden Club of America by Alice G. B. Lockwood. New York: Published for the Garden Club of America by Scribner, 1931–34. 2 vols., illus., plans, bibliog.

Gothein, Marie Luise. *A History of Garden Art.* Edited by Walter P. Wright. New York: Hacker Art Books, c1966, 1979. 2 vols (867 pp.), illus., plans, bibliog.

Hopkins, Alfred. *An Architectural Monograph on Fences and Fence Posts of Colonial Times.* St. Paul: White Pine Bureau, 1922. 16 pp., illus. ◆ White Pines Series of Architectural Monographs, 8:6. Includes fences, gates and fence posts.

Hubbard, Henry V., and Theodora Kimball. *An Introduction to the Study of Landscape Design.* Rev. ed. 1929. Reprint. Boston: Hubbard Educational Trust, 1959. 419 pp., illus., plates, bibliog.

Jackson, John Brinckerhoff. *American Space: The Centennial Years, 1865–1876.* New York: Norton, c1972. 254 pp., illus.

Jakle, John A. *Past Landscapes: A Bibliography for Historic Preservationists Selected from the Literature of Historical Geography.* Monticello, Ill.: Council of Planning Librarians, 1974. 56 pp. ◆ Exchange Bibliography no. 651.

Jellicoe, Geoffrey A., and Susan Jellicoe. *The Landscape of Man: Shaping the Environment from Prehistory to the Present Day.* New York: Viking Press, 1975. 383 pp., illus., bibliog. notes. ◆ Includes section on American landscape architecture.

Kassler, Elizabeth Bauer. *Modern Gardens and the Landscape.* New York: Museum of Modern Art, distr. by Doubleday, Garden City, c1964. 96 pp., illus.

Laurie, Michael. *An Introduction to Landscape Architecture.* New York: American Elsevier Pub. Co., c1975. 214 pp., illus., bibliog., index.

The Man-made Landscape. Prepared in cooperation with the International Federation of Landscape Architects. Paris: UNESCO, 1977. 178 pp., illus., bibliogs. ◆ Museums and Monuments—X.

Martin, George A. *Fences, Gates and Bridges: A Practical Manual.* 1887. Reprint. Brattleboro, Vt.: Stephen Greene Press, 1974. 191 pp., illus. ◆ Description of fences and other landscape structures; new foreword and index.

Matthews, William Henry. *Mazes and Labyrinths: Their History and Development.* 1922. Reprint. New York: Dover Publications, 1970. 253 pp., illus., bibliog., appendix.

Nelson, John A. *History of Landscape Architecture from Western Traditions Since 1800.* Monticello, Ill.: Council of Planning Librarians, September 1977. 15 pp. ◆ Exchange Bibliography no. 1355.

Newton, Norman T. *Design on the Land: The Development of Landscape Architecture.* Cambridge, Mass.: Belknap Press of Harvard University Press, 1971. 714 pp., illus., map, plans, bibliog.

Nichols, Frederick D., and Ralph E. Griswold. *Thomas Jefferson, Landscape Architect.* Charlottesville: University Press of Virginia, 1978. 196 pp., illus., bibliog., index.

Olmsted, Frederick Law. *Frederick Law Olmsted, Landscape Architect, 1822–1903.* Edited by Frederick Law Olmsted, Jr., and Theodora Kimball. 1922–28. Reprint. New York: Benjamin Blom, 1970. 2 vols. in 1 (131, 575 pp.), illus., bibliog., maps. ◆ *Forty Years of Landscape Architecture,* 1922 edition half title. Volume 2 on Central Park, published 1928 by Putnam, New York, also reprinted by MIT Press, 1973.

Olmsted, Frederick Law. *Landscape into Cityscape: Frederick Law Olmsted's Plans for a Greater New York City.* Edited and with an introductory essay and notes by Albert Fein. Ithaca, N.Y.: Cornell University Press, c1967,

1968. 490 pp., illus., maps, plans, bibliog. footnotes. ◆ Cornell Reprints in Urban Studies.

Reed, Henry Hope, and Sophia Duckworth. *Central Park: A History and Guide.* 2nd rev. ed. New York: Clarkson N. Potter, c1967, 1972. 166 pp., illus., maps, appendices, bibliog.

Roper, Laura Wood. *FLO: A Biography of Frederick Law Olmsted.* Baltimore: Johns Hopkins University Press, 1973. 555 pp., illus., appendix, bibliog. references, index.

Schmidt, Carl F. *Fences, Gates and Garden Houses.* Rochester, N.Y.: 1963. 106 pp., illus., drawings, diagrams, index. ◆ Available from Landmark Society of Western New York.

Scott, Frank J. *Victorian Gardens: The Art of Beautifying Suburban Home and Grounds, A Victorian Guidebook of 1870.* Watkins Glen, N.Y.: American Life Foundation, 1977. 274 pp., illus.

Simonds, John O. *Landscape Architecture: The Shaping of Man's Natural Environment.* New York: F. W. Dodge Corp., 1961. 244 pp., illus.

Smith, Isadore Leighton Luce [i.e. Ann Leighton]. *American Gardens in the Eighteenth Century: "for Use or for Delight."* Boston: Houghton Mifflin, 1976. 514 pp., illus., bibliog., index.

Smith, Isadore Leighton Luce [i.e. Ann Leighton]. *Early American Gardens: for Meate or Medicine.* Boston: Houghton Mifflin, 1970. 441 pp., illus., bibliog.

Stevenson, Elizabeth. *Park Maker: A Life of Frederick Law Olmsted.* New York: Macmillan, 1977. 484 pp., plates, illus., bibliog. notes.

Stewart, Ian R. *Nineteenth Century American Public Landscape Design.* Monticello, Ill.: Council of Planning Librarians, 1969. 20 pp. ◆ Exchange Bibliography no. 68.

Thacker, Christopher. *The History of Gardens.* Berkeley: University of California Press, 1979. 288 pp., illus., bibliog., index.

Tobey, George B. *A History of Landscape Architecture: The Relationship of People to Environment.* New York: American Elsevier Pub. Co., 1973. 305 pp., illus., bibliog.

Tunnard, Christopher. *Gardens in the Modern Landscape.* 2nd rev. ed. New York:

Scribner's Sons, 1948. 184 pp., illus., bibliog., index.

U.S. Office of Archeology and Historic Preservation. *Landscape Architecture and the Allied Arts: An Annotated Bibliography of Articles and Notes Appearing in the Bulletin or Newsletter of the Association for Preservation Technology.* Compiled by Rebecca L. Keim and Lourie Hammel. Washington, D.C.: U.S. Department of the Interior, National Park Service, 1977. 5 pp. ◆ Technical Preservation Services Reading List; includes additional entries by Andrea Nadel, January 1977.

Vance, Mary. *Landscape, Landscape Architecture and Landscape Gardening: A Selective List of Books.* Monicello, Ill.: Vance Bibliographies, 1980. 61 pp., indexes. ◆ Architecture Series, Bbiliography A197.

Victorian Landscape Gardening: *A Facsimile of Jacob Weidenmann's Beautifying Country Homes.* With a new introduction by David Schuyler. 1870. Reprint. Watkins Glen, N.Y.: American Life Foundation, 1978. 140 pp., illus., diagrams.

Williams, Dorothy Hunt. *Historic Virginia Gardens: Preservations by the Garden Club of Virginia.* Charlottesville: University Press of Virginia, 1975. 350 pp., illus., bibliog.

NOTES

American Landscape Architect. monthly, 1929–1932. American Landscape Architect Co., 608 South Dearborn Street, Chicago, Illinois 60605. ◆ Vols. 1–7 (July 1929–October 1932); no issues for August-September 1932. Indexed in *Art Index.*

American Society of Landscape Architects, Edward H. Able, Jr., Executive Director, 1733 Connecticut Avenue, N.W., Washington, D.C. 20009. Founded in 1899, it is a professional society of landscape architects and is organized into regional chapters. It seeks to strengthen existing and proposed courses in landscape architecture as the official accrediting agency. It offers counsel to new schools, encourages state registration of landscape architects, maintains a traveling exhibition of works of landscape architects. It conducts research, and presents a medal annually for excellence in design. Its committees are Civil Service, National Capital, Historic Preservation, Federal Agency Programs, Private Practice, Public Relations, and Student Affairs. Publications include *Landscape Architecture* (bimonthly); *LAND* (Landscape Architecture News Digest, monthly); *LATIS* (Landscape Architecture Technical Information Series); Handbook of Professional Practice; Membership roster, and monographs. It holds a biennial meeting and convention.

Landscape. 1951, 3/yr., subscription. Box 7107, Berkeley, California 94707.

Landscape Architecture. 1910, bimonthly, subscription. American Society of Landscape Architects, 1190 East Broadway, Louisville, Kentucky 40204.

Urban Design and Planning

Abrams, Charles, and Robert Kolodny. *The Language of Cities: A Glossary of Terms.* New York: Viking Press, Inc., 1971. 365 pp., index.

The American City: *From the Civil War to the New Deal.* By Georgio Ciucci, et al., trans. by Barbara Luigra la Penta. Cambridge, Mass.: MIT Press, c1979. 563 pp., illus., bibliog. references, index.

Bacon, Edmund N. *Design of Cities.* Rev. ed. New York: Penguin, c1974, 1976. 336 pp., illus., maps, diagrams.

Barnett, Jonathan. *An Introduction to Urban Design.* Cambridge and New York: Harper & Row, 1982. 260 pp., illus., index.

Barnett, Jonathan. *Urban Design as Public Policy: Practical Methods for Improving Cities.* New York: Architectural Record Books, 1974. 200 pp., illus.

Berk, Emanuel. *Downtown Improvement Manual.* Chicago: ASPO Press, 1976. 734 pp. in various pagings, illus., bibliog., index.

Burby, Raymond J., III, and Shirley F. Weiss. *New Communities U.S.A.* Lexington, Mass.: Lexington Books, c1976. 593 pp., illus., bibliog., index.

Chapin, F. Stuart, Jr., and Edward J. Kaiser. *Urban Land Use Planning.* 3rd ed. Urbana: University of Illinois Press, c1979. 656 pp., illus., index.

Cullen, Gordon. *The Concise Townscape.* New York: Van Nostrand Reinhold, c1961, 1971. 199 pp., illus., drawings, index.

Cutler, Laurence S., and Sherrie S. Cutler. *Recycling Cities for People—The Urban Design Process.* Boston: CBI Publishing Co., c1976. 250 pp., illus., bibliog., index.

De Chiara, Joseph, and Lee Koppelman. *Urban Planning and Design Criteria.* 3rd ed. New York: Van Nostrand Reinhold, c1982. 732 pp., illus., index.

Dober, Richard P. *Environmental Design.* 1969. Reprint. Huntington, N.Y.: R. E. Krieger Pub. Co., 1975. 278 pp., illus., maps, index.

Eldredge, Hanford Wentworth, ed. *Taming Megalopolis.* Garden City, N.Y.: Anchor Books, 1967. 2 vols. (1166 pp.,), index.

Encyclopedia of Urban Planning. Arnold Whittick, ed. 1974. Reprint. New York: R. E. Krieger Pub. Co., 1980. 1218 pp., illus., bibliog. references, index.

Fishman, Robert. *Urban Utopias in the Twentieth Century: Ebenezer Howard, Frank Lloyd Wright, Le Corbusier.* New York: Basic Books, c1977. 332 pp., illus., bibliog., index.

Gallion, Arthur B., and Simon Eisner. *The Urban Pattern: City Planning and Design.* 3rd ed. New York: Van Nostrand, c1975. 528 pp., illus., bibliog., index.

Geddes, Patrick. *Cities in Evolution: An Introduction to the Town Planning Movement and to the Study of Civics.* 1915. Reprint. New York: H. Fertig, 1968. 409 pp., illus., maps, plans, bibliog.

Gibberd, Frederick. *Town Design.* 5th ed., rev. New York: Praeger Publishers, 1967. 372 pp., illus., plans.

Golany, Gideon. *New Towns Planning and Development: A World-wide Bibliography.* Washington, D.C.: Urban Land Institute, 1973. 256 pp., illus. ◆ ULI Research Report 20. Classified listing of towns from early times to the present; emphasis is on developments in the U.S. and England.

Goodman, Percival, and Paul Goodman. *Communitas: Means of Livelihood and Ways of Life.* 2nd rev. ed. New York: Vintage Books, 1960. 248 pp., illus., appendices.

Halprin, Lawrence B. *Cities.* Rev. ed. Cambridge, Mass.: MIT Press, 1973. 240 pp., illus.

Hayden, Dolores. *Seven American Utopias: The Architecture of Communitarian Socialism, 1790–1975.* Cambridge, Mass.: MIT Press, c1976. 401 pp., illus., bibliog., index.

Hegemann, Werner, and Elbert Peets. *The American Vitruvius: An Architect's Handbook of Civic Art.* 1922. Reprint. New York: Benjamin Blom, 1972. 298 pp., illus., plans, bibliog. ♦ History and case studies of city plans, street design, gardens and parks, and groupings of buildings.

Howard, Ebenezer. *Garden Cities of Tomorrow.* Cambridge, Mass.: MIT Press, 1965. 168 pp., illus.

International City Management Association. *The Practice of Local Government Planning.* Edited by Frank S. So, Israel Stollman, Frank Bead and David S. Arnold. Washington, D.C.: The Association, 1979. 676 pp., illus., maps, bibliog., index.

Jacobs, Jane. *The Death and Life of Great American Cities.* New York: Random House, Vintage Books, 1961. 458 pp., index.

Jacobs, Stephen W., and Barclay G. Jones. *City Design Through Conservation: Methods for the Evaluation and Utilization of Aesthetic and Cultural Resources.* Berkeley, Calif.: University of California, 1960. 2 vols., illus., plans, maps, bibliog. footnotes. ♦ Limited publication; mimeo copies distributed by authors to 100 libraries.

Jeanneret-Gris, Charles Edouard. *The Radiant City: Elements of a Doctrine of Urbanism to be Used as the Basis of Our Machine Age Civilization,* by Le Corbusier [pseud.]. New York: The Orion Press, 1967. 344 pp., illus., maps, plans.

Keller, Suzanne. *The Urban Neighborhood: A Sociological Perspective.* New York: Random House, 1968. 201 pp., bibliog.

Krier, Rob. *Urban=Stadtraum.* Trans. by Christine Czechowski and George Black. New York: Rizzoli International Publications, 1979. 174 pp., illus., bibliog.

Lynch, Kevin. *The Image of the City.* Cambridge, Mass.: MIT Press, c1960, 1966. 194 pp., illus., drawings, diagrams, maps. ♦ Publications of the Joint Center for Urban Studies.

Lynch, Kevin. *Site Planning.* Rev. 2nd ed. Cambridge, Mass.: MIT Press, c1962, 1971. 348 pp., illus., diagrams, bibliog.

Lynch, Kevin. *A Theory of Good City Form.* Cambridge, Mass.: MIT Press, 1981. 504 pp., illus., bibliog., index.

Mumford, Lewis. *The Culture of Cities.* New York: Harcourt, Brace Jovanovich, c1938, 1970. 586 pp., illus., maps, bibliog., index.

Peets, Elbert. *On the Art of Designing Cities: Selected Essays of Elbert Peets.* Edited by Paul D. Spreiregen. Cambridge, Mass.: MIT Press, 1968. 234 pp., illus., map.

Proshansky, Harold M.; William H. Ittleson; and Leeanne G. Rivlin, eds. *Environmental Psychology: People and Their Physical Setting.* 2nd ed. New York: Holt, Rinehart & Winston, c1976. 632 pp., illus., bibliog., indexes.

Rasmussen, Steen Eiler. *Towns and Buildings Described in Drawings and Words.* Cambridge, Mass.: MIT Press, c1951, 1969. 203 pp., illus., maps, plans.

Reps, John W. *Cities of the American West: A History of Frontier Urban Planning.* Princeton, N.J.: Princeton University Press, 1979. 827 pp., illus., bibliog., index.

Reps, John W. *The Making of Urban America: A History of City Planning in the United States.* Princeton, N.J.: Princeton University Press, 1965. 574 pp., illus., maps, plans.

Reps, John W. *Town Planning in Frontier America.* Princeton, N.J.: Princeton University Press, c1965, 1969. 473 pp., illus., diagrams, maps, bibliog., index.

Rifkind, Carole. *Main Street: The Face of Urban America.* New York: Harper & Row, 1977. 267 pp., illus., bibliog., index.

Robinson, Charles Mulford. *Modern Civic Art: Or, the City Made Beautiful.* 4th ed. 1903. Reprint. New York: Arno Press, 1970. 381 pp., illus., maps, plan.

Scott, Mellier Goodin. *American City Planning Since 1890: A History Commemorating the Fiftieth Anniversary of the American Institute of Planners.* Berkeley: University of California Press, 1969. 745 pp., illus., maps, plans, bibliog., index.

Sitte, Camillo. *The Art of Building Cities: City Building According to Its Artistic Fundamentals.* Trans. by Charles T. Stewart. Westport, Conn.: Hyperion Press, c1945, 1979. 128 pp., illus., index.

Spreiregen, Paul D. *Urban Design: The Architecture of Towns and Cities.* New York: McGraw-Hill, 1965. 243 pp., illus., bibliog.

Stein, Clarence S. *Toward New Towns for America.* 3rd ed. Cambridge, Mass.: MIT Press, 1966. 263 pp., illus., maps, bibliog.

Tunnard, Christopher. *The City of Man: A New Approach to the Recovery of Beauty in American Cities.* 2nd ed. New York: Charles Scribner's Sons, 1970. 424 pp., illus., plans, maps, bibliog. references.

Tunnard, Christopher, and Boris Pushkarev. *Man-made America: Chaos or Control: An Inquiry into Selected Problems of Design in the Urbanized Landscape.* New Haven, Conn.: Yale University Press, 1963. 479 pp., illus., maps, bibliog.

Tunnard, Christopher, and Henry Hope Reed. *American Skyline: The Growth and Form of Our Cities and Towns.* New York: New American Library, c1953, 1956. 224 pp., illus., drawings, bibliog., index.

Weber, Max. *The City.* Trans. and edited by Don Martindale and Gertrud Newwirth. New York: Free Press, c1958, 1966. 242 pp., bibliog.

Wright, Frank Lloyd. *The Living City.* New York: Horizon Press, 1958. 222 pp., illus., maps.

Yeates, Maurice, and Barry Garner. *The North American City.* 3rd ed. San Francisco: Harper & Row, c1980. 557 pp., illus., bibliog., index.

Ziegler, Arthur P., Jr., and Walter C. Kidney. *Historic Preservation in Small Towns: A Manual of Practice.* Nashville, Tenn.: American Association for State and Local History, c1980. 146 pp., illus., bibliog., index.

Zucker, Paul. *Town and Square: From the Agora to the Village Green.* Cambridge, Mass.: MIT Press, 1970. 287 pp., plates, figures, bibliog., index.

NOTE

CPL Bibliographies, Council of Planning Librarians, Jean S. Gottlieb, Editor, 1313 East 60th Street, Chicago, Illinois 60637. Begun 1979; succeeds Exchange Bibliographies, 1959–1978. Comprehensive Index to CPL Exchange Bibliographies Nos. 1–1565 (1958–July 1978), in three parts: subject, author, numerical.

Regional Architecture

New England

Architecture in Colonial Massachusetts: *A Conference held by the Colonial Society of Massachusetts, September 10 and 20, 1974.* Boston: The Society; Charlottesville, distr. by University Press of Virginia, 1979. 234 pp., illus., bibliog. references, index. ♦ Publications of the Colonial Society of Massachusetts, vol. 51.

Armstrong, John Borden. *Factory Under the Elms: A History of Harrisville, New Hampshire, 1744–1969.* Cambridge, Mass.: MIT Press, published for the Merrimack Valley Textile Museum, 1969. 320 pp., illus., bibliog.

Boston Society of Architects. *Architecture, Boston.* New York: Clarkson N. Potter, distr. by Crown Publishers, 1976. 192 pp., illus., maps, bibliog., index.

Brown, Elizabeth Mills. *New Haven: A Guide to Architecture and Urban Design.* New Haven, Conn.: Yale University Press, 1976. 228 pp., illus., indexes.

Bunting, Bainbridge. *Houses of Boston's Back Bay: An Architectural History, 1840–1917.* Cambridge, Mass.: Belknap Press of Harvard University Press, 1967. 494 pp., illus., appendix, index.

Cambridge, Mass. Historical Commission. *Survey of Architectural History In Cambridge: Report 1—East Cambridge; Report 2—Mid-Cambridge; Report 3—Cambridgeport; Report 4—Old Cambridge; Report 5—Northwest Cambridge.* Boston: MIT Press for Cambridge, Massachusetts, Historical Commission, 1965–1977. 5 vols., illus., drawings, diagrams, maps, bibliog.

Congdon, Herbert Wheaton. *Old Vermont*

Houses. Peterborough, N.H.: Noone House, 1968. 192 pp., illus., glossary, index.

Coolidge, John. *Mill and Mansion: A Study of Architecture and Society in Lowell, Mass., 1820–1865.* 1942. Reprint. New York: Russell & Russell, 1967. 261 pp., illus., bibliog., index.

Cummings, Abbott Lowell. *The Framed Houses of Massachusetts Bay, 1625–1725.* Cambridge, Mass.: Belknap Press, 1979. 261 pp., illus., bibliog. references, index.

Downing, Antoinette F., and Vincent J. Scully, Jr. *The Architectural Heritage of Newport, Rhode Island, 1640–1912.* 2nd ed., rev. New York: Bramhall House, Clarkson N. Potter, c1952, 1970. 526 pp., illus., drawings, maps, appendices.

Forman, Henry Chandlee. *Early Nantucket and Its Whale Houses.* New York: Hastings House, 1966. 291 pp., illus., bibliog.

Garvan, Anthony. *Architecture and Town Planning in Colonial Connecticut.* New Haven, Conn.: Yale University Press, 1951. 166 pp., illus., bibliog., index.

Garvin, James L. *Historic Portsmouth: Early Photographs from the Collection of Strawbery Banke, Inc.* Somersworth, N.H.: New Hampshire Publishing Co., 1974. 144 pp., illus., bibliog.

Giffen, Daniel H. "Historic American Buildings Survey Catalog, Merrimack and Hillsborough Counties, New Hampshire," *Historical New Hampshire,* 22:3 (Autumn 1967), pp. 2–21.

Greater Portland Landmarks. *Portland.* Portland, Me.: Greater Portland Landmarks, 1973. 236 pp., illus., glossary.

Historic American Buildings Survey. *Historic Buildings of Massachusetts: Photographs from the Historic American Buildings Survey.* New York: Charles Scribner's Sons, c1976. 141 pp., 126 leaves of plates.

Historic American Buildings Survey. *Maine Catalogue: A List of Measured Drawings, Photographs and Written Documentation in the Survey, 1974.* Compiled with an introductory essay "The Historic Architecture of Maine" by Denys Peter Myers. Augusta: Maine State Museum, c1974. 254 pp., illus., bibliog., index.

Historic American Buildings Survey. *New Haven Architecture.* Washington, D.C.: National Park Service, 1970. 159 pp., illus., maps, plans, bibliog. ♦ Selections no. 9.

Hitchcock, Henry-Russell. *Rhode Island Architecture.* 1939. Reprint. New York: DaCapo Press, 1968. 230 pp., illus.

Howells, John Mead. *The Architectural Heritage of the Merrimack: Early Houses and Gardens.* 1941. Reprint. Bowie, Md.: Heritage Books, 1978. 229 pp., illus., index. ♦ Photo essay on architecture, gardens, interiors and details of the river valley in Massachusetts and New Hampshire.

Howells, John Mead. *Architectural Heritage of the Piscataqua: Houses and Gardens of the Portsmouth District of Maine and New Hampshire.* New York: Architectural Book Publishing Co., c1937, 1965. 217 pp., illus.

Isham, Norman M., and Albert F. Brown. *Early Connecticut Houses: An Historical and Architectural Study.* 1900. Reprint. New York: Dover Publications, 1965. 303 pp., drawings, diagrams, maps, bibliog. footnotes, appendices, index.

Kelly, John Frederick. *Early Domestic Architecture of Connecticut.* 1924. Reprint. New York: Dover Publications, 1963. 210 pp., illus., drawings, diagrams, index.

Kuckro, Anne Crofoot. *Hartford Architecture: Hartford Architecture Conservancy Survey.* Hartford, Conn.: The Conservancy, c1978. 3 vols., illus., bibliog., index.

Lancaster, Clay. *The Architecture of Historic Nantucket.* New York: McGraw-Hill, 1972. 286 pp., illus., drawings, diagrams, maps, glossary, list of architects, appendices, bibliog.

Lancaster, Clay. *Nantucket in the Nineteenth Century: 180 Photographs and Illustrations.* New York: Dover Publications, 1979. 125 pp., illus.

"New Hampshire Catalogue, Historic American Buildings Survey, Records in the Library of Congress," *Historical New Hampshire,* 18:2 (October 1963), pp. 1–7.

Tolles, Bryant F., Jr., and Carolyn K. Tolles. *New Hampshire Architecture: An Illustrated Guide.* Hanover, N.H.: Published for the New Hampshire Historical Society by the University Press of New England, 1979. 393 pp., illus., bibliog., indexes.

Tucci, Douglass S. *Built in Boston: City and Suburb, 1800–1950.* 1st ed. Boston: New York Graphic Society, 1978. 269 pp., illus., bibliog., index.

Middle Atlantic

American Institute of Architects, New York Chapter. *AIA Guide to New York City.* Norval White and Elliot Willensky, editors. Rev. ed. New York: Macmillan, 1978. 653 pp., illus., maps, indexes.

Bailey, Rosalie Fellows. *Pre-Revolutionary Dutch Houses and Families in Northern New Jersey and Southern New York.* 1936. Reprint. New York: Dover Publications, 1968. 612 pp., illus., genealogical index, bibliog.

Buffalo Architecture: A Guide. Reyner Banham, et al. Cambridge, Mass.: MIT Press, c1981. 336 pp., bibliog., index.

Burnham, Alan, ed. *New York Landmarks: A Study and Index of Architecturally Notable Structures in Greater New York.* Middletown, Conn.: Published under the auspices of the Municipal Art Society of New York by Wesleyan University Press, c1963, 1970. 430 pp., illus., bibliog., indexes.

District of Columbia Catalog, 1974. Compiled by Nancy B. Schwartz. Charlottesville, Va.: Published for the Columbia Historical Society by the University Press of Virginia, 1976. 193 pp., illus., index.

Dorsey, John R., and James D. Dilts. *A Guide to Baltimore Architecture.* 2nd ed., rev. and enl. Centreville, Md.: Tidewater Publishers in cooperation with the Peale Museum, 1981. 327 pp., illus., maps, glossary, appendices, indexes.

Dutchess County Planning Board. *Landmarks of Dutchess County, 1683–1867: Architecture Worth Saving in New York State.* New York: New York State Council on the Arts, 1969. 242 pp., illus., maps.

Eberlein, Harold Donaldson. *Historic Houses and Buildings of Delaware.* 2nd ed. By Harold Donaldson Eberlein and Cortlandt Van Dyke Hubbard. Dover, Del.: Public Archives Commission, c1962, 1963. 227 pp., illus., maps, plans.

Eberlein, Harold Donaldson. *Historic Houses of George-Town and Washington City.* By Harold Donaldson Eberlein and Cortlandt Van Dyke Hubbard. Richmond, Va.: Dietz Press, 1958. 480 pp., illus., map, bibliog.

Eberlein, Harold Donaldson. *Manor Houses and Historic Homes of Long Island and Staten Island.* Port Washington, N.Y.: Ira J. Friedman, Inc., c1928, 1966. 318 pp., illus. ◆ Empire State Historical Publications Series no. 40.

Everest, Allan S. *Our North Country Heritage: Architecture Worth Saving in Clinton and Essex Counties.* Plattsburgh, N.Y.: Tundra Books, 1972. 143 pp., illus., maps, glossary, appendices, bibliog.

Foerster, Bernd. *Architecture Worth Saving in Rensselaer County, New York.* Troy, N.Y.: Rensselaer Polytechnic Institute, 1965. 207 pp., illus., bibliog.

Forman, Henry. *Early Manor and Plantation Houses of Maryland.* Easton, Md.: The Author, 1934. 271 pp.

Forman, Henry Chandlee. *Maryland Architecture: A Short History from 1634 through the Civil War.* Cambridge, Md.: Tidewater Publishers, 1968. 102 pp., illus., drawings, bibliog., glossary.

Forman, Henry Chandlee. *Old Buildings, Gardens, and Furniture in Tidewater Maryland.* Cambridge, Md.: Tidewater Publishers, 1967. 326 pp., illus., drawings.

Forman, Henry Chandlee. *Tidewater Maryland Architecture and Gardens.* New York: Architectural Book Publishing Co., 1956. 208 pp., illus., bibliog. ◆ Sequel to or continuation of *Early Manor and Plantation Houses* (cited above), first published survey of the state's historic buildings. Part of author's Maryland Trilogy, with *Maryland Architecture . . .* , and *Old Buildings, Gardens . . .* , cited above.

Gayle, Margot. *Cast-Iron Architecture in New York: A Photographic Survey.* New York: Dover Publications, 1974. 190 pp., illus., maps, index.

Goldberger, Paul. *The City Observed: New York, A Guide to the Architecture of Manhattan.* New York: Random House, 1979. 347 pp., illus., index.

Goldstone, Harmon H., and Martha Dalrymple. *History Preserved: A Guide to New York City Landmarks and Historic Districts.* New

York: Simon & Schuster, 1974. 576 pp., illus., bibliog.

Gowans, Alan. *Architecture in New Jersey, A Record of American Civilization.* Princeton, N.J.: D. Van Nostrand Co., 1964. 161 pp., illus., bibliog., index. ◆ New Jersey Historical Series vol. 6.

Greiff, Constance M.; Mary W. Gibbons; and Elizabeth G. C. Menzies. *Princeton Architecture: A Pictorial History of Town and Campus.* Princeton, N.J.: Princeton University Press, 1967. 200 pp., illus., glossary, bibliog., index.

A Guide to the Architecture of Washington, D.C. Written and edited by Warren J. Cox and others, for the Washington Metropolitan Chapter of the American Institute of Architects. 2nd ed., rev. and expanded. New York: McGraw-Hill, 1974. 246 pp., illus., bibliog. references.

Historic American Buildings, New York. Introduction by David G. DeLong. New York: Garland Publishing Co., 1979–. 8 vols., chiefly illus., bibliog. references, index. ◆ Includes reproductions of the drawings in the Historic American Buildings Survey.

Historic American Buildings Survey. *New Jersey Catalog: A List of Measured Drawings, Photographs and Written Documentation in the Survey.* Compiled by William B. Bassett; edited by John Poppeliers. Newark: New Jersey Historical Society, 1977. 210 pp., illus.

Historic American Buildings Survey. *Philadelphia Preserved: Catalog of the Historic American Buildings Survey.* By Richard J. Webster. Philadelphia, Pa.: Temple University Press, 1976. 411 pp., 33 leaves of plates, illus., bibliog. references, index.

Historic American Buildings Survey. *Washington, D.C. Architecture—Market Square.* Washington, D.C.: National Park Service, 1969. 151 pp., illus. ◆ Selections from the Historic American Buildings Survey no. 8.

Huxtable, Ada Louise. *The Architecture of New York: A History and Guide.* Garden City, N.Y.: Anchor Books, 1964–. 1 vol., illus., glossary, bibliog., index. ◆ Vol. 1—*Classic New York: Georgian Gentility to Greek Elegance.* 142 pp.

Jacobs, Stephen W. *Wayne County, The Aesthetic Heritage of a Rural Area: A Catalog for the Environment.* Lyons, N.Y.: Wayne County Historical Society, distr. by Publishing Center for Cultural Resources, c1979. 287 pp., illus., maps, bibliog.

Lancaster, Clay. *Old Brooklyn Heights: New York's First Suburb, Including Detailed Analyses of 619 Century-Old Houses.* 2nd ed., with a supplement of new photos. By Edmund V. Gillon, Jr. New York: Dover Publications, 1979. 223 pp., illus., bibliog., index.

Maddex, Diane. *Historic Buildings of Washington, D.C.* Pittsburgh, Pa.: Ober Park Associates, Inc., 1973. 192 pp., illus., bibliog., appendix, index.

Malo, Paul. *Landmarks of Rochester and Monroe County: A Guide to Neighborhoods and Villages.* Syracuse, N.Y.: Syracuse University Press, 1974. 277 pp., illus., bibliog., appendices.

New York (State). Office of Planning Coordination. The Metropolitan New York District Office. *Long Island Landmarks.* Albany, N.Y.: New York State Office of Planning Coordination, 1969. 122 pp., illus., maps, appendix—Architectural Landmark Evaluation and Index.

Onondaga Landmarks: *A Survey of Historic and Architectural Sites in Syracuse and Onondaga County.* Prepared by the Syracuse-Onondaga County Planning Agency. Rev. ed. Syracuse, N.Y.: Cultural Resources Council of Syracuse and Onondaga County, 1981. 111 pp., illus., maps, appendix.

Philadelphia Art Alliance. *Philadelphia Architecture in the 19th Century.* Theo B. White, ed. By William P. Harbeson and others. 2nd rev. ed. Philadelphia: Art Alliance Press, 1973. 36 [86] pp., illus.

Philadelphia Museum of Art. *Two Centuries of Philadelphia Architectural Drawings.* Catalogue of the Exhibit held at the Philadelphia Museum of Art by the Society of Architectural Historians. James C. Massey, editor. Philadelphia: 1964. 112 pp., illus., plans, bibliog. references.

Prokopoff, Stephen S., and Joan C. Siegfried. *The Nineteenth-Century Architecture of Saratoga Springs: Architecture Worth Saving in New York State.* New York: New York State Council on the Arts, 1970. 104 pp., illus.

Raymond, Eleanor. *Early Domestic Architecture of Pennsylvania.* With a new introduction by John Miner. Princeton, N.J.: Pyne Press, c1931, 1973. 1 vol., unpaged, illus., measured drawings.

Reynolds, Helen Wilkinson. *Dutch Houses in the Hudson Valley Before 1776.* 1929. Reprint. New York: Dover Publications, 1965. 467 pp., illus., maps, index.

Sanchis, Frank E. *American Architecture, Westchester County, New York: Colonial to Contemporary.* Croton-on-Hudson, N.Y.: North River Press, 1977. 563 pp., illus., indexes.

Schmidt, Carl F. *Greek Revival Architecture in the Rochester Area.* Scottsville, N.Y.: C. F. Schmidt, 1946. 200 pp., illus., measured drawings, appendix.

Schull, Diantha Dow. *Landmarks of Otsego County.* Syracuse, N.Y.: Syracuse University Press, 1980. 285 pp., illus., map.

Shelgren, Olaf W.; Cary Lattin; and Robert W. Frasch. *Cobblestone Landmarks of New York State.* Syracuse, N.Y.: Syracuse University Press, 1978. 163 pp., illus.

Stotz, Charles Morse. *The Architectural Heritage of Early Western Pennsylvania: A Record of Buildings Before 1860.* Pittsburgh: University of Pittsburgh Press, 1966. 293 pp., illus.

Syracuse University. School of Architecture. *Architecture Worth Saving in Onondaga County.* New York: New York State Council on the Arts, 1964. 202 pp., illus., drawings, diagrams, maps.

Tatum, George B. *Penn's Great Town: 250 Years of Philadelphia Architecture Illustrated in Prints and Drawings.* Philadelphia: University of Pennsylvania Press, 1961. 352 pp., plates, bibliog., index.

Teitelman, Edward and Richard W. Longstreth. *Architecture in Philadelphia.* Cambridge, Mass.: MIT Press, 1974. 284 pp., illus., bibliog.

U.S. Commission of Fine Arts. *Georgetown Commercial Architecture, M Street, Northwest Washington, District of Columbia.* Issued jointly by the Commission and Historic American Buildings Survey. Arlington, Va.: Washington Planning and Service Center, 1967. 130 pp., illus. ◆ Historic American Buildings Survey Selections no. 2. See also: *Georgetown Commercial Architecture—Wisconsin Avenue . . . ,* HABS Selections no. 3, 1967, 108

pp.; *Georgetown Architecture—The Waterfront . . . ,* HABS Selections no. 4, 1968, 297 pp.; *Georgetown Residential Architecture—Northeast . . . ,* HABS Selections no. 5, 1969, 233 pp.; *Georgetown Architecture—Northwest . . . ,* HABS Selections no. 6, 1971, 661 pp.; *Georgetown Architecture—Northwest Washington . . . ,* HABS Selections no. 10, 1970, 291 pp.

U.S. Commission of Fine Arts and Office of Archeology and Historic Preservation. *Georgetown Historic Waterfront, Washington, D.C.: A Review of Canal and Riverside Architecture.* Washington, D.C.: for sale by Supt. of Docs., U.S. Government Printing Office, 1968. 92 pp., illus., maps, plans, bibliog. ◆ Written by Constance W. Werner from research by Daniel D. Reiff, and architectural analysis by William R. Gwinn.

U.S. Commission of Fine Arts. *Massachusetts Avenue Architecture, Volume I, Northwest Washington, District of Columbia.* Washington, D.C.: Commission of Fine Arts, 1973. 472 pp., illus., bibliog., glossary.

Van Trump, James D., and Arthur P. Ziegler, Jr. *Landmark Architecture of Allegheny County, Pennsylvania.* Pittsburgh: Pittsburgh History and Landmarks Foundation, 1967. 294 pp., illus., maps, bibliog.

Villas on the Hudson: *A Collection of Photo-Lithographs of Thirty-one Country Residences.* 1860. Reprint. New York: DaCapo Press, 1977. 10, 53 pp., chiefly illus.

South

Andrews, Wayne. *Pride of the South: A Social History of Southern Architecture.* New York: Atheneum, 1979. 181 pp., illus., bibliog., index.

The Architectural Legacy of the Lower Chattahoochee Valley in Alabama and Georgia. D. Gregory Jeane, ed.; Douglas C. Purcell, associate ed., et al. University: Published for the Historic Chattahoochee Commission by the University of Alabama Press, c1978. 280 pp., illus., bibliog., index.

Brumbaugh, Thomas B.; Martha I. Strayhorn; and Gary G. Gore, eds. *Architecture of Middle Tennessee: The Historic American Buildings Survey.* Nashville, Tenn.: Vanderbilt University Press, 1974. 170 pp., illus., drawings, bibliog.

Cerwinske, Laura. *Tropical Deco: The Architecture and Design of Old Miami Beach.* New York: Rizzoli, 1981. 95 pp., illus., bibliog.

Cochran, Gifford A. *Grandeur in Tennessee: Classical Revival Architecture in a Pioneer State.* New York: J. J. Augustin, 1946. 132 pp., illus., bibliog.

Coffin, Lewis A., Jr., and Arthur C. Holden. *Brick Architecture of the Colonial Period in Maryland and Virginia.* 1919. Reprint. New York: Dover Publications, 1970. 29 pp., 118 plates, illus., plans, bibliog.

Crocker, Mary Wallace. *Historic Architecture in Mississippi.* Jackson: University and College Press of Mississippi, c1973. 194 pp., illus., appendix, notes, bibliog. references.

Davidson, William H. *Pine Log and Greek Revival: Houses and People of Three Counties in Georgia and Alabama.* Alexander City, Ala.: Outlook Publishing Co., 1964. 396 pp., illus., diagrams, maps. ♦ Chattahoochee Valley Historical Society Publication no. 6.

Dulaney, Paul S. *The Architecture of Historic Richmond.* Charlottesville: University Press of Virginia, 1976. 218 pp., illus., maps, appendices, index.

Forman, Henry Chandlee. *The Architecture of the Old South: The Medieval Style, 1585–1850.* New York: Russell & Russell, c1948, 1967. 203 pp., illus., diagrams, bibliog.

Forman, Henry Chandlee. *Virginia Architecture in the Seventeenth Century.* Williamsburg: Virginia 350th Anniversary Celebration Corp., 1957. 79 pp., illus., bibliog.

Hammond, Ralph. *Ante-Bellum Mansions of Alabama.* New York: Architectural Book Publishing Co., 1951. 196 pp., illus.

Historic American Buildings Survey. *Historic Architecture of the Virgin Islands.* 1966. Reprint. Springfield, Va.: 1970? 1 vol., unpaged. ♦ Historic American Buildings Survey Selections no. 1.

Historic American Buildings Survey. *Records of Buildings in Charleston and the South Carolina Low Country.* Harley J. McKee, comp. Philadelphia: Eastern Office, Design and Construction, National Park Service, 1965. 26 pp., photocopy.

Historic American Buildings Survey. *Virginia Catalog: A List of Measured Drawings, Photographs, and Written Documentation in the Survey.* Compiled by Virginia Historic Landmarks Commission and the Historic American Buildings Survey. Charlottesville: Published for the Historic American Buildings Survey by the University Press of Virginia, 1976. 461 pp., illus.

Historic Savannah Foundation, Inc. *Historic Savannah: Survey of Significant Buildings in the Historic and Victorian Districts of Savannah, Georgia.* Edited by Mary L. Morrison, 2nd ed. Savannah: Historic Savannah Foundation, The Junior League of Savannah, 1979. 299 pp., illus., maps, indexes.

Johnston, Frances Benjamin. *The Early Architecture of North Carolina: A Pictorial Survey.* With an architectural history by Thomas Tilton Waterman. Chapel Hill: University of North Carolina Press, c1947, 1958. 290 pp., illus., diagrams, maps, index.

Lancaster, Clay. *Antebellum Houses of the Bluegrass.* Lexington: University of Kentucky Press, 1961. 186 pp., 34 plates, illus., drawings, map, glossary, bibliog.

Lancaster, Clay. *Eutaw: The Builders and Architecture of an Ante-Bellum Southern Town.* Eutaw, Ala.: Greene County Historical Society, c1979. 208 pp., illus., bibliog. references, index.

Lancaster, Clay. *Vestiges of the Venerable City: A Chronicle of Lexington, Kentucky, Its Architectural Development and Survey of Its Early Streets and Antiquities.* Lexington, Ky.: Lexington-Fayette County Historic Commission, c1978. 282 pp., illus., bibliog., index.

Linley, John. *Architecture of Middle Georgia: The Oconee Area.* Athens: University of Georgia Press, 1972. 194 pp., illus., maps, plans, bibliog., index.

Lyle, Royster, Jr., and Pamela Hemenway Simpson. *The Architecture of Historic Lexington.* Charlottesville: Published for the Historic Lexington Foundation by the University Press of Virginia, 1977. 314 pp., illus., bibliog., index.

Manucy, Albert. *The Houses of St. Augustine: Notes on the Architecture from 1565 to 1821.* St. Augustine, Fla.: St. Augustine Historical Society, 1962. 179 pp., illus., bibliog.

Morgan, William. *Louisville: Architecture and the Urban Environment.* Dublin, N.H.: W. L. Bauhan, 1979. 96 pp., illus.

Mumford, Lewis. *The South in Architecture.* 1941. Reprint. New York: DaCapo Press, 1967. 147 pp.

New Orleans Architecture. Text by Samuel Wilson, Jr. and Bernard Lemann. Compiled and edited by Mary Louise Christovich, Roulhac Toledano, and Betty Swanson. Gretna, La.: Friends of the Cabildo, distr. by Pelican Pub. Co., 1971–1981. 6 vols., illus., plates, bibliog., inventory of architects, index.

Newcomb, Rexford. *Architecture in Old Kentucky.* Urbana: University of Illinois Press, 1953. 185 pp., illus., bibliog.

Nichols, Frederick D. *The Architecture of Georgia.* Photos by Van Jones Martin and Frances Benjamin Johnston; drawings by Frederick Spitzmiller; special research by Elizabeth MacGregor; edited by Mills Lane. Savannah, Ga.: Beehive Press, c1976. 436 pp., illus., bibliog. references, index.

O'Neal, William Bainter. *Architecture in Virginia: An Official Guide to Four Centuries of Building in the Old Dominion.* New York: Walker & Co., for the Virginia Museum, 1968. 192 pp., illus., maps, bibliog.

Overdyke, William Darrell. *Louisiana Plantation Homes: Colonial and Antebellum.* New York: Architectural Book Pub. Co., 1965. 206 pp., illus.

Patrick, James A. *Architecture in Tennessee, 1768–1897.* Photography by Michael A. Tomlan. Knoxville: University of Tennessee Press, 1981. 273 pp., illus.

Sawyer, Elizabeth M., and Jane Foster. *The Old in New Atlanta: A Directory of Houses, Buildings, and Churches Built Prior to 1915, Still Standing in Atlanta and Environs.* Atlanta, Ga.: JEMS Publications, c1976. 134 pp., illus., bibliog., index.

Severens, Kenneth. *Southern Architecture: 350 Years of Distinctive American Buildings.* New York: E.P. Dutton, 1981. 208 pp., illus., bibliog. references, index.

Simons, Albert, and Samuel Lapham, Jr., eds. *The Early Architecture of Charleston: Introduction by Samuel Gaillard Stoney.* 2nd ed. 1927. Reprint. Columbia: University of South Carolina Press, 1970. 223 pp., illus., drawings, plans, maps, bibliog., index.

Smith, Eugenia B. *Centreville, Virginia, Its History and Architecture.* Fairfax, Va.: Fairfax County Office of Planning, 1973. 117 pp., illus., bibliog., appendices.

Smith, Joseph Frazer. *White Pillars: Early Life and Architecture of the Lower Mississippi Valley Country.* New York: W. Helburn, Inc., 1941. 252 pp., illus., diagrams, bibliog.

Stoney, Samuel Gaillard. *Plantations of the Carolina Low Country.* 7th rev. ed. Edited by Albert Simons and Samuel Lapham, Jr. Intro. by John Mead Howells. Charleston, S.C.: Carolina Art Association, 1977. 247 pp., illus, diagrams, maps, bibliog.

Stoney, Samuel Gaillard. *This is Charleston: A Survey of the Architectural Heritage of a Unique American City.* Rev. ed. Charleston, S.C.: Carolina Art Association, 1976. 139 pp., illus., maps.

Virginia. Historic Landmarks Commission. *Virginia Landmarks Register.* 2nd ed. Richmond, Va.: The Commission, 1976. 216 pp.

Waterman, Thomas T. *The Mansions of Virginia, 1706–1776.* Chapel Hill: University of North Carolina Press, 1946. 456 pp., illus., diagrams, glossary, bibliog., index.

Waterman, Thomas T., and John A. Barrows. *Domestic Colonial Architecture of Tidewater Virginia.* 1932. Reprint. New York: Dover Publications, 1969. 191 pp., illus., drawings, diagrams, glossary, index.

Wells, Sharon. *Portraits, Wooden Houses of Key West.* Key West, Fla.: Historic Key West Preservation Board, Florida Department of State, 1979. 64 pp., illus., bibliog.

Whiffen, Marcus. *The Eighteenth Century Houses of Williamsburg: A Study of Architecture and Building in the Colonial Capital of Virginia.* Williamsburg, Va.: Colonial Williamsburg, distr. by Holt, Rinehart & Winston, c1960, 1969. 223 pp., illus., drawings, diagrams, bibliog. notes, index.

Midwest

American Institute of Architects. Columbus Chapter. Foundation. *Architecture: Columbus.*

A Project of the Foundation of the Columbus Chapter of the American Institute of Architects. Robert E. Samuelson, Project Director. 1st ed. Columbus, Ohio: The Foundation, 1976. 305 pp., illus., maps, bibliog., index.

American Institute of Architects. Kansas City Chapter. *Kansas City.* Kansas City, Mo.: Kansas City Chapter, American Institute of Architects, c1979. 256 pp., illus., maps, indexes.

Campen, Richard N. *Ohio—An Architectural Portrait.* Chagrin Falls, Ohio: West Summit Press, 1973. 320 pp., illus., maps, bibliog. references, index.

Chicago's Famous Buildings: A Photographic Guide to the City's Architectural Landmarks and Other Notable Buildings. 3rd ed., rev. and enl. Edited by Ira J. Bach, with the assistance of Roy Forrey. Chicago: University of Chicago Press, 1980. 265 pp., bibliog., indexes.

Detroit Architecture: A.I.A. Guide. Katherine Mattingly Meyer, ed.; American Institute of Architects, Detroit Chapter. Rev. ed. Martin C.P. McElroy, ed. Detroit: Wayne State University Press, 1980. 264 pp., illus., maps, index.

Drury, John. *Historic Midwest Houses.* Chicago: University of Chicago Press, c1947, 1977. 246 pp., illus., maps, index.

Drury, John. *Old Illinois Houses.* 1948. Reprint. Chicago: University of Chicago Press, c1941, 1977. 220 pp., illus., index. ◆ Reprint of 1948 edition published by Illinois State Historical Society in a series as Publication no. 51.

Ehrlich, George. *Kansas City, Missouri, An Architectural History, 1826–1976.* Kansas City, Mo.: Historic Kansas City Foundation, c1979. 185 pp., illus., bibliog., index.

Ferry, W. Hawkins. *The Buildings of Detroit: A History.* Rev. ed. Detroit: Wayne State University Press, 1980. 498 pp., illus., index.

Frary, Ihna Thayer. *Early Homes of Ohio.* 1936. Reprint. New York: Dover Publications, 1970. 334 pp., illus., drawings, diagrams, appendix, bibliog., index.

Gebhard, David, and Tom Martinson. *A Guide to the Architecture of Minnesota.* Minneapolis: Published by the University of Minnesota Press for the University Gallery of the University of Minnesota and the Minnesota Society of Architects, c1977. 469 pp., illus., bibliog., index.

Historic American Buildings Survey. *Historic American Buildings Survey: Chicago and Nearby Illinois Areas, List of Measured Drawings, Photographs and Written Documentation in the Survey 1966.* Compiled and edited by the Historic American Buildings Survey, Eastern Office, Design and Construction, National Park Service, Department of the Interior. J. William Rudd, comp. Park Forest, Ill.: The Prairie School Press, 1966. 52 pp., illus., drawings, diagrams, index.

Historic American Buildings Survey. *Indiana Catalog: A List of Measured Drawings, Photographs, and Written Documentation in the Survey.* Compiled by William P. Thompson; edited by Nancy K. Beinke. Preliminary ed. Washington, D.C.: Historic American Buildings Survey, Division of Architecture, Office of Archeology and Historic Preservation, National Park Service, U.S. Department of the Interior, 1971. 54 pp.

Historic American Buildings Survey. *The Iowa Catalog: Historic American Buildings Survey.* Compiled by Wesley I. Shank. Iowa City: University of Iowa Press, 1979. 158 pp., illus., bibliog. references, index.

Historic American Buildings Survey. *Michigan: List of Measured Drawings, Photographs, and Documentation in the Survey of 1965, and Complete Listings of Michigan's HABS Records.* Harley J. McKee, comp. Lansing: Historical Society of Michigan and Detroit Society of Architects, 1965. 65 pp., illus., bibliog. footnotes.

Historic American Buildings Survey. *Wisconsin Architecture: A Catalog of Buildings Represented in the Library of Congress with Illustrations from Measured Drawings.* Narrative by Richard W. E. Perrin. Washington, D.C.: U.S. Government Printing Office, 1966. 80 pp., illus., measured drawings, diagrams, maps, bibliog.

Indianapolis Architecture. By Rick A. Ball, et al. Indianapolis: Architectural Foundation, c1975. 261 pp., illus., bibliog.

Johannesen, Eric. *Cleveland Architecture, 1876–1976.* Cleveland, Ohio: Western Reserve Historical Society, 1979. 268 pp., illus., diagrams.

Keyes, Margaret N. *Nineteenth Century Home Architecture of Iowa City.* Iowa City: University of Iowa Press, 1966. 126 pp., illus., glossary, bibliog.

Kidney, Walter C. *Historic Buildings of Ohio: A Selection from the Records of the Historic American Buildings Survey, National Park Service.* Pittsburgh, Pa.: Ober Park Associates, Inc., 1972. 130 pp., illus., measured drawings, diagrams, maps, bibliog. notes, index.

Koeper, Frederick. *Illinois Architecture from Territorial Times to the Present: A Selective Guide.* Chicago: University of Chicago Press, 1968. 304 pp., illus.

Koeper, H. F. *Historic St. Paul Buildings: A Report of the Historic Sites Committee, A Special Citizens Group Named by the St. Paul City Planning Board.* St. Paul, Minn.: St. Paul City Planning Board, 1964. 116 pp., illus.

McCue, George. *The Building Art in St. Louis: Two Centuries, A Guide to the Architecture of the City and Its Environs.* Rev. and enl. ed. St. Louis, Mo.: St. Louis Chapter, American Institue of Architects, 1967. 104 pp., illus., maps.

Madden, Betty I. *Arts, Crafts, and Architecture in Early Illinois.* Urbana: University of Illinois Press, 1974. 297 pp., illus., appendices, bibliog., index.

Minneapolis. Institute of Arts. *A Century of Minnesota Architecture.* Organized by the Minneapolis Institute of Arts as a contribution to the Minnesota Statehood Centennial. . . . Selection of architectural monuments and text by Donald R. Torbert. Minneapolis: Minneapolis Society of Fine Arts, 1958. 64 pp., illus.

Newcomb, Rexford. *Architecture of the Old Northwest Territory: A Study of Early Architecture in Ohio, Indiana, Illinois, Michigan, Wisconsin and Part of Minnesota.* Chicago: University of Chicago Press, 1950. 775 pp., plates, glossary, bibliog., index.

Oringderff, Barbara. *True Sod: Sod Houses of Kansas.* North Newton, Kans.: Mennonite Press, c1976. 168 pp., illus., bibliog.

Peat, Wilbur D. *Indiana Houses of the Nineteenth Century.* Indianapolis: Indiana Historical Society, 1962. 195 pp., illus.

Perrin, Richard W. E. *The Architecture of Wisconsin.* Madison: State Historical Society of Wisconsin, 1967. 175 pp., illus., bibliog. references.

Perrin, Richard W. E. *Historic Wisconsin Buildings: A Survey of Pioneer Architecture*

1835–1870. 2nd ed., rev. Milwaukee, Wisc.: Milwaukee Public Museum Press, 1981. 123 pp., illus., index.

Peterson, Charles E. *The Houses of French St. Louis.* Urbana: University of Illinois Press, 1965. 40 pp., illus. ◆ Reprinted from *The French in the Mississippi Valley,* edited by John Francis McDermott (Urbana: University of Illinois Press, 1965).

Randall, Frank Alfred. *History of the Development of Building Construction in Chicago.* 1949. Reprint. New York: Arno Press, 1972. 388 pp.

Schmitt, Peter, and Balthazar Korab. *Kalamazoo: Nineteenth-Century Homes in a Midwestern Village.* Kalamazoo, Mich.: Kalamazoo City Historical Commission, c1976. 240 pp., illus.

Scott, James Allen. *Duluth's Legacy—Volume 1, Architecture.* Duluth, Minn.: City of Duluth, Office of the Department of Research and Planning, c1974. 165 pp., illus., maps, index of architects.

Skjelver, Mabel Cooper. *Nineteenth Century Homes of Marshall, Michigan.* Marshall, Mich.: Marshall Historical Society, 1971. 208 pp., illus., drawings, maps, bibliog., index.

Tallmadge, Thomas E. *Architecture in Old Chicago.* 1941. Reprint. Chicago: University of Chicago Press, 1975. 218 pp., illus., notes, index.

van Ravenswaay, Charles. *The Art and Architecture of German Settlements in Missouri: A Survey of a Vanishing Culture.* Columbia: University of Missouri Press, 1977. 533 pp., plates, illus., bibliog., index.

Wilson, Richard Guy, and Sidney K. Robinson. *The Prairie School in Iowa.* Ames: Iowa State University Press, 1977. 127 pp., illus., bibliog. references.

Southwest

Alexander, Drury Blakeley. *Texas Homes of the Nineteenth Century.* Austin: University of Texas Press for the Amon Carter Museum of Western Art, 1966. 276 pp., plates, bibliog.

Barnstone, Howard. *The Galveston That Was.* New York: Macmillan, 1966. 224 pp., illus.

Bunting, Bainbridge. *Early Architecture in New Mexico.* 1st ed. Albuquerque: University of New Mexico Press, c1976. 122 pp., bibliog., index.

Bunting, Bainbridge. *Taos Adobes: Spanish Colonial and Territorial Architecture of the Taos Valley.* Santa Fe: Museum of New Mexico Press, 1964. 80 pp., illus.

Clark, Anne, comp. *Historic Homes of San Augustine.* Edited by Carolyn Allen. Austin, Tex.: San Augustine Historical Society, 1972. 72 pp., illus., bibliog.

Conron, John P., and Anthony Alofson. *Socorro, A Historic Survey.* Albuquerque: University of New Mexico Press, c1980. 124 pp., illus., bibliog. references.

Current, William, and Vincent Scully. *Pueblo Architecture of the Southwest: A Photographic Essay.* Austin: University of Texas Press for the Amon Carter Museum of Western Art, 1971. 97 pp., illus.

Florin, Lambert. *Arizona Ghost Towns.* Seattle: Superior Publishing Co., 1971. 80 pp., illus.

Heimsath, Clovis. *Pioneer Texas Buildings: A Geometry Lesson.* Austin: University of Texas Press, 1968. 158 pp., illus., map.

Henderson, Arn; Frank Parman; and Dortha Henderson. *Architecture in Oklahoma: Landmark and Vernacular.* Norman, Okla.: Point Riders Press, c1978. 215 pp., illus., bibliog.

Historic American Buildings Survey. *Texas Catalog: A List of Measured Drawings, Photographs and Written Documentation in the Survey, 1974.* Compiled by Paul Goeldner; edited by Lucy Pope Wheeler and S. Allen Chambers, Jr. San Antonio, Tex.: Trinity University Press, 1974. 247 pp., illus., index.

Historic American Buildings, Texas. Intro. by David G. DeLong. New York: Garland Publishing Co., 1979. 2 vols., chiefly illus., bibliog. references, index.

Houston: An Architectural Guide. Houston, Tex.: Houston Chapter, American Institute of Architects, 1972. 168 pp., illus.

Junior League of Tulsa. *Tulsa Art Deco: An Architectural Era, 1925–1942.* Tulsa, Okla.: Junior League of Tulsa, 1980. 203 pp., illus., maps, notes, bibliog., index.

Kowert, Elise. *Old Homes and Buildings of Fredericksburg.* Fredericksburg, Tex.: Fredericksburg Publishing, 1977. 205 pp., illus., bibliog. references, index.

LaZar, Arthur, and Bainbridge Bunting. *Of Earth and Timbers Made; New Mexico Architecture.* Albuquerque: University of New Mexico Press, 1974. 85 pp., illus.

Meredith, Howard L., and Mary Ellen Meredith, eds. *Of the Earth: Oklahoma Architectural History.* Oklahoma City: Oklahoma Historical Society, 1980. 134 pp.

Niemann, Charles L. *Spanish Times and Boom Times: Toward an Architectural History of Socorro, New Mexico.* Socorro, N.M.: Socorro County Historical Society, 1972. 100 pp., illus., bibliog.

Sanford, Trent Elwood. *The Architecture of the Southwest: Indian, Spanish, American.* 1950. Reprint. Westport, Conn.: Greenwood Press, 1971. 312 pp., illus., appendix.

Stewart, Janet Ann. *Arizona Ranch Houses: Southern Territorial Styles, 1867–1900.* Edited by John Bret Harte. Tucson: Arizona Historical Society, 1974. 121 pp., illus., bibliog.

West

American Institute of Architects. Portland, Oregon Chapter. *A Guide to Portland Architecture.* Portland, Ore.: American Institute of Architects, Portland Chapter, 1968. 74 pp., illus., bibliog.

Baer, Morley. *Adobes in the Sun: Portraits of a Tranquil Era.* Text by Augusta Fink, with Amelie Elkinton. San Francisco: Chronicle Books, 1972. 144 pp., illus.

Baird, Joseph Armstrong, Jr. *Time's Wondrous Changes: San Francisco Architecture 1776–1915.* San Francisco: California Historical Society, 1962. 67 pp., 164 plates, maps, bibliog.

Balcom, Mary G. *Ghost Towns of Alaska.* Chicago: Adams Press, 1965. 80 pp., illus., maps, bibliog.

Bangs, Edward G. *Portals West: A Folio of Late Nineteenth Century Architecture in California.* San Francisco: California Historical Society, 1960. 86 pp., illus.

Banham, Reyner. *Los Angeles: The Architecture of Four Ecologies.* New York: Harper & Row, 1971. 256 pp., illus.

Bernhardi, Robert. *The Buildings of Berkeley.* Oakland, Calif.: The Holmes Book Company, 1972. 116 pp., illus., bibliog., index.

Bernhardi, Robert C. *Great Buildings of San Francisco: A Photographic Guide.* New York: Dover Publications, 1979. 96 pp., illus., map.

Brettell, Richard R. *Historic Denver: The Architects and the Architecture, 1858–1893.* Denver, Colo.: Historic Denver, Inc., c1973. 240 pp., illus., notes, bibliog., index.

Bruce, Curt, and Thomas Aidala. *The Great Houses of San Francisco.* New York: A. A. Knopf, 1974. 200 pp., illus.

Chambers, S. Allen. *The Architecture of Carson City, Nevada.* Washington, D.C.: Historic American Buildings Survey, 1972. 194 pp., illus., bibliog. references. ◆ Historic American Buildings Survey Selections no. 14.

Crumb, Lawrence N. *Historic Preservation in the Pacific Northwest: A Bibliography of Sources, 1947–1978.* Chicago, Ill.: Council of Planning Librarians, 1979. 57 pp., index. ◆ CPL Bibliography no. 11.

Dallas, Sandra. *Cherry Creek Gothic: Victorian Architecture in Denver.* Norman: University of Oklahoma Press, 1971. 292 pp., illus., bibliog., index.

Fairfax, Geoffrey W. *The Architecture of Honolulu.* Norfolk Island, Australia: Island Heritage, Ltd., distr. by W. W. Distributors, Honolulu, 1971. 120 pp., illus., bibliog.

Freudenheim, Leslie M., and Elizabeth Sussman. *Building with Nature: Roots of the San Francisco Bay Region Tradition.* Santa Barbara, Calif.: Peregrine Smith, 1974. 112 pp., illus, bibliog. references, index.

Gebhard, David; Roger Montgomery; Robert Winter; John Woodbridge; and Sally Woodbridge. *A Guide to Architecture in San Francisco and Northern California.* Santa Barbara, Calif.: Peregrine Smith, Inc., 1973. 557 pp., illus., maps, glossary, index.

Gebhard, David, and Robert Winter. *A Guide to Architecture in Los Angeles and Southern California.* Santa Barbara, Calif.: Peregrine Smith, 1977. 728 pp., illus., bibliog., index.

George Washington Smith, 1876–1830: The Spanish Colonial Revival in California. Santa Barbara, Calif.: Art Gallery, University of California, 1964. 1 vol., unpaged, illus. ◆ Catalog of an exhibition organized by David Gebhard.

Goeldner, Paul. *Utah Catalog: Historic American Buildings Survey.* Salt Lake City: Utah Heritage Foundation, 1969. 76 pp., illus., drawings, diagrams, bibliog. footnotes, index.

Haglund, Karl T., and Philip F. Notarianni. *The Avenues of Salt Lake City.* Salt Lake City: Utah State Historical Society, c1980. 166 pp., illus., bibliog. references, index.

Hart, Arthur A. *Historic Boise: An Introduction to the Architecture of Boise, Idaho: 1863–1938.* Boise, Idaho: Boise City Historic Preservation Commission, 1979. 82 pp., illus., index.

Heimann, Jim, and Rip Georges. *California Crazy: Roadside Vernacular Architecture.* San Francisco: Chronicle Books, 1980. 139 pp., chiefly illus., bibliog., index.

Historic American Buildings, California. Intro. by David G. DeLong. New York: Garland Publishing, 1980. 4 vols., chiefly illus., bibliog. references, index.

Jackson, Olga. *Architecture/Colorado.* George Thorson, ed. Denver: American Institute of Architects, Colorado Chapter, 1966. 96 pp., illus., maps. ◆ Cover title: Mountains, Mines & Mansions: An Architectural Guide to Colorado.

Judd, Walter F. *Palaces and Forts of the Hawaiian Kingdom: From Thatch to American Florentine.* Palo Alto, Calif.: Pacific Books, 1975. 176 pp., illus., bibliog., index.

Kirker, Harold. *California's Architectural Frontier: Style and Tradition in the Nineteenth Century.* 1960. Reprint. New York: Russell & Russell, 1970. 224 pp., illus., bibliog., index.

McCoy, Esther. *Case Study Houses, 1945–1962.* 2nd ed. Los Angeles: Hennessey & Ingalls, 1977. 217 pp., illus., bibliog., index. ◆ Originally from "The Case Study House Program" of *Arts and Architecture* magazine.

Morris, Langdon E., Jr. *Denver Landmarks.* Denver, Colo.: Charles W. Cleworth, 1979. 324 pp., illus., indexes.

Regnery, Dorothy F. *An Enduring Heritage:*

111

Historic Buildings of the San Francisco Peninsula. Stanford, Calif.: Stanford University Press, 1976. 124 pp., illus., bibliog., index.

Reitzes, Lisa B. *Paris: A Look at Idaho Architecture.* Boise: Idaho State Historic Preservation Office, 1981. 104 pp.

Society of Architectural Historians. Northern Pacific Coast Chapter. *Festschrift: A Collection of Essays on Architectural History.* Salem, Ore.: Northern Pacific Coast Chapter, Society of Architectural Historians, 1978. 80 pp., illus.

Stoehr, C. Eric. *Bonanza Victorian: Architecture and Society in Colorado Mining Towns.* Albuquerque: University of New Mexico Press, c1975. 173 pp., illus., bibliog., index.

Vaughan, Thomas, and Virginia Guest Ferriday, eds. *Space, Style, and Structure: Building in Northwest America.* Portland, Ore.: Oregon Historical Society, 1974. 2 vols. (750 pp.), illus., bibliog., index.

Vaughan, Thomas, and George A. McMath. *A Century of Portland Architecture.* Portland: Oregon Historical Society, 1967. 226 pp., illus., bibliog. references.

Venturi, Robert; Denise Scott Brown; and Steven Izenour. *Learning From Las Vegas: The Forgotten Symbolism of Architectural Form.* Cambridge, Mass.: MIT Press, c1977. 192 pp., illus., bibliog.

Waldhorn, Judith L., and Sally Woodbridge. *Victoria's Legacy: Tours of San Francisco Bay Area Architecture.* San Francisco: 101 Productions, distr. by Scribner's, N.Y., c1978. 224 pp., illus., bibliog., indexes.

Winter, Robert. *The California Bungalow.* Los Angeles, Calif.: Hennessey & Ingalls, 1980. 96 pp., bibliog., index. ◆ California Architecture and Architects no. 1.

Woodbridge, John Marshall, and Sally Byrne Woodbridge, comps. *Buildings of the Bay Area: A Guide to Architecture of the San Francisco Bay Region.* New York: Grove Press, 1960. 1 vol., unpaged, drawings, illus., maps.

Woodbridge, Sally B., and Robert Montgomery. *A Guide to Architecture in Washington State: An Environmental Perspective.* Seattle: University of Washington Press, 1980. 483 pp., illus., bibliog., index. ◆ Includes essay on landscape design by David S. Streatfield.

Wright, Patricia A. *Twin Falls Country: A Look at Idaho Architecture.* Boise: Idaho State Historical Society, Preservation Office, 1979. 84 pp., illus.

4

Technology and Crafts

Imagine trying to handle in a single chapter all the research references extending from the Golden Age of Homespun through the First Industrial Revolution to the Second Industrial Revolution. In other words, man's technological progress during the last 200 years, from handcrafts to telecommunication. That is what is attempted here. The content is based on the well-established outline used for the "Current Bibliography" compiled by Jack Goodwin in *Technology and Culture,* the quarterly journal of the Society for the History of Technology, an interdisciplinary organization founded in 1958.

"Technology" comprises a host of subjects—and there could have been more, as the expert may point out. In order to make work on this chapter feasible, limits had to be set. The guiding principle could not be completeness; it had to be service to those people who needed help in their research in the major branches of a complex subject.

Eugene S. Ferguson in his *Bibliography of the History of Technology,* which the editors consider to be a "must" item on the Basic Reference Shelf, has many wise points to make in his Preface. He (with an assist from another expert, Brooke Hindle) helps to define the relatively new field, which deals with "things," their making and doing. Viewed in that light, those who consult this chapter will better understand its major thrust.

Professor Ferguson has done the editors a further favor by unearthing a quotation that can serve as their final word in the final chapter of the final volume of this *Bibliography.* In 1846, Johann Beckmann in the 4th edition of his book *A History of Inventions,* published in London, had this to say:

> In executing this task I shall aim at more than the character of a diligent collector; for to bring together information of this kind, to arrange it, and to make it useful, requires no less readiness of thought than the labours of those who assume the character of original thinkers, and who imagine that they render others inferior to themselves when they bestow on them the appellation of compilers.

Basic Reference Shelf

Ardrey, Robert L. *American Agricultural Implements: A Review of Invention and Development in the Agricultural Implement Industry of the United States.* 1894. Reprint. New York: Arno Press, 1972. 236 pp., illus. ◆ In two parts: General History of Invention; Pioneer Manufacturing Centers.

Bridenbaugh, Carl. *The Colonial Craftsman.* Chicago: University of Chicago Press, c1950, 1961. 214 pp., illus., bibliog. references. ◆ A cultural survey based on the craft and craftsmen.

Brown, M. L. *Firearms in Colonial America: The Impact on History and Technology, 1492–1792.* Washington, D.C.: Smithsonian Institution Press, 1981. 450 pp., illus., bibliog., appendices, index. ◆ Historical analysis of contributions made by firearms manufacturing in various fields of technology and industrialization.

Condit, Carl W. *American Building: Materials and Techniques from the First Colonial Settlement to the Present.* 2nd ed. Chicago: University of Chicago Press, 1982. 329 pp., illus., drawings, diagrams, bibliog., index. ◆ Survey of architectural construction methods and materials used in the U.S. from the colonial period to the present. In four parts: colonial building development, agricultural republic, rise of the industrial republic, and industrial and urban expansion in the 20th century.

Derry, Thomas Kingston, and Trevor I. Williams. *A Short History of Technology from the Earliest Times to A.D. 1900.* London and New York: Oxford University Press, c1961, 1970. 783 pp., illus., bibliog. ◆ A popular reference and textbook based on the 5-volume *History of Technology,* edited by Charles Singer, et al.

Ferguson, Eugene S. *Bibliography of the History of Technology.* Cambridge, Mass.: Society for the History of Technology, 1968. 347 pp., index. ◆ Society for the History of Technology Monograph Series no. 5. The basic bibliography on the history of technology. Kept up to date by annual bibliography in *Technology and Culture.*

Giedion, Siegfried. *Mechanization Takes Command: A Contribution to Anonymous History.* 1948. Reprint. New York: W. W. Norton & Co., 1969. 743 pp., illus., diagrams, bibliog. footnotes, index. ◆ Basic work on the effects of industrialization, especially as it relates to development of mechanization of complicated crafts, the organic (agriculture, etc.), the household, etc., and including early industrial assembly lines.

Hindle, Brooke. *Technology in Early America: Needs and Opportunities for Study.* With a directory of artifact collections by Lucius Ellsworth. Chapel Hill: University of North Carolina Press for the Institute of Early American Culture at Williamsburg, Va., 1966. 145 pp., bibliog. footnotes, index. ◆ Interpretive essay and extensive bibliography surveying the chronology and major characteristics of American technology before 1850. Directory covers raw materials production, manufacturing, tools and instruments, power, transportation, communication.

Hodges, Henry. *Artifacts: An Introduction to Early Materials and Technology.* Atlantic Highlands, N.J.: Humanities Press, c1964, 1981. 248 pp., illus., bibliog., index. ◆ A review of materials used by early man and methods of working them. In two parts: materials and techniques; technological examination of artifacts.

Hudson, Kenneth. *A Pocket Book for Industrial Archaeologists.* London: J. Baker, 1976. 134 pp., illus., map, plans, index. ◆ A guide to field work and research; emphasis on need to investigate also the industrial archeology of the Second Industrial Revolution, e.g., electricity, petroleum, plastics, etc.

Hunter, Louis C. *A History of Industrial Power in the United States, 1780–1930.* Charlottesville, Va.: Published for the Eleutherian Mills-Hagley Foundation by the University Press of Virginia, c1979–. illus., plans, bibliog. references, index. ◆ Vol. 1—*Waterpower in the Century of the Steam Engine.* 606 pp., illus., appendix, index. Covers stationary power as used in industrial production in mills, mines and factories; analyzes technological achievement, management industrialization, and urban change and growth.

Jacobs, David, and Anthony E. Neville. *Bridges, Canals and Tunnels: The Engineering Conquest of America.* New York: American Heritage Publishing Co., distr. by Van Nostrand, 1968. 159 pp., illus., diagrams, maps, appendix, bibliog., index. ◆ Illustrated history of American civil engineering by topics.

Lewis, Walter David. *Iron and Steel in*

America. Greenville, Del.: Hagley Museum, c1976. 64 pp., illus., bibliog., index. ◆ Surveys all aspects of this basic technology from colonial ironmaking to World War II.

Moxon, Joseph. *Mechanik Exercises; or, The Doctrine of Handy-Works, applied to the Arts of Smithing, Joinery, Carpentry, Turning, Bricklaying, to which is added, Mechanick Dyalling. . . .* 1703. Reprint, with an introduction, table of contents, and captions explaining the 26 plates by Benno Forman. Edited by Charles F. Montgomery. New York: Praeger, 1970. 352 pp., illus. ◆ An 18th century how-to-do-it book. Includes a glossary and bibliography in each section.

Mystic Seaport Museum. *Mystic Seaport Museum Watercraft.* By Michael Bray. Mystic, Conn.: Mystic Seaport Museum, c1979. 280 pp., illus., bibliogs., indexes. ◆ Definitive reference work.

Passer, Harold. *The Electrical Manufacturers, 1875–1900: A Study in Competition, Entrepreneurship, Technical Change, and Economic Growth.* 1953. Reprint. New York: Arno Press, 1972. 412 pp., bibliog. ◆ Study of the rise of U.S. firms from about 1880 and of their response to innovations and needs in light, power, and railway traction.

Rae, John B. *The Road and the Car in American Life.* Cambridge, Mass.: MIT Press, 1971. 390 pp., bibliog. ◆ Evolution of the transportation system in the U.S.

Russell, Carl P. *Firearms, Traps and Tools of the Mountain Men.* Albuquerque: University of New Mexico Press, c1967, 1977. 448 pp., illus., bibliog., index. ◆ Covers implements, utensils, equipment for the fur trade, and firearms.

Salaman, R. A. *Dictionary of Tools used in the Woodworking and Allied Trades, c.1700–1900.* New York: Scribner, c1975. 545 pp., illus., bibliog., index. ◆ The *Bibliography of Tools,* reprinted from *Dictionary. . . ,* reproduced by permission of Charles Scribner's Sons, by Early American Industries Association.

Sande, Theodore A. *Industrial Archeology: A New Look at the American Heritage.* 1976. Reprint. New York: Penguin Books, c1976, 1978. 152 pp., illus., bibliog., index. ◆ Documentation and description of America's first industrial artifacts: bridges, mills, mines, dams, factories, etc.; also a descriptive roster of sites from 49 states.

Sharrer, G. Terry, comp. *1001 References for the History of American Food Technology.* Davis: Agricultural History Center, University of California, 1978. 103 pp., index.

Technology and Culture. 1960, quarterly, subscription. Society for the History of Technology, University of Chicago Press, 5801 South Ellis Avenue, Chicago, Illinois 60637. ◆ Includes annual update of Ferguson bibliography, begun 1964, Jack Goodwin, editor.

Technology in Western Civilization. Edited by Melvin Kranzberg and Carroll W. Pursell, Jr. New York: Oxford University Press, 1967. 2 vols., illus., maps, bibliog. ◆ A comprehensive work. Vol. 1—*The Emergence of Modern Industrial Society, Earliest Times to 1900;* Vol. 2—*Technology in the Twentieth Century.*

Usher, Abbott Payson. *A History of Mechanical Inventions.* Rev. ed. Boston: Beacon Press, c1954, 1959. 450 pp., illus., bibliog., index. ◆ Covers theory of invention, connections with society, and topics such as clocks, textiles, power, printing, machine tools; from antiquity to the 20th century.

White, John H., Jr. *The American Railroad Passenger Car.* Baltimore: Johns Hopkins University Press, c1978. 699 pp., illus., appendices, bibliog., index. ◆ Includes technical details, information on companies that built cars, biographical sketches of car designers and builders.

Technology/Craft Organizations and Periodicals

Association for Preservation Technology, Ann Falkner, Executive Secretary, Box 2487 Station D, Ottawa, Ontario K1P 5W6, Canada. Founded in 1968, the Association's membership includes preservationists, architects, furnishings consultants, museum curators, architectural educators, archeologists, craftsmen and other persons directly or indirectly involved in preservation activities. Its objectives are to improve the quality of professional practices in the field of historic preservation in North America; to promote research and gather technical information in all aspects of historic preservation; to encourage the training of craftsmen in the traditional techniques and skills required for historic preservation; to encourage the establishment of national and local collections of reference materials, tools and artifacts for study purposes; to encourage government and private participation and support of these activities; and to maintain a listing of professional restorationists, consultants, curators, conservationists, craftsmen and sources of supply and other services related to historic preservation. It presents awards; maintains a speakers bureau and placement service; and offers specialized education. The Association publishes a *Bulletin* (4/yr.), books, monographs and numerous topical bulletins, and holds an annual meeting.

In 1975, the Foundation for Preservation Technology was incorporated to assist in the dissemination of knowledge on all subjects related to the technology of historic preservation. It has developed a number of projects and has affiliated with the Association for Preservation Technology to meet its goals. It supports varied historic preservation research and education programs through donations and grants; prepared "Suggested Guidelines for Training in Architecture Conservation"; reprinted the 1865 Russell & Erwin Hardware Catalogue; publishes *Communiqué;* begun "Building Early North America" project (6 essays on history of building technology); reprinted the two-volume, 1743 Builder's Dictionary; and begun a project on guidelines for rehabilitation of existing buildings.

Association of Science-Technology Centers, Sheila Grinell, Executive Director, 1016 16th Street, N.W., Washington, D.C. 20036. The Association, founded in 1973, is a not for profit organization of science and technology museums dedicated to furthering public understanding and appreciation of science and technology. It seeks to improve operations of museums of science and technology; serve as a vehicle for cooperative projects of mutual interest to members; and advance the role of science and technology centers in society. It conducts educational and instructional workshops to assist museum professionals in administration and program development and implementation; in-service training; research in areas of museum administration, facilities, educational programs and exhibits. It represents science and technology centers in relations with government agencies, industry, foundations, and other museum organizations.

The Association has established an internship program, traveling exhibition services, and provides consultation, placement and referral services. It maintains a library, compiles statistics, holds an annual meeting and sponsors special interest workshops. Publications include *Newsletter* (bimonthly), directories, brochures, guidelines, surveys, monographs and pamphlets. It is affiliated with the American Association of Museums and the International Council of Museums.

Bulletin of APT. 1969, quarterly, membership. Association for Preservation Technology, Ann Falkner, Executive Secretary, Box 2487 Station D, Ottawa, Ontario K1P 5W6, Canada.

Communiqué. 1975, monthly, membership. Association for Preservation Technology, c/o Barbara L. Daniels-Swannack, Editor, P. O. Box 2165, Albuquerque, New Mexico 87103. ♦ Succeeds *Newsletter* (1972–1975).

Engineering News-Record. 1874, weekly, subscription. McGraw-Hill Publications Co., 1221 Avenue of the Americas, New York, New York 10020. ♦ Originally issued as *Engineering News* (1874–1917), with minor variations. Selective indexes, 1874–1890; and 1890–1899; semiannual index.

Franklin Institute. *Journal.* 1826, monthly, subscription. Pergamon Press, Maxwell House, Fairview Park, Elmsford, New York 10523. ♦ "New Series," and "Third Series."

Isis: *International Review Devoted to the History of Science and Its Cultural Influences.* 1912, 5/yr., subscription. History of Science Society, Arnold Thackray, Editor, 215 South 34th Street, D6, Philadelphia, Pennsylvania 19104. ♦ Technology included in annual "Critical Bibliography."

Newcomen Society for the Study of the History of Engineering and Technology, Science Museum, London SW7 2DD, England. Publishes *Transactions* (1920, annual), papers on the history of engineering, technology and industry; *The Newcomen Bulletin* (3/yr. to members), articles on elements of basic technology and important figures in the history of technology.

Newcomen Society in North America, c/o Charles Penrose, Jr., President, P. O. Box 113, Downingtown, Pennsylvania 19335. Founded in 1923, membership includes business and professional men in education and industry in the U.S. and Canada. It studies material history, as distinguished from political history, in terms of beginnings, growth and contribution of industry, transportation, communication, mining, agriculture, banking, insurance, education, invention, law and related historical fields. It presents awards to college and graduate students for essays and theses in industrial history and for proficiency in mathematics, chemistry and physics. The Society maintains the Thomas Chester Newcomen Memorial Library and Museum in Steam Technology and Industrial History, in Chester County, Pennsylvania. Publications include *Newcomen Addresses* (irregular); *Pamphlet* series, studies of business, industrial, educational and other institutions; *Annual Report; Index of Publications, 1933–61* (West Chester, Pa.: 1961, 28 pp.). It holds bimonthly regional meetings.

Old-Time New England: *Devoted to the Ancient Buildings, Household Furnishings, Domestic Arts, Manners and Customs, and Minor Antiquities of the New England People.* 1910, quarterly, subscription. Society for the Preservation of New England Antiquities, 141 Cambridge Street, Boston, Massachusetts 02114.

Scientific American. 1845, monthly, subscription. Scientific American, Inc., 415 Madison Avenue, New York, New York 10017.

Society for the History of Technology, c/o Carroll W. Pursell, Secretary, Department of History, University of California, Santa Barbara, California 93106. The Society was founded in 1958 in response to a growing need for systematic investigation into the history of technology and its impact on society and culture. Its objectives are to promote the study of technological change, to increase public understanding of the relationship between technology and civilization, and to encourage international cooperation and communication among historians, scientists, technologists, engineers, and other individuals. An interdisciplinary organization, the Society is concerned not only with the history of technological devices and process but also with the relations of technology to science, politics, social change, the arts and humanities, and economics. Membership is open to individuals, organizations, corporations and institutions interested in the purposes and activities of the Society. It gives prizes for scholarly work in the field, and for an outstanding book on the history of technology;

sponsors symposia; encourages the preservation of technological artifacts and documents; and prepares bibliographic materials on the history of technology. Publications include *Technology and Culture* (quarterly); *Newsletter* (quarterly); monograph series in the History of Technology. It holds an annual meeting, occasionally with related organizations. The Society is affiliated with the American Association for the Advancement of Science, the American Council of Learned Societies, and the American Historical Association.

Technology and Culture. 1960, quarterly subscription. Society for the History of Technology, University of Chicago Press, 5801 South Ellis Avenue, Chicago, Illinois 60637. ◆ Includes annual update of Ferguson bibliography (begun 1964), Jack Goodwin, editor. *An Annotated Index to Vols. 1–10 of Technology and Culture* (1959–1969), edited by Barton C. Hacker.

Technology In Society: *An International Journal.* 1979, quarterly, subscription. Pergamon Press, Journals Division, Maxwell House, Fairview Park, Elmsford, New York 10523. ◆ Provides focus for wide range of interdisciplinary fields: technology assessment; science, technology and society; economics of technology; technology transfer; appropriate technology and economic development; ethical and value implications of science and technology; and technology forecasting.

Reference Books and Guides to Sources

American Men of Science: *A Biographical Dictionary.* Jacques Cattell, ed. 1st ed. Lancaster, Pa.: Science Press, 1906–. 364 pp. ◆ 9th edition begins 3 vols.: Physical Sciences; Biological Sciences; Social Sciences. Continued as: *American Men and Women of Science,* 12th ed. New York: R. R. Bowker, 1971–. Issued in two sections, Physical and Biological Sciences; Social and Behavioral Sciences. Current edition, 15th, 1982. 7 vols. Edited by Jacques Cattell Press.

Black, George W., Jr. *American Science and Technology: A Bicentennial Bibliography.* Carbondale: Southern Illinois University Press, c1979. 170 pp., indexes.

Carter, Ernest F. *Dictionary of Inventions and*

Discoveries. 2nd rev. ed. New York: Crane, Russak, c1966, 1974. 208 pp.

Cutliffe, Stephen H.; Judith A. Mistichelli; and Christine M. Roysdon. *Technology and Values in American Civilization: A Guide to Information Sources.* Detroit: Gale Research Co., c1980. 704 pp., indexes.

Diderot, Denis. *Recueil des Planches, sur les Sciences, les Arts Liberaux, et les Arts Méchaniques, avec leur Explication.* Paris: Cercle du Livre Précieux, 1964–66. ◆ 6 vols., reprints of plates. Also published by Readex Microprint Corporation, 1969, 1 volume. Contains all plates and with explanation.

A Diderot Pictorial Encyclopedia of Trades and Industry: *Manufacturing and the Technical Arts in Plates Selected from "L'Encyclopédie, ou Dictionnaire Raisonné des Sciences, des Arts et des Metiers" of Denis Diderot.* Edited by Charles Coulston Gillespie. New York: Dover Publications, 1959. 2 vols., 485 plates, bibliog.

Edinburgh Encyclopaedia. *The Edinburgh Encyclopaedia.* Conducted by David Brewster . . . the first American edition, corrected and improved. . . . Philadelphia: Joseph and Edward Parker, 1832. 18 vols., diagrams, maps.

Eleutherian Mills Historical Library, Greenville, Del. *A Guide to the Manuscripts in the Eleutherian Mills Historical Library; Accessions through the Year 1965.* By John Beverley Riggs. Greenville, Del.: 1970. 1205 pp. ◆ See also: Supplement. 1978.

Elliott, Clark A. *Biographical Dictionary of American Science: The Seventeenth through the Nineteenth Centuries.* Westport, Conn.: Greenwood Press, 1979. 360 pp., bibliog. references, index.

Encyclopaedia Britannica: *A Dictionary of Arts, Sciences, Literature and General Information.* 9th ed. New York: Encyclopaedia Britannica Co., 1910–1911. 29 vols., illus., maps, diagrams, index. ◆ Best edition for historical information on technology.

Ferguson, Eugene S. *Bibliography of the History of Technology.* Cambridge, Mass.: Society for the History of Technology, 1968. 347 pp., index. ◆ Society for the History of Technology Monograph series no. 5.

Harvard University. Graduate School of Business Administration. Baker Library. *Studies in Enterprise: A Selected Bibliography of American and Canadian Company Histories and Biographies of Businessmen.* Lorna M. Daniells, comp. Boston: 1957. 169 pp. ◆ Expanded edition of business biographies and company histories compiled by Baker Library in 1948.

Hindle, Brooke. *Technology in Early America: Needs and Opportunities for Study.* With a directory of artifact collections by Lucius Ellsworth. Chapel Hill: University of North Carolina Press for the Institute of Early American Culture at Williamsburg, Va., 1966. 145 pp., directory, bibliog. footnotes, index.

John Crerar Library, Chicago. *A List of Books on the History of Industry and Industrial Arts, January 1915.* Prepared by Aksel G. S. Josephson. 1915. Reprint. Detroit: Gale Research Co., 1966. 9, 486 pp.

Klein, Bernard, ed. *Guide to American Scientific and Technical Directories.* 10th ed. Rye, N.Y.: B. Klein Publications, Inc., 1972. 324 pp.

Knight, Edward H. *Knight's American Mechanical Dictionary: Being a Description of Tools, Instruments, Machines, Processes, and Engineering; History of Inventions; General Technological Vocabulary; and a Digest of Mechanical Appliances in Science and the Arts.* New York: J. B. Ford & Company, 1874–1876. 3 vols., drawings, diagrams. ◆ Vol. 4, a supplement, was published in 1884 (A to Zoo), reprinted in 1980 in limited edition of 600 copies by Early American Industries Association and Mid-West Tool Collector's Association.

National Museum of History and Technology. *Guide to the Manuscript Collections in the National Museum of History and Technology.* Washington, D.C.: Smithsonian Institution Press, 1978. 143 pp., index. ◆ Archives and Special Collections of the Smithsonian Institution no. 3.

Rees, Abraham, ed. *The Cyclopaedia; or, Universal Dictionary of Arts, Sciences and Literature.* Philadelphia: Samuel F. Bradford and Murray, Fairman and Co., 1810–1824. 41 vols., plates in 6 vols.

Rider, Kenneth J. *History of Science and Technology, a Select Bibliography for Students.* 2nd ed. London: Library Association, 1970. 75 pp., index.

Rink, Evald. *Technical Americana: A Checklist of Technical Publications Printed Before 1831.* Foreword by Eugene S. Ferguson; sponsored by the Eleutherian Mills Historical Library. Millwood, N.Y.: Kraus International Publications, 1981. 776 pp., index.

Romaine, Lawrence B. *A Guide to American Trade Catalogs, 1744–1900.* 1960. Reprint. New York: Arno Press, 1976. 422 pp., bibliog., index.

Sarton, George. *A Guide to the History of Science: A First Guide for the Study of the History of Science, with Introductory Essays on Science and Tradition.* New York: Ronald Press, 1952. 316 pp., illus., bibliog.

Smithsonian Institution. *Guide to the Smithsonian Archives.* Washington, D.C.: Smithsonian Institution Press, 1978. 298 pp., index. ◆ Archives and Special Collections of the Smithsonian no. 2. Catalog of records and manuscripts accessioned as of mid-1977; supersedes 1971 Preliminary Guide to the Smithsonian Archives.

Special Libraries Association. Transportation Division. *Transportation Libraries in the United States and Canada: An SLA Directory.* 3rd ed. New York: Special Libraries Association, 1978. 221 pp., index.

Technology in Industrial America: *The Committee on Science and the Arts of The Franklin Institute, 1824–1900.* Edited by A. Michal McMahon and Stephanie A. Morris. Wilmington, Del.: Scholarly Resources, Inc., 1977. 400 pp. ◆ Guide and calendar of records of the Institute's Committee on Science and the Arts. Includes comprehensive name and subject index. Investigative records of the Committee available on 28 rolls of microfilm. Address: Scholarly Resources, Inc., 104 Greenhill Avenue, Wilmington, Delaware 19805.

U.S. Patent Office. *Subject-Matter Index of Patents for Inventions Issued by the United States Patent Office from 1790 to 1873, Inclusive.* Edited by M. D. Leggett. 1874. Reprint. New York: Arno Press, 1976. 3 vols.

Ure, Andrew. *Dictionary of Arts, Manufactures, and Mines: Containing a Clear Exposition of their Principles and Practice.* By Robert Hunter, assisted by F. W. Rudler. 7th ed., completely rev. and greatly enlarged. London: Longmans, Green and Co., 1875–1879. 4 vols., illus. ◆ See also: *Supplement of Recent Improvements to the Present Time,* by Robert Hunter, ed. 1850. First edition published in London, 1839.

NOTES

Applied Science and Technology Index. 1958, monthly (except July), service basis. H. W. Wilson, 950 University Avenue, Bronx, New York 10452. ◆ A cumulative subject index to English language periodicals in the fields of aeronautics and space science, automation, chemistry, construction, earth sciences, electricity and electronics, etc.

"Current Bibliography in the History of Technology." In *Technology and Culture,* April issue, beginning Winter 1964. Compiled by Jack Goodwin, Chief, Collections Management Division, Smithsonian Institution, Washington, D.C. 20560. ◆ Annotated; catalogs current publications on the history of technology from prehistory to the present day; within each historical division works are classified by subject areas such as biography, civil engineering, transportation, materials and processes, energy conversion, military technology, and economic, business, political and social history. Spring 1966 issue includes list of journals.

History of Technology. 1976, annual. Mansell Publishing, 3 Bloomsbury Place, London WC1A 2QA, England. ◆ Distributed in U.S. by Mansell, Merrimack Book Service, 99 Main Street, Salem, New Hampshire 03079.

Smithsonian Studies in History and Technology, Smithsonian Institution Press, Washington, D.C. 20560. Series begun in 1969, and studies issued irregularly, with 45 issued to date. Topics covered include musical instruments, textiles, canals, meteorological instruments, agricultural implements, military artifacts, medical instruments, mechanical devices, photographic arts and printing. A list of titles is available from the Series Section of the Press. Requests to be put on the mailing list to receive publications should be directed to the Distribution Section.

U.S. Patent Office Records. Finding aids, manuscript records, patent models, and searching of patents in the U.S. are discussed in Ferguson, *Bibliography of the History of Technology* (cited above), Chapter 7, pp. 102–107. See also: Nathan Reingold, "U.S. Patent Office Records as Sources for the History of Invention and Technological Property," *Technology and Society,* 1:2 (Spring 1960), pp. 156–167.

Technology and Invention: General Works

America's Wooden Age: *Aspects of Its Early Technology.* Edited by Brooke Hindle. Tarrytown, N.Y.: Sleepy Hollow Restoration, 1975. 218 pp., illus., maps, bibliog. references.

Bigelow, Jacob. *The Useful Arts, Considered in Connexion with the Applications of Science.* 1842. Reprint. New York: Arno Press, 1972. 2 vols. in 1, illus.

Burke, James. *Connections.* 1st American ed. Boston: Little, Brown and Company, c1978. 304 pp., illus., bibliog., index. ♦ Presents history of technology as a continuing and interconnected process.

Burlingame, Roger. *Engines of Democracy: Inventions and Society in Mature America.* 1940. Reprint. New York: Arno Press, 1976. 606 pp., illus., plates, bibliog., index. ♦ Social history of American invention to ca.1865; sequel to Burlingame, *March of the Iron Men,* cited below.

Burlingame, Roger. *March of the Iron Men.* 1938. Reprint. New York: Arno Press, 1976. 500 pp., illus., plates, bibliog., index. ♦ Includes "Events and Inventions, A Reference List."

Byrn, Edward W. *The Progress of Invention in the Nineteenth Century.* 1900. Reprint. New York: Russell & Russell, 1970. 476 pp., illus.

Cohen, I. Bernard. *From Leonardo to Lavoisier, 1450–1800.* New York: Scribner, c1980. 298 pp., illus., bibliog., index.

Daumas, Maurice, ed. *A History of Technology and Invention: Progress Through the Ages.* Trans. by Eileen B. Hennessy. New York: Crown Publishers, c1969–. 3 vols., illus., bibliogs. ♦ Vol. 1—*The Origins of Technological Civilization* (1969); Vol. 2—*The First Stages of Mechanization* (1969); Vol. 3—*The Expansion of Mechanization, 1725–1860* (1980).

Derry, Thomas Kingston, and Trevor I. Williams. *A Short History of Technology from the Earliest Times to A.D. 1900.* London and New York: Oxford University Press, c1961, 1970. 783 pp., illus., bibliog. ♦ Based on five-volume *History of Technology* by Charles Singer.

Eco, Umberto, and G. B. Zorzoli. *The Picture History of Inventions from Plough to Polaris.* Trans. from Italian by Anthony Lawrence. New York: Macmillan, c1962, 1963. 360 pp., illus., maps, diagrams, plans.

Ferguson, Eugene S. *Oliver Evans: Inventive Genius of the American Industrial Revolution.* Greenville, Del.: The Hagley Museum, c1980. 72 pp., illus., bibliog. references, index.

Forbes, Robert James. *Man the Maker: A History of Technology and Engineering.* New York: Schuman, 1950. 355 pp., illus., bibliog., index.

Francois, William. *Automation: Industrialization Comes of Age.* New York: Collier Books, 1964. 192 pp., bibliog. footnotes.

Freedley, Edwin Troxell. *A Treatise on the Principal Trades and Manufactures of the United States.* 1856. Reprint, with new introduction by Michael Hudson. New York: Garland Publishing, 1974. 614 pp. ♦ Pp. 477–614, advertisements.

Giedion, Siegfried. *Mechanization Takes Command: A Contribution to Anonymous History.* 1948. Reprint. New York: W. W. Norton & Co., 1969. 743 pp., illus., diagrams, bibliog. footnotes, index.

Gies, Joseph, and Frances Gies. *The Ingenious Yankees: The Men, Ideas & Machines that Transformed a Nation, 1776–1876.* New York: Thomas Y. Crowell, c1976. 376 pp., illus., bibliog., index.

Habakkuk, H. J. *American and British Technology in the Nineteenth Century: The Search for Labour-Saving Inventions.* Cambridge and New York: Cambridge University Press, c1962, 1967. 222 pp., bibliog., index.

Hall, Courtney R. *History of American Industrial Science.* 1954. Reprint. New York: Arno Press, 1972. 453 pp., bibliog.

Hughes, Thomas P. *The Development of Western Technology Since 1500.* New York: Macmillan, 1964. 149 pp.

Jewkes, John; David Sawers; and Richard Stillerman. *The Sources of Invention.* 2nd ed., rev. and enl. New York: W. W. Norton, c1969, 1971. 372 pp., bibliog. references.

Kaempffert, Waldemar Bernhard. *A Popular History of American Invention.* 1924. Reprint. New York: AMS Press, 1975. 2 vols., illus., diagrams. ♦ Vol. 1—*Transportation, Communication, and Power;* Vol. 2—*Material Resources, Labor Saving Machines.*

Kouwenhoven, John A. *The Arts in Modern American Civilization.* New York: W. W. Norton and Co., c1948, 1967. 259 pp., illus., drawings, diagrams, bibliog., index. ♦ Original title: *Made in America.* Relationship of art, largely art in structures and industrial products, to American life.

Layton, Edwin R., Jr., ed. *Technology and Social Change in America.* New York: Harper & Row, 1973. 181 pp., bibliog.

Morison, Elting E. *From Know-How to Nowhere: The Development of American Technology.* New York: Basic Books, 1974, 1975. 199 pp., illus., bibliog.

Morison, Elting E. *Men, Machines and Modern Times.* Cambridge, Mass.: MIT Press, 1966. 235 pp.

Mumford, Lewis. *Technics and Civilization.* New York: Harcourt Brace & World, c1934, 1963. 495 pp., illus., bibliog., index. ♦ Includes chronological list of inventions.

Noble, David F. *America by Design: Science, Technology, and the Rise of Corporate Capitalism.* New York: Knopf, 1977. 384 pp., bibliog. references, index.

One Hundred Years' Progress of the United States *(with an Appendix Entitled Marvels that Our Grandchildren Will See, or One Hundred Years' Progress in the Future), by eminent literary men.* 1870. Reprint. New York: Arno Press, 1972. 546 pp., illus.

Pursell, Carroll W., Jr., ed. *Technology in America: A History of Individuals and Ideas.* Cambridge, Mass.: MIT Press, 1981. 265 pp., illus. ♦ Eighteen contributions by noted historians of science which discuss the technological innovations of Thomas Jefferson, Eli Whitney, Cyrus McCormick and others.

Rosenberg, Nathan. *Technology and American Economic Growth.* New York: Harper & Row, 1972. 211 pp., bibliog. references, index.

Schmookler, Jacob. *Patents, Inventions and Economic Change: Data and Selected Essays.* Edited by Zvi Griliches and Leonid Hurwicz. Cambridge, Mass.: Harvard University Press, 1972. 292 pp., illus., bibliog.

Science in America since 1820. Nathan Reingold, ed. New York: Science History Publications, 1976. 334 pp., illus., bibliog. references. ♦ Selection of articles from *Isis.*

Sinclair, Bruce. *Philadelphia's Philosopher Mechanics: A History of the Franklin Institute, 1824–1865.* Baltimore: Johns Hopkins University Press, 1974. 353 pp., illus., bibliog. ♦ Johns Hopkins Studies in the History of Technology.

Singer, Charles, et al., eds. *A History of Technology.* Oxford: Clarendon Press, 1954–1958. 5 vols., illus., maps, bibliog. ♦ See also Vols. 6 & 7, cited below.

Singer, Charles J. *A History of Technology: Vols. 6 & 7: The Twentieth Century.* Edited by Trevor Williams. Oxford: Clarendon Press, 1978. 1530 pp., illus., bibliog. ♦ Extension of Singer's five-volume work, covers 1900 to 1950.

Singer, Charles J. *A Short History of Scientific Ideas to 1900.* Oxford: Oxford University Press, 1959. 525 pp., illus., maps, diagrams, index.

The Smithsonian Book of Invention. Washington, D.C.: Smithsonian Institution, distr. by W. W. Norton, 1978. 256 pp., illus., index.

Struik, Dirk Jan. *Yankee Science in the Making.* New rev. ed. New York: Collier Books, 1962. 544 pp., bibliog. notes, bibliog.

Susskind, Charles. *Understanding Technology.* Baltimore: Johns Hopkins University Press, 1973. 164 pp., bibliog. notes, index.

Technology in Western Civilization. Edited by Melvin Kranzberg and Carroll W. Pursell, Jr. New York: Oxford University Press, 1967. 2 vols., illus., maps, bibliog. ♦ Vol. 1—*The Emergence of Modern Industrial Society;* Vol. 2—*Technology in the Twentieth Century.*

Ure, Andrew. *Philosophy of Manufactures; or, An Exposition of the Scientific, Moral and Commercial Economy of the Factory System of Great Britain.* 1861. Reprint. 3rd ed., continued in its details to the present time by P. L. Simmonds. New York: B. Franklin, 1969. 766 pp., illus., bibliog. references.

United States. Patent Office. *The Growth of Industrial Art.* Arranged and compiled under the supervision of Benjamin Butterworth, with a new introduction by Mark Kramer. 1892. Reprint. New York: Alfred A. Knopf, 1972. 200 pp., illus., folio.

Usher, Abbott Payson. *A History of Mechanical Inventions.* Rev. ed. Boston: Beacon Press, c1954, 1959. 450 pp., illus., bibliog., index.

Welsh, Peter C. *United States Patents, 1790–1870: New Uses for Old Ideas.* Washington, D.C.: Smithsonian Institution; for sale by Supt. of Docs., U.S. Government Printing Office, 1965. 110–151 pp., illus., bibliog. footnotes. ◆ U.S. National Museum Bulletin 241; Contributions from the Museum of History and Technology Paper 48.

Wolf, Abraham. *A History of Science, Technology, and Philosophy in the Eighteenth Century.* 2nd ed., rev. by D. McKie. New York: Harper, c1952, 1961. 2 vols. (814 pp.), illus.

NOTE

Companies and Men: Business Enterprise in America, series. Advisory editors: Stuart Bruchey and Vincent P. Carosso. New York: Arno Press, 1976. 38 titles in the series; reprints of publications, 1937–1976. Includes such company histories as Goodyear, Norwalk Truck Line Company, Pennsylvania Railroad, Reed & Barton, Standard Oil Co., IBM, General Electric, Anaconda, Ford, Marshall Field, etc.

Crafts and Trades

Andrews, Edward C. *The Community Industries of the Shakers.* 1932. Reprint. Philadelphia: Porcupine Press, 1972. 322 pp., illus., bibliog. ◆ Issued as Handbook 15 of the New York State Museum.

Arbor, Marilyn. *Tools and Trades of America's Past: The Mercer Collection.* Doylestown, Pa.: The Bucks County Historical Society, 1981. 116 pp., illus.

Arnold, James. *The Shell Book of Country Crafts.* 1st American ed. New York: Hastings House, 1969. 358 pp., illus., drawings, bibliog., museum list, index.

Bealer, Alex W. *The Art of Blacksmithing.* Rev. ed. New York: Funk and Wagnalls, 1976. 438 pp., illus., bibliog., index.

Bealer, Alex W. *Old Ways of Working Wood.* Rev. ed. Barre, Mass.: Barre Pub. Co., c1980. 255 pp., illus., bibliog., index.

Bridenbaugh, Carl. *The Colonial Craftsman.* Chicago: University of Chicago Press, c1950, 1961. 214 pp., illus., bibliog. references.

Butts, Isaac Ridler. *The Tinman's Manual and Builder's and Mechanic's Hand Book, Designed for Tinmen, Japanners, Coppersmiths, Engineers . . . etc., with compositions and receipts for other useful and important purposes in the practical arts.* 9th ed. Boston: Cupples & Hurd, c1888. 204 pp., illus.

Chisholm, K. Lomneth. *The Candlemaker's Primer.* New York: Dutton, 1973. 130 pp., illus.

Christopher, Frederick J. *Basketry.* Edited by Marjorie O'Shaughnessy. New York: Dover Publications, c1952. 108 pp., illus.

Edlin, Herbert L. *Woodland Crafts in Britain: An Account of the Traditional Uses of Trees and Timbers in the British Countryside.* New ed. Newton Abbot: David & Charles, 1973. 182 pp., illus., index.

Fields, Curtis P. *The Forgotten Art of Building a Stone Wall: An Illustrated Guide to Dry Wall Construction.* Dublin, N.H.: Yankee, 1971. 61 pp., illus., appendix. ◆ Forgotten Arts series.

The Foxfire Book: Hog Dressing, Log Cabin Building, Mountain Crafts and Foods, Planting by the Signs, Snake Lore, Hunting, Faith Healing, Moonshining and Other Affairs of Plain Living. Edited by Eliot Wigginton. Garden City, N.Y.: Doubleday and Company, 1972. 384 pp., illus., index. ◆ See also: *Foxfire Two* (1973); *Foxfire Three* (1975); *Foxfire Four* (1977); *Foxfire Five* (1979); *Foxfire Six* (1980); *Foxfire Seven,* Paul Gillespie, ed. (1982).

Freese, Stanley. *Windmills and Millwrighting.* South Brunswick, N.J.: Great Albion Books, c1971, 1972. 168 pp., illus., bibliog.

Hazen, Edward. *The Panorama or [sic] Professions and Trades; or Every man's Book.* 1837. Reprint. Watkins Glen, N.Y.: Century House, c1970. 320 pp., illus.

A Historical Guide to Wagon Hardware and Blacksmith Supplies. Edited by Towana Spivey. Lawton, Okla.: Museum of the Great

Plains, 1979. 202 pp., illus., index. ◆ Selected pages from the 1909 catalog of the George Worthington Company.

Jenkins, John Geraint. *The Craft Industries.* London: Longman, 1972. 128 pp., illus., bibliog., index. ◆ Describes series of surviving handicraft industries in Britain that help to explain their successor factory industries.

Jenkins, John Geraint. *Traditional Country Craftsmen.* Rev. ed. London and Boston: Routledge & Kegan Paul, 1978. 253 pp., illus., bibliog., index.

Kauffman, Henry J. *The American Pewterer: His Techniques and His Products.* Camden, N.J.: T. Nelson, 1970. 158 pp., illus., bibliog.

Kauffman, Henry J. *The Colonial Silversmith: His Techniques and His Products.* Camden, N.J.: T. Nelson, 1969. 176 pp., illus., bibliog.

Kauffman, Henry J. *Early American Ironware; Cast and Wrought.* Rutland, Vt.: C. E. Tuttle Co., 1966. 166 pp., illus., bibliog. ◆ Study of the crafts, techniques, and products of the blast furnace, forge, iron foundry, blacksmith, whitesmith, edge toolmaker, cutler, locksmith, gunsmith, nailer, wheelwright, and tinsmith.

Kidwell, Claudia B. *Cutting a Fashionable Fit: Dressmakers' Drafting Systems in the United States.* Washington, D.C.: Smithsonian Institution Press, 1979. 163 pp., illus., bibliog., index. ◆ Smithsonian Studies in History and Technology no. 42. Technical information on three main drafting systems and the tools.

Kilby, Kenneth. *The Cooper and His Trade.* New York: Fernhill, 1971. 192 pp., illus., bibliog., index.

Lasansky, Jeannette. *To Draw, Upset, and Weld: The Work of the Pennsylvania Rural Blacksmith, 1742–1935.* Lewisburg, Pa.: Oral History Traditions Project of the Union County Historical Society, c1980. 80 pp., illus., bibliog., index.

Manners, John E. *Country Crafts Today.* Detroit: Gale Research Co., 1974. 208 pp., illus., drawings, bibliog., appendices, index. ◆ Surviving handcrafts in villages in the United Kingdom.

Moxon, Joseph. *Mechanik Exercises; or, The Doctrine of Handy-Works, applied to the Arts of Smithing, Joinery, Carpentry, Turning, Bricklaying . . . , to which is added, Mechanick Dyalling. . . .* 1703. Reprint, with an introduction, table of contents, and captions explaining the 26 plates by Benno Forman. Edited by Charles F. Montgomery. New York: Praeger, 1970. 352 pp., illus., glossary, bibliog.

"Navajo Silversmithing." Reprinted from *El Palacio,* 77:2 (1971), entire issue. 20 pp., illus.

Noel Hume, Ivor. *James Geddy and Sons, Colonial Craftsmen.* Williamsburg, Va.: Colonial Williamsburg Foundation, 1970. 45 pp., illus., diagrams, bibliog. footnotes. ◆ Colonial Williamsburg Archaeological series no. 5.

Sachs, Hans, and Jost Amman. *The Book of Trades (Ständebuch).* 1568. Reprint, with a new introduction by Benjamin A. Rifkin. New York: Dover Publications, 1973. 127 pp., illus.

Sayward, Elliot M. *The Cooper and His Work; Definitions, Operations, Materials, Tools.* Levittown, N.Y.: 1972. 63 pp., illus. ◆ Reprinted for the Early Trades and Crafts Society. Originally published in 1969.

Simmons, Marc, and Frank Turley. *Southwestern Colonial Ironwork: The Spanish Blacksmithing Tradition from Texas to California.* Santa Fe: Museum of New Mexico Press, 1980. 199 pp., illus., drawings, bibliog., glossary. ◆ Southwestern Culture Series no. 2. Examines products and processes of colonial smithy in the southwest.

Sloane, Eric. *ABC Book of Early Americana: A Sketchbook of Antiquities and American Firsts.* Garden City, N.Y.: Doubleday, 1963. 61 pp., illus. ◆ Definitions and illustrations of building, tools and other objects.

Steinmetz, Rollin C., and Charles S. Rice. *Vanishing Crafts and their Craftsmen.* New Brunswick, N.J.: Rutgers University Press, 1959. 160 pp., illus.

Streeter, Donald. *Professional Smithing, Traditional Techniques for Decorative Ironworks, Whitesmithing, Hardware, Toolmaking, and Locksmithing.* New York: Charles Scribner's Sons, 1980. 133 pp., illus., index.

Sturt, George. *The Wheelwright's Shop.* Cambridge: Cambridge University Press, c1923, 1963. 235 pp., illus.

Teleki, Gloria Roth. *The Baskets of Rural America.* New York: Dutton, 1975. 202 pp., illus., bibliog.

Tunis, Edwin. *Colonial Craftsmen and the Beginnings of American Industry.* New York: Harper & Row, c1965, 1976. 160 pp., illus.

Untracht, Oppi. *Metal Techniques for Craftsmen: A Basic Manual for Craftsmen on the Methods of Forming and Decorating Metals.* 1st ed. Garden City, N.Y.: Doubleday, 1968. 509 pp., illus., drawings, diagrams, tool list, glossary, bibliog., index.

Vance, Mary A. *Cabinet Work and Cabinet Workers: A Bibliography.* Monticello, Ill.: Vance Bibliographies, 1981. 11 pp.

Watson, Aldren Auld. *The Village Blacksmith.* New York: Thomas Y. Crowell, 1968. 125 pp., illus., bibliog.

Williamson, Scott Graham. *The American Craftsman.* New York: Crown Publishers, c1940. 239 pp., illus., maps. ◆ Numerous illustrations from photographs and contemporary prints.

NOTES

Chronicle: *The Journal of the Early American Industries Association.* 1933, quarterly, subscription. c/o John S. Watson, Treasurer, P. O. Box 2128 Empire State Plaza, Albany, New York 12220.

Colonial Williamsburg, Craft Series. Begun in 1955, titles include: *The Apothecary in Eighteenth Century Williamsburg; The Blacksmith . . . ; The Bookbinder . . . ; The Cabinetmaker. . . ; The Leather Worker . . . ; The Miller . . . ; The Printer . . . ; The Silversmith . . . ; The Wigmaker. . . .*

Early American Industries Association, P. O. Box 2128 Empire State Plaza, Albany, New York 12220. Founded in 1933, membership includes museums, dealers, libraries, historical societies and interested individuals. Its purpose is to encourage the study and better understanding of early American industries in the home, in the shop, on the farm, and on the sea; also, to discover, identify, classify, preserve and exhibit obsolete tools, implements, utensils, vehicles, and mechanical devices which were used in early America. It conducts a program for the identification of unknown tools and devices, and holds a semiannual meeting. Publications include *Chronicle* (quarterly); *Shavings from the Chronicle* (6/yr.), newsletter; membership directory; books and publications program to study and record for future use the history of tools and industry in America.

Forgotten Arts series. Articles published in *Yankee* magazine, September 1973 (no. 1) through November 1978 (no. 54). Also published, Book series (1969–), by Richard M. Bacon, Curtis P. Fields, Julia Older, Vrest Orton.

Foxfire. 1967, quarterly, subscription. B. Eliot Wigginton, Editor, Foxfire Fund, Inc., Rabun Gap, Georgia 30468.

Hand Tools

Bealer, Alex W. *The Tools that Built America.* Barre, Mass.: Barre Publishing, distr. by Crown Publishers, N.Y., c1976. 212 pp., illus., bibliog.

Blackburn, Graham. *The Illustrated Encyclopedia of Woodworking Handtools, Instruments and Devices: Containing a Full Description of Tools Used by Carpenters, Joiners, and Cabinet Makers, with Many Examples of Tools Used by Other Woodworkers Such as Woodsmen, Sawyers, Coach Makers, Wheelwrights, Shipwrights, Wainwrights, Coopers, Turners, Pattern Makers and Whittlers.* New York: Simon & Schuster, 1974. 238 pp., illus., bibliog.

Blandford, Percy. *Country Crafts Tools.* New York: T. Y. Crowell, c1975, 1976. 240 pp., illus., glossary, bibliog., index. ◆ Groups implements by form or function rather than craft.

Evans, George E. *Tools of Their Trades: An Oral History of Men at Work c.1900.* New York: Taplinger Pub. Co., c1970, 1971. 296 pp., illus., bibliog.

Goodman, William Louis. *The History of Woodworking Tools.* New York: David McKay Co., c1964, 1966. 208 pp., illus., bibliog., index.

Hodgkinson, Ralph. "Tools of the Woodworker: Axes, Adzes and Hatchets," *History News,* 20:5 (May 1965), Technical Leaflet no. 28.

Horsley, John. *Tools of the Maritime Trades.* Newton Abbot: David & Charles, 1978. 304 pp., illus.

Hummel, Charles F. *With Hammer in Hand: The Dominy Craftsmen of East Hampton, New York.* 1968. Reprint. Charlottesville: Published for the Henry Francis duPont Winterthur Museum by the University Press of Virginia, 1976. 424 pp., illus., diagrams, charts, appendices, bibliog., index. ◆ Tools of the cabinetmaker and clockmaker, 1760–1840.

Kauffman, Henry J. *American Axes, A Survey of their Development and their Makers*. Brattleboro, Vt.: Stephen Greene Press, 1972. 151 pp., illus., drawings, glossary, bibliog., index.

Kebabian, Paul B., and Dudley Witney. *American Woodworking Tools*. Boston: New York Graphic Society, c1978. 213 pp., illus., bibliog., index.

Kline, John B. *Tobacco Farming and Cigar Making Tools*. Landisville, Pa.: The Author, 1975. 52 pp., illus.

Mercer, Henry C. *Ancient Carpenter's Tools*. 5th ed. Doylestown, Pa.: Horizon Press for the Bucks County Historical Society, 1975. 339 pp., illus.

Miller, Robert W. *Pictorial Guide to Early American Tools and Implements*. Des Moines, Iowa: Wallace-Homestead, c1980. 160 pp., illus.

Rempel, John I. "Tools of the Woodworker: Hand Planes," rev. ed., *History News*, 26:9 (September 1971), Technical Leaflet no. 24.

Roberts, Kenneth D. *Some 19th Century English Woodworking Tools; Edge and Joiner Tools and Bit Braces*. Fitzwilliam, N.H.: K. Roberts Pub. Co., 1980. 482 pp., illus., index.

Roberts, Kenneth D. *Wooden Planes in 19th Century America*. Fitzwilliam, N.H.: K. Roberts Pub. Co., 1975. 218 pp., illus., bibliog. ◆ K. Roberts Publishing Company, P. O. Box 151, Fitzwilliam, New Hampshire 03447 has reprinted numerous early tool catalogues; quantity and availability varies.

Roberts, Kenneth D., and Jane W. Roberts. *Planemakers and Other Edge Tool Enterprises in New York State in the Nineteenth Century*. Cooperstown: New York State Historical Association and Early American Industries Association, c1971. 230 pp., bibliog.

Salaman, R. A. *Dictionary of Tools Used in Woodworking and Allied Trades, c.1700–1970*. New York: Scribner, c1975. 545 pp., illus., bibliog., index. ◆ A Bibliography of Tools,

reprinted from *Dictionary . . . ,* reproduced by permission of Charles Scribner's Sons, by Early American Industries Association.

Sellens, Alvin. *The Stanley Plane: A History and Descriptive Inventory*. South Burlington, Vt.: Early American Industries Association, 1975. 216 pp., illus., bibliog. references, index.

Sellens, Alvin. *Woodworking Planes: A Descriptive Register of Wooden Planes*. Augusta, Kan.: distr. by Alvin Sellens, c1978. 323 pp., illus., bibliog. references, index.

Shelburne, Vt., Museum. *Woodworking Tools at Shelburne Museum*. By Frank H. Wildung. Shelburne, Vt.: Shelburne Museum, 1957. 79 pp., illus., index of tools. ◆ Museum Pamphlet Series no. 3.

Sloane, Eric. *A Museum of Early American Tools*. New York: Ballantine Books, c1964, 1974. 108 pp., illus., index.

Smith, H. R. Bradley. *Blacksmiths' and Farriers' Tools at Shelburne Museum; a History of their Development from Forge to Factory*. Shelburne, Vt.: Shelburne Museum, 1966. 272 pp., illus., bibliog. ◆ See also: Supplement, "Chronological Development of Nails," 12 pp. insert.

Tomlinson, Charles. *Illustrations of Trades*. 1860. Reprint. Ambridge, Pa.: Early American Industries Association, 1972. 106 pp., illus. ◆ Includes tools and products of the building, agricultural, furniture, and transport trades.

Tools and Technologies: America's Wooden Age. Edited by Paul B. Kebabian and William C. Lipke. Hanover, N.H.: Published for the Robert Hull Fleming Museum of the University of Vermont by the University Press of New England, 1979. 111 pp., illus. ◆ Book to accompany exhibit of woodworking tools.

Tools of the Glassmaker. Photography by Raymond F. Errett and Nicholas L. Williams. Corning, N.Y.: Corning Museum of Glass, c1980. 16 pp., illus.

Welsh, Peter C. *Woodworking Tools, 1600–1900*. Washington, D.C.: Smithsonian Institution, 1966. 52 pp., illus., drawings, diagrams, bibliog. ◆ U.S. National Museum Bulletin 241; Contributions from the Museum of History and Technology, Paper 51.

Agriculture and Food Technology

Ardrey, Robert L. *American Agricultural Implements: A Review of Invention and Development.* 1894. Reprint. New York: Arno Press, 1972. 236 pp., illus.

Baron, Stanley W. *Brewed in America: A History of Beer and Ale in the United States.* 1962. Reprint. New York: Arno Press, 1972. 424 pp., illus., bibliog.

Bateman, James A. *Animal Traps and Trapping.* Harrisburg, Pa.: Stackpole Books, 1971. 286 pp., illus., bibliog., index.

Blandford, Percy W. *Old Farm Tools and Machinery: An Illustrated History.* Fort Lauderdale, Fla.: Gale Research Co., c1976. 188 pp., illus., bibliog., index.

Bogue, Allan G. *From Prairie to Corn Belt: Farming on the Illinois and Iowa Prairies in the Nineteenth Century.* Chicago: University of Chicago Press, 1963. 310 pp., maps, diagrams, tables, bibliog. references. ♦ Includes a chapter on innovations in farm machinery.

Browning, Robert J. *Fisheries of the North Pacific: History, Species, Gear and Processes.* Rev. ed. Anchorage: Alaska Northwest, 1980. 423 pp., illus., map.

Carosso, Vincent P. *The California Wine Industry, 1830–1895: A Study of the Formative Years.* 1951. Reprint. Berkeley, Los Angeles and London: University of California Press, 1976. 241 pp., bibliog.

Clifton, Robert T. *Barbs, Prongs, Points, Prickers, and Stickers: A Complete and Illustrated Catalogue of Antique Barbed Wire.* Norman: University of Oklahoma Press, 1970. 418 pp., illus., bibliog., indexes.

Danhof, Clarence H. *Change in Agriculture: The Northern United States, 1820–1870.* Cambridge, Mass.: Harvard University Press, 1969. 322 pp., illus., bibliog., index.

Deane, Samuel. *The New-England Farmer; or Georgical Dictionary.* 1822. Reprint. New York: Arno Press, 1972. 532 pp. ♦ Reprint of 3rd edition; early farmer's guide.

Downard, William L. *Dictionary of the History of the American Brewing and Distilling Industries.* Westport, Conn.: Greenwood Press, 1980. 268 pp., bibliog., appendices, index.

Evans, Oliver. *The Young Mill-Wright and Miller's Guide.* 13th ed., with additions and corrections by Thomas P. Jones. With a Description of an Improved Merchant Flour-Mill, with engravings, by C. & O. Evans, engineers. 1850. Reprint. New York: Arno Press, 1972. 400 pp., 38 plates. ♦ Pioneering treatise on theory of American milling, first published 1795; many editions in 19th century.

Fussell, George E. *Crop Nutrition: Science and Practice Before Liebig.* Lawrence, Kan.: Coronado Press, 1971. 232 pp., bibliog.

Fussell, George E. *The Farmer's Tools, 1500–1900: The History of British Farm Implements, Tools and Machinery Before the Tractor Came.* London: Andrew Melrose, 1952. 246 pp., illus., bibliog.

Fussell, George E. *Farming Technique from Prehistoric to Modern Times.* 1st ed. New York: Pergamon Press, c1965. 269 pp., illus., bibliog.

Gray, Roy B. *The Agricultural Tractor, 1855–1950.* St. Joseph, Mo.: American Society of Agricultural Engineers, 1975. 91, 60 pp., illus., indexes.

Heimann, Robert K. *Tobacco and Americans.* New York: McGraw-Hill, 1960. 265 pp., illus., maps, diagrams, bibliog.

Herndon, George Melvin. *William Tatham and the Culture of Tobacco. Including a facsim. reprint of An Historical and Practical Essay on the Culture and Commerce of Tobacco, by William Tatham.* Coral Gables, Fla.: University of Miami Press, 1969. 506 pp., illus., bibliog.

Holbrook, Stewart Hall. *Machines of Plenty: Chronicle of an Innovator in Construction and Agricultural Equipment.* Updated by Richard G. Charlton. Rev. ed. New York: Macmillan, c1955, 1976. 269 pp., illus., bibliog. ♦ History of the J. I. Case Company, Racine, Wisconsin.

Jefferson, Thomas. *Thomas Jefferson's Farm Book, with Commentary and Relevant Extracts from other Writings.* Edited by Edwin M. Betts. 1953. Reprint. Charlottesville: University Press of Virginia, 1976. 168, 552 pp., illus., bibliog. ♦ Photoreproduction of the manuscript of Jefferson's Farm Book (168 pp.).

Jefferson, Thomas. *Thomas Jefferson's Garden Book, 1766–1824, with Relevant Extracts from his other Writings, annotated by Edwin*

Morris Betts. Philadelphia: American Philosophical Society, 1944. 704 pp., tables, diagrams, bibliog.

Johnson, Paul C. *Farm Inventions in the Making of America*. Des Moines, Iowa: Wallace-Homestead Book Co., c1976. 128 pp., illus., bibliog. ◆ Pictorial history of farm machinery.

Johnson, Paul. *Farm Power in the Making of America*. Des Moines, Iowa: Wallace-Homestead Book Co., c1978, 1979. 136 pp., illus., diagrams ◆ Includes advertising matter.

Kuhlmann, Charles B. *The Development of the Flour-milling Industry in the United States, with Special Reference to the Industry in Minneapolis*. 1929. Reprint. Clifton, N.J.: A. M. Kelley, 1973. 349 pp., bibliog. ◆ Library of Early American Business and Industry vol. 32.

Lampard, Eric E. *The Rise of the Dairy Industry in Wisconsin: A Study in Agricultural Change, 1820–1920*. Madison: State Historical Society of Wisconsin, 1963. 466 pp., map, tables, bibliog.

McCallum, Henry D., and Frances T. McCallum. *The Wire that Fenced the West*. Norman: University of Oklahoma Press, c1965, 1979. 285 pp., illus. ◆ Development of various patents, suits, and growth of industry.

Mousette, Marcel. *Fishing Methods Used in the St. Lawrence River and Gulf*. Ottawa: National Historic Parks and Sites Branch, Parks Canada, 1979. 171 pp., illus., bibliog. ◆ History and Archaeology no. 22. Description of the subsistence and commercial fishing devices and methods.

National Museum of History and Technology. *Agricultural Implements and Machines in the Collection of the National Museum of History and Technology*. By John T. Schlebecker. Washington, D.C.: Smithsonian Institution Press; for sale by Supt. of Docs., U.S. Government Printing Office, 1972. 57 pp., illus. ◆ Smithsonian Studies in History and Technology no. 17.

Nearing, Helen, and Scott Nearing. *The Maple Sugar Book: Together with Remarks on Pioneering as a Way of Living in the Twentieth Century*. New York: Schocken Books, c1970. 273 pp., illus., bibliog.

Norwak, Mary. *Kitchen Antiques*. New York: Praeger Publishers, 1975. 135 pp., illus., index. ◆ Equipment for cooking, dairying, laundry, etc. for history of domestic technology.

Partridge, Michael. *Farm Tools Through the Ages*. New York: Promontory Press, c1973. 240 pp., illus., bibliog., index.

Quick, Graeme, and Wesley Buchele. *The Grain Harvesters*. St. Joseph, Mich.: American Society of Agricultural Engineers, 1978. 269 pp., bibliog.

Robinson, James. *The Whole Art of Curing, Pickling, and Smoking Meat and Fish*. 1847. Reprint. New York: Gordon Press, 1973. 153 pp.

Rossiter, Margaret. *The Emergence of Agricultural Science: Justus Liebig and the Americans, 1840–1880*. New Haven, Conn.: Yale University Press, 1975. 275 pp., illus., bibliog., index.

Russell, Carl P. *Firearms, Traps and Tools of the Mountain Men*. Albuquerque: University of New Mexico Press, c1967, 1977. 448 pp., illus., bibliog., index.

Schmitt, Frederick P.; Cornelius deJong; and Frank H. Winter. *Thomas Welcome Roys: America's Pioneer of Modern Whaling*. Charlottesville: Published for the Mariners Museum, Newport News, Virginia, by the University Press of Virginia, 1980. 253 pp., illus., map, bibliog. references, index. ◆ Mariners Museum Publication no. 38.

Science and Technology in Agriculture: *A Symposium*. Edited by C. Clyde Jones and Homer E. Socolofsky. Washington, D.C.: Agricultural History Society, 1980. 230 pp.

Selitzer, Ralph. *The Dairy Industry in America*. New York: Magazines for Industry, c1976. 502 pp., bibliog., index.

Seufert, Francis. *Wheels of Fortune*. Edited by Thomas Vaughan. Portland: Oregon Historical Society, 1980. 282 pp., illus. ◆ Salmon fishing techniques and history of Seufert Bros. Company, a 19th century canning firm.

Sharrer, G. Terry, comp. *1001 References for the History of American Food Technology*. Davis: Agricultural History Center, University of California, 1978. 103 pp., index.

Sloane, Eric. *The Seasons of America Past*. New York: T. Y. Crowell, 1958. 150 pp., illus. ◆ Illustrates the farmer's year.

Stewart, Hilary. *Indian Fishing: Early Methods on the Northwest Coast.* Seattle: University of Washington Press, 1977. 181 pp., illus., bibliog., index.

Stewart, Robert E. *Seven Decades That Changed America: A History of the American Society of Agricultural Engineers, 1907–1977.* St. Joseph, Mich.: The Society, c1979. 432 pp., illus., bibliog. references, index.

Technical Information Systems (U.S.). *Guide to Manuscripts in the National Agricultural Library.* Compiled by Alan E. Fusonie. Washington, D.C.: Technical Information Systems, Science and Education Administration, U.S. Department of Agriculture, 1979. 39 pp., index. ◆ U.S. Department of Agriculture Misc. Pub. no. 1374.

Tilley, Nannie May. *The Bright-Tobacco Industry, 1860–1929.* 1948. Reprint. New York: Arno Press, 1972. 754 pp., illus., bibliog.

Whitehead, Vivian B., comp. *A List of References for the History of Agricultural Technology.* Davis: Agricultural History Center, University of California, 1979. 76 pp., bibliogs.

Wik, Reynold M. *Steam Power on the American Farm.* Philadelphia: University of Pennsylvania Press, c1953, 1959. 288 pp., illus., bibliog.

Williams, Robert C. "Antique Farm Equipment: Researching and Identifying," *History News,* 32:11 (November 1977), Technical Leaflet no. 101.

NOTE

American Society of Agricultural Engineers, J. L. Butt, Executive Vice President, P. O. Box 410, St. Joseph, Michigan 49085. Founded in 1907, the Society has regional, state and local groups. It is a professional society of agricultural engineers employed in industries serving agriculture and in public service. It develops engineering standards used in agriculture; sponsors national techniques meetings and continuing education; maintains biographical archives and a placement service. It sponsors competitions and conferences, and holds semiannual meetings. Publications include *Travel Historic Rural America,* a guide to agricultural museums in the U.S. and Canada including annual fairs and shows; *Agricultural Engineering* (1920, monthly); *ASAE Transactions* (1958, bimonthly); Year-

book; proceedings. It is affiliated with the American Association of Engineering Societies, and Council for Agricultural Science and Technology.

Engineering: General Works

American Society of Mechanical Engineers. *Mechanical Engineers in America Born Prior to 1861: A Biographical Dictionary.* Sponsored by the History and Heritage Committee. New York: American Society of Mechanical Engineers, c1980. 330 pp., bibliog.

Armytage, W. H. G. *A Social History of Engineering.* 4th ed. Boulder, Colo.: Westview Press, 1976. 381 pp., illus., bibliog., index. ◆ Summary, from ancient world to 20th century, with emphasis since 1700.

Burstall, Aubrey Frederic. *A History of Mechanical Engineering.* Cambridge, Mass.: MIT Press, 1965. 456 pp., illus., bibliog., index.

Finch, James Kip. *Engineering and Western Civilization.* New York: McGraw-Hill, 1951. 397 pp., illus., maps, bibliog.

Finch, James Kip. *The Story of Engineering.* Garden City, N.Y.: Doubleday, 1960. 528 pp., illus.

Kirby, Richard Shelton, et al. *Engineering in History.* New York: McGraw-Hill, 1956. 530 pp., illus., bibliog. references.

Latrobe, Benjamin Henry. *The Engineering Drawings of Benjamin Henry Latrobe.* Edited with an introductory essay by Darwin H. Stapleton. New Haven, Conn.: Published for the Maryland Historical Society by Yale University Press, 1980. 256 pp., illus., bibliog., index.

Marshall, John. *A Biographical Dictionary of Railway Engineers.* North Pomfret, Vt.: David & Charles, c1978. 247 pp., index. ◆ Biographies from Britain, Europe, North America.

Merritt, Raymond H. *Engineering in American Society, 1850–1875.* Lexington: University Press of Kentucky, 1969. 199 pp., bibliog. essay, index.

Roysdon, Christy, and Linda A. Khatri. *American Engineers of the Nineteenth Century: A Biographical Index.* New York: Garland Publishing, 1978. 247 pp.

Sellers, George Escol. *Early Engineering Reminiscences, 1815–1840.* Edited by Eugene S. Ferguson. Washington, D.C.: Smithsonian Institution, 1965. 202 pp., illus., maps, bibliog. notes, index. ◆ U.S. National Museum Bulletin 238.

Sinclair, Bruce, and James P. Hull. *A Centennial History of the American Society of Mechanical Engineers, 1880–1980.* Toronto and Buffalo: Published for the American Society of Mechanical Engineers by University of Toronto Press, 1980. 256 pp., illus., bibliog. references, index.

NOTES

American Society of Mechanical Engineers, Dr. Rogers B. Finch, Executive Director, 345 East 47th Street, New York, New York 10017. Founded in 1880, membership includes individuals, local and regional groups. It is a technical society of mechanical engineers that conducts research, develops codes and serves as sponsor for American National Standards Institute. The Society maintains a library; sponsors a National Historic Mechanical Engineering program; and holds an annual meeting. It has 19 committees on research and 30 divisions. Publications include *Applied Mechanics Reviews* (monthly); *Mechanical Engineering* (monthly); *Transactions* (quarterly); *A Biographical Dictionary,* cited above; *Centennial History,* cited above; and *National Historic Mechanical Engineering Landmarks* (1979, 146 pp., illus.).

Canadian Engineering Heritage Record (CEHR), Department of Indian and Northern Affairs, 365 Laurier Avenue West, 16th Floor, Ottawa, Ontario K1A 0H4, Canada. In 1972 the Canadian government and the Engineering Institute of Canada agreed to jointly undertake a national survey of historic engineering achievements to be known as the Canadian Engineering Heritage Record. Its goals are the identification and recording of remains of technological and engineering achievements; apprising the responsible authorities of those tangible remains which warrant consideration for commemoration due to national, provincial or local significance; and the unearthing of significant documents and objects. Initially the surveying and recording will be done by volunteer groups of the Institute. The National Historic Sites Service will provide recording forms, arrange for records preservation, and

take appropriate steps to commemorate or preserve significant landmarks.

U.S. Army. Corps of Engineers. In 1966, the Corps began the publication of official histories of all its districts, divisions, and special experiment stations. Some were written by the districts or through arrangements with professional historians. Scope and intent has grown from promotional pieces to more complex studies examining the Corps in full context of political and environmental questions.

U.S. National Park Service, Historic American Engineering Record (HAER), National Register Programs, Washington, D.C. 20240. The Historic American Engineering Record was begun in 1969. The National Park Service conducts a national program of intensive surveys of engineering works on a shared-fund basis with professional engineering societies, state and local governments, historical societies, and preservation groups. The purpose of HAER is to record a complete summary of engineering technology for surveying significant examples of engineering solutions which demonstrate the work of the various branches of the engineering profession: civil, mechanical, architectural, electrical, hydraulic. The program began with the Historic American Buildings Survey in 1933, which included a variety of works such as bridges, dams, projects in industrial archeology, and mill complexes. In 1964 the American Society of Civil Engineers set up a Committee on the History and Heritage of American Civil Engineering. It has designated engineering landmarks, worked on a series of books on engineering history, and published a biographical dictionary of civil engineers.

When the HAER was established in 1969, an agreement similar to that of the HABS was entered into, with the National Park Service administering the program and conducting the research, the American Society of Civil Engineers providing the professional counsel and financial assistance, and the Library of Congress keeping the records and making them available for study and copying through its Prints and Photographs Division. In 1971 the American Society of Mechanical Engineers formed a History and Heritage Committee, which also assists the HAER.

Two types of surveys are conducted: a regional survey identifying landmarks on a geographic basis which may begin as an inventory; and an industrial survey which identifies landmarks on the basis of the type of industry and may focus on a particular firm or cover a given industry entirely within a particular area. Survey records include architectural and engineering drawings, photographic and photogrammetric records, and historical research and technical documentation. Some documentary reports on the surveys have been published; state catalogs of the material are also being produced. See references cited in the Industrial Archeology section of this chapter.

Civil Engineering

General Works

American Society of Civil Engineers. Committee on History and Heritage of American Civil Engineers. *A Biographical Dictionary of American Civil Engineers.* New York: 1972. 163 pp. ♦ ASCE Historical Publication no. 2.

American Society of Civil Engineers. Committee on History and Heritage of American Civil Engineering. *The Civil Engineer: His Origins.* New York: The Society, 1970. 116 pp., illus., bibliog. references. ♦ ASCE Historical Publication no. 1.

Calhoun, Daniel H. *The American Civil Engineer: Origins and Conflict.* Cambridge, Mass.: Technology Press, Massachusetts Institute of Technology; distr. by Harvard University Press, 1960. 295 pp., illus., map, bibliog. notes, appendix, index.

Condit, Carl W. *American Building: Materials and Techniques from the First Colonial Settlement to the Present.* 2nd ed. Chicago: University of Chicago Press, 1982. 329 pp., illus., drawings, diagrams, bibliog., index.

Condit, Carl W. *American Building Art: The Nineteenth Century.* New York: Oxford University Press, 1960. 371 pp., illus., drawings, diagrams, notes, bibliog., index.

Condit, Carl W. *American Building Art: The Twentieth Century.* New York: Oxford University Press, 1961. 427 pp., illus., drawings, diagrams, tables, notes, bibliog., index.

Merdinger, Charles J. *Civil Engineering through the Ages.* Washington, D.C.: Society of American Military Engineers, 1963. 159 pp., illus.

Pannell, J. P. M. *Man the Builder: An Illustrated History of Engineering.* 1965. Reprint. London: Thames and Hudson, 1977. 256 pp., illus., maps, bibliog., index.

Rowe, Robert S. *Bibliography of Rivers and Harbors and Related Fields in Hydraulic Engineering.* Princeton, N.J.: Rivers and Harbors Section, Department of Civil Engineering, Princeton University, 1953. 407 pp. ♦ 500 copies printed.

Straub, Hans. *A History of Civil Engineering: An Outline from Ancient to Modern Times.* English translation by Erwin Rockwell. Cambridge, Mass.: MIT Press, 1964. 258 pp., illus., chronological table, bibliog.

NOTE

American Society of Civil Engineers, 345 East 47th Street, New York, New York 10017. Founded in 1852, it is the oldest national professional engineering society in the U.S. Members in the U.S. and overseas are organized into local sections. Through the Society's History and Heritage of American Civil Engineering Program significant engineering landmarks, including canals, tunnels, powerhouses, bridges, railroad and highway structures, are cited for national recognition. Local section committees locate and document landmarks before proposing them to the national committee for approval and inclusion on the ASCE listing. The Society also cooperates in documenting and recording civil engineering landmarks in the Historic American Engineering Record. A published *Guide to the History and Heritage Program* (1974), and *National Historic Landmarks of the Civil Engineering Profession* (1979) are available. The Society also publishes *Civil Engineering,* monthly, which includes the column "Benchmarks" featuring historic engineering subjects; *Biographical Dictionary of American Civil Engineers* (1972); and an historical publications series. The Society maintains a library; and has a slide program on the history of the engineering profession.

Building Construction

Benson, Tedd, and James Gruber. *Building the Timber Frame House: The Revival of a Forgotten Craft.* New York: Charles Scribner's Sons, 1980. 211 pp., bibliog., index..

Birkmire, William H. *Skeleton Construction in Buildings: With Numerous Practical Illustrations of High Buildings.* 2nd ed. 1894. Reprint. New York: Arno Press, 1972. 237 pp., illus.

Briggs, Martin Shaw. *A Short History of the Building Crafts.* London: Clarendon Press, 1945. 296 pp., illus., bibliog. footnotes.
♦ Includes brickwork, masonry, concrete, carpentry, joinery, ironwork, roof coverings, plasterwork, external plumbing and glazing.

Bruce, Alfred, and Harold Sandbank. *The History of Prefabrication.* 1944. Reprint. New York: Arno Press, 1977. 80 pp., illus., bibliog.
♦ Original edition reprinted from series of articles in *Architectural Forum* beginning December 1942.

Brunskill, Ronald, and Alec Clifton-Taylor. *English Brickwork.* London: Ward Lock, 1977. 160 pp., illus., bibliog., index.

Building Early America: Contributions Toward the History of a Great Industry. The Carpenters' Company of the City and County of Philadelphia; Charles E. Peterson, ed. Radnor, Pa.: Chilton Book Co., c1976. 407 pp., illus., bibliog. references, index. ♦ Proceedings of a symposium on the occasion of the 250th anniversary of the Carpenters' Company . . . , sponsored by the Company, Philadelphia, March 27–29, 1974.

Carpenter's Company of the City and County of Philadelphia. *The Rules of Work of the Carpenters' Company of the City and County of Philadelphia, 1786.* 1786. Reprint. Annotated, with an introduction by Charles E. Peterson. Princeton, N.J.: The Pyne Press, 1971. 47 pp., plates, prints, diagrams, tables, notes on the facsimile, index.

Cowan, Henry J. *The Master Builders: A History of Structural and Environmental Design from Ancient Egypt to the Nineteenth Century.* New York: Wiley, 1977. 299 pp., illus., bibliog. references, indexes.

Cowan, Henry J. *Science and Building: Structural and Environmental Design in the Nineteenth and Twentieth Centuries.* New York: Wiley, c1978. 374 pp., illus., bibliog. references, indexes.

Davey, Norman. *A History of Building Materials.* New York: Drake Publishers, 1970. 260 pp., illus., drawings.

Dent, Roger N. *Principles of Pneumatic Architecture.* New York: Halsted Press Division, Wiley, 1972. 236 pp., illus., tables, bibliog.
♦ History and characteristics of air-supported structures.

Encyclopedia of Architectural Technology. Editor: Pedro Guedes. New York: McGraw-Hill, c1979. 313 pp., illus., index.

Hansen, Hans Jürgen, ed. *Architecture in Wood: A History of Wood Building and Its Techniques in Europe and North America.* New York: Viking Press, 1971. 288 pp., plates, illus., drawings, bibliog., index.

Herbert, Gilbert. *Pioneers of Prefabrication: The British Contribution in the Nineteenth Century.* Baltimore: Johns Hopkins University Press, c1978. 228 pp., illus., glossary, bibliog., index.

Hewett, Cecil Alec. *The Development of Carpentry, 1200–1700: An Essex Study.* New York: Augustus M. Kelley, 1969. 232 pp., illus., drawings, glossary, bibliog. references, appendices, index.

Hopson, Rex C. *Adobe: A Comprehensive Bibliography.* Santa Fe, N.M.: Lightening Tree, c1979. 127 pp., indexes.

Hudson, Kenneth. *Building Materials.* London: Longman, 1972. 122 pp., bibliog., index.

McKaig, Thomas H. *Building Failures: Case Studies in Construction and Design.* New York: McGraw-Hill Book Co., 1962. 261 pp., plans, bibliog., index. ♦ Case studies on concrete failures; steel failures; miscellaneous construction failures; failures caused by alterations; foundation failures; negligence and ignorance; old buildings and overload; wind, fire and explosion, etc.

McKee, Harley J. *Introduction to Early American Masonry: Stone, Brick, Mortar, and Plaster.* Washington, D.C. National Trust for Historic Preservation, 1973. 92 pp., illus., diagrams, drawings, tables, bibliog. footnotes, appendix, bibliog., index. ♦ National Trust—Columbia University Series on the Technology of Early American Buildings no. 1.

Masonry, Carpentry, Joinery: The Art of Architecture, Engineering, and Construction in 1899. 1899. Reprint. Chicago: Chicago Review Press, 1980. (103 pp.), illus. ♦ Selections from the International Library of Technology published by the International Textbook Co., Scranton, Pa. beginning in 1899.

"Masonry Issue." *Bulletin of APT*, XI:3 (1979), pp. 3–100.

Materials in the Architecture of Arizona, 1870–1920. With contributions by Jon P. Anderson, et al.; edited with an introduction by Bernard Michael Boyle. Tempe: College of Architecture, Arizona State University, 1976. 119 pp., illus., bibliogs.

Morris, Anthony E. J. *Precast Concrete in Architecture.* New York: Whitney Library of Design, 1978. 571 pp., illus.

Oerhlein, Mary, ed. *Publications of the National Bureau of Standards Related to Preservation Technology, Part 1, 1901–June 30, 1960.* Compiled by Thomas H. Taylor, Jr. and Christopher A. Sowick. Ottawa, Ontario: Association for Preservation Technology, 1980. 120 pp. ◆ Annotated list with subject index to research related to building technology; includes lists of NBS catalogs, addresses of depository libraries in U.S., and Department of Commerce field offices.

Putnam, Robert E., and G. E. Carlson. *Architectural and Building Trades Dictionary.* 3rd ed. Chicago: American Technical Society, 1974. 510 pp. ◆ Legal terms and building material sizes as well as definition of terms.

Rempel, John I. *Building with Wood, and Other Aspects of Nineteenth-Century Building in Central Canada.* Rev. ed. Toronto: University of Toronto Press, 1980. 454 pp., illus., drawings, diagrams, charts, bibliog., index.

Santa Fe. Museum of New Mexico. *Adobe: Past and Present.* Reprinted from *El Palacio*, 77:4 (1972), 20 pp., illus., drawings, bibliog. notes. ◆ Publication of the Museum of New Mexico, Santa Fe.

Schmidt, Carl F. *Cobblestone Masonry.* Scottsville, N.Y.: The Author, 1966. 326 pp., illus., drawings, diagrams, index.

U.S. Office of Archeology and Historic Preservation. *A Selected Bibliography on Early Wood Framing Systems.* Rev. ed. Robert A. Mack, comp. Washington, D.C.: U.S. Department of the Interior, National Park Service, 1974, 1977. 4 pp. ◆ Technical Preservation Services Reading List.

Vogel, Robert M. *Elevator Systems of the Eiffel Tower, 1899.* Washington, D.C.: Smithsonian Institution, 1961. 1–40 pp. ◆ U.S. National Museum Bulletin 228, Paper 19.

Volz, John R. "Brick Bibliography," *Bulletin of APT*, 7:4 (1975), pp. 38–49.

Wachsmann, Konrad. *The Turning Point of Building: Structure and Design.* Trans. by Thomas E. Burton. New York: Reinhold Publishing Co., 1961. 239 pp., illus.

Waite, Diana S., comp. *Architectural Elements, The Technological Revolution: Galvanized Iron Roof Plates and Corrugated Sheets; Cast Iron Facades, Columns, Door and Window Caps, Sills and Lintels; Galvanized Cornices; Marbleized Mantels; Plumbing and Heating Supplies and Fixtures; Staircases, Balconies, Newels and Balusters in Wood and Iron; Cut and Etched Glass Transoms and Sidelights.* Princeton, N.J.: Pyne Press, distr. by Scribner's, 1972. 1 vol., various pagings, illus., bibliog. ◆ American Historical Catalog Collection; reproduces facsimile plates and several manufacturers catalogs.

Woodforde, John. *Bricks to Build a House.* London: Routledge & Kegan Paul, 1976. 208 pp., illus., bibliog., index. ◆ History of brickmaking in Britain with references to American brickmaking.

METALS IN BUILDINGS

Geerlings, Gerald K. *Metal Crafts in Architecture: Bronze, Brass, Cast Iron, Copper, Lead, Lighting Fixtures, Tin, Specifications.* New York: Scribner's, c1929, 1972. 202 pp., illus., bibliog.

Geerlings, Gerald K. *Wrought Iron in Architecture: Wrought Iron Craftsmanship, Historical Notes and Illustrations.* New York: Charles Scribner's Sons, c1929, 1972. 202 pp., illus., drawings, diagrams, bibliog., index.

Kühn, Fritz. *Wrought Iron.* Translated by Charles B. Johnson. 2nd Eng. ed. New York: Architectural Book Publishing Co., c1969, 1974. 120 pp., chiefly illus.

Metals in America's Historic Buildings. Washington, D.C.: U.S. Department of Interior, Heritage Conservation and Recreation Service, Technical Preservation Services Division, 1980. 170 pp., illus., bibliog. ◆ Contents: *A Historical Survey of Use,* by Margot Gayle and David W. Look; *Deterioration and Methods of Preservation.* HCRS Publication no. 29.

Priess, Peter J. *An Annotated Bibliography for the Study of Building Hardware.* Ottawa: Parks

Canada, available from Printing and Publishing, Supply and Services Canada, 1978. 79 pp.

Robertson, Edward Graeme, and Joan Robertson. *Cast Iron Decoration: A World Survey.* New York: Whitney Library of Design, 1977. 336 pp., illus., bibliog., index.

Southworth, Susan, and Michael Southworth. *Ornamental Ironwork: An Illustrated Guide to Its Design, History and Use in American Architecture.* Boston: David R. Godine, 1978. 202 pp., illus., bibliog., index.

U.S. Office of Archeology and Historic Preservation. *Inventory of Metal Building Component Catalogs in the Library of Congress.* David W. Look, comp. Washington, D.C.: U.S. Department of the Interior, National Park Service, August 1975. 5 pp. ◆ Technical Preservation Services Reading List.

Wallace, Phillip B. *Colonial Ironwork in Old Philadelphia: The Craftsmanship of the Early Days of the Republic.* 1930. Reprint. New York: Dover Publications, 1970. 147 pp., chiefly illus., measured drawings, index.

Wickersham, John B. *Victorian Ironwork: A Catalogue.* 1857. Reprint. With a new introduction by Margot Gayle. Philadelphia: Athenaeum of Philadelphia and the American Life Foundation, 1977. 112 pp., illus.

Bridges/Harbors/Tunnels

Auvil, Myrtle. *Covered Bridges of West Virginia: Past and Present.* 3rd ed. with additional material. Parsons, W. Va.: McClain Print Co., 1977. 249 pp., illus., index.

Beaver, Patrick. *A History of Tunnels.* Secaucus, N.J.: Citadel, c1972, 1976. 155 pp., illus., bibliog.

Billington, David P. *Robert Maillart's Bridges.* Princeton, N.J.: Princeton University Press, c1979. 148 pp., illus., bibliog. references, index. ◆ Concrete construction.

Cockrell, Nick, and Bill Cockrell. *Roofs Over Rivers: A Guide to Oregon's Covered Bridges.* Beaverton, Ore.: Touchstone Press, 1978. 122 pp., maps and drawings, bibliog.

Comp, T. Allan, and Donald Jackson. "Bridge Truss Types: A Guide to Dating and

Identifying," *History News,* 32:5 (May 1977), Technical Leaflet no. 95.

Deibler, Dan Grove. *A Survey and Photographic Inventory of Metal Truss Bridges in Virginia: 1865–1932.* Charlottesville: Virginia Highway and Transportation Research Council, 1975–. illus., bibliog. references. ◆ Unique project in U.S. which included establishing criteria and a rating system; 8 vols. to date. Vol. 1—*An Examination of the Development of the Truss Form including an Annotated List of Nineteenth and Twentieth Century Bridge Companies;* remaining volumes are surveys within each construction district.

Gies, Joseph. *Bridges and Men.* New York: Grosset & Dunlap, c1963, 1966. 343 pp., illus., diagrams, appendix, bibliog., index.

Graton, Milton S. *The Last of the Covered Bridge Builders.* Plymouth, N.H.: Clifford-Nichol, c1978. 147 pp., illus., plates. ◆ Author-contractor who worked on 22 bridges, primarily in New England.

Jacobs, David, and Anthony E. Neville. *Bridges, Canals and Tunnels: The Engineering Conquest of America.* New York: American Heritage Publishing Co., distr. by Van Nostrand, 1968. 159 pp., plates, illus., diagrams, maps, appendix, bibliog., index.

Kassler, Elizabeth (Bauer). *The Architecture of Bridges.* By Elizabeth B. Mock. 1949. Reprint. New York: Published for the Museum of Modern Art by Arno Press, 1972. 127 pp., illus., glossary.

McCullough, David G. *The Great Bridge.* New York: Simon & Schuster, 1972. 636 pp., illus., bibliog., index. ◆ History of the building of the Brooklyn Bridge.

Plowden, David. *Bridges: The Spans of North America.* New York: Viking Press, 1974. 328 pp., illus., plans, bibliog., index.

Sanström, Gösta E. *Tunnels.* 1st ed. New York: Holt, Rinehart & Winston, c1963. 427 pp., illus., maps, bibliog.

Scott, Quinta, and Howard S. Miller. *The Eads Bridge.* Columbia: University of Missouri Press, 1979. 142 pp., illus., bibliog. references, index. ◆ First American bridge to employ "steel" in its principal members.

Shank, William H. *Historic Bridges of Pennsylvania.* 3rd ed. York, Pa.: American Canal and Transportation Center, 1980. 70 pp., illus., bibliog.

Steinman, David B. *The Builders of the Bridge: The Story of John Roebling and His Son.* 1950. Reprint. New York: Arno Press, 1972. 457 pp., illus., bibliog.

Steinman, David B., and Sara Ruth Watson. *Bridges and their Builders.* Rev. and expanded ed. New York: Dover Publications, 1957. 401 pp., illus.

Vogel, Robert M. *Tunnel Engineering, A Museum Treatment.* Washington, D.C.: Smithsonian Institution; for sale by Supt. of Docs., U.S. Government Printing Office, 1964. 203–239 pp., illus., map, plans, bibliog. ♦ U.S. National Museum Bulletin 240, Contributions from the Museum of History and Technology Paper 41.

Water Supply/Dams

Billings, William R. *Some Details of Water-Works Construction.* 3rd ed. 1898. Reprint. Park Ridge, N.J.: Noyes Press, 1972. 96 pp., illus. ♦ Noyes Press Series in History of Technology vol. 2. Based on a series of articles in the Engineering Record.

Blake, Nelson M. *Water for the Cities: A History of the Urban Water-Supply Problem in the United States.* Syracuse, N.Y.: Syracuse University Press, 1956. 341 pp., illus., maps, bibliog. references. ♦ Development of public water supply in eastern cities 1776 to 1876.

Green, Donald E. *Land of the Underground Rain: Irrigation on the Texas High Plains, 1910–1970.* Austin: University of Texas Press, 1973. 295 pp., illus., bibliog.

Lankton, Larry D. *The "Practicable" Engineer: John B. Jervis and the Old Croton Aqueduct.* Chicago: Public Works Historical Society, 1977. 30 pp., illus., bibliog. references.

Leffel, J., & Co. *Construction of Mill Dams.* 1881. Reprint. Park Ridge, N.J.: Noyes Press, 1972. 152 pp., illus. ♦ Noyes Press Series in History of Technology vol. 1. ♦ Reprinted from the 1881 ed. which was published together with another work under title: Leffel's Construction of Mill Dams, and Bookwalter's Millwright and Mechanic.

Smith, Norman A. F. *A History of Dams.* Se-

caucus, N.J.: Citadel Press, 1972. 279 pp., illus., maps, bibliog., glossary. ♦ Includes water supply, irrigation, hydraulic and hydroelectric power, canal supply and all other functions.

Vogel, Robert M. *Roebling's Delaware & Hudson Canal Aqueduct.* Washington, D.C.: Smithsonian Institution Press; for sale by Supt. of Docs., U.S. Government Printing Office, 1971. ♦ Smithsonian Institution Studies in History and Technology no. 10.

Water for the Southwest: *Historical Survey and Guide to Historic Sites.* By T. Lindsay Baker and others. New York: American Society of Civil Engineers, 1973. 205 pp., illus., bibliog. ♦ ASCE Historical Publication no. 3. Prepared in cooperation with HAER and the Water Resources Center, Texas Tech University. Sites range from prehistoric relics and Spanish-American works to 20th-century engineering projects.

Surveying/Mapping

Bagrow, Leo. *History of Cartography.* Rev. & enl. by R. A. Skelton. Cambridge, Mass.: Harvard University Press, 1964. 321 pp., illus., bibliog.

Ernst, Joseph W. *With Compass and Chain: Federal Land Surveyors in the Old Northwest, 1785–1816.* New York: Arno Press, c1958, 1979. 319 pp., maps, bibliog.

Harvey, P. D. A. *The History of Topographical Maps: Symbols, Pictures, and Surveys.* London: Thames & Hudson, c1980. 199 pp., illus., maps, bibliog. references.

Hodgman, Francis. *A Manual of Land Surveying: Comprising an Elementary Course of Practice with Instruments and a Treatise Upon the Survey of Public and Private Lands.* 1891. Reprint. Columbus, Ohio: Buckner Historical Surveying Book Reprints, 1976. 424 pp., illus., diagrams. ♦ Reprint of 1891 edition with revisions to 1913.

Stewart, Lowell O. *Public Land Surveys.* 1935. Reprint. New York: Arno Press, 1979. 202 pp., plates, illus., bibliog., index. ♦ History, instructions and methods.

Thompson, Morris M. *Maps for America: Cartographic Products of the U.S. Geological Survey and Others.* Reston, Va.: The Survey; for sale by the Supt. of Docs., U.S. Government Printing Office, Washington, D.C., 1979. 265

pp., illus., maps, bibliog. ◆ Development of American mapping from early days of the William Young transit to satellite programs used for mapping the moon.

Tooley, Ronald Vere, comp. *Tooley's Dictionary of Mapmakers.* New York: A. R. Liss; Amsterdam: Meridian Pub. Co., c1979. 684 pp., illus., bibliog. ◆ Entries cover persons from earliest times to 1900.

Transportation

General Works

Baer, Christopher T. *Canals and Railroads of the Mid-Atlantic States, 1800–1860.* Wilmington, Del.: Regional Economic History Center, Eleutherian Mills-Hagley Foundation, 1981. 51 pp., 29 pp., illus., maps, bibliog.

Dunbar, Seymour. *A History of Travel in America.* 1915. Reprint. Westport, Conn.: Greenwood Press, 1968. 4 vols., paged continuously, illus., maps, bibliog. ◆ Subtitle: Showing the Development of Travel and Transportation from the Crude Methods of the Canoe and the Dog-Sled to the Highly Organized Railway Systems of the Present, Together with a Narrative of the Human Experiences and Changing Social Conditions that Accompanied this Economic Conquest of the Continent.

Faulk, Odie B. *Destiny Road: The Gila Trail and the Opening of the Southwest.* New York: Oxford University Press, 1973. ◆ Development of transportation and communication in the Gadsden Purchase from early Spanish expeditions to early 20th century.

Hill, Forest G. *Roads, Rails and Waterways: The Army Engineers and Early Transportation.* 1957. Reprint. Westport, Conn.: Greenwood Press, 1977.

Hofsommer, Donovan Lowell. *Prairie Oasis: The Railroads, Steamboats, and Resorts of Iowa's Spirit Lake Country.* Des Moines, Iowa: Waukon and Mississippi Press, c1975. 159 pp., illus., maps, bibliog. references, index.

Meyer, Balthaser H. *History of Transportation in the United States before 1860.* Washington, D.C.: Carnegie Institution of Washington, 1917. 678 pp., maps, bibliog. ◆ Carnegie Institution of Washington Publications no. 215C. Reprinted by Peter Smith, Gloucester, Mass., 1948.

Powered Vehicles. By Reginald Carpenter, et al. New York: Crown Publishers, 1974. 240 pp., illus., bibliog. ◆ Survey of air, land and sea vehicles.

Taylor, George R. *The Transportation Revolution, 1815–1860.* White Plains, N.Y.: M. E. Sharpe, c1951, 1977. 490 pp., illus., maps, bibliog. ◆ Economic History of the United States vol. 4.

Transportation in the Puget Sound Region: *Past, Present & Future.* Edited by James W. Scott. Bellingham: Center for Pacific Northwest Studies, Western Washington State College, 1977. 127 pp., maps, tables, charts, bibliog. references.

NOTE

Journal of Transport History. 1953, new series 1971, semiannual, subscription. Manchester University Press, Oxford Road, Manchester M13 9PL, England. ◆ Beginning 1962, includes a short annual "Transport Bibliography."

Land Transportation

The American Car Since 1775, *The Most Complete Survey of the American Automobile Ever Published.* By the editors of Automobile Quarterly. New York: L. S. Bailey, distr. by Dutton, 1971. 504 pp., illus.

American Railway Master Mechanics' Association. *Locomotive Dictionary: An Illustrated Vocabulary of Terms which Designate American Railroad Locomotives, Their Parts, Attachments and Details of Construction, with Definitions and Illustrations of Typical British Locomotive Practice; five thousand one hundred and fortyeight illustrations.* Compiled for the American Railway Master Mechanics' Association by George L. Fowler. 1906. Reprint. Novato, Calif.: Newton K. Gregg, 1972. 523 pp., illus., advertising supplement. ◆ 15 editions produced between 1906 and 1956.

Berkebile, Donald H., ed. *American Carriages, Sleighs, Sulkies, and Carts: 168 Illustrations from Victorian Sources.* New York: Dover Publications, 1977. 167 pp., chiefly illus.

Berkbile, Donald H. *Carriage Terminology: An Historical Dictionary.* Washington, D.C.: Smithsonian Institution Press, 1978. 487 pp., illus., bibliog.

Condit, Carl W. *The Port of New York.* Chicago: University of Chicago Press, 1980–82. 2 vols., illus., maps, plans, bibliog. ◆ Vol. 1—*A History of the Rail Terminal System from the Beginnings of Pennsylvania Station;* Vol. 2—*A History of the Rail Terminal System from the Grand Central Electrification to the Present.*

Detroit. Public Library. Automotive History Collection. *The Automotive History Collection of the Detroit Public Library: A Simplified Guide to Its Holdings.* Boston: G. K. Hall, 1966. 2 vols. ◆ Dictionary catalog of books, periodicals, automobile catalogs, and special collections.

Fletcher, William. *English and American Steam Carriages and Traction Engines.* 1903. Reprint, with a new intro. by W. J. Hughes. North Pomfret, Vt.: David & Charles Reprints, 1973. 427 pp., illus. ◆ Continuation and update of earlier work, *The History and Development of Steam Locomotion on Common Roads* (1891).

Forney, Matthias N. *The Railroad Car Builder's Pictorial Dictionary.* 1897. Reprint, with a new intro. by John F. Stover. New York: Dover Publications, 1974. 491 pp., illus. ◆ Also available, reprints of 1888 and 1906 editions by Gregg Reprints, Kentfield, Calif.

Hilton, George W., and John F. Due. *The Electric Interurban Railways in America.* Stanford, Calif.: Stanford University Press, 1960. 463 pp., illus., maps, bibliog. references.

Hitt, Rodney. *Electric Railway Dictionary: Definitions and Illustrations of the Parts and Equipment of Electric Railway Cars and Trucks.* Compiled under the direction of a committee appointed by the American Electric Railway Association. 1911. Reprint. Novato, Calif.: Newton K. Gregg, 1972. 63, 292 pp., illus. ◆ Includes dictionary and advertising sections.

Hofsommer, Donovan L., comp. *Railroads of the Trans-Mississippi West: A Selected Bibliography.* Plainview, Tex.: Wayland College, 1974. 45 pp.

McCall, Walter P. *American Fire Engines since 1900.* Glen Ellyn, Ill.: Crestline Pub., c1976. 384 pp., illus.

Middleton, William D. *When the Steam Railroads Electrified.* Milwaukee: Kalmbach Books, 1974. 439 pp., illus., index.

Moloney, James H. *Encyclopedia of American Cars, 1930–42.* Editing and design by George H. Dammann. Glen Ellyn, Ill.: Crestline Pub., c1977. 383 pp., illus.

Oliver, Smith Hempstone, and Donald H. Berkebile. *Wheels and Wheeling: The Smithsonian Cycle Collection.* Washington, D.C.: Smithsonian Institution Press, for sale by Supt. of Docs., U.S. Government Printing Office, 1974. 104 pp., illus., bibliog. ◆ Smithsonian Studies in History and Technology no. 24.

Rae, John B. *The American Automobile: A Brief History.* Chicago: University Press, 1965. 265 pp., illus., maps, bibliog.

Rae, John B. *The Road and the Car in American Life.* Cambridge, Mass.: MIT Press, 1971. 390 pp., bibliog.

Ritchie, Andrew. *King of the Road: An Illustrated History of Cycling.* Berkeley, Calif.: Ten Speed Press, 1975. 192 pp., bibliog., index.

Seebree, Mac, and Paul Ward. *The Trolley Coach in North America.* Cerritos, Calif.: I. L. Swett, 1974. 416 pp., illus., bibliog. ◆ Companion volume to authors' *Transit's Stepchild: The Trolley Coach* (1973).

Sharp, Archibald. *Bicycles and Tricycles: An Elementary Treatise on Their Design and Construction, with Examples and Tables.* 1896. Reprint. Cambridge, Mass.: MIT Press, c1977. 536 pp., illus., index.

Smith, J. Bucknall. *A Treatise Upon Cable or Rope Traction, as Applied to the Working of Street and Other Railways.* 2nd ed., with additional materials by George W. Hilton. 1887. Reprint. Philadelphia, Pa.: Owlswick Press, 1977. 200 pp., illus., bibliog. references, index.

Tuplin, William A. *The Steam Locomotive: Its Form and Function.* New York: Scribners, 1974. 158 pp., illus., index.

White, John H., Jr. *The American Railroad Passenger Car.* Baltimore: Johns Hopkins University Press, c1978. 699 pp., illus., bibliog., appendices, index.

White, John H., Jr. *A History of the American Locomotive: Its Development, 1830–1880.* 1968. Reprint. New York: Dover Publications, 1979. 504 pp., illus., appendices, bibliog., index.

White, John H., Jr., ed. *Horse Cars, Cable Cars and Omnibuses: All 107 Photographs* *from the John Stephenson Company Album, 1888.* New York: Dover Publications, 1974. 33 pp., 54 leaves of plates, bibliog.

Wixom, Charles W. *ARBA Pictorial History of Roadbuilding.* Washington, D.C.: American Road Builder's Association, c1975. 207 pp., chiefly illus., bibliog.

NOTE

Automobile Quarterly. 1962, 4/yr., subscription. Automobile Quarterly, Inc., 221 Nassau Street, Princeton, New Jersey 08540.

Railroad History. 1921, semiannual, membership/subscription. Railway and Locomotive Historical Society, Division of Transportation, Smithsonian Institution, Washington, D.C. 20560. Cumulative index 1921–71, then every two years. Formerly: Railway and Locomotive Historical Society. *Bulletin.*

Marine Transportation

Adney, Edwin Tappan, and Howard I. Chapelle. *The Bark Canoes and Skin Boats of North America.* Washington, D.C.: Smithsonian Institution, 1964. 242 pp., illus., bibliog., appendix, index. ◆ U.S. National Museum Bulletin 230.

Ansel, Willits D. *The Whaleboat: A Study of Design, Construction and Use from 1850 to 1970.* Mystic, Conn.: Mystic Seaport Museum, c1978. 147 pp., illus., bibliog., index.

Blandford, Percy W. *An Illustrated History of Small Boats: A History of Oared, Poled and Paddled Craft.* Bourne End, Eng.: Spurbooks, distr. by Transatlantic Arts, Levittown, N.Y., 1974. 130 pp., illus., bibliog., index.

Bockstoce, John R. *Steam Whaling in the Western Arctic.* With contributions by William A. Baker and Charles F. Batchelder. New Bedford, Mass.: Old Dartmouth Historical Society, 1977. 127 pp., illus., maps, bibliog. ◆ Catalog for special exhibition at the Whaling Museum.

Brown, Alexander Crosby. *Juniper Waterway: A History of the Albemarle and Chesapeake Canal.* Charlottesville: Published for the Mariners' Museum and the Norfolk County Historical Society by the University Press of Virginia, 1981. 255 pp., illus., bibliog., index.

Chapelle, Howard I. *The American Fishing Schooner, 1825–1935.* New York: Norton, 1973. 690 pp., illus.

Chapelle, Howard I. *American Sailing Craft.* 1936. Reprint. Camden, Me.: International Marine, 1975. 239 pp., illus., bibliog. references, index.

Chapelle, Howard I. *Boatbuilding: A Complete Handbook of Wooden Boat Construction.* New York: W. W. Norton & Co., c1941. 624 pp., illus., plans, diagrams.

Chapelle, Howard I. *The National Watercraft Collection.* 2nd ed. Washington, D.C.: Smithsonian Institution Press, 1976. 299 pp., illus., bibliog., index. ◆ Describes and illustrates the collection of ship models.

Cutler, Carl C. *Greyhounds of the Sea; the Story of the American Clipper Ship.* Annapolis: U.S. Naval Institute, c1930, 1961. 592 pp., illus.

Cutler, Carl C. *Queens of the Western Ocean; the Story of America's Mail and Passenger Sailing Lines.* Annapolis: U.S. Naval Institute, 1961. 672 pp., illus., plans, bibliog. references.

Greenhill, Basil. *Archaeology of the Boat: A New Introductory Study.* With chapters by John S. Morrison and Sean McGrail. Middletown, Conn.: Wesleyan University Press, 1976. 320 pp., illus., maps, plans, bibliogs., glossary, index.

Harris, Robert. *Canals and Their Architecture.* New York: Frederick A. Praeger, 1969. 223 pp., illus., drawings, bibliog., appendices, maps, index.

Holland, Francis Ross. *America's Lighthouses: Their Illustrated History Since 1716.* Brattleboro, Vt.: Stephen Greene Press, 1972. 226 pp., illus., bibliog., index.

Hunter, Louis C. *Steamboats on the Western Rivers: An Economic and Technological History.* 1949. Reprint. New York: Octagon Books, 1969. 684 pp., illus., maps, bibliog. footnotes. ◆ Covers period 1810–1880; the Mississippi River and its tributaries.

May, William E., and Leonard Holder. *A History of Marine Navigation.* With a chapter on modern developments by Leonard Holder. New York: Norton, 1973. 280 pp., illus., maps, bibliog. ◆ History of marine navigation instruments; emphasis on British developments.

The Medley of Mast and Sail: *A Camera Record: 407 Photographic Illustrations of Many of the World's Vanished Sailing Craft, Both Great and Small.* Accompanied by comment and description by Frank G. G. Carr, et al. Annapolis: Naval Institute Press, c1976. 330 pp., illus.

Millar, John Fitzhugh. *American Ships of the Colonial and Revolutionary Periods.* New York: Norton, c1978. 356 pp., illus., bibliog., indexes.

Mystic Seaport Museum. *Mystic Seaport Museum Watercraft.* By Michael Bray. Mystic, Conn.: Mystic Seaport Museum, c1979. 280 pp., illus., bibliogs., indexes.

Sanderlin, Walter S. *The Great National Project: A History of the Chesapeake and Ohio Canal.* 1946. Reprint. New York: Arno Press, 1976. 331 pp., illus., bibliog., index. ◆ Originally issued as Johns Hopkins University Studies in History and Political Science Series 64, no. 1.

Shank, William H. *The Amazing Pennsylvania Canals.* 3rd ed. York, Pa.: American Canal and Transportation Center, 1981. 128 pp., bibliog.

Shaw, Ronald E. *Erie Water West: A History of the Erie Canal, 1792–1854.* Lexington: University of Kentucky Press, 1966. 449 pp., illus., map, bibliog. essay.

Strobridge, Truman R. *Chronology of Aids to Navigation and the Old Lighthouse Service, 1716–1939.* Washington, D.C.: Public Affairs Division, U.S. Coast Guard, 1974. 39 pp., bibliog. ◆ U.S. Coast Guard Historical Chronology Program CG458.

Taylor, E. G. R., and M. W. Richey. *The Geometrical Seaman: A Book of Early Nautical Instruments.* London: Published by Hollis & Carter for the Institute of Navigation, 1962. 111 pp., illus.

U.S. Coast Guard. *Complete List of Lights and Other Marine Aids, Atlantic Coast of the United States.* Washington, D.C.: U.S. Government Printing Office, 1943–. annual. ◆ See also: *Pacific Coast.* 1912–.

The Visual Encyclopedia of Nautical Terms Under Sail. Principal advisors: George P. B. Naish, Alan Villiers, Basil W. Bathe, et al. New York: Crown, 1978. 250 pp. in various pagings, illus., maps, bibliog., index.

NOTES

Aids to Navigation Records. The National Archives, Record Group 26, contains records of United States aids to navigation from 1786. Sources for research on lighthouses and lightships include surviving papers, personnel ledgers, correspondence, journals, record books, and files.

American Canal Society, c/o William H. Shank, President, 809 Rathton Road, York, Pennsylvania 17403. Founded in 1972, membership includes persons interested in historic and operating canals of the Americas. Its purposes are to encourage the preservation, restoration and use of navigation canals; to save threatened canals; and to provide an exchange of canal information on an international basis. It collects and disseminates historical and engineering information on canals, conducts detailed research on the indexing of canals and canal structures. Publications include *American Canals* (quarterly bulletin); American Canal Guide series; books, and index sheets on many canals.

American Neptune: *A Quarterly Journal of Maritime History.* 1941, quarterly, subscription. Peabody Museum of Salem, East India Marine Hall, Salem, Massachusetts 01970.

Journal of Navigation. 1947, 3/yr., subscription. Royal Institute of Navigation, Cambridge University Press, Box 110, Cambridge CB2 3RL, England. ◆ Formerly: Institute of Navigation. *Journal.*

Mariner's Mirror. 1911, quarterly, membership/subscription. Society for Nautical Research, Meadow Bank, 26 Lucastes Road, Haywards Heath, West Sussex, England.

Steamship Historical Society of America, Alice S. Wilson, Secretary, 414 Pelton Avenue, Staten Island, New York 10310. Founded in 1935 to bring together professional and amateur historians, collectors and others interested in the history and development of steam or other power driven vessels. It maintains a Photo Bank of steamship and steamboat photographs including many private collections, and a library. Publications include *Steamboat Bill* (quarterly); books and pamphlets including the Lytle List, a compendium of all steam vessels known to exist before the first government list was issued in 1868. It holds an annual meeting, spring and fall interim meetings.

Air and Space Transportation

Anderson, John D., Jr. *Introduction to Flight: Its Engineering and History*. New York: McGraw-Hill Book Co., c1978. 432 pp., illus., index.

Constant, Edward W., II. *The Origins of the Turbojet Revolution*. Baltimore: Johns Hopkins University Press, c1980. 311 pp., illus., technical appendix, bibliog. references, index.

Emme, Eugene M., ed. *The History of Rocket Technology: Essays on Research, Development, and Utility*. By William M. Bland, Jr., et al. Detroit: Wayne State University Press, 1964. 320 pp., illus., bibliog. references. ◆ Published in cooperation with the Society for the History of Technology; many articles previously published in *Technology and Culture*, 4:4 (Fall 1963). Extensive bibliographic note by Arthur G. Renstrom.

Gibbs-Smith, Charles Harvard. *Flight through the Ages: A Complete, Illustrated Chronology from the Dreams of Early History to the Age of Space Exploration*. New York: Crowell, 1974. 240 pp., illus., bibliog., index.

Robertson, Bruce. *Aviation Archaeology: A Collector's Guide to Aeronautical Relics*. Cambridge: Stephens, 1977. 152 pp., illus., maps.

Smithsonian Annals of Flight. Vol. 1–. Washington, D.C.: Smithsonian Institution; for sale by Supt. of Docs., U.S. Government Printing Office, 1964–. illus., charts, maps. ◆ Short monographs.

The Wright Brothers: Heirs of Prometheus. Edited by Richard P. Hallion; with contributions by Roger E. Bilstein, et al. Washington, D.C. Published by the National Air and Space Museum, Smithsonian Institution, distr. by Smithsonian Institution Press, 1978. 146 pp., illus., bibliog.

NOTES

Aerospace Historian. 1954, quarterly, subscription. c/o Robin Higham, Editor, Eisenhower Hall, Kansas State University, Manhattan, Kansas 66506. ◆ Formerly: *Airpower Historian*. Cumulative index 1954–72 (published 1974).

American Aviation Historical Society, Thomas S. Britton, President, P. O. Box 99, Garden Grove, California 92642. Founded in 1956, the membership and regional groups include individuals interested in aircraft and research in aviation history; aviation and aerospace museums, and libraries with aviation research sections. The Society documents important personnel and events in aviation history; provides referral assistance to authors; bestows annual awards for best article and best artwork; and holds an annual meeting. It sponsors AAHS Book Service, providing members with discounts on aviation related books. It maintains a resource collection of negatives and slides on aircraft and aircraft markings and a library on aviation history, military unit histories and biographies. Publications include *Journal* (quarterly); *Newsletter* (quarterly); decennial cumulative index for the Journal and Newsletter; catalogs of the Negative Lending Library (irregular); and monographs.

Energy Conversion

General Works

Ayres, Eugene, and Charles A. Scarlott. *Energy Sources, The Wealth of the World*. New York: McGraw-Hill, 1952. 344 pp., illus., bibliog.

Ewbank, Thomas. *A Descriptive and Historical Account of Hydraulic and Other Machines for Raising Water, Ancient and Modern, Including the Progressive Development of the Steam Engine*. 1842. Reprint. New York: Arno Press, 1972. 582 pp., illus., bibliog. references.

Klotz, Louis H., ed. *Energy Sources: the Promises and Problems*. Durham, N.H.: Center for Industrial and Institutional Development, University of New Hampshire, 1980. 388 pp. in various pagings, illus., bibliogs. ◆ Traces energy development; titles in series include water power, coal, gas, nuclear, oil, solar, tidal, wind and wood.

McNeil, Ian. *Hydraulic Power*. London: Longman, 1972. 197, 12 pp., map, plan, bibliog., index.

Rouse, Hunter. *Hydraulics in the United States, 1776–1976*. Iowa City: Institute of Hydraulic Research, University of Iowa, c1976. 238 pp., illus., bibliogs., index.

Smith, Norman A. F. *Man and Water: A History of Hydro-Technology.* New York: Scribner's, c1975. 239 pp., illus., bibliog., index. ◆ Covers antiquity to the present; irrigation, water supply, water power, and general problems today.

Wind and Water Power

Beedell, Suzanne M. *Windmills.* New York: Scribner, c1975. 143 pp., illus., bibliog., index. ◆ Primarily British windmills; some American examples.

Garber, D. W. *Waterwheels and Millstones: A History of Ohio Gristmills and Milling.* Columbus: Ohio Historical Society, 1970. 139 pp., illus., glossary.

Hamilton, Edward P. *The Village Mill in Early New England.* Sturbridge, Mass.: Old Sturbridge Village, c1964. 23 pp., illus. ◆ Booklet Series no. 18.

Howell, Charles, and Allan Keller. *The Mill of Philipsburg Manor, Upper Mills and a Brief History of Milling.* Tarrytown, N.Y.: Sleepy Hollow Restorations, 1977. 192 pp., illus., glossary.

Howell, Kenneth T., and Einar W. Carlson. *Empire Over the Dam: The Story of Waterpowered Industry, Long Since Passed from the Scene.* Chester, Conn.: The Pequot Press, c1974. 269 pp., illus., appendices, bibliog. ◆ Waterpowered industries in northwestern Connecticut.

Hunter, Louis C. *A History of Industrial Power in the United States, 1780–1930.* Charlottesville: Published for the Eleutherian Mills-Hagley Foundation by the University Press of Virginia, c1979–. ◆ Vol. 1—*Waterpower in the Century of the Steam Engine.* 606 pp., illus., maps, plans, bibliog. references, appendix, index.

Jaray, Cornell, comp. *The Mills of Long Island.* Southampton, N.Y.: Yankee Peddler Book Co., c1962, 1975. 44 pp., illus. ◆ Part 1—Windmills of Eastern Long Island, by Rex Wailes; Part 2—The Water Mills on Long Island, by Bernice Marshall.

Priamo, Carol. *Mills of Canada.* Toronto and New York: McGraw-Hill Ryerson, c1976. 192 pp., illus., bibliog., index.

Rawson, Marion N. *Little Old Mills.* New York: Johnson Reprint Corp., c1963, 1970. 366 pp.,

illus. ◆ History of mills and mill-work of all kinds, map of mill beginnings, basic forces, hand and animal power, tide mills, dams and waterways, windmills.

Reynolds, John. *Windmills and Watermills.* New York: Praeger Publishers, 1970. 196 pp., illus., glossary, bibliog.

Sweeny, F. R. J. *The Burden Water-Wheel.* Washington, D.C.: Society for Industrial Archeology, 1973. 12 pp., illus., diagrams. ◆ Occasional Publication no. 2. Reprinted from the 1915 Transactions of the American Society of Civil Engineers with additional illustrations, and an introduction by Robert M. Vogel.

Torrey, Volta. *Wind-Catchers, American Windmills of Yesterday and Tomorrow.* Brattleboro, Vt.: Stephen Greene Press, c1976, 1981. 226 pp., illus., bibliog. references, appendix, index.

Tyrwhitt, Janice; William Fox; and Bill Brooks. *The Mill.* Toronto: McClelland and Stewart, c1976. 224 pp., chiefly illus., bibliog., index. ◆ Grist, saw, and other mills in Canada and the U.S.

Vance, Mary. *Windmills and Wind Power: A Bibliography.* Monticello, Ill.: Vance Bibliographies, 1981. 59 pp.

Wailes, Rex. *The English Windmill.* London: Routledge & K. Paul; New York: Augustus M. Kelley, 1967. 246 pp., illus., bibliog.

Wailes, Rex. *A Source Book of Windmills and Watermills.* London: Ward Lock, 1979. 128 pp., illus., index.

Wilson, Paul N. *Water Turbines.* London: H. M. Stationery Office, distr. by Pendragon House, Palo Alto City, Calif., 1974. 31 pp., illus. ◆ A London Science Museum booklet.

Zimiles, Martha, and Murray Zimiles. *Early American Mills.* New York: Clarkson N. Potter, 1973. 290 pp., illus., bibliog., index.

NOTE

Society for the Preservation of Old Mills, c/o Donald W. Martin, President, Box 435, Wiscasset, Maine 04578. The Society was founded in 1972 to promote interest, both public and private, in old mills and other Americana. It encourages the preservation, restoration and adaptive use of such structures, and honors individuals whose work and ideas made the mills possible. It compiles lists of old mills still standing and of those still grinding specialty flours; bestows a Millstone Award; and holds an annual meeting. It publishes *Old Mill News* (1972, quarterly).

Engines

American Society of Mechanical Engineers. Gas Turbine Division. *Bibliography on Gas Turbines, 1896–1948.* New York: American Society of Mechanical Engineers, 1962. 134 pp.

Buchanan, Robert A., and George Watkins. *The Industrial Archaeology of the Stationary Steam Engine.* London: Allen Lane, 1976. 199 pp., illus., diagrams, bibliog., index. ◆ Includes technological development and evolution with emphasis on form and details; the British builders, under headings by type.

Cardwell, David Stephen Lowell. *Steam Power in the Eighteenth Century: A Case Study in the Application of Science.* London and New York: Sheed and Ward, 1963. 98 pp., bibliog. ◆ Study of the Newcomen and Watt engines.

Cummins, C. Lyle, Jr. *Internal Fire.* Lake Oswego, Ore.: Carnot Press, 1976. 351 pp., illus., 38 leaves of plates, bibliog., index.

Dickenson, Henry Winram. *A Short History of the Steam Engine.* 1938. Reprint, with a new intro. by A. E. Musson. London: F. Cass, 1963. 255 pp., illus., charts, diagrams, index. ◆ Savery, Newcomen, Watt, pressure, boilers, turbine engines.

King, William James. *Beam Engines.* Dearborn, Mich.: Henry Ford Museum and Greenfield Village, 1974. 24 pp., illus. ◆ Describes examples, mostly British, preserved at the Museum.

Major, John Kenneth. *Animal-Powered Engines.* London: B. T. Batsford, 1978. 168 pp., illus., bibliog., index. ◆ Roles of these devices in agriculture, industry and mining.

Pursell, Carroll W., Jr. *Early Stationary Steam Engines in America: A Study in the Migration of a Technology.* Washington, D.C.: Smithsonian Institution Press, 1969. 152 pp., illus., diagrams, charts, bibliog., index.

Rolt, Lionel T. C., and J. S. Allen. *The Steam Engine of Thomas Newcomen.* New York: Science History, 1977. 160 pp., illus., maps, bibliog.

Thurston, Robert H. *A History of the Growth of the Steam-Engine.* 1939. Reprint. With a supplementary chapter by William N. Barnard. Port Washington, N.Y.: Kennikat Press, 1972. 555 pp., illus., diagrams, tables, index.

Walker, Graham. *Stirling Machines.* New York: Oxford University Press, 1980. 532 pp., illus., bibliog., indexes. ◆ Study of the hot-air engine.

Watkins, George. *The Stationary Steam Engine.* Newton Abbot: David & Charles, 1968. 119 pp., illus.

Watkins, George. *The Steam Engine in Industry.* Ashbourne, Eng.: Mooreland Publishing Co., c1978–79. 2 vols. (128, 128 pp.), illus., glossary. ◆ Vol. 1—*The Public Services;* Vol. 2—*Mining and the Metal Trades.* British examples.

Watkins, George. *The Textile Mill Engine.* Newton Abbot: David & Charles, 1970. 2 vols., illus.

Woodall, Frank. *Steam Engines and Waterwheels: A Pictorial Study of Some Early Mining Machines.* Buxton, Eng.: Mooreland Publishing Co., 1975. 96 pp., illus., bibliog. references, index. ◆ Pumping engines and other English mining machinery.

Heating/Ventilation/Refrigeration

Anderson, Oscar E. *Refrigeration in America: A History of a New Technology and Its Impact.* Port Washington, N.Y.: Kennikat Press, c1953, 1972. 344 pp., illus., bibliog.

Cummings, Richard Osborn. *The American Ice Harvests: A Historical Study in Technology 1800–1918.* Berkeley: University of California Press, 1949. 184 pp., illus., drawings, appendices, bibliog. footnotes, index.

Edgerton, Samuel Y., Jr. "Heating Stoves in Eighteenth Century Philadelphia," *Bulletin of APT,* III:2–3 (1971), pp. 15–104 (special issue).

Hall, Henry. *The Ice Industry of the United States, with a Brief Sketch of Its History.* 1888. Reprint. Burlington, Vt.: Early American Industries Association, 1974. 43 pp., illus. ◆ Reprinted from U.S. Department of the Interior, Census Division, Tenth Census, 1880, v. 22.

Hough, Walter. *Collection of Heating and Lighting Utensils in the United States National Museum.* 1928. Reprint. Talcottville, Conn.: Rushlight Club, 1981. 113 pp., illus., plates, bibliog. references, index. ◆ Originally published as Smithsonian Institution, National Museum Bulletin 141.

Ingels, Margaret. *Willis Haviland Carrier, Father of Air-Conditioning.* 1952. Reprint. New York: Arno Press, 1972. 170 pp., illus., bibliog. ◆ Includes chronological tables of events which led to modern air conditioning, 1500–1952.

Jones, Joseph C. *American Ice Boxes: A Book on the History, Collecting and Restoration of Ice Boxes.* Humble, Tex.: Jobeco Books, 1981. 100 pp., illus., bibliog. ◆ Includes manufacturers and illus. from advertisements; available from Box 3323, Humble, Texas 77347.

Orton, Vrest. *Observations on the Forgotten Art of Building a Good Fireplace: The Story of Sir Benjamin Thompson, Count Rumford, an American Genius, & His Principles of Fireplace Design Which Have Remained Unchanged for 174 Years.* 2nd ed. Dublin, N.H.: Yankee, 1974. 60 pp., illus.

Peirce, Josephine Halvorson. *Fire on the Hearth: The Evolution and Romance of the Heating Stove.* With 145 illus. from photos and drawings showing an amazing variety of heating devices; also entertaining anecdotes, excerpts from old diaries and other papers, alluring advertisments and interesting bits of information pertaining to their manufacture and uses. Intro. by Robert W. G. Vail. Springfield, Mass.: Pond-Ekberg Co., 1951. 254 pp., illus., bibliog., appendices, index.

Rowsome, Frank, Jr. *The Bright and Glowing Place.* Brattleboro, Vt.: S. Greene Press, 1975. 212 pp., illus. ◆ History of stove and fireplace in U.S.

Stifler, Susan Martha (Reed). *The Beginnings of a Century of Steam and Water Heating by the H. B. Smith Company.* Westfield, Mass.: H. B. Smith Co., 1960. 163 pp., illus., bibliog.

Wright, Lawrence. *Home Fires Burning: The History of Domestic Heating and Cooking.* London: Routledge & K. Paul, c1964, 1968. 219 pp., illus., bibliog., index.

Electricity

Benjamin, Park. *A History of Electricity.* 1898. Reprint. New York: Arno Press, 1975. 611 pp., illus., bibliog. references.

Bright, Arthur A., Jr. *The Electric-Lamp Industry; Technological Change and Economic Development from 1800 to 1947.* 1949. Reprint. New York: Arno Press, 1972. 526 pp., illus., bibliog.

Dibner, Bern. *Benjamin Franklin: Electrician.* In celebration of the two hundredth year of the nation he helped found. Norwalk, Conn.: Burndy Library, 1976. 48 pp., illus., bibliog. references. ◆ Burndy Library Publication no. 30.

Dunsheath, Percy. *A History of Electrical Power Engineering.* Cambridge, Mass.: MIT Press, c1962, 1969. 368 pp., illus., bibliog.

Edison, Thomas A. *The Beginning of the Incandescent Lamp and Lighting System: An Autobiographical Account.* Introduction by Robert G. Koolakian. Dearborn, Mich.: Greenfield Village and Henry Ford Museum, c1976. 29 pp., illus.

Hennessey, Roger A. S. *The Electric Revolution.* Newcastle upon Tyne: Oriel, 1972. 190 pp., diagrams, plates, maps, bibliog.

Hubbard, Howard G., comp. *A Complete Check list of Household Lights Patented in the United States, 1792–1862.* South Hadley, Mass.: 1935. 24 leaves. ◆ Reproduced from typewritten copy.

King, William James. *The Development of Electrical Technology in the 19th Century.* Washington, D.C.: Smithsonian Institution, 1962. 231–407 pp., illus. ◆ U.S. National Museum Bulletin 228; Contributions from the Museum of History and Technology, Paper 28, 30.

Mottelay, Paul Fleury, comp. *Bibliographical History of Electricity and Magnetism.* 1922. Reprint. New York: Arno Press, 1975. 673 pp., illus.

Passer, Harold. *The Electrical Manufacturers, 1875–1900: A Study in Competition, Entrepreneurship, Technical Change, and Economic Growth.* 1953. Reprint. New York: Arno Press, 1972. 412 pp., bibliog.

Sharlin, Harold. *The Making of the Electrical Age; From Telegraph to Automation.* London and New York: Abelard-Schuman, c1963, 1964. 248 pp., illus., bibliog. references. ◆ Two parts, communication and power; includes telegraph, telephone, central power station, electric motor, and automation.

Smithsonian Institution. Division of Electricity and Nuclear Energy. *Manuscripts in U.S. Depositories Relating to the History of Electrical Science and Technology.* Compiled by David A. Hounshell. Washington, D.C.: 1973. 115 pp.

Turning Points in American Electrical History. Edited by James E. Brittain. New York: IEEE Press, distr. by Wiley, c1977. 399 pp., illus., bibliog. references, indexes. ◆ Reprints 64 papers beginning with Benjamin Franklin.

Materials and Processes

General Works

Bishop, John L. *A History of American Manufactures from 1608 to 1860.* 3rd ed., rev. and enl. 1868. Reprint. New York: A. M. Kelley, 1966. 3 vols., illus., bibliog. footnotes, appendix—statistics of the principal manufacturing centers, index.

Clark, Victor S. *The History of Manufactures in the United States from 1607 to 1928.* 1916–1928. Reprint. New York: Peter Smith, 1949. 3 vols., illus., graphs, charts, appendices, bibliog. ◆ Originally published, Carnegie Institution of Washington, 1916, Publication no. 215B.

Gregory, Cedric E. *A Concise History of Mining.* New York: Pergamon Press, c1980. 259 pp., illus., maps, bibliog., index.

Hodges, Henry. *Artifacts: An Introduction to Early Materials and Technology.* Atlantic Highlands, N.J.: Humanities Press, c1964, 1981. 248 pp., illus., bibliog., index.

Hollister, Ovando James. *The Mines of Colorado.* 1867. Reprint. New York: Arno Press, 1973. 450 pp., map.

Lindsay, Jean. *A History of the North Wales Slate Industry.* North Pomfret, Vt.: David & Charles, 1974. 376 pp., illus., map, bibliog.

Richardson, John Bryning. *Metal Mining.* London: Allen Lane, 1974. 207 pp., illus., 16 pp. of plates, maps, bibliog., index.

Rowe, John. *The Hard-Rock Men; Cornish Immigrants and the North American Mining Frontier.* New York: Barnes & Noble, 1974. 322 pp., illus., maps, bibliog., index.

Russell & Erwin Manufacturing Company, New Britain, Conn. *Illustrated Catalogue of Early American Hardware.* 1865. Reprint. Introduction by Lee H. Nelson. Ottawa, Ont.: Association for Preservation Technology, 1980. 436 pp., illus. ◆ Unabridged reprint of the 1865 edition published by Francis Hart & Co., N.Y. Hardware ranges from tools to cutlery, hinges to nails, kettles to guns.

Smith, Duane A. *Colorado Mining: A Photographic History.* Albuquerque: University of New Mexico Press, c1977. 176 pp., illus., maps, bibliog., index.

Wyman, Mark. *Hard Rock Epic: Western Miners and the Industrial Revolution, 1860–1910.* Berkeley: University of California Press, c1979. 331 pp., illus., maps, notes, bibliog., index.

Yankee Enterprise: *The Rise of the American System of Manufactures.* Otto Mayr and Robert C. Post, eds. Washington, D.C.: Smithsonian Institution Press, 1981. 236 pp., illus., bibliog.

Metals and Metallurgy

Aitchison, Leslie. *A History of Metals.* New York: Interscience Publishers, 1960. 2 vols. (647 pp.), illus., maps, diagrams, bibliogs.

Barraclough, Kenneth C., comp. *Sheffield Steel.* Buxton, Derbyshire: Moorland, 1976. 112 pp., illus., map, plans, bibliog., index.

Bining, Arthur Cecil. *Pennsylvania Iron Manufacture in the Eighteenth Century.* 2nd ed. Harrisburg: Pennsylvania Historical and Museum Commission, 1973. 215 pp., illus., map, bibliog., index.

Chaput, Donald. *The Cliff; America's First Great Copper Mine.* Kalamazoo, Mich.: Sequoia Press, 1971. 116 pp., illus., diagrams, drawings, maps, bibliog., index. ◆ Mining in the Upper Peninsula, 1845–1903.

Dennis, William H. *A Hundred Years of Metal-*

lurgy. Chicago: Aldine Pub. Co., c1963, 1964. 342 pp., illus., bibliogs.

Hoare, William E.; E. S. Hedges; and B. T. K. Barry. *The Technology of Tinplate.* New York: St. Martin's Press, 1965. 420 pp., illus., bibliog. references.

Kauffman, Henry J. *American Copper and Brass.* Camden, N.J.: Thomas Nelson & Sons, 1968. 288 pp., illus., bibliog.

Lathrop, William G. *The Brass Industry in the United States; A Study of the Origin and the Development of the Brass Industry in the Naugatuck Valley and Its Subsequent Extension over the Nation.* 1926. Reprint. New York: Arno Press, 1972. 174 pp., illus., bibliog.

Lewis, Walter David. *Iron and Steel in America.* Greenville, Del.: Hagley Museum, c1976. 64 pp., illus., bibliog., index.

McHugh, Jeanne. *Alexander Holley and The Makers of Steel.* Baltimore: Johns Hopkins University Press, c1980. 402 pp., illus., bibliog., index.

Mulholland, James A. *A History of Metals in Colonial America.* University: University of Alabama Press, 1981. 215 pp., illus., bibliog., index.

St. Clair, Hillary W. *Mineral Industry in Early America.* Washington, D.C.: U.S. Department of the Interior, Bureau of Mines; for sale by Supt. of Docs., U.S. Government Printing Office, 1977. 62 pp., illus., bibliog.

Sorby Centennial Symposium on the History of Metallurgy, Cleveland, 1963. *The Sorby Centennial Symposium on the History of Metallurgy, Cleveland, Ohio, October 22–23, 1963: Proceedings.* Edited by Cyril Stanley Smith. New York: Gordon and Breach Science Publishers, 1965. 558 pp., illus., bibliogs. ◆ Symposium sponsored by Society for the History of Technology, American Society for Metals, and the Metallurgical Society, American Institute of Mining, Metallurgical and Petroleum Engineers.

Swank, James M. *History of the Manufacture of Iron in All Ages, and Particularly in the United States from Colonial Times to 1891. Also a short history of early coal mining in the United States. . . .* 2nd ed. 1892. Reprint. Philadelphia: B. Franklin, 1965. 554 pp., tables, index of people.

Temin, Peter. *Iron and Steel in Nineteenth-Century America: An Economic Inquiry.* Cambridge, Mass.: MIT Press, 1964. 304 pp., bibliog.

Chemical Industries

American Chemists and Chemical Engineers. Wyndham D. Miles. Washington, D.C.: American Chemical Society, 1976. 544 pp., bibliog. references, index.

Bishop, Philip W. *Petroleum.* Washington, D.C.: Smithsonian Institution Press for the Museum of History and Technology, 1969. 31 pp., illus., diagrams, glossary, bibliog.

Blakey, Arch Fredric. *The Florida Phosphate Industry: A History of the Development and Use of a Vital Mineral.* Cambridge, Mass.: Wertheim Committee, Harvard University, distr. by Harvard University Press, 1973. 197 pp., illus., maps, bibliog. references.

Clow, Archibald, and Nan L. Clow. *The Chemical Revolution: A Contribution to Social Technology.* 1952. Reprint. Freeport, N.Y.: Books for Libraries Press, 1970. 680 pp., illus., bibliog.

Eklund, Jon. *The Incompleat Chymist: Being an Essay on the Eighteenth-Century Chemist in His Laboratory, with a Dictionary of Obsolete Chemical Terms of the Period.* Washington, D.C.: Smithsonian Institution Press, 1975. 49 pp., illus., bibliog. references. ◆ Smithsonian Studies in History and Technology no. 33.

Farber, Eduard. *History of Phosphorous.* Washington, D.C.: Smithsonian Institution; for sale by Supt. of Docs., U.S. Government Printing Office, 1965. ◆ U.S. National Museum Bulletin 240, Contributions from the Museum of History and Technology, Paper 40.

Haynes, Williams. *American Chemical Industry.* New York: Van Nostrand, 1945–54. 6 vols., illus., bibliogs.

Kaufman, Morris. *The First Century of Plastics: Celluloid and Its Sequel.* London: Plastics Institute, distr. by Iliffe Books, 1963. 130 pp., illus. ◆ Covers celluloid, synthetic resins, thermoplastics, and includes examples outside Britain.

Kaufman, Morris. *Giant Molecules: The Technology of Plastics, Fibers, and Rubber.*

Garden City, N.Y.: Doubleday, 1968. 187 pp., illus., bibliog.

Multhauf, Robert P. *Neptune's Gift: A History of Common Salt.* Baltimore: Johns Hopkins University Press, c1978. 325 pp., illus., bibliog., index.

Multhauf, Robert P. *The Origins of Chemistry.* New York: F. Watts, 1967. 412 pp., bibliog.

Munn, Robert F. *The Coal Industry in America: A Bibliography and Guide to Studies.* 2nd ed. Morgantown: West Virginia University Library, 1977. 351 pp., index.

Owen, Edgar Wesley. *Trek of the Oil Finders: A History of Exploration for Petroleum.* Tulsa, Okla.: American Association of Petroleum Geologists, 1975. 1647 pp., illus., bibliogs., index. ◆ American Association of Petroleum Geologists, Memoir no. 6.

Shreve, R. Norris, and Joseph A. Brink, Jr. *Chemical Process Industries.* 4th ed. New York: McGraw-Hill, c1977. 814 pp., illus., bibliogs., index.

Taylor, Frank Sherwood. *A History of Industrial Chemistry.* 1957. Reprint. New York: Arno Press, 1972. 467 pp., illus., bibliog.

Van Gelder, Arthur Pine, and Hugo Schlatter. *History of the Explosives Industry in America.* 1927. Reprint. New York: Arno Press, 1972. 1132 pp., illus., bibliog. references.

Welsh, Peter C. *Tanning in the United States to 1850: A Brief History.* Washington, D.C.: Museum of History and Technology, Smithsonian Institution, 1964. 99 pp., illus., bibliog. ◆ U.S. National Museum Bulletin 242.

White, Wayne E., et al. *From Salt Kettles to Nuclear Fuels Chemistry in Oklahoma.* Tulsa, Okla.: Tulsa Section, American Chemical Society, c1976. 135 pp., illus., bibliog. references.

Wilkinson, Norman B. *Explosives in History: The Story of Black Powder.* Wilmington, Del.: Hagley Museum and Rand McMally, 1966. 63 pp., illus.

Williamson, Harold F., and Arnold R. Daum. *The American Petroleum Industry.* Evanston, Ill.: Northwestern University Press, 1959–1968. 2 vols., illus., maps, diagrams, tables, bibliog. references. ◆ Vol. 1—*Age of Illumination, 1859–99* (1959); Vol. 2—*Age of Energy, 1900–1959* (1968).

Ceramics/Glass/Cement

Architectural Stained Glass. Edited by Brian Clarke. New York: Architectural Record Books, c1979. 234 pp., illus., bibliog., index.

Barnard, Julian. *Victorian Ceramic Tiles.* London: Studio Vista, 1972. 184 pp., illus., bibliog., glossary. ◆ Includes listing of English and American manufacturers.

Bivins, John, Jr. *The Moravian Potters in North Carolina.* Winston Salem, N.C.: Published for Old Salem, Inc. by the University of North Carolina Press, Chapel Hill, 1972. 300 pp., illus., bibliog.

Campbell, James Edward. *Pottery and Ceramics: A Guide to Information Sources.* Detroit: Gale Research Co., c1978. 241 pp., indexes.

Cooper, Emmanuel. *A History of Pottery.* New York: St. Martin's Press, 1972. 276 pp., illus., maps, bibliog., index.

Cox, Warren E. *The Book of Pottery and Porcelain.* Rev. ed. New York: Crown Publishers, c1970. 2 vols. (1158 pp.), illus.

Cummings, Keith. *The Technique of Glass Forming.* London: Batsford; North Pomfret, Vt.: David & Charles, 1980. 168 pp., illus., bibliog., index.

Jackson, Charles S. *The Singack and Mead's Basin Brickyards in Wayne Township.* Wayne, N.J.: Wayne Township Historical Commission, c1978. 58 pp., illus., bibliog.

Lesley, Robert W., et al. *History of the Portland Cement Industry in the United States.* With appendices covering the progress of industry by years, and an Outline of the Organization and Activities of the Portland Cement Association. 1924. Reprint. New York: Arno Press, 1972. 330 pp., illus. ◆ Includes production methods, and use of Portland cement in water works, tunnels, and domestic and industrial buildings.

McCollam, C. Harold. *The Brick and Tile Industry in Stark County, 1809–1976.* Kent, Ohio: Published for the Stark County Historical Society by Kent State University Press, 1976. 337 pp., maps, illus., notes.

McKearin, George S., and Helen McKearin. *American Glass.* New York: Crown Publishers, c1943, 1966. 634 pp., illus., drawings, bibliog. ♦ Treats technology, products and patterns.

Newman, Harold. *An Illustrated Dictionary of Glass.* With an introductory survey of the history of glass-making by Robert J. Charleston. New York: Thames and Hudson, c1977. 351 pp., illus. ♦ On title page: 2,442 entries including definitions of wares, materials, processes, forms and decorative styles; and entries on principal glass-makers, decorators, and designers, from antiquity to the present.

Plaut, James S. *Steuben Glass: A Monograph.* 3d rev. & enl. ed. New York: Dover Publications, 1972. 111 pp., illus.

Powell, Elizabeth. *Pennsylvania Pottery: Tools and Processes.* Doylestown, Pa.: Bucks County Historical Society, 1972. 20 pp., illus.

Revi, Albert C. *American Cut and Engraved Glass.* New York: T. Nelson, 1965. 497 pp., illus., bibliog.

Revi, Albert C. *American Pressed Glass and Figure Bottles.* New York: T. Nelson and Sons, 1964. 446 pp., illus., bibliog., indexes. ♦ Includes glass patents, history of firms.

Revi, Albert C. *Nineteenth Century Glass: Its Genesis and Development.* 1959. Reprint. New York: Schiffer, 1981. 270 pp., illus.

Reyntiens, Patrick. *The Technique of Stained Glass.* New York: Watson-Guptill, 1967. 192 pp., illus., diagrams, bibliog. ♦ Technical handbook with glossary, and sources of supply.

Scoville, Warren Chandler. *Revolution in Glassmaking: Entrepreneurship and Technological Change in the American Industry, 1880–1920.* 1948. Reprint. New York: Arno Press, 1972. 398 pp., illus., bibliog.

A Selection of Historic American Papers on Concrete: 1876–1926. Edited by Howard Newlon, Jr. Detroit, Mich.: American Concrete Institute, c1976. 334 pp., illus., index. ♦ Publication SP52. Landmark papers commonly referred to in work on the history of cement and concrete, all published before 1926.

Switzer, Ronald R. *The Bertrand Bottles; A Study of 19th-Century Glass and Ceramic Containers.* Washington, D.C.: National Park Service; for sale by Supt. of Docs., U.S. Government Printing Office, 1974. 100 pp., illus., bibliog. ♦ Publications in Archeology no. 12.

NOTES

Concrete History Committee, American Concrete Institute, P. O. Box 19150, Detroit, Michigan 48219. Organized in 1972, its purpose is to study and report on the history of concrete; to assemble records of achievements or failures significant in the development of design and construction practices and materials technology; to record personal contributions of those involved; to assist in the identification and encouraging the preservation of important structures and artifacts and assurance of access thereto for future study or inspection.

Journal of Glass Studies. 1959, annual, subscription. Corning Museum of Glass, Corning Glass Center, Corning, New York 14831. Includes annual bibliography of books and articles published in preceding year. Index to Vols. 1–15 (1959–1973), compiled by Marie-Anne Honeywell, published 1976.

Paper

Clapperton, Robert H. *The Paper-making Machine, Its Invention, Evolution, and Development.* 1st ed. New York: Pergamon Press, 1967. 365 pp., illus.

Davis, Charles T. *The Manufacture of Paper: Being a Description of the Various Processes for the Fabrication, Coloring, and Finishing of Every Kind of Paper....* 1886. Reprint. New York: Arno Press, 1972. 608 pp., illus., bibliog. references. ♦ Subtitle: ... Including the Different Raw Materials and the Methods for Determining Their Values: The Tools, Machines, and Practical Details Connected with an Intelligent and Profitable Prosecution of the Art, With Special Reference to the Best American Practice. To Which are added a History of Paper, Complete Lists of Paper-making Materials, Lists of American Machines, Tools, and Processes Used in Treating the Raw Materials, and in Making, Coloring, and Finishing Paper.

Gravell, Thomas L., and George Miller. *A Catalogue of American Watermarks, 1690–1835.* New York: Garland Pub., 1979. 230 pp., illus., bibliog., indexes. ♦ Text includes study of the paper mills.

Hunter, Dard. *The Literature of Papermaking, 1390–1800.* 1925. Reprint. New York: B. Franklin, 1971. 47 pp., illus.

Hunter, Dard. *Papermaking in Pioneer America.* With a new introduction by Leonard Schlosser. 1952. Reprint. New York: Garland Publishing, 1981. 178 pp., illus., bibliog. references, index.

Hunter, Dard. *Papermaking: The History and Technique of an Ancient Craft.* 2nd ed., rev. & enl. 1947. Reprint. New York: Dover Publications, 1978. 611 pp., illus., bibliog., index.

Morris, Henry. *The Paper Maker: A Survey of Lesser-known Hand Paper Mills in Europe and North America.* North Hills, Pa.: Bird & Bull Press, 1974. 128 pp., illus., samples. ◆ Includes selective index to the *Paper Maker*, 1932–70, compiled by J. L. Anderson and H. Morris.

Smith, David C. *A History of Papermaking in the United States (1691–1969).* New York: Lockwood Pub. Co., c1971. 693 pp., illus., bibliog.

Sutermeister, Edwin. *The Story of Papermaking.* Boston: S. D. Warren Co., 1954. 200 pp., illus.

Wilkinson, Norman B. *Papermaking in America.* Greenville, Del.: The Hagley Museum, c1975. 64 pp., illus., bibliog., index.

Lumber

Carranco, Lynwood, and John T. Labbe. *Logging the Redwoods.* Caldwell, Idaho: Caxton Printers, 1975. 145 pp., illus., map, index.

Clarke, Kenneth, and Ira Kohn. *Kentucky's Age of Wood.* Lexington: University Press of Kentucky, c1976. 77 pp., illus., index.

Davis, Richard C., comp. *North American Forest History: A Guide to Archives and Manuscripts in the United States and Canada.* Santa Barbara, Calif.: Published under contract with the Forest History Society, Inc. by Clio Books, c1977. 376 pp., bibliog., index. ◆ Lists 3830 groups or collections.

Fahl, Ronald J. *North American Forest and Conservation History: A Bibliography.* Santa Barbara, Calif.: Published under contract with the Forest History Society by ABC-Clio Press, c1977. 408 pp., index. ◆ Companion volume to

Richard C. Davis, . . . *Guide to Archives* (1977), cited above.

Holbrook, Stewart Hall. *The American Lumberjack.* Enl. ed. New York: Collier Books, 1962. 254 pp. ◆ Originally published under title: Holy Old Mackinaw, A Natural History of the American Lumberjack.

Hutchinson, W. H. *California Heritage: A History of Northern California Lumbering.* Rev. ed. Santa Cruz, Calif.: Forest History Society, 1974. 32 pp., illus., map. ◆ Activities of 6 firms, with chapter on flumes and fluming.

Lucia, Ellis. *The Big Woods: Logging and Lumbering, From Bull Teams to Helicopters, in the Pacific Northwest.* Garden City, N.Y.: Doubleday, 1975. 222 pp., illus., 24 leaves of plates, bibliog., index.

McCulloch, Walter F. *Wood Words: A Comprehensive Dictionary of Loggers Terms.* Portland, Ore.: Oregon Historical Society, 1958. 219 pp.

Roberge, Earl. *Timber Country.* Caldwell, Idaho: Caxton Printers, 1973. 182 pp., illus. ◆ Logging methods and equipment in the far Northwest.

Smith, David Clayton. *A History of Lumbering in Maine, 1861–1960.* Orono: University of Maine Press, 1972. 468 pp., illus., bibliog. ◆ University of Maine Studies no. 93.

Wood, Richard G. *A History of Lumbering in Maine, 1820–1861.* 1935. Reprint, with a new introduction by David C. Smith. Orono: University of Maine Press, c1971. 267 pp. ◆ See companion volume by David C. Smith, cited above.

NOTE

Forest History Society, Elwood R. Maunder, Executive Director, P. O. Box 1581, Santa Cruz, California 95061. The Society was organized in 1955 to search out original source materials and seek to get them deposited and catalogued for use by scholars; to interest scholars in research and writing on North American forest history; to educate the forest-related community in the importance of its history; to publish books and shorter works produced by scholars and professional writers; to make tape-recorded interviews; to compile and publish bibliographies and other aids to scholars. Membership is open to interested individuals, institutions, and corporations. It publishes Forest History (1957, quarterly), and holds an annual meeting.

Textiles

Baines, Patricia. *Spinning Wheels: Spinners and Spinning.* New York: Scribner, c1977, 1978. 252 pp., illus., bibliog., index

Bendure, Zelma, and Gladys Pfeiffer. *America's Fabrics: Origin and History, Manufacture, Characteristics and Uses.* New York: Arno Press, c1946, 1972. 688 pp., illus.

Catling, Harold. *The Spinning Mule.* North Pomfret, Vt.: David & Charles, 1970. 207 pp., illus., bibliog.

Channing, Marion L. *The Textile Tools of Colonial Homes: From Raw Materials to Finished Garments, Before Mass Production in the Factories.* 2nd ed. Marion, Mass.: Channing Books, 1971. 64 pp., illus., bibliog.

Dockstader, Frederick J. *Weaving Arts of the North American Indian.* London and New York: J. J. Kery, 1978. 223 pp., illus., bibliog., index.

Dunwell, Steve. *The Run of the Mill: A Pictorial Narrative of the Expansion, Dominion, Decline, and Enduring Impact of the New England Textile Industry.* Boston: D. R. Godine, 1978. 299 pp., illus., bibliog., index.

Encyclopedia of Textiles. By the editors of American Fabrics and Fashions Magazine. 3rd ed. Englewood Cliffs, N.J.: Prentice-Hall, c1980. 636 pp., illus., index. ◆ Sections on various fibers, history of textiles, design, manufacturing, and a comprehensive dictionary of textile terms.

English, Walter. *The Textile Industry: An Account of the Early Inventions of Spinning, Weaving, and Knitting Machines.* Harlow: Longmans, 1969. 242 pp., illus., glossary, bibliog., index. ◆ Includes list of British museums with textile collections.

Gordon, Beverly. *Shaker Textile Arts.* Hanover, N.H.: University Press of New England, 1980. 329 pp., illus., bibliog. references, index. ◆ In cooperation with the Merrimack Valley Textile Museum and Shaker Community, Inc.

Groves, Sylvia. *The History of Needlework Tools and Accessories.* Newton Abbot: David

& Charles, 1973. 136, 64 pp., illus., bibliog. references, index.

Hargrove, John. *The Weavers Draft Book and Clothiers Assistant.* 1792. Reprint. With a new introduction by Rita J. Adrosko. Worcester, Mass.: American Antiquarian Society, distr. by University Press of Virginia, Charlottesville, 1979. 18, 28 pp., bibliog. references.

Jeremy, David J. *Transatlantic Industrial Revolution: The Diffusion of Textile Technologies between Britain and America, 1790–1830s.* North Andover, Mass.: Merrimack Valley Textile Museum; Cambridge, Mass.: MIT Press, c1981. 384 pp., illus., drawings, bibliog., index. ◆ Covers cotton spinning, power loom weaving, calico printing, and woollen manufacturing.

Kopycinski, Joseph V. *Textile Industry: Information Sources; An Annotated Guide to the Literature of Textile Fibers, Dyes and Dyeing, Design and Decoration, Weaving, Machinery, and Other Subjects.* Detroit: Gale Research Co., c1964. 194 pp., bibliog.

Leavitt, T. W., comp. *The Hollingworth Letters: Technical Change in the Textile Industry, 1826–1837.* Cambridge, Mass.: Published jointly by the Society for the History of Technology and MIT Press, 1969. 120 pp., illus., geneal. table, bibliog. ◆ Society for the History of Technology Monograph series no. 6.

MacMurray, Robert R. *Technological Change in the American Cotton Spinning Industry, 1790 to 1836.* New York: Arno Press, c1971, 1977. 669 pp., illus., bibliog. references, index.

Merrimack Valley Textile Museum, North Andover, Mass. *Homespun to Factory Made: Woolen Textiles in America, 1776–1876.* Peter M. Molloy. North Andover, Mass.: The Museum, c1977. 102 pp., illus. ◆ Revised exhibition catalog.

Partridge, William *A Practical Treatise on Dying of Woollen, Cotton, and Skein Silk with the Manufacture of Broadcloth and Cassimere, including the Most Improved Methods in the West of England.* Edington, Wiltshire: Pasold Research Fund, 1973. 264 pp., illus. ◆ Reissue of 1823, New York, edition, with a new introduction and notes by Julia de Lacy Mann and technical notes by K. G. Ponting.

Wilson, Kax. *A History of Textiles.* Boulder,

Colo.: Westview Press, c1979. 357 pp., illus., bibliogs., index.

NOTES

Textile History. 1968, 2/yr., subscription. Butterworth Scientific Ltd., Journals Division, Box 63, Westbury House, Bury Street, Guildford, Surrey GU2 5BH, England. Edited by K. G. Ponting; supported by the Pasold Research Fund.

Textile Museum Journal. 1962, annual, purchase. Textile Museum, 2320 S Street, N.W., Washington, D.C. 20008. Supersedes: *Workshop Notes.*

Mechanical Technology

General Works

Alth, Max. *All About Locks and Locksmithing.* New York: Hawthorn Books, 1972. 180 pp., illus., drawings, glossary.

Beeching, Wilfred A. *Century of the Typewriter.* New York: St. Martin's Press, 1974. 276 pp., illus., bibliog., index.

Bowers, Q. David, ed. *Encyclopedia of Automatic Musical Instruments.* Vestal, N.Y.: Vestal Press, c1967, 1972. 1008 pp., illus., bibliog.

Cooper, Grace Rogers. *The Sewing Machine: Its Invention and Development.* 2nd ed. rev. and expanded. Washington, D.C.: Smithsonian Institution Press for the National Museum of History and Technology, 1976. 238 pp., illus., bibliog.

Dummer, Geoffrey W. A. *Electronic Inventions and Discoveries.* 2nd rev. and expanded ed. Oxford and New York: Pergamon Press, 1978. 204 pp., illus., bibliog. references, index.

Edison Institute (Henry Ford Museum and Greenfield Village), Dearborn, Mich. *Mechanical Arts at the Henry Ford Museum.* Dearborn, Mich.: Edison Institute, 1974. 128 pp., illus., index.

Hennessy, Thomas F. *Early Lock and Lockmakers of America.* Des Plaines, Ill.: Nickerson & Collins Pub. Co., Locksmith Ledger Division, c1976. 149 pp., illus., bibliog. references.

Ord-Hume, Arthur W. J. G. *Clockwork Music: An Illustrated History of Mechanical Musical Instruments from the Musical Box to the Pianola, from Automaton Lady Virginal Players to Orchestrion.* New York: Crown Publishers, 1973. 334 pp., illus., appendix.

Streeter, Donald. "Early American Wrought Iron Hardware: Norfolk Latches," *Bulletin of APT,* 3:4 (1971), pp. 12–30. ♦ See also rest of series on locks, etc.: 5:1 (1973); 5:2 (1973); 6:1 (1974).

Machines and Machine Tools

Battison, Edwin A. *Screw-thread Cutting by the Master-Screw Method since 1480.* Washington, D.C.: Smithsonian Institution; for sale by Supt. of Docs., U.S. Government Printing Office, 1964. 106–119 pp., illus. ♦ U.S. National Museum Bulletin 240, Contributions from the Museum of History and Technology Paper 37.

Bradley, Ian. *A History of Machine Tools.* Hemel Hempstead: Model and Allied Publications, distr. by International Publications Service, N.Y., 1972. 224 pp., illus.

Holtzapffel, John J. *Hand or Simple Turning: Principles and Practice.* 1881. Reprint. New York: Dover Publications, 1976. 592 pp., illus. ♦ Reprint of 1881 ed. published by Holtzapffel, London, which was issued as Vol. 4 of Turning and Mechanical Manipulation by C. Holtzapffel.

Holtzapffel, John J. *The Principles and Practice of Ornamental or Complex Turning.* 1894. Reprint. New York: Dover Publications, 1973. ♦ Reprint of 1894 ed. published by Holtzapffel, London, as Vol. 5 of Turning and Mechanical Manipulation by C. Holtzapffel.

Rolt, Lionel T. C. *A Short History of Machine Tools.* Cambridge, Mass.: MIT Press, 1965. 256 pp., illus., bibliog., index. ♦ Machine tool development in Great Britain and U.S.

Steeds, William. *A History of Machine Tools, 1799–1910.* Oxford: Clarendon Press, 1969. 181 pp., 153 plates, illus., bibliog.

Strandh, Sigvard. *The History of the Machine.* New York: A & W Publications, 1979. 240 pp., illus., bibliog.

Wagoner, Harless D. *The U.S. Machine Tool*

Industry from 1900 to 1950. Cambridge, Mass.: MIT Press, 1968. 421 pp., illus., bibliog.

White, James. *A New Century of Inventions: Being Designs and Descriptions of One Hundred Machines, Relating to Arts, Manufactures, and Domestic Life.* 2nd ed. 1822. Reprint. New York: Burt Franklin, 1967. 394 pp., illus.

Woodbury, Robert S. *Studies in the History of Machine Tools.* Cambridge, Mass.: MIT Press, c1972. 4 vols. in 1 (557 pp.), illus., diagrams, tables, bibliogs., indexes. ◆ Includes: *History of the Gear-Cutting Machine: A Historical Study in Geometry and Machines* (1958); *History of the Grinding Machine: A Historical Study in Tools and Precision Production* (1959); *History of the Milling Machine: A Study of Technical Development* (1960); *History of the Lathe to 1850: A Study in the Growth of a Technical Element of an Industrial Economy* (1961).

Timekeepers

Bailey, Chris H. *Two Hundred Years of American Clocks and Watches.* Englewood Cliffs, N.J.: Prentice-Hall, 1975. 254 pp., illus., bibliogs, index.

Basserman-Jordan, Ernst von. *The Book of Old Clocks and Watches.* 4th ed. fully rev. by Hans von Bertele. New York: Crown Publishers, 1964. 522 pp., illus., bibliog.

Britten, Frederick J. *Britten's Old Clocks and Watches and their Makers: A Historical and Descriptive Account of Different Styles of Clocks and Watches of the Past in England and Abroad Containing a List of Nearly Fourteen Thousand Makers.* 8th ed. by Cecil Clutton, the late G. H. Baillie, and C. A. Ilbert. Rev. & enl. by Cecil Clutton. New York: Dutton, 1973. 532 pp., illus., bibliog.

Britten, Frederick J. *Britten's Watch & Clock Maker's Handbook: Dictionary and Guide.* 16th ed., rev. by Richard Good. New York: Arco Pub. Co., c1978. 459 pp., illus., bibliog., indexes.

Crom, Theodore R. *Horological Shop Tools, 1700–1900.* Melrose, Fla.: T. R. Crom, 1980. 678 pp., illus., bibliog., index.

Eckhardt, George H. *United States Clock and Watch Patents, 1790–1890; The Record of a Century of American Horology and Enterprise.*

New York: privately printed, 1960. 231 pp., illus.

Rees, Abraham. *Rees's Clocks, Watches, and Chronometers (1819–20); A Selection from the Cyclopaedia, or Universal Dictionary of Arts, Sciences, and Literature.* Rutland, Vt.: C. E. Tuttle Co., 1970. 295 pp., illus. ◆ Reprint of extracts from 1st ed., London, 1819.

Roberts, Kenneth D. *Eli Terry and the Connecticut Shelf Clock.* Fitzwilliam, N.H.: K. Roberts Publishing Co., 1973. 320 pp., illus., bibliog. essay.

Tyler, Eric John. *The Craft of the Clockmaker.* New York: Crown Publishers, c1973, 1974. 96 pp., illus., appendices, bibliog., index.

Wyke, John. *A Catalogue of Tools for Watch and Clock Makers.* Introduction and technical commentary by Alan Smith. Charlottesville: Published for the Henry Francis du Pont Winterthur Museum by the University Press of Virginia, 1978. 153 pp., illus.

Scientific Instruments

Babbage, Charles. *Charles Babbage and His Calculating Engines: Selected Writings by Babbage and Others.* Edited with an introduction by Philip Morrison and Emily Morrison. New York: Dover Publications, 1961. 400 pp., illus., bibliog.

Bedini, Silvio. *Early American Scientific Instruments and their Makers.* Washington, D.C.: Museum of History and Technology, Smithsonian Institution; for sale by Supt. of Docs., U.S. Government Printing Office, 1964. 184 pp., illus., bibliog. ◆ U.S. National Museum Bulletin 231.

Bedini, Silvio. *Thinkers and Tinkers: Early American Men of Science.* New York: Scribner, 1975. 520 pp., illus., glossary, bibliog., index.

Bennion, Elisabeth. *Antique Medical Instruments.* London: Sotheby Parke Bernet; Berkeley: University of California Press, 1979. 355 pp., illus., bibliog., index. ◆ Includes veterinary and dental devices, feeding apparatus, and toilet articles.

Cohen, I. Bernard. *Some Early Tools of American Science: An Account of the Early Scientific Instruments and Mineralogical and Biological Collections in Harvard University.*

New York: Russell & Russell, c1950, 1967. 201 pp., illus., bibliog.

Hughes, Barbara. *Catalog of the Scientific Apparatus at the College of Charleston, 1800–1940.* Edited with additional material by Ralph Melnick. Charleston, S.C.: College of Charleston Library Associates, 1980. 94 pp., illus., bibliog., index.

Middleton, William E. Knowles. *The History of the Barometer.* Baltimore: Johns Hopkins University Press, 1964. 489 pp., illus., diagrams, bibliog. footnotes.

Padgitt, Donald L. *A Short History of the Early American Microscopes.* London and Chicago: Microscope Publications, 1975. 147 pp., illus., bibliog. references, index. ◆ The Microscope Series, vol. 12.

Richeson, Allie W. *English Land Measuring to 1800: Instruments and Practices.* Cambridge, Mass.: Published jointly by the Society for the History of Technology and MIT Press, 1966. 214 pp., illus., map, bibliog. ◆ Society for the History of Technology Monograph series no. 2.

Smart, Charles E. *The Makers of Surveying Instruments in America Since 1700.* Troy, N.Y.: Regal Art Press, 1962–67. 2 vols. (282 pp.), illus.

NOTE

Historical Technology. 1970, irregular, purchase. Historical Technology, Inc., 6 Mugford Street, Marblehead, Massachusetts 01945. Catalogs of instruments in all areas (astronomy, scientific, surveying, clocks and clockmaking, etc.); descriptions include date, maker, special notes, illustrations. Bound volumes of Catalogs 101–110 (500 pp.), and Catalogs 111–120 (575 pp.), available to private customers, dealers, museums, libraries.

Weights/Measures/Standards

Eaches, Albert R. "Scales and Weighing Devices: An Aid to Identification," *History News,* 27:3 (March 1972), Technical Leaflet no. 59.

Frazier, Arthur H. *Water Current Meters in the Smithsonian Collections of the National Museum of History and Technology.* Washington, D.C.: Smithsonian Institution Press, for sale by Supt. of Docs., U.S. Government Printing Office, 1974. 95 pp., illus., bibliog. references.

Kisch, Bruno. *Scales and Weights: A Historical Outline.* New Haven, Conn.: Yale University Press, 1965. 297 pp., illus., charts, bibliog., appendices, index.

Rossini, Frederick D. *Fundamental Measures and Constants for Science and Technology.* Cleveland: CRC Press, 1974. 132 pp., illus., bibliog. references.

Zupko, Ronald E. *British Weights and Measures: A History from Antiquity to the Seventeenth Century.* Madison: University of Wisconsin Press, 1977. 248 pp., illus., bibliog., index.

Zupko, Ronald W. *French Weights and Measures Before the Revolution: A Dictionary of Provincial and Local Units.* Bloomington: Indiana University Press, c1978. 208 pp., bibliog.

NOTE

International Scale Society, c/o Albert R. Eaches, R. D. 3 , Phoenixville, Pennsylvania 19460.

Communication

Printing and Graphic Reproduction

American Dictionary of Printing and Bookmaking: *Containing a History of These Arts in Europe and America, with Definitions of Technical Terms and Biographical Sketches.* Edited by W. W. Pasko. 1894. Reprint. Detroit: Gale Research Co., 1967. 592 pp., illus.

Annenberg, Maurice. *Type Foundries of America and Their Catalogs.* Baltimore: Marian Printing Services, 1975. 245 pp., illus., bibliog.

Brunner, Felix. *A Handbook of Graphic Reproduction Processes.* 3rd ed. New York: Hastings House Publishers, 1968. 379 pp., illus., bibliog.

Day, Kenneth, ed. *Book Typography, 1815–1965, in Europe and the United States of America.* Chicago: University of Chicago Press, 1966. 401 pp., plates.

Huss, Richard E. *The Development of Printers' Mechanical Typesetting Methods, 1822–1925.* Charlottesville: Published for the Bibliographical Society of the University of Virginia by the University Press of Virginia, 1973. 307 pp., illus., appendices, bibliog., index.

Lehmann-Haupt, Hellmut, ed. *Bookbinding in America: Three Essays.* 1941. Reprint, with new supplements by the authors. New York: R. R. Bowker, 1967. 293 pp., illus., bibliog. references. ♦ Authors: Hannah French, Joseph E. Rogers, Hellmut Lehmann-Haupt.

Lehmann-Haupt, Hellmut. *One Hundred Books about Bookmaking: A Guide to the Study and Appreciation of Printing.* 1949. Reprint. Westport, Conn.: Greenwood Press, 1975. 83 pp., index.

McMurtrie, Douglas C. *History of Printing in the United States; the Story of the Introduction of the Press and of its History and Influence During the Pioneer Period of each State of the Union. Vol. II: Middle and South Atlantic States.* 1939. Reprint. New York: Burt Franklin, 1969. 462 pp., bibliog. ♦ No other volumes published.

Middleton, Bernard C. *A History of English Craft Bookbinding Technique.* Rev. ed. New Castle, Del.: Oak Knoll, 1978. 326 pp., illus., diagrams, bibliog. footnotes.

Moran, James. *Printing Presses: History and Development from the Fifteenth Century to Modern Times.* Berkeley: University of California Press, 1973. 263 pp., illus., bibliog., index, index of presses and machines.

Moxon, Joseph. *Mechanick Exercises on the Whole Art of Printing (1683–4).* Edited by Herbert Davis and Harry Carter. 2nd ed. New York: Dover Publications, c1962, 1978. 487 pp., illus., bibliog., index.

Ross, John, and Clare Romano. *The Complete Printmaker: The Art and Technique of the Relief Print, the Intaglio Print, the Collagraph, the Lithograph, the Screen Print, the Dimensional Print, Photographic Prints, Children's Prints, Collecting Prints, Print Workshop.* New York: Free Press, 1972. 306 pp., illus., bibliog.

Saff, Donald, and Deli Sacilotto. *Printmaking: History and Processes.* New York: Holt, Rinehart & Winston, c1978. 436 pp., illus., bibliog., index.

Silver, Rollo G. *The American Printer, 1787–1825.* Chatlottesville: Published for the Bibliographical Society of the University of Virginia

by the University Press of Virginia, 1967. 189 pp., illus., bibliog. footnotes.

Silver, Rollo G. *Typefounding in America, 1787–1825.* Charlottesville: Published for the Bibliographical Society of the University of Virginia by the University Press of Virginia, 1965. 139 pp., illus., bibliog. footnotes.

Thompson, John Smith. *History of Composing Machines: A Complete Record of the Art of Composing Type by Machinery; Also Lists of Patents on Composing Machines, American and British, Chronologically Arranged.* 1904. Reprint. New York: Arno Press, 1972. 200 pp., illus.

Winckler, Paul A. *A History of Books and Printing: A Guide to Information Sources.* Detroit: Gale Research Co., c1979. 209 pp., indexes.

Wroth, Lawrence C. *The Colonial Printer.* 2nd ed., rev. & enl. Charlottesville: Dominion Books, distr. by University Press of Virginia, c1938, 1964. 368 pp., illus., bibliog.

Photography

Crawford, William. *The Keepers of Light: A History and Working Guide to Early Photographic Processes.* Dobbs Ferry, N.Y.: Morgan & Morgan, c1979. 318 pp., illus., bibliog., index.

Gernsheim, Helmut, and Alison Gernsheim. *The History of Photography from the Camera Obscura to the Beginning of the Modern Era.* 2nd ed. New York: Mc-Graw-Hill, 1969. 599 pp., illus., bibliog.

Gernsheim, Helmut, and Alison Gernsheim. *L. J. M. Daguerre: The History of the Diorama and the Daguerreotype.* Rev. ed. New York: Dover Publications, 1968. 226 pp., illus., bibliog. references.

Gosser, H. Mark. *Selected Attempts at Stereoscopic Moving Pictures and Their Relationship to the Development of Motion Picture Technology, 1852–1903.* New York: Arno Press, c1975, 1977. 340 pp., illus., bibliog.

Hunt, Robert. *A Popular Treatise on the Art of Photography; Including Daguerreotype and All the New Methods of Producing Pictures by the Chemical Agency of Light.* 1841. Reprint. Facsim. ed., with intro. and notes by James Yingpeh Tong. Athens: Ohio University Press,

c1973. 96 pp., illus., bibliog. references.
• Treatise on all known techniques on paper, glass and metal.

Jenkins, Reese V. *Images and Enterprise: Technology and the American Photographic Industry, 1839 to 1925.* Baltimore: Johns Hopkins University Press, c1975. 371 pp., illus., bibliog., index.

Jones, John. *Wonders of the Stereoscope.* New York: Knopf, distr. by Random House, 1976. 2 vols., illus., bibliog. • Vol. 1—survey of history of the stereoscope; Vol. 2—box containing stereoscope and 48 reproductions of views.

Tubbs, Douglas B. *The Illustrated History of the Camera from 1839 to the Present.* By Michel Auer; trans. and adapted by D. B. Tubbs. Boston: New York Graphic Society, 1975. 285 pp., illus.

Telephone/Radio/Television/ Phonograph

Aitken, Hugh G. J. *Syntony and Spark: The Origins of Radio.* New York: John Wiley & Sons, c1976. 347 pp., illus., bibliog. references, index.

Barnouw, Erik. *Tube of Plenty: The Evolution of American Television.* New York: Oxford University Press, 1975. 518 pp., illus., bibliog., index. • Condensed and updated version of previous 3 vols. on history of broadcasting.

Bell Telephone Laboratories, Inc. *A History of Engineering and Science in the Bell System.* Prepared by members of the technical staff, Bell Telephone Laboratories; M. D. Fagen, ed. New York: The Laboratories, 1975–78. 2 vols. (1073 pp.), illus., bibliogs., indexes. • Vol. 1—*The Early Years, 1875–1925;* Vol. 2—*National Service in War and Peace, 1925–1975.*

Boettinger, Henry M. *The Telephone Book: Bell, Watson, Vail and American Life, 1876–1976.* Croton-on-Hudson, N.Y.: Riverwood Publishers, c1977. 189 pp., illus., plates, bibliog. references, index.

Langley, Ralph H. *Radio Collector's Guide, 1924–1932; Ralph H. Langley's Set Catalog and Index.* Edited and expanded by Morgan E. McMahon. Palos Verdes Peninsula, Calif.: Vintage Radio, 1973. 264 pp., illus. • Reprint of

work first published in 1933; dates of introduction and technical specifications for radios. Address: Box 2045, Palos Verdes Peninsula, Calif. 90274.

Lichty, Lawrence W., and Malachi C. Topping, comps. *American Broadcasting: A Source Book on the History of Radio and Television.* New York: Hastings House Publishers, 1975. 723 pp., illus., bibliog.

Maclaurin, William R. *Invention and Innovation in the Radio Industry.* 1949. Reprint. New York: Arno Press, 1971. 304 pp., illus., bibliog.

Prescott, George Bartlett. *Bell's Electric Speaking Telephone: Its Invention, Construction, Application, Modification, and History.* 1884. Reprint. New York: Arno Press, 1972. 526 pp., illus.

Read, Oliver, and Walter L. Welch. *From Tin Foil to Stereo: Evolution of the Phonograph.* 2nd ed. Indianapolis, Ind.: Howard W. Sams & Co., 1976. 550 pp., illus., bibliog., index.

Thompson, Robert Luther. *Wiring a Continent: The History of the Telegraph Industry in the United States, 1832–1866.* 1947. Reprint. New York: Arno Press, 1972. 544 pp., illus., bibliog.

NOTES

Historical Studies in Telecommunications, series. Editors: John M. Kittross, George Shiers, and Elliott Sivowitch. New York: Arno Press, 1977. 5 books in 6 vols., illus., bibliog. references; each an anthology of reprinted, significant articles (1858–1970). Titles: *The Electric Telegraph; The Telephone; The Development of the Wireless to 1920; Technical Development of Television; Documents in American Telecommunications Policy* (2 vols.). Brochure available from The Ayer Company, Inc., Publishers & Booksellers, Harborview, Sag Harbor, New York 11963.

History of Broadcasting: Radio to Television, series. New York: Arno Press, 1971. 32 titles; reprints (1901–1958). Titles available individually; brochure available from The Ayer Company, Inc., Publishers & Booksellers, Harborview, Sag Harbor, New York 11963. See also: Dissertations in Broadcasting, series. Advisory Editor, Christopher H. Sterling. 26 books, 1979.

Telecommunications, series. New York: Arno

Press, 1974. 34 titles; reprints (1875–1974). Titles available individually; brochure available from The Ayer Company, Inc., Publishers & Booksellers, Harborview, Sag Harbor, New York 11963.

Military Technology

Bailey, De Witt. *Percussion Guns & Rifles: An Illustrated Reference Guide.* Harrisburg, Pa.: Stackpole, 1972. 79 pp., illus., bibliog.

Brown, M. L. *Firearms in Colonial America: The Impact on History and Technology, 1492–1792.* Washington, D.C.: Smithsonian Institution Press, 1981. 450 pp., illus., bibliog., appendices, index.

Butler, David F. *The American Shotgun.* New York: Winchester Press, 1973. 243 pp., illus.

Butler, David F. *United States Firearms: The First Century, 1776–1875.* New York: Winchester Press, 1971. 249 pp., illus.

Dillin, John G. W. *The Kentucky Rifle, A Study of the Origin and Development of a Purely American Type of Firearm, Together with Accurate Historical Data Concerning Early Colonial Gunsmiths, and Profusely Illustrated with Photographic Reproduction of Their Finest Work.* 6th ed. York, Pa.: G. Shumway, 1975. 201 pp., illus.

Duffy, Christopher. *Fire and Stone: The Science of Fortress Warfare, 1660–1860.* Newton Abbot: David & Charles; N. Y.: Hippocrene, 1975. 207 pp., illus., maps, plans, bibliog.

Gill, Harold B., Jr. *The Gunsmith in Colonial Virginia.* Williamsburg, Va.: Colonial Williamsburg Foundation; Charlottesville: distr. by University Press of Virginia, 1974. 139 pp., illus., bibliog., index.

Hartzler, Daniel D. *Arms Makers of Maryland.* York, Pa.: G. Shumway, 1977. 310 pp., illus.

Held, Robert. *The Age of Firearms; A Pictorial History from the Invention of Gunpowder to the Advent of the Modern Breechloader.* Research assistance by Nancy Held; revision edited by Joseph J. Schroeder, Jr. New & rev. ed. Northfield, Ill.: Gun Digest Co., 1970. 192 pp., illus., bibliog.

The History of Winchester Firearms, 1866–1980. By Duncan Barnes, et al. Tulsa: Winchester Press, c1980. 237 pp., illus.

Jinks, Roy G., and Robert J. Neal. *Smith and Wesson, 1857–1945.* Rev. ed. South Brunswick, N.J.: A. S. Barnes, 1975. 434 pp., illus., bibliog.

Lindsay, Merrill. *The New England Gun: The First Two Hundred Years.* New Haven, Conn.: New Haven Colony Historical Society, distr. by David McKay, N.Y., 1975. 187 pp., illus., bibliog., index.

McAfee, Michael J. *Artillery of the American Revolution; 1775–1783.* Washington, D.C.: American Defense Preparedness Association, 1974. 16 pp., illus., bibliog.

Peterson, Harold L., ed. *Encyclopedia of Firearms.* New York: Dutton, 1964. 367 pp., illus., bibliog.

Peterson, Harold L. *Round Shot and Rammers.* Harrisburg, Pa.: Stackpole Books, 1969. 128 pp., illus., bibliog. ◆ All forms of muzzle-loading land artillery in America.

Peterson, Harold L. *The Treasury of the Gun.* Technical consultation by Howard L. Blackmore, Claude Blair, and William Reid. New York: Golden Press, 1962. 249 pp., illus., bibliog.

Quick, John. *Dictionary of Weapons and Military Terms.* New York: McGraw-Hill Book Co., 1973. 515 pp., illus., bibliog.

Russell, Carl P. *Guns on the Early Frontiers; A History of Firearms from Colonial Times Through the Years of the Western Fur Trade.* 1957. Reprint. Lincoln: University of Nebraska Press, 1980. 395 pp., illus., maps, diagrams, glossary, bibliog., index.

Serven, James Edsall. *200 Years of American Firearms.* Edited by Joseph J. Schroeder, Jr. Chicago: Follett Publ. Co., c1975. 224 pp., illus.

Smith, Merritt Roe. *Harpers Ferry Armory and the New Technology: The Challenge of Change.* Ithaca, N.Y.: Cornell University Press, 1976. 363 pp., illus., bibliog., index.

Smith, Walter H. B., and Joseph E. Smith. *The Book of Rifles.* 4th ed. Harrisburg, Pa.: Stackpole, 1972. 689 pp., illus.

Wilson, Robert L., and R. E. Hable. *Colt Pistols, 1836–1976.* Dallas: J. Arms, c1976. 380 pp., illus.

Military Engineer. 1920, bimonthly, membership/subscription. Society of American Military Engineers, 740 15th Street, N.W., Washington, D.C. 20005. Supersedes: *Professional Memoirs,* 1909–1919 (11 vols.).

Industrial Archeology

Bracegirdle, Brian. *The Archaeology of the Industrial Revolution.* Rutherford, N.J.: Fairleigh Dickinson University Press, 1973. 207 pp., illus., bibliog. ◆ Covers entire range of structures; explains industrial processes.

Buchanan, Robert A. *Industrial Archaeology in Britain.* 1st ed., reprinted. London: Allen Lane, 1974. 446 pp., illus., maps, plans, bibliog., index. ◆ Includes additional plates.

Butt, John, and Ian Connachie. *Industrial Archaeology in the British Isles.* New York: Barnes & Noble Books, 1979. 307 pp., illus., bibliog., index.

Cossons, Neil. *The BP Book of Industrial Archaeology.* Newton Abbot, Eng. and North Pomfret, Vt.: David & Charles, c1975. 496 pp., illus., bibliog., index.

Grube, Oswald W. *Industrial Buildings and Factories.* New York: Praeger Publishers, 1971. 199 pp., illus.

Hudson, Kenneth. *The Archaeology of Industry.* New York: Scribner, c1976. 128 pp., illus., bibliog., index. ◆ Discusses sites, including factories and mills.

Hudson, Kenneth. *Exploring Our Industrial Past.* London: Hodder and Stoughton, 1975. 214 pp., illus. ◆ Introduction to techniques of preparing case studies, collecting information, etc. Also available from David McKay Co., N.Y.

Hudson, Kenneth. *Food, Clothes and Shelter: Twentieth Century Industrial Archaeology.* London: J. Baker, 1978. 160 pp., illus., bibliog., index.

Hudson, Kenneth. *A Guide to the Industrial Archaeology of Europe.* 1st American Edition. Madison, N.J.: Fairleigh Dickinson University Press, 1971. 186 pp., plates, illus.

Hudson, Kenneth. *Industrial Archaeology: A New Introduction.* 3rd rev. and reset ed. London: J. Baker, 1976. 240 pp., illus., maps,

plans, bibliog., index. ◆ Contents: definition, what to look for, research methods.

Hudson, Kenneth. *A Pocket Book for Industrial Archaeologists.* London: J. Baker, 1976. 134 pp., illus., map, plans, index. ◆ Supersedes *Handbook* . . . (1967). Emphasizes need to investigate industrial archaeology of Second Industrial Revolution: electricity, petroleum, plastics, etc.

Industrial Archaeologists's Guide, 1971–73. 2nd ed. Edited by Neil Cossons and Kenneth Hudson. Newton Abbot, Eng.: David & Charles, c1971, 1972. 201 pp., illus., drawings, diagrams, maps, charts, bibliog.

Kidney, Walter C. *Working Places: The Adaptive Use of Industrial Buildings.* A Handbook sponsored by the Society for Industrial Archeology. 1st ed. Pittsburgh: Ober Park Associates, 1976. 171 pp., illus., plans, bibliog., index.

Koch, Jean A. *Industrial Archaeology: A Selected Bibliography.* Monticello, Ill.: Council of Planning Librarians, 1977. 17 pp. ◆ Exchange Bibliography no. 1382.

Major, John Kenneth. *Fieldwork in Industrial Archaeology.* London: Batsford, 1975. 176 pp., illus., bibliog., index.

Massey, James C., ed. *An Introductory Bibliography in Industrial Archeology.* Washington, D.C.: Society for Industrial Archeology, April 1977. 7 pp.

Pannell, John Percival. *The Techniques of Industrial Archaeology.* 2nd ed. Edited by J. Kenneth Major. Newton Abbot, Eng.: David & Charles, 1974. 200 pp., illus., maps, bibliog., index. ◆ Includes sources, surveying, measuring up machines and structures, records; British emphasis.

Raistrick, Arthur. *Industrial Archaeology: An Historical Survey.* New York: Harper & Row, 1972. 314 pp., illus., bibliog.

Sande, Theodore A. *Industrial Archeology: A New Look at the American Heritage.* 1976. Reprint. New York: Penguin Books, c1976, 1978. 152 pp., illus., bibliog., index. ◆ Documentation and description of America's first industrial artifacts: bridges, mills, mines, dams, factories; also roster of sites from 49 states.

Tann, Jennifer. *The Development of the Factory.* London: Cornmarket Press, Ltd., 1970.

175 pp., illus., bibliog., index. ◆ Includes reproductions of 18th and 19th century engineering drawings.

Waite, John G., comp. *Iron Architecture in New York City: Two Studies in Industrial Archeology.* Edited by John G. Waite. Albany: New York State Historic Trust and Society for Industrial Archeology, 1972. ◆ 83 pp., illus., diagrams, map, appendix of architectural drawings and chronology, bibliog. references. ◆ Contents: The Edgar Laing Stores (1849), by John G. Waite; The Cooper Union (1853–59), compiled by William Rowe, III.

Wallace, Anthony F. C. *Rockdale: The Growth of an American Village in the Early Industrial Revolution.* New York: Knopf, c1978. 553 pp., illus., bibliog., index.

Weitzman, David. *Traces of the Past: A Field Guide to Industrial Archaeology.* New York: Scribner's, 1980. 229 pp., illus., maps, bibliog., index. ◆ Seven sections: locomotives, maps, bridges, roofs, oil rigs, and the furnaces used to produce and mold iron; serves as a guide through areas recently considered just blighted.

Surveys and Inventories

Cleveland: *An Inventory of Historic Engineering and Industrial Sites.* Edited by Daniel M. Bluestone. Washington, D.C.: Historic American Engineering Record, Heritage Conservation and Recreation Service, U.S. Department of the Interior; for sale by Supt. of Docs., U.S. Government Printing Office, 1978. 118 pp., illus., bibliog. references, index. ◆ Cosponsored by Cleveland Landmarks Commission, Industrial Valley Study Advisory Committee, Cleveland Foundation/Greater Cleveland Associated Foundation, Cleveland State University.

Comp, T. Allan, ed. *New England: An Inventory of Historic Engineering and Industrial Sites.* Washington, D.C.: Historic American Engineering Record, Office of Archeology and Historic Preservation, National Park Service, U.S. Department of the Interior, 1974. 87 pp., illus.

Connecticut: *An Inventory of Historic Engineering and Industrial Sites.* Author and project director, Matthew Roth. Washington, D.C.: Society for Industrial Archeology, 1981. 279 pp., illus., index. ◆ Sponsored by Historic

American Engineering Record and Connecticut Historical Commission.

Eleutherian Mills-Hagley Foundation, Greenville, Del. *Delaware: An Inventory of Historic Engineering and Industrial Sites.* Edited by Selma Thomas; preliminary inventory by Tommy Guider; graphics by Bruce Gavin. Washington, D.C.: U.S. Department of the Interior, 1975. 47 pp., illus., index. ◆ Cosponsored by the Eleutherian Mills-Hagley Foundation and Historic American Engineering Record.

Ellifritt, Duane S. *An Inventory of Historic Engineering Sites in Oklahoma.* Stillwater, Okla.: Oklahoma State University, School of Civil Engineering, 1974. 21, 12 pp., illus., map, bibliog.

Hall, Stephen P., and David A. Walker. *Duluth-Superior Harbor Cultural Resources Study.* St. Paul: Minnesota Historical Society, 1976. 151 pp., illus., maps, bibliog. ◆ Authorized by Dept. of Army, St. Paul District, Corps of Engineers; includes mills, fur trade posts, roads, shanties, docks, terminals, warehouses, etc.

Historic American Buildings Survey. *The New England Textile Mill Survey.* Edited by Ted Sande. Washington, D.C.: Historic American Buildings Survey, Division of Historic Architecture, Office of Archeology and Historic Preservation, 1971. 176 pp., illus., drawings, charts, maps, case studies, bibliog. HABS Selections no. 4.

Historic American Engineering Record. *Great Falls, Sum Survey: A Report on the First Summer's Work, 1973.* Washington, D.C.: 1973. 80 pp., illus. ◆ In cooperation with the Great Falls Development Corporation, Paterson, N.J.

Historic American Engineering Record. *Historic American Engineering Record Catalog, 1976.* Compiled by Donald E. Sackheim. Washington, D.C.: National Park Service, for sale by Supt. of Docs., U.S. Government Printing Office, 1976. 193 pp., illus., index. ◆ Illustrated and annotated listing of structures recorded as of 1969 thru 1975; future catalogs issued by state.

Kulik, Gary, and Julia Bonham. *Rhode Island: An Inventory of Historic Engineering and Industrial Sites.* Editorial assistance provided by the Rhode Island Historical Preservation Commission. Washington, D.C.: U.S. Department of the Interior, Heritage Conservation and Recreation Service, Office of Archeology and Historic Preservation; for sale by Supt. of Docs., U.S. Government Printing Office, 1978. 296 pp., illus., bibliog. ◆ Cosponsored by Slater Mill Historic Site and the Rhode Island Historical Preservation Commission.

Long Island: *An Inventory of Historic Engineering and Industrial Sites.* Directed by John A. Gable, with the assistance of Dennis R. Wood, Robert B. MacKay, T. Allan Comp; edited by Peter H. Stott. Washington, D.C.: U.S. Department of the Interior, National Park Service, 1975. 75 pp., illus., index. ◆ Cosponsored by the Society for the Preservation of Long Island Antiquities and Historic American Engineering Record.

Lower Peninsula of Michigan: *An Inventory of Historic Engineering and Industrial Sites.* Directed by Charles K. Hyde; edited by Diane B. Abbott. Washington, D.C.: Historic American Engineering Record, Office of Archeology and Historic Preservation, National Park Service, U.S. Department of the Interior, 1976. 322 pp., illus., maps, bibliog. references, index. ◆ Cosponsored by Michigan History Division, Michigan Department of State, Wayne State University, and the Michigan Society of Professional Engineers.

Malone, Patrick M. *The Lowell Canal System.* Lowell, Mass.: Lowell Museum, 1976. 27 pp., illus., bibliog. ◆ Product of Lowell Canal Survey conducted by HAER.

Molloy, Peter M., ed. *Lower Merrimack River Valley: An Inventory of Historic Engineering and Industrial Sites.* Washington, D.C.: Historic American Engineering Record, 1976. 110 pp., illus., bibliog., index. ◆ Sponsored by the Merrimack Valley Textile Museum, North Andover, Mass., and the Historic American Engineering Record.

North Carolina: *An Inventory of Historic Engineering and Industrial Sites.* Edited by Brent D. Glass. Washington, D.C.: Historic American Engineering Record, National Park Service, U.S. Department of the Interior, 1975. 105 pp., illus. ◆ Cosponsored by North Carolina Division of Archives and History, Department of Cultural Resources and Historic American Engineering Record.

The Upper Peninsula of Michigan: *An Inventory of Historic Engineering and Industrial Sites.* Directed by Charles K. Hyde; manu-

script preparation by Diane B. Abbott. Washington, D.C.: Historical American Engineering Record, Office of Archeology and Historic Preservation, Heritage Conservation and Recreation Service, U.S. Department of the Interior; for sale by Supt. of Docs., U.S. Government Printing Office, 1978. 236 pp., illus., bibliog., indexes. ◆ Cosponsored by the Michigan History Division, Michigan Department of State, and Northern Michigan University.

Vogel, Robert M., ed. *Report on the Mohawk-Hudson Area Survey: A Selective Recording Survey of the Industrial Archeology of the Mohawk and Hudson River Valleys in the Vicinity of Troy, New York, June-September 1969.* Washington, D.C.: Smithsonian Press, for sale by Supt. of Docs., U.S. Government Printing Office, 1973. 210 pp., illus., bibliogs. ◆ Cosponsored by Smithsonian Institution, the National Museum of History and Technology, American Society of Civil Engineers, and the New York State Office of Parks and Recreation. Smithsonian Studies in History and Technology no. 26.

NOTES

Association for Industrial Archaeology, c/o Neil Cossons, Secretary, The Wharfage, Ironbridge, Telford, Salop TF8 7AW, England. Founded in 1973, the Association's purposes are to promote the study of industrial archaeology, and to encourage improved standards of recording, research, publication and conservation. It aims to assist and support regional and specialist survey and research groups and bodies involved in the preservation of industrial monuments; to represent the interests of industrial archaeology at a national level; to hold conferences and seminars, and to publish the results of research. The Association holds an annual conference. Publications include AIA *Bulletin* (6/yr.), *Industrial Archaeology Review* (3/yr.).

IA: The Journal of the Society for Industrial Archeology. 1975, annual, membership/subscription. Society for Industrial Archeology, National Museum of American History, Room 5020, Smithsonian Institution, Washington, D.C. 20560.

Industrial Archaeology Review. 1976, 3/yr., subscription. Association for Industrial Archaeology (cited above); subscriptions to: Oxford University Press, Journal Subscriptions

Department, Press Road, Neasden, London NW 10, England. Supersedes: *Industrial Archaeology;* largely British in scope.

Society for Industrial Archeology, National Museum of American History, Room 5020, Smithsonian Institution, Washington, D.C. 20560. Founded in 1971, the Society is a non-profit organization open to all those interested in the study and preservation of the industrial past. The membership, individuals and local chapters, includes historians, architects, engineers, museum professionals, preservationists and students. The study, preservation and commemoration of historically significant factories, machinery, bridges, canals, vehicles and power sources that are the physical remains of early industry form the core of the Society's purposes. The Society encourages research and field investigation of vanishing works and processes; promotes identification,

interpretation, preservation and use of surviving industrial structures and equipment. In 1960, the SIA extracted from the Advisory List to the National Register of Historic Places those sites related to its interests and has distributed this compilation widely in order to encourage preservation of industrial sites. It holds an annual conference and tour, and field trips. Publications include *Newsletter* (1972, quarterly), also supplementary issues; *IA,* annual journal; occasional monographs, Data Sheets; Publications List (6th ed., December 1979).

Society for Industrial Archeology. *Newsletter.* 1972, quarterly, membership. c/o Carol Poh Miller, Editor, Program for the History of Science and Technology, Mather House, Case Western Reserve University, Cleveland, Ohio 44107.

APPENDIX
Periodicals Cited

Aerospace Historian. 1954, quarterly, subscription. c/o Robin Higham, Editor, Eisenhower Hall, Kansas State University, Manhattan, Kansas 66506. Formerly: *Airpower Historian.*

Agricultural History. 1927, quarterly, subscription. Agricultural History Society, James Shideler, Editor, University of California Press, 2223 Fulton Street, Berkeley, California 94720.

AIA Journal. 1944, monthly, subscription. American Institute of Architects, Octagon, 1735 New York Avenue, N.W., Washington, D.C. 20006. Formerly: American Institute of Architects. *Journal.*

America: History and Life: *A Guide to Periodical Literature About U.S. and Canadian History, Prehistory to the Present.* 1964, quarterly, subscription. American Bibliographic Center-Clio Press, Riviera Campus, 2040 Alameda Padre Serra, Santa Barbara, California 93103.

American Anthropologist. 1898, quarterly, membership. American Anthropological Association, 1703 New Hampshire Avenue, N.W., Washington, D.C. 20009.

American Antiquarian Society. *Proceedings.* 1812, semiannual, subscription. American Antiquarian Society, 185 Salisbury Street, Worcester, Massachusetts 01609.

American Antiquity. 1935, quarterly, membership. Society for American Archaeology, 1703 New Hampshire Avenue, N.W., Washington, D.C. 20009.

The American Archivist. 1938, quarterly, subscription. Society of American Archivists, Ann Morgan Campbell, Executive Director, Suite 810, 330 South Wells Street, Chicago, Illinois 60606.

American Heritage. 1949, bimonthly, subscription. American Heritage Publishing Co., McGraw-Hill Publications, 1221 Avenue of the Americas, New York, New York 10020.

American Historical Review. 1895, 5/yr., subscription. American Historical Association, 400 A Street, S.E., Washington, D.C. 20003.

American Landscape Architect. 1929–1932, monthly. American Landscape Architect Co., 608 South Dearborn Street, Chicago, Illinois 60605.

American Neptune: *A Quarterly Journal of Maritime History.* 1941, quarterly, subscription. Peabody Museum of Salem, East India Marine Hall, Salem, Massachusetts 01970.

American Quarterly. 1949, 5/yr., membership/subscription. American Studies Association, 4025 Chestnut Street, Philadelphia, Pennsylvania 19174.

American Studies International. 1965, 4/yr., subscription. American Studies Program, George Washington University, Washington, D.C. 20052. Formerly: *American Studies News* (1965–1970); *American Studies: An International Newsletter* (supplement to the *American Quarterly,* 1970–1975).

American West. 1964, bimonthly, subscription. Western History Association, 20380 Town Center Lane, Suite 160, Cupertino, California 95014.

Annotation. 1973, quarterly, limited circulation. National Historical Publications and Records Commission, National Archives Building, Washington, D.C. 20408.

Antiques. 1922, monthly, subscription. Straight Enterprises, Inc., 551 Fifth Avenue, New York, New York 10017.

Applied Science and Technology Index. 1958, monthly (except July), service basis. H. W. Wilson Co., 950 University Avenue, Bronx, New York 10452.

Archaeology. 1948, bimonthly, subscription.

Archaeological Institute of America, 53 Park Place, Room 802, New York, New York 10007.

Architectural Periodicals Index. 1972, quarterly, subscription. Royal Institute of British Architects, 66 Portland Place, London W1N 4AD, England. Supersedes: Sir Banister Fletcher Library, *RIBA Library Bulletin*, vols. 1–26 (1946–1972) and Royal Institute of British Architects, London, *RIBA Annual Review of Periodical Articles*, vols. 1–7 (1965–1972).

Architectural Record. 1891, monthly, subscription. Architectural Record, 1221 Avenue of the Americas, New York, New York 10020.

Art Index: *An Author and Subject Index to Domestic and Foreign Art Periodicals and Museum Bulletins Covering Archaeology, Architecture, Art History, Arts and Crafts, City Planning, Fine Arts, Graphic Arts, Industrial Design, etc.* 1929, quarterly, service basis. H. W. Wilson Co., 950 University Avenue, Bronx, New York 10452.

Automobile Quarterly. 1962, 4/yr., subscription. Automobile Quarterly, Inc., 221 Nassau Street, Princeton, New Jersey 08540.

Biography Index: *A Quarterly Index to Biographical Material in Books and Magazines.* 1946, quarterly, subscription. H. W. Wilson Co., 950 University Avenue, Bronx, New York 10452.

Blueprints. 1981, quarterly, membership. National Building Museum, Pension Building, 440 G Street, N.W., Washington, D.C. 20001.

Bulletin of APT. 1969, quarterly, membership. Association for Preservation Technology, Ann Falkner, Executive Secretary, Box 2487 Station D, Ottawa, Ontario K1P 5W6, Canada.

Canadian Historic Sites: *Occasional Papers in Archaeology and History.* 1970, irregular. Canadian Government Publishing Centre, Supply and Services Canada, Hull, Quebec, K1A OS9, Canada. Also in French: *Lieux historiques canadians: cahiers d'archéologie et d'histoire.*

Choice. 1964, 11/year., subscription. Choice, 100 Riverview Center, Middletown, Connecticut 06457.

Chronicle: *The Journal of the Early American Industries Association.* 1933, quarterly, subscription. c/o John Watson, Treasurer, P.O. Box 2128 Empire State Plaza, Albany, New York 12220.

Civil War History: *A Journal of the Middle Period.* 1955, quarterly, subscription. Kent State University Press, Kent, Ohio, 44242.

Classical America. 1972, 2/yr., membership. Society for a Classical America, 10–41 51st Avenue, Long Island City, New York 11101.

Communiqué. 1975, monthly, membership. Association for Preservation Technology, c/o Barbara L. Daniels-Swannack, Editor, P.O. Box 2165, Albuquerque, New Mexico 87103. Succeeds: *Newsletter* (1972–1975).

Computers and the Humanities. 1966, bimonthly, subscription. Pergamon Press, Inc., Maxwell House, Fairview Park, Elmsford, New York 10523.

Council on America's Military Past. *Periodical.* 1967, quarterly, membership/subscription. c/o Secretary, Box 1151, Fort Myer, Virginia 22211. Subscription includes *Headquarters Heliogram*, monthly, tabloid format.

Cumulative Book Index: *A World List of Books in the English Language.* 1928/32, 10/yr., subscription. H. W. Wilson Co., 950 University Avenue, Bronx, New York 10452.

Early Man. 1979, quarterly, membership/subscription. Center for American Archeology, 1911 Ridge Avenue, Evanston, Illinois 60201.

El Palacio. 1913, quarterly, subscription. Museum of New Mexico, P.O. Box 2087, Santa Fe, New Mexico 87501.

Engineering News-Record. 1874, weekly, subscription. McGraw-Hill Publications Co., 1221 Avenue of the Americas, New York, New York 10020.

Family Records Today: *The Journal of American Family Records.* 1980, quarterly, membership/subscription. American Family Records Association, 311 East Twelfth Street, Kansas City, Missouri 64106.

Folklife Center News. 1978, quarterly, free. American Folklife Center, U.S. Library of Congress, Washington, D.C. 20540.

Folklore Forum. 1968, 3/yr., subscription. Folklore Forum, Inc., 504 North Fess Street, Bloomington, Indiana 47405.

Folklore Institute. *Journal.* 1964, 3/yr., subscription. The Folklore Institute, Indiana University, 504 North Fess Street, Bloomington, Indiana 47405. Formerly: Indiana University. Folklore Institute. *Journal.*

Forest History. 1957, quarterly, subscription. Forest History Society, P.O. Box 1581, Santa Cruz, California 95061.

Foxfire. 1967, quarterly, subscription. Foxfire Fund, Inc., B. Eliot Wigginton, Editor, Rabun Gap, Georgia 30568.

Franklin Institute. *Journal.* 1826, monthly, subscription. Pergamon Press, Maxwell House, Fairview Park, Elmsford, New York 10523.

The Genealogical Helper. 1947, bimonthly, subscription. Everton Publishers, P.O. Box 368, Logan, Utah 84321.

Genealogical Journal. 1972, quarterly, subscription. Utah Genealogical Association, Box 1144, Salt Lake City, Utah 84110.

Historic Preservation. 1949, quarterly, membership. National Trust for Historic Preservation, 1785 Massachusetts Avenue, N.W., Washington, D.C. 20036.

Historical Archaeology. 1967, annual, membership. Society for Historical Archaeology, 1703 New Hampshire Avenue, N.W., Washington, D.C. 20009.

Historical Methods. 1967, quarterly, subscription. Heldref Publications, 4000 Albemarle Street, N.W., Washington, D.C. 20016. Formerly: *Historical Methods Newsletter* (1967–1977).

Historical New Hampshire. 1946, quarterly, membership. New Hampshire Historical Society, 30 Park Street, Concord, New Hampshire 03301.

Historical Technology. 1970, irregular, purchase. Historical Technology, Inc., 6 Mugford Street, Marblehead, Massachusetts 01945.

History and Archaeology. 1975, occasional. Canadian Government Publishing Centre, Supply and Services Canada, Hull, Quebeck K1A OS9, Canada. Also in French: *Histoire et archéologie.*

History News. 1941, monthly, membership. American Association for State and Local History, 708 Berry Road, Nashville, Tennessee 37204.

History of Technology. 1976, annual. Mansell Publishing, 3 Bloomsbury Place, London WC1A 2QA, England. Distributed in U.S. by Mansell, Merrimack Book Service, 99 Main Street, Salem, New Hampshire 03079.

History: Reviews of New Books. 1972, 10/yr., subscription. Heldref Publications, 4000 Albemarle Street, N.W., Washington, D.C. 20016.

The History Teacher. 1967, quarterly, subscription. Society for History Education, California State University, Long Beach, California 90840.

Humanities. 1965, bimonthly, free. National Endowment for the Humanities, 806 15th Street, N.W., Washington, D.C. 20506.

IA: The Journal of the Society for Industrial Archaeology. 1975, annual, membership/subscription. Society for Industrial Archeology, Room 5020, National Museum of American History, Smithsonian Institution, Washington, D.C. 20560.

The Indian Historian. 1964, quarterly, subscription. The American Indian Historical Society, 1451 Masonic Avenue, San Francisco, California 94117.

Industrial Archaeology Review. 1976, triennial, subscription. Association for Industrial Archaeology, The Wharfage, Ironbridge, Telford, Salop TF8 7AW, England. Subscriptions to Oxford University Press, Journal Subscriptions Department, Press Road, Neasden, London, NW 10, England. Supersedes: *Industrial Archaeology.*

International Journal of Nautical Archaeology and Underwater Exploration. 1972, 4/yr., subscription. Council for Nautical Archaeology, Academic Press, Inc., 111 Fifth Avenue, New York, New York 10003.

International Journal of Oral History. 1980, 3/yr., subscription. Meckler Publishing, P.O. Box 405, Saugatuck Station, Westport, Connecticut 06880.

Isis: *International Review Devoted to the History of Science and Its Cultural Influences.* 1912, 5/yr., subscription. History of Science Society, Arnold Thackray, Editor, 215 South 34th Street D6, Philadelphia, Pennsylvania 19104.

Journal of American Ethnic History. 1981, semiannual, membership/subscription. Immigration History Society, c/o Minnesota Historical Society, 690 Cedar Street, St. Paul, Minnesota 55101.

Journal of American Folklore. 1888, quarterly, membership/subscription. American

Folklore Society, 1703 New Hampshire Avenue, N.W. Washington, D.C. 20009.

Journal of American History. 1914, quarterly, membership. Organization of American Historians, Indiana University, Ballantine Hall, Bloomington, Indiana 47401. Formerly: *Mississippi Valley Historical Review.*

Journal of Cultural Geography. 1980, semiannual, subscription. Popular Culture Association, Alvar W. Carlson, Editor, Bowling Green State University, Bowling Green, Ohio 43403.

The Journal of Economic History. 1941, quarterly, membership. Economic History Association, Eleutherian Mills Historical Library, Wilmington, Delaware 19807.

Journal of Family History: *Studies in Family, Kinship, and Demography.* 1976, quarterly, subscription. National Council on Family Relations, 1219 University Avenue, S.E., Minneapolis, Minnesota 55414. Supersedes: *Family in Historical Perspective.*

Journal of Field Archaeology. 1974, quarterly, membership. Association for Field Archaeology, Boston University, 745 Commonwealth Avenue, Boston, Massachusetts 02215.

Journal of Glass Studies. 1959, annual, subscription. Corning Museum of Glass, Corning Glass Center, Corning, New York 14831.

Journal of Library History, *Philosophy and Comparative Librarianship.* 1966, quarterly, subscription. University of Texas Press, Donald G. Davis, Jr., Editor, Austin, Texas 78712.

Journal of Navigation. 1947, 3/yr., subscription. Royal Institute of Navigation, Cambridge University Press, Box 110, Cambridge CB2 3RL, England. Formerly: Institute of Navigation. *Journal.*

Journal of Popular Culture. 1967, quarterly, subscription. Popular Culture Association, 100 University Hall, Bowling Green State University, Bowling Green, Ohio 43402.

Journal of Social History. 1967, quarterly, subscription. Carnegie-Mellon University Press, Schenley Park, Pittsburgh, Pennsylvania 15213.

The Journal of Southern History. 1935, quarterly, subscription. Southern Historical Association, Bennett H. Wall, Secretary-Treasurer, c/o History Department, Tulane University, New Orleans, Louisiana 70118.

Journal of the Society of Architectural Historians. 1941, quarterly, membership. Society of Architectural Historians, Room 716, 1700 Walnut Street, Philadelphia, Pennsylvania 19103.

Journal of Transport History. 1953, n.s. 1971, semiannual, subscription. Manchester University Press, Oxford Road, Manchester M13 9PL, England.

Journal of Urban History. 1974, quarterly, subscription. Sage Publications, Inc., 275 South Beverly Drive, Beverly Hills, California 90212.

Landscape. 1951, 3/yr., subscription. Landscape, Box 7107, Berkeley, California 94707.

Landscape Architecture. 1910, bimonthly, subscription. American Society of Landscape Architects, 1190 East Broadway, Louisville, Kentucky 40204.

Library Journal. 1876, semimonthly (Sept.-June), monthly (July-Aug.), subscription. R. R. Bowker Co., 1180 Avenue of the Americas, New York, New York 10036.

Library Trends. 1952, quarterly, subscription. University of Illinois at Urbana-Champaign, Graduate School of Library Science, Urbana, Illinois 61801.

The London Archaeologist. 1968, quarterly, subscription. London Archaeologist Association, 7, Coalecroft Road, S.W. 15, London, England.

Magazine of Bibliographies. 1972, quarterly, subscription. Lalla Campbell Critz, Editor, 1209 Clover Lane, Fort Worth, Texas 76107.

Man In The Northeast. 1971, semiannual, subscription. Man in the Northeast, Inc., Department of Anthropology, Franklin Pierce College, Rindge, New Hampshire 03461.

Mariner's Mirror. 1911, quarterly, membership/subscription. Society for Nautical Research, Meadow Bank, 26 Lucastes Road, Haywards Heath, West Sussex, England.

MASCA Journal. 1965, 1–2/yr., free. Applied Science Center for Archaeology, The University Museum, University of Pennsylvania, 33rd and Spruce Streets, Philadelphia, Pennsylvania 19104. Formerly: *ASCA Newsletter; MASCA Newsletter.*

Media and Methods: *Exploration in Education.* 1965, monthly, subscription. North American Publishing Co., 134 North 13th Street, Philadelphia, Pennsylvania 19107.

Mid-Continental Journal of Archaeology.
1976, 2/yr., subscription. Kent State University
Press, Kent, Ohio 44242. Cover title: *MCJA.*

Military Collector and Historian. 1951, quar-
terly, membership/subscription. Company of
Military Historians, North Main Street,
Westbrook, Connecticut 06498.

Military Engineer. 1920, bimonthly,
membership/subscription. Society of Military
Engineers, 740 15th Street, N.W., Washington,
D.C. 20005. Supersedes: *Professional
Memoirs* (1909–1919).

Museum News. 1924, 9/yr., membership.
American Association of Museums, 1055
Thomas Jefferson Street, N.W., Washington,
D.C. 20007.

Names: *Journal of the American Name Soci-
ety.* 1953, quarterly, membership. American
Name Society, State University of New York at
Potsdam, Potsdam, New York 13676.

National Genealogical Society Quarterly.
1912, quarterly, membership. National
Genealogical Society, 1921 Sunderland Place,
N.W., Washington, D.C. 20036. Supersedes:
*The New England Historical and Genealogical
Register* (1847–1911).

Newsletter of APT. See: *Communiqué.*

**Newsletter of the Society of Architectural
Historians.** 1957, bimonthly, membership.
Society of Architectural Historians, 1700 Walnut Street, Suite 716, Philadelphia, Pennsylvania 19103.

North American Archaeologist. 1979, quarterly, subscription. Baywood Publishing, Inc.,
120 Marine Street, Box D, Farmingdale, New
York 11735.

Northeast Historical Archaeology. 1971,
semiannual, membership/subscription.
Council for Northeast Archaeology, c/o University Museum, University of Pennsylvania,
33rd and Spruce Streets, Philadelphia,
Pennsylvania 19104.

**Northwest Anthropological Research
Notes.** 1967, semiannual, subscription. Laboratory of Anthropology, Roderick Sprague,
Editor, University of Idaho, Moscow, Idaho
83843.

The Old House Journal: Renovation and
Maintenance Ideas for the Antique House.
1973, monthly, subscription. Old House Journal, 69A Seventh Avenue, Brooklyn, New York
11217.

Old-Time New England. 1910, quarterly,
membership. Society for the Preservation of
New England Antiquities, Harrison Gray Otis
House, 141 Cambridge Street, Boston, Massachusetts 02114.

Oral History Association. *Newsletter.* 1967,
quarterly, membership. Oral History Association Newsletter, c/o Thomas Carlton, Editor,
Baylor University, Box 228, Waco, Texas
76798.

Oral History Review. 1973, annual, member-
ship. Oral History Association, Ronald E. Mar-
cello, Executive Secretary, Box 13734, North
Texas State University, Denton, Texas 76203.
Formerly: National Colloquium on Oral History.
Proceedings.

**Pacific Coast Archaeological Society Quar-
terly.** 1965, quarterly, subscription. Pacific
Coast Archaeological Society, Inc., Box
10926, Costa Mesa, California 92627. Includes: *PCAS Newsletter.*

Pacific Historical Review. 1932, quarterly,
subscription. Pacific Coast Branch, American
Historical Association, University of California
Press, 2223 Fulton Street, Berkeley, California
94720.

Pioneer America: *The Journal of American
Historic Material Culture.* 1968, semiannual,
subscription. M. B. Newton, Jr., Editor,
Geography-Anthropology Department, Box
22230, Louisiana State University, Baton
Rouge, Louisiana 70893.

Popular Archaeology. 1972, bimonthly, subscription. Life and Lettres Publishers, Inc.,
P.O. Box 4211, Arlington, Virginia 22204. Includes: *American Archaeologist.*

Progressive Architecture. 1920, monthly,
subscription. John Morris Dixon, Editor,
Penton–IPC, Box 95759, Cleveland, Ohio
44101.

Prologue. 1968, quarterly, subscription. U.S.
National Archives and Records Service, Washington, D.C. 20408.

The Public Historian. 1979, quarterly, subscription. University of California Press, 2223
Fulton Street, Berkeley, California 94720.

Railroad History. 1921, semiannual,
membership/subscription. Railway and
Locomotive Historical Society, Smithsonian
Institution, Division of Transportation, Wash-
ington, D.C. 20560. Subscriptions to: H. Arnold
Wilder, Lowell Road, Westford, Massachusetts

01886. Formerly: Railway and Locomotive Historical Society. *Bulletin.*

Readers' Guide to Periodical Literature: *Author and Subject Index to a Selected List of Periodicals . . .* 1900/1904, monthly, subscription. H. W. Wilson Co., 950 University Avenue, Bronx, New York 10452.

Report. 1975, 8/yr., on request. Advisory Council on Historic Preservation, 1522 K Street, N.W., Washington, D.C. 20005. Succeeds: *Newsletter* (1973–1974).

Reviews in American History. 1973, quarterly, subscription. Johns Hopkins University Press, 34th and Charles Streets, Baltimore, Maryland 21218.

Scientific American. 1845, monthly, subscription. Scientific American, Inc., 415 Madison Avenue, New York, New York 10017.

SEHA Newsletter and Proceedings. 1951, 6/yr., membership. Ross T. Christensen, Editor, Department of Anthropology and Archaeology, 140 Maeser Building, Brigham Young University, Provo, Utah 84602. Formerly: *UAS Newsletter.*

Smithsonian. 1970, monthly, subscription. Smithsonian Associates, 900 Jefferson Drive, S.W., Washington, D.C. 20560. Succeeds: *The Smithsonian Journal of History* (1966–1969).

Society for Historical Archaeology. *Newsletter.* 1968, quarterly, subscription. Society for Historical Archaeology, 1703 New Hampshire Avenue, N.W., Washington, D.C. 20009. Includes subscription to *Historical Archaeology.*

Society for Industrial Archeology. *Newsletter.* 1972, bimonthly, membership. Society for Industrial Archeology, National Museum of American History, Room 5020, Smithsonian Institution, Washington, D.C. 20560.

Sound Heritage. 1974, quarterly, subscription. Provincial Archives of British Columbia, Victoria, British Columbia V8V 1X4, Canada.

Southern Exposure. 1973, quarterly, subscription. Institute of Southern Studies, P.O. Box 230, Chapel Hill, North Carolina 27514.

Southwestern Anthropological Association Newsletter. 1960, quarterly, membership/subscription. c/o American Anthropological Association, 1703 New Hampshire Avenue, N.W., Washington, D.C. 20009.

Studies in Conservation. 1952, quarterly, membership/subscription. International Institute for Conservation of Historic and Artistic Works, 6 Buckingham Street, London WC2N 6BA, England.

Technology and Culture. 1960, quarterly, membership. Society for the History of Technology, University of Chicago Press, 5801 S. Ellis Avenue, Chicago, Illinois 60637.

Technology In Society: *An International Journal.* 1979, quarterly, subscription. Pergamon Press, Journals Division, Maxwell House, Fairview Park. Elmsford, New York 10523.

Textile History. 1968, 2/yr., subscription. Butterworth Scientific, Ltd., Journals Division, Box 63, Westbury House, Bury Street, Guildford, Surrey GU2 5BH, England.

Textile Museum Journal. 1962, annual, purchase. Textile Museum, 2320 S Street, N.W., Washington, D.C. 20008. Supersedes: *Workshop Notes.*

Vernacular Architecture Newsletter. 1979, quarterly, membership/subscription. c/o Ellen Coxe, Secretary-Treasurer, 406 Second Street, Annapolis, Maryland 21403.

Western History Quarterly. 1970, quarterly, subscription. Western History Association, Utah State University of Agriculture and Applied Science, Logan, Utah 84322.

William and Mary Quarterly: *A Magazine of Early American History.* 1892, quarterly, subscription. Institute of Early American History and Culture, Box 220, Williamsburg, Virginia 23185.

Index

American and British Genealogy and Heraldry
. . . , 41
American and British Technology in the
Nineteenth Century . . . , 120
American and English Popular Entertainment . . . ,
39
American Anthropological Association, 47
American Architects From the Civil War to the
First World War; First World War to the Present,
80
American Architectural Books . . . Before 1895,
67, 72
American Architectural Books, 1775–c1899 . . . ,
74
American Architectural Drawings: A Catalog . . . ,
72
American Architectural Styles, 1600–1940, 84
American Architecture, 78
American Architecture and Art . . . , 73
American Architecture and Other Writings, 79
American Architecture and Urbanism, 79
American Architecture Now, 79
The American Architecture of Today, 89
American Architecture Since 1780: A Guide to the
Styles, 68, 84
American Architecture, 1607–1976, 79
American Architecture, Westchester County, New
York . . . , 105
American Association for State and Local History,
descr., 7
American Association of Museums, descr., 7
American Association of Architectural Bibliog-
raphers, 69, 71
The American Automobile: A Brief History, 136
American Aviation Historical Society, 139
American Axes, a Survey of Their Development
and Their Makers, 125
American Bibliography, 16
American Bibliography: A Preliminary Checklist
for 1801–1819, 17
The American Book of Days . . . , 20
American Broadcasting . . . , 153
American Building Art . . . , 130
American Building: Materials and Techniques
. . . , 114, 130
American Building, 1: The Historical Forces . . . ;
Environmental Forces . . . , 67, 78
American Buildings and Their Architects . . . , 86,
88, 89
American Canal Society, 138
The American Car Since 1775 . . . , 135
American Carriages, Sleighs, Sulkies, and Carts
. . . , 135
American Catalogue of Books . . . [1861–1871], 16
American Catalogue of Books, 1876–1910, 15
American Century: 100 Years of Changing Life
Style in America, 36
American Chemical Industry, 144
American Chemical Society, 54
American Chemists and Chemical Engineers, 144
The American City . . . , 99
American City Planning Since 1890 . . . , 100
The American Civil Engineer . . . , 130
The American Civil War, 29

American Civilization: An Introduction to Research
and Bibliography, 15
American Colonial Architecture . . . , 86
The American Colonies: From Settlement to Inde-
pendence, 26
American Common Houses: A Selected Bibliog-
raphy of Vernacular Architecture, 85
American Copper and Brass, 144
The American Counties . . . , 20
The American Craftsman, 124
American Cut and Engraved Glass, 146
American Diaries: An Annotated Bibliography
. . . , 21
American Diaries in Manuscript, 1580–1954 . . . ,
20
American Dictionary of Printing and Bookmaking
. . . , 151
American Diner, 94
American Economic and Business History Infor-
mation Sources . . . , 31
American Education: The Colonial Experience
. . . ; The National Experience, 37
American Engineers of the Nineteenth Century
. . . , 128
American Fabrics and Fashions Magazine, 148
American Family Records Association, 43
The American Farmhouse, 90
American Fire Engines since 1900, 136
The American Fishing Schooner, 1825–1935, 137
American Folk Architecture: A Selected Bibliog-
raphy, 68, 85
American Folklife Center, 4
American Folklore, 25
American Folklore Society, 4
American Forts: Architectural Form and Function,
79
American Gardens in the Eighteenth Century . . . ,
98
The American Genealogical-Biographical Index
. . . , 40
American Genealogical Periodicals . . . , 40
American Genealogical Research Institute, 39
American Geographical Society of New York, 19
American Georgian Architecture, 86
American Glass, 146
American Gothic . . . , 87
American Government: Problems and Readings in
Political Analysis, 27
American Heritage, 24, 27, 28, 29, 31, 36, 37
American Heritage Book of the Revolution, 28
The American Heritage Cookbook and Illustrated
History of American Eating and Drinking, 36
The American Heritage Dictionary of the English
Language, 9
The American Heritage History of American Busi-
ness and Industry, 31
The American Heritage History of Railroads in
America, 31
The American Heritage History of Seafaring
America, 26
The American Heritage History of the American
People, 36
The American Heritage History of the Confident
Years, 26

Architectural Styles, 84–90. (*See also* Regional Architecture)
Architectural Styles, 84
Architecture: history of, 77–79; organizations, 68–70; regional studies, 101–112; research methods, 70–71; styles, 84–90; types, 78, 90–96
Architecture, Ambition and Americans . . . , 67, 78
Architecture and Town Planning in Colonial Connecticut, 102
The Architecture Book, 73
Architecture, Boston, 101
Architecture/Colorado, 111
Architecture: Columbus, 108
Architecture in America . . . , 78
Architecture in Britain, 1530 to 1830, 78
Architecture in Colonial Massachusetts . . . , 101
Architecture in New Jersey . . . , 104
Architecture in Oklahoma . . . , 110
Architecture in Old Chicago, 109
Architecture in Old Kentucky, 107
Architecture in Philadelphia, 105
Architecture in Tennessee . . . , 107
Architecture in the United States . . . , 84
Architecture in Virginia . . . , 107
Architecture in Wood . . . , 131
Architecture: Nineteenth and Twentieth Centuries, 67, 77
The Architecture of America: A Social and Cultural History, 78
The Architecture of Bridges, 133
The Architecture of Carson City, Nevada, 111
The Architecture of Choice: Eclecticism . . . , 88
The Architecture of Colonial America, 86
The Architecture of Country Houses . . . , 87
The Architecture of Georgia, 107
The Architecture of Historic Lexington, 106
The Architecture of Historic Nantucket, 102
The Architecture of Historic Richmond, 106
The Architecture of Honolulu, 111
Architecture of Middle Georgia . . . , 106
Architecture of Middle Tennessee . . . , 105
The Architecture of New York . . . , 104
Architecture of the Old Northwest Territory . . . , 109
The Architecture of the Old South . . . , 106
The Architecture of the Southwest . . . , 110
The Architecture of the Well-Tempered Environment, 89
Architecture of the Western Reserve, 1800–1900, 108
The Architecture of Wisconsin, 109
Architecture Since 1945 . . . , 89
Architecture Through the Ages, 77
Architecture U.S.A., 89
Architecture Worth Saving in Onondaga County, 105
Architecture Worth Saving in Rensselaer County, 103
Archives, research in, 19–23, 32; genealogical, 40–44
Archives of American Art, 12
Ardrey, Robert L., 114, 126
Arizona Ghost Towns, 110

Arizona Ranch Houses . . . , 110
Arms and Men: A Study in American Military History, 29
Arms Makers of Maryland, 154
Armstrong, Ellis L., 34
Armstrong, John Borden, 101
Armytage, W. H. G., 128
Arnold, David S., 100
Arnold, J. Barto, III, 62, 63
Arnold, James, 122
Art and Archaeology Technical Abstracts, 56
Art and Architecture in Spain and Portugal and Their American Dominions . . . , 86
The Art and Architecture of German Settlements in Missouri . . . , 109
Art and Life in America, 38
Art Deco, 89, 106, 110
The Art of Blacksmithing, 122
The Art of Building Cities . . . , 101
"Art of the United States: Architecture," 78
Arthur, Eric, 90
Artifacts: An Introduction to Early Materials and Technology, 114, 143
Artillery of the American Revolution . . . , 154
Artistic Country-Seats . . . , 87
Arts and Crafts Movements, 36, 90
Arts, Crafts, and Architecture in Early Illinois, 109
Arts in America: A Bibliography, 36
The Arts in America: The Nineteenth Century, 36
The Arts in Early American History, 37, 72
The Arts in Modern American Civilization, 121
Asch, David L., 53
Ash, Lee, 19
Ashby, Charlotte M., 22
Ashmore, Wendy, 47, 59
Association for Field Archaeology, 48
Association for Industrial Archaeology, 157
Association for Preservation Technology, 115
Association of Science-Technology Centers, 116
At Odds: Women and Family in America . . . , 2, 34
Atkinson, Richard John Coplan, 50
The Atlantic Economy and Colonial Maryland's Eastern Shore . . . , 30
The Atlantic Migration, 1607–1860 . . . , 34
Atlas of Early American History . . . , 24
Atlas of the Historical Geography of the United States, 26
Atlases, 19, 21, 22, 24, 26, 41
Auer, Michel, 153
Automation: Industrialization Comes of Age, 120
Automobile Quarterly, 135
Automobiles, 135–137
The Automotive History Collection of the Detroit Public Library . . . , 136
Auvil, Myrtle, 133
The Avenues of Salt Lake City, 111
Avery, Thomas Eugene, 52
Avery Obituary Index of Architects and Artists, 79
Avery Index to Architectural Periodicals, 71
Aviation, 139
Aviation Archaeology . . . , 139
Ayres, Eugene, 139

Babbage, Charles, 150
Bach, Ira J., 108
Back, Kathryn, 14
Backus, William, and Samuel D. Backus, 75
Bacon, Edmund N., 99
Badekas, John, 52
Badger, Daniel D., 75, 76
Badger's Illustrated Catalogue of Cast-Iron Architecture, 75
Baer, Christopher T., 135
Baer, Morley, 110
Bagrow, Leo, 134
Bailey, Chris H., 150
Bailey, De Witt, 154
Bailey, Lynn Robison, 55
Bailey, Rosalie Fellows, 103
Bailey, Thomas A., 36
Baines, Patricia, 148
Baird, Joseph Armstrong, Jr., 110
Baker, Paul R., 82
Baker, T. Lindsay, 134
Balcom, Mary G., 110
Baldwin, Charles C., 83
Ball, Berenice M., 90
Ball, Rick A., 108
Bangs, Edward G., 110
Banham, Reyner, 89, 103, 111
Barbs, Prongs, Points, Prickers, and Stickers . . . Catalogue of Antique Barbed Wire, 126
The Bark Canoes and Skin Boats of North America, 137
Barker, Philip A., 50
Barlow, Elizabeth, 96
The Barn: A Vanishing Landmark in America, 90
Barnard, Henry, 92
Barnard, Julian, 145
Barnard, William N., 141
Barnes, Duncan, 154
Barnes, Edward Larrabee, 79
Barnett, Jonathan, 79, 99
Barnouw, Erik, 37, 153
Barns. (*See* Farm Buildings)
Barns of California: A Collection, 91
Barns of Chester County, Pennsylvania, 90
Barns of Wisconsin, 90
Barns, Sheds and Outbuildings, 76
Barns: Their History, Preservation and Restoration, 91
Barnstone, Howard, 83, 109
Baron, Stanley W., 126
Barr, Matthew, 94
Barraclough, Kenneth C., 143
Barrows, John A., 107
Barry, B. T. K., 144
Bartis, Peter, 9, 19
Bartlett, Richard A., 34
Barzun, Jacques, 2, 9
Basic Reference Shelf: archeology, 46–47; architecture, 67–68; history, 2–3; technology and crafts, 114–115
Basketry, 122
The Baskets of Rural America, 123
Bass, George F., 46, 62
Basserman-Jordan, Ernst von, 150

Bassett, Margaret, 27
Bassett, William B., 104
Bastian, Robert W., 85
Bateman, James A., 126
Bathe, Basil W., 138
Battison, Edwin A., 149
The Bauhaus: Weimar, Dessau, Berlin, Chicago, 90
Baum, Willa K., 2, 14
Beach, Mark, 37
Bead, Frank, 100
Bealer, Alex W., 90, 122, 124
Beam Engines, 141
Beard, Timothy F., 39
Beatty, Betty, 73
The Beauties of Modern Architecture, 76
Beaver, Patrick, 133
Beck, Curt W., 54
Bedini, Silvio, 150
Beecher, Catharine E., 75
Beeching, Wilfred A., 149
Beedell, Suzanne M., 140
Beginning in Archaeology, 52
The Beginning of the Incandescent Lamp and Lighting System . . . , 142
The Beginnings of a Century of Steam and Water Heating by the H. B. Smith Company, 142
Behavioral Archeology, 47, 54
Beinke, Nancy, 94, 108
Beirne, Rosamond Randall, 80
Bell, James B., 2, 39
Bell, Robert E., 60
Bell, Whitfield J., Jr., 37
Bell Telephone Laboratories, Inc., 153
Belle Grove Excavations . . . , 62
Bell's Electronic Speaking Telephone . . . , 153
Bemis, Samuel F., 27
Benchley, Elizabeth, 60
Bendure, Zelma, 148
Beneath the Footnote . . . , 9
Beneath the Waters of Time . . . , 63
Benes, Peter, 60
Benjamin, Asher, 75
Benjamin, Park, 142
Benjamin Franklin: Electrician, 142
Bennion, Elizabeth, 150
Benson, Tedd, 130
Benton, Mildred, 19
Berg, Gary, 58
Berg, Walter G., 94
Berk, Emanuel, 99
Berkebile, Donald H., 135, 136
Bernhardi, Robert C., 111
Bertele, Hans von, 150
Berthoff, Rowland T., 34
The Bertrand Bottles: A Study of 19th-Century Glass . . . , 146
The Best Remaining Seats . . . , 38
Betts, Benjamin F., 95
Betts, Edwin M., 126
Betts, John Rickards, 37
The Bibliographer's Manual of American History . . . , 15

Russell, Carl P., 115, 127, 154
Russell, Francis, 26
Russell, Howard S., 32
Russell & Erwin Manufacturing Company, 143
Russo, David J., 10, 11
Ryder, Michael L., 53

Saarinen, Aline B., 82
Saarinen, Eero, 79, 82, 84
Saarinen, Eliel, 82
Sabin, Joseph, 17
Sabloff, Jeremy A., 54, 59
Sachs, Hans, 123
Sacilotto, Deli, 152
Sackheim, Donald E., 156
Sadler, Julius Trousdale, Jr., 81, 88
Saff, Donald, 152
Sahli, Nancy, 11
St. Clair, Hillary W., 144
St. Joseph, John K. S., 53
Salaman, R. A., 115, 125
Salem Possessed; The Social Origins of Witch-craft, 34
Salmon, Lucy M., 11
Salt, 145
Salvage Archeology, 60, 64–65
"Salvage Archaeology and History Preservation," 64
Salvage Archaeology in Painted Rocks Reservoir . . . , 65
Sampling of Archaeology, 53
San Augustin, First Cathedral Church in Arizona, 91
Sanchis, Frank E., 105
Sandbank, Harold, 131
Sande, Theodore A., 115, 155
Sandeen, Ernest R., 38
Sanderlin, Walter S., 138
Sandström, Gösta E., 133
Sanford, Trent Elwood, 110
Santa Fe. Museum of New Mexico, 132
Sarton, George, 119
Saum, Lewis O., 39
Savelle, Max, 39
Sawers, David, 120
Sawyer, Elizabeth M., 107
Saylor, Henry H., 73
Sayward, Elliot M., 123
"Scales and Weighing Devices . . . , 151
Scales and Weights . . . , 151
Scammon, Richard M., 27
Scarff, John Henry, 80
Scarlott, Charles A., 139
Schapsmeier, Edward L., and Frederick H. Schapsmeier, 3, 32
Scheitlin, Thomas E., 61
Schiffer, Michael B., 46, 47, 50, 54, 55, 64
Schindler, Rudolph M., 80, 82, 83
Schlatter, Hugo, 145
Schlebecker, John T., 32, 127
Schlereth, Thomas J., 71, 93
Schlesinger, Arthur M., 34
Schlesinger, Arthur M., Jr., 28
Schmeckebier, Lawrence F., 21

Schmidt, Carl F., 87, 88, 91, 98, 105, 132
Schmitt, Frederick P., 127
Schmitt, Peter, 109
Schmookler, Jacob, 121
Schneir, Miriam, 34
Schob, David E., 32
Scholars as Contractors . . . , 65
Scholars as Managers . . . , 65
School Architecture, 92
Schoolhouses and Their Equipment . . . , 92
Schools: architecture, 77, 87, 92–93; history of, 37–39
Schools for the New Needs . . . , 92
Schroeder, Joseph J., Jr., 154
Schudson, Michael, 39
Schulke, Flip, 63
Schull, Diantha Dow, 105
Schuyler, Montgomery, 79
Schuyler, Robert L., 19, 46, 57, 58
Schwartz, Anna J., 31
Schwartz, Bernard, 28
Schwartz, Nancy B., 84, 103
Science: applied, 119, 120–122; and technology, 117–119; history of, 31–32, 37–39, 119; in agriculture, 126, 127; in archeology, 50–55
Science and Building . . . , 131
Science and Technology in Agriculture . . . , 127
Science in America since 1820, 121
Science in American Society . . . , 37
Science in Archaeology . . . , 50
Science in the British Colonies of America, 39
Scientific Instruments, 150–151
The Scientist and Archaeology, 53
Scott, Frank J., 98
Scott, James Allen, 109
Scott, James W., 135
Scott, Mellier Goodin, 100
Scott, Quinta, 133
Scoville, Warren Chandler, 146
Screw-thread Cutting by the Master-Screw Method . . . , 149
Scroll Ornaments of Early Victorian Period, 76
Scudiere, Paul J., 63
Scully, Arthur, 80
Scully, Vincent, 68, 79, 88, 89, 90, 102, 110
Seale, William, 93
Sealock, Richard B., 17
Search and Research; the Researcher's Handbook . . . , 21
Search for the Cittie of Ralegh . . . , 61
Searching for Your Ancestors . . . , 2, 39
Sears, Stephen W., 35
A Season of Youth: The American Revolution and the Historical Imagination, 35
The Seasons of America Past, 127
Sebree, Mac, 136
The Second National Colloquium on Oral History, 12
Secrets of the Past: Nuclear Energy Applications . . . , 52
Sedlak, Michael W., 37
Seeds of Liberty: The Genesis of the American Mind, 39
Seely, Pauline A., 17